LESSON PLANS FOR

DYNAMIC PHYSICAL EDUCATION FOR ELEMENTARY SCHOOL CHILDREN

TENTH EDITION

Robert P. Pangrazi

Arizona State University
Tempe, Arizona

Victor P. Dauer

Washington State University
Pullman, Washington

Macmillan Publishing Company
New York

Maxwell Macmillan Canada
Toronto

Maxwell Macmillan International
New York   Oxford   Singapore   Sydney

Macmillan Publishing Company
866 Third Avenue, New York, New York 10022

Macmillan Publishing Company is part of
the Maxwell Communication Group of Companies.

Maxwell Macmillan Canada, Inc.
1200 Eglinton Avenue East
Suite 200
Don Mills, Ontario M3C 3N1
Printing: 1 2 3 4 5 6 7   Year: 2 3 4 5 6 7 8

ISBN   0-02-390685-5

How to Use the Lesson Plans

Lesson Plans for Dynamic Physical Education for Elementary School Children is designed for use with the text, *Dynamic Physical Education for Elementary School Children,* Tenth Edition *(DPE)*. The activities presented in the plans are covered in detail in the text. The lesson plans provide a guide for presenting movement experiences in a sequential and orderly manner and can serve as a suggested curriculum. Teachers still need to plan lessons and reshape curriculums based on individual and school needs.

Vertical Parts of the Lesson Plan

Each lesson plan is divided into four activity parts as described in Chapter 5 of *DPE*. Each plan offers an outline of activities for one week. This means that not every small detail, teaching hint, or technique point is included. Teachers should read the textual material as referenced in *DPE* and enhance each lesson plan to meet personal needs.

Briefly, the four instructional parts of the lesson plan and major purposes of each are as follows:
1. **Introductory Activity:** Occupies 2 or 3 minutes for the purpose of physiologically preparing children and ensuring that they immediately become involved in activity when entering the gymnasium or activity area. Activities used in this section demand little instruction and allow time for practicing class management skills. Descriptions of introductory activities can be found in *DPE*, Chapter 12.
2. **Fitness Development Activity:** This part of the lesson plan takes 7 to 9 minutes of a 30-minute lesson. The sole purpose of this section is to develop physical fitness. The activities should be demanding and progressive in nature, and should exercise all parts of the body. Allied to the workout should be brief discussions about the values of fitness for a healthy life-style. A comprehensive discussion of fitness principles, activities, and routines is in *DPE*, Chapter 13.
3. **Lesson Focus Activities:** The purpose of the lesson focus is to help children attain major program objectives such as hand–eye coordination, body management competency, and basic and specialized skills (e.g., folk dancing, shooting a basket, and catching an object). The lesson focus uses 15–20 minutes of the daily lesson, depending on the length of the teaching period. Lesson focus activities are organized into units and vary in length, depending on the developmental level of children.

   The movement experiences in *DPE* and *Lesson Plans* are organized in a developmental sequence, with the first activity being the easiest and the last activity the most difficult. Usually, instruction should start with the first activity and then proceed forward regardless of grade level. The implications are twofold: The teacher will ensure that each unit begins with success, since all children are capable of performing the beginning activities. It also assures that proper progression and sequence will be followed in the presentation of activities. Older or more skilled children will progress further along the continuum of activities than younger or less capable children. A wide variety of activities for developing a well-balanced curriculum is offered in *DPE*.
4. **Game Activity:** This part of the lesson plan takes place at the closing of the lesson, utilizing the last 5–7 minutes of the period. The game can be a culminating activity for practicing skills emphasized in the lesson focus or can be something entirely different, taught as a separate entity, with fun and enjoyment the overriding consideration. The activity should leave children with a positive feeling so they look forward with anticipation to the next lesson. If the lesson has been physically demanding, a less active game can be played and vice versa. In some cases, a low-key, relaxing activity might be chosen so that children can unwind before returning to the classroom.

Horizontal Parts of the Lesson Plan

The material and organization in the lesson plan format are broken into three columns.
1. **Movement Content—Experience:** This column lists the movement sequences that will be taught in the lesson. They are not described in detail but do provide the instructor guidance with respect to the learning sequences that will be presented during the week.

2. **Organization and Teaching Hints:** This section provides points for efficient organization of the class and important learning cues. Emphasis in this column is on teaching for quality of movement rather than quantity. Page numbers in this section refer to the *DPE* text, which should be used for in-depth discussions and teaching techniques.

3. **Expected Student Objectives and Outcomes:** Objectives that students should be expected to achieve are listed in this area. The objectives are written in the three learning domains: psychomotor, cognitive, and affective. The objectives are not listed as concise behavioral objectives, but they do offer direction for student learning. The affective learning objectives should offer direction for discussions that can enhance fitness and skill learning.

Using the Lesson Plans

Three sets of lesson plans are included to cover three developmental levels. Optional plans are offered and can be substituted into the suggested yearly plan. Yearly plans for each of the three developmental levels are listed on pages 1–3, 111–113, and 217–219. Most teachers do not use the lesson plans during the actual class presentation; rather, they place activities to be taught on 4- by 6-inch note cards. Writing the activities on cards encourages the teacher to mentally organize the lesson and results in a more effective presentation. All lesson presentations should be mentally rehearsed to prevent excessive use of written notes. Lesson plan notes should remind the teacher of the next activity rather than cause a break in the continuity of instruction.

The introductory activities are changed weekly and should be presented at the beginning of each daily lesson. The duration of the fitness development units varies depending on the developmental level of youngsters. Younger children need frequent change, while older children can see improvement by staying with a fitness routine for 2–4 weeks. The same fitness activities are used each day throughout the duration of the routine. Only the work load is modified.

Lesson focus activities are changed weekly except when continuity of instruction demands longer units. Enough activities are placed in the lesson focus section to accommodate three to four teaching periods. A large variety of games are offered so children will not be restricted to a narrow range of enjoyable closing activities.

Attention to quality of movement should be given throughout the lesson. Youngsters should be taught skills in a manner that is mechanically correct. However, steps in the movement progressions should allow opportunity for creativity and exploration. Note that throughout the lesson plans activities are offered to allow youngsters a chance to explore the range of movement possibilities.

Acknowledgments and appreciation go to Debbie Pangrazi, physical education resource teacher for the Mesa School District, for her many contributions to *Lesson Plans*. Connie Orlowicz, Mesa School District, also field-tested and contributed much to the plans. A hearty thank you goes to Donald Hicks, Kyrene School District; Nicki Rippee, professor at University of Nevada-Reno; and Carole Castin, professor at California State University-Dominguez Hills, for their important contributions to *Lesson Plans*.

Self-Evaluation Guide

The following points can be used for evaluating the daily lesson.

1. Did you prepare ahead of time? Few lessons can be properly taught without prior mental preparation.
2. Did you understand the "whys" behind your lesson? Did they lead you in the direction you wanted the class to go?
3. Was the equipment necessary for your lesson arranged before class? If so, it will allow more time to chat with students.
4. Did you constantly change positions in relationship to the class while you were teaching? This allows you to be close to all students so that you can attempt to acknowledge each of them on a daily basis.
5. Did you carefully observe for the child who was having trouble performing the activities? He or she needs help but doesn't want a big fuss made in order to receive aid.
6. Did you tell the class what your goals for the lesson are? Students must be told what the purpose of the activity is so that they believe it is relevant and useful.
7. Were you excited and enthusiastic about the lesson? If not, the student probably didn't enjoy the lesson. Remember that enthusiasm begets enthusiasm.
8. Did you praise children for the improvement or effort they made during the lesson? Finding something positive to tell children when you know they are putting forth an effort will make them try harder next time.
9. Did you give sufficient attention to the development of student independence and creativity? You must allow time for students to create.
10. Did you give students a sense of responsibility? Using student leaders and allowing the class an opportunity to make decisions about choice of activity is a start.
11. Were enough activities in the lesson plan? Did you cover enough in the lesson or too much?
12. Did you teach for quality of movement or just quantity of movement? Usually, activities must be performed more than once if they are going to be learned.
13. Did you ask for student evaluation of the lesson? This doesn't have to be done every lesson; however, students should be able to provide feedback about the presentation.
14. What activities used in this lesson were effective or ineffective? Why?
15. What overt signs of misbehavior, if any, were present? Who were the students directly involved? To what causes, either the teaching or the personalities, can this misbehavior be attributed?
16. Was the major objective of the lesson reached? Did the students grasp the idea or ideas presented? If not, why not?

Finally, put down any other comments that will make the lesson more effective in the future. Constant updating and evaluation of the lesson plans will make them more useful and in line with your style of teaching.

Contents

Page numbers for individual Lesson Plans appear on pages 1–3, 111–113, and 217–219.

LESSON PLANS FOR THE SCHOOL YEAR
Developmental Level I

WEEK	INTRODUCTORY ACTIVITY	FITNESS DEVELOPMENT ACTIVITY	LESSON FOCUS ACTIVITY	GAME ACTIVITY	PAGE
1	Orientation and Class Management Games				4
2	Move and Assume Pose	Parachute Fitness	Manipulative Skills Using Beanbags	Midnight Leap the Brook Parachute Activity	6
3	Locomotor Movements and Freeze	Movement Challenges	Fundamental Skills Using Individual Mats	Mat Game Red Light Sneak Attack	9
4	Hoops—Free Activity	Walk, Trot, and Sprint	Kicking, Trapping, Bowling, and Rolling	Back to Back Change Sides Musical Ball Pass	13
5	European Running	Jump Rope Exercises	Educational Movement (1)	Jack Frost and Jane Thaw Marching Ponies Tag Games	16
6	Magic Number Challenges	Mini-Challenge Course	Rhythmic Movement (1)	Squirrel in the Trees Stop Ball	21
7	Crossing the River	Circuit Training	Long-Rope Jumping Skills	Ball Passing Hot Potatoes Aviator	24
8	Combination Movements	Movement Challenges	Manipulative Skills Using Playground Balls	Teacher Ball The Scarecrow and the Crows	26
9	Bend, Stretch, and Shake	Fitness Games and Challenges	Educational Movement Using Rope Patterns	Tag Games Charlie over the Water Flowers and Wind	29
10	Marking	Parachute Fitness	Educational Movement (2)	Fire Fighter Animal Tag Sneak Attack	31
11	Individual Movement with Manipulation	Four-Corners Movement	Individual Rope Jumping Skills	Tommy Tucker's Land Change Sides	36
12	Movement Varieties	Circuit Training	Educational Movement (3)	Rollee Pollee Mix and Match	38
13	New Leader Warm-Up	Jump Rope Exercises	Fundamental Skills Using Benches	Hill Dill Bottle Kick Ball	42
14	Group Over and Under	Astronaut Drills	Throwing Skills (1)	Red Light Sneak Attack	45
15	Countdown	Animal Movements and Fitness Challenges	Stunts and Tumbling Skills (1)	Circle Straddle Ball Statues Soap Bubbles	48

1

DYNAMIC PHYSICAL EDUCATION LESSON PLAN
Orientation and Class Management Games
Level I

Note: See Chapters 6 and 7 in *Dynamic Physical Education for Elementary School Children*, Tenth Edition.

ORIENTATION LESSON PLAN

This week should be used to get students involved in the system you are going to use throughout the year. The following are reminders you might find useful in establishing your organizational schemes.

1. Tell the class what is expected with regard to entry and exit behavior. If you are using the squad method, it might be helpful to place four cones (one per squad) in the same area each day and ask the squads to get into line behind the cones.
2. Discuss with the class your interest in them and that you are anxious to learn their names. State that you are going to ask them their names many times to expedite learning them quickly. It also might be helpful to ask classroom teachers to put name tags on students before they come to physical education class. Having students write their names on a piece of masking tape is a quick and easy way to make name tags.
3. Explain briefly the lesson plan format to the class. Each lesson will contain an introductory activity, fitness activity, lesson focus, and game activity. In that way, they will know what to expect and won't have to ask if "we're going to play a game today," etc.
4. When classes come to the activity area, explain briefly what you are going to do in the day's lesson. It should be short and concise, but they should know what you have planned for them.
5. Establish rules and expectations. Usually, basic rules state that students must listen when you are speaking and vice versa, and they must act in a socially sound manner, respecting the rights of other students.
6. If you are going to test, let the students know the reason for the test and what it will involve on their behalf.
7. Emphasize the value of fitness and take them through a fitness routine. Set expectations high—it is always easier to lower them later. Practice various formations such as open-squad and closed-squad, so they know what to do when you ask them to assume these positions. Try formations such as square, triangle, and rectangle.
8. Discuss issue, distribution, and care of equipment and where and how it is to be stored. Students should play an integral part in handling materials.
9. Decide how excuses for nonparticipation should be handled. Children should know where they go to be excused and where they go after they are excused.
10. Establish a signal to stop the class and gain attention. Usually a whistle and a hand signal are most effective. Practice gaining the attention of the class with the signal during this orientation period. Activity should be started by verbal command.
11. Select activities for this week in which you know all students will be successful. This is one of the best ways to develop enthusiasm for a program in its early stages. The corollary of this rule is to teach a few games and activities you enjoy.
12. The orientation week usually requires more explanation than is normal. After the first week, keep talking to a minimum and activity to a maximum. Remember that when you are talking or children are standing in line, there is no way they can learn and practice new physical skills.
13. Circulate among students as you develop movement experiences and skills. This allows for individualized instruction and attention to the lesser skilled. Avoid spending the majority of teacher time "at the podium" in front of the class.

14. In each of the lessons, read the reference areas in *Dynamic Physical Education* to provide quality teaching and more depth of the movement patterns.
15. Frequent reference should be made as needed to Chapter 7, "Effective Class Management," in *Dynamic Physical Education for Elementary School Children*. This chapter applies to all activities taught and offers strategies and techniques to enhance the teaching process.
16. Safety is an important issue to be covered in the first week. Children should receive safety rules to be followed on large apparatus as well as similar rules for playground and gymnasium conduct. Proper use of equipment should be emphasized. Rules should be posted in the gymnasium and throughout the school. See Chapter 9 in *Dynamic Physical Education* for an in-depth discussion.
17. It is crucial to the success of the teacher that good student management skills be developed early in the school year. During the first week, students should practice getting into various formations quickly and without talking, getting into groups of different sizes, and stopping on signal quickly (within 5 seconds). Games, such as those that follow, are excellent for teaching class management skills.

ACTIVITY

Play a few favorite games after a fitness routine has been introduced. The following games make good introductory activities and offer the students a chance to get to know each other.

1. Stoop Tag, p. 518
2. Back to Back, p. 516
3. Midnight, p. 516
4. Red Light, p. 523
5. One, Two, Button My Shoe, p. 517
6. Skunk Tag, p. 518

DYNAMIC PHYSICAL EDUCATION LESSON PLAN
Manipulative Skills Using Beanbags
Level I

Supplies and Equipment Needed:
One beanbag per child — Music
One parachute — Tape player

MOVEMENT EXPERIENCE—CONTENT	ORGANIZATION AND TEACHING HINTS	EXPECTED STUDENT OBJECTIVES AND OUTCOMES

INTRODUCTORY ACTIVITY (2 – 3 MINUTES)

Move and assume pose:

1. Have children move using a variation of a locomotor movement. Freeze on signal and assume a pose using the following commands:
   a. Balance on different body parts
   b. Stretch
   c. Curl
   d. Bridge
   e. Push-up position
   f. V-sit position, try seat circles
   g. Stork stand
   Many challenges can be found in reference at right.

DPE p. 219

Scatter formation. Emphasize proper method of stopping quickly.

Discourage falling and lack of body control.

Encourage creativity in various poses

Try continuous movement without freeze command. Different poses and locomotor movements can be named.

PM.—The student will be able to perform the basic poses on command.

Cog.—The student will be able to recognize the basic command names and nonlocomotor movement.

PM.—The student will be able to stop quickly with good balance.

Aff.—Physical activity is an excellent means of releasing tension. Students will begin to appreciate the importance of exercise to enhance wellness.

FITNESS DEVELOPMENT ACTIVITIES (7 – 8 MINUTES)

Parachute Fitness

1. Jog in circle with chute held in left hand.
2. Shake the chute.
3. Slide to the right; return slide to the left.
4. Sit and perform situps - 30 seconds.
5. Skip for 20 seconds.
6. Freeze, face the center, and stretch the chute tightly. Hold for 8–12 seconds. Repeat five to six times.
7. Run in place while holding the chute taut at different levels.
8. Sit with legs under the chute. Do a seat walk toward the center. Return to the perimeter. Repeat four to six times.
9. Place the chute on the ground. Jog away from the chute and return on signal. Repeat for 30 seconds.
10. Shake the chute and jump in place.
11. Lie on back with feet under the chute. Shake the chute with the feet.
12. Hop to the center of the chute and return. Repeat for 20 seconds.

DPE pp. 244 – 245

Evenly space youngsters around the chute.

Use different grips to add variation to the activities.

Develop group morale by encouraging students to move together.

Use music to motivate youngsters.

To cool down, allow youngsters a minute to perform parachute stunts like the Dome or Mushroom.

Cog.—The student will be able to explain verbally why correct form is important when performing fitness activities.

PM.—The student will be able to perform all activities at the teacher established level.

Aff.—One of the reasons for fitness activities now is to establish patterns for later life. Establish the need for fitness throughout life through example and brief comments.

MOVEMENT EXPERIENCE— CONTENT	ORGANIZATION AND TEACHING HINTS	EXPECTED STUDENT OBJECTIVES AND OUTCOMES

13. Sit with feet under the chute. Stretch by touching the toes with the chute. Relax with other stretches while sitting.

LESSON FOCUS (15 – 20 MINUTES)

Beanbag Activities

DPE pp. 365 – 368

A. *In Place, Tossing to Self*
   1. Toss and catch with both hands—right hand, left hand.
   2. Toss and catch with the back of hands. This will force children to give and thus tend to develop "soft hands."
   3. Toss the beanbag to increasingly high levels, *emphasizing* a good straight throw. (To force the child to throw the beanbag directly overhead, have the child sit down.)
   4. Exploratory activity

Scatter formation.

Stress soft catch.

Keep eyes on the bag.

Try all challenges in sitting, back, or side positions.

Try all the toss and catch activities with the feet and combinations of feet, hands, and body parts.

PM.—The student will enhance his development of visual concentration on a moving object.

PM.—The student will be able to demonstrate "giving" with body to create a soft home for beanbag.

Cog.—The student will be able to recite the necessary ingredients for successful catching.

B. *In Place, Adding Stunts*
   1. Toss overhead and perform the following stunts and catch bag.
      a. 1/4 and 1/2 turns, right and left
      b. Full turn
      c. Touch floor
      d. Clap hands
      e. Clap hands around different parts of body, behind back, under legs
      f. Heel click
      g. Sit down, get up
      h. Look between legs

Emphasize keeping eyes on object while performing stunts.

Give them two or three activities to attempt so that you have time to move around and help children in need.

Catching is more important than the stunt.

Make sure that students are making good throws and catching the bag.

Use a change-of-pace activity. For example, place the beanbags on the floor and hop over five blue beanbags. Use different challenges.

Cog.—The student will be able to verbalize the importance of visually tracking moving projectiles.

Cog.—The student will be able to explain why catching is more difficult when the person is moving.

C. *Toss, Move, and Catch*
   1. Toss overhead, move to another spot, and catch.
   2. Toss, do a locomotor movement, and catch.
   3. Move from side to side.
   4. Toss overhead behind self, move, and catch.

Encourage the class to look where they are moving. This will force them to take their eyes off the object, recover, focus, and catch the bag, which is a more advanced skill.

PM.—The student will be able to propel the body and balance an object simultaneously.

D. *Balance the Beanbag*
   1. Balance on the following body parts:
      a. Head
      b. Back of hand
      c. Shoulder
      d. Knee
      e. Foot
      f. Elbow
      g. Exploratory activity
   2. Balance and move as follows:
      a. Walk
      b. Run
      c. Skip

Look for new and exciting ways of balancing the bags. Allow students to show their ideas to the rest of the class.

See who can balance her bag the longest on various body parts while moving.

If time allows, go back and polish some of the activities performed earlier in the week.

Aff.—Visual–tactile coordination demands a great deal of practice and repetition if the student is going to improve. Discuss the importance of tenacity and persistence in achieving a goal.

MOVEMENT EXPERIENCE—CONTENT	ORGANIZATION AND TEACHING HINTS	EXPECTED STUDENT OBJECTIVES AND OUTCOMES

    d. Gallop
    e. Sit down
    f. Lie down
    g. Turn around
    h. Combinations
    i. Exploratory activity

E. *Challenge Activities*
    1. Hold the beanbag between knees and play tag with a partner or small group.
    2. Place the beanbag on tummy and shake it off.
    3. Place the beanbag on back and Mule Kick it off.
    4. Push the beanbag across the floor with different body parts.
    5. Toss the beanbag up and touch specified body parts.
    6. Put beanbags on floor. Rotate various body parts on a beanbag.
    7. Beanbag balance tag—balance a beanbag on selected body parts. The color called identifies those who are it and try to tag others.

GAME (5 – 7 MINUTES)

Make this an active game in order to assure the class receives enough cardiovascular activity. The following are suggested:

1. Midnight, p. 516
2. Leap the Brook, p. 522
3. Parachute Activity, pp. 365 – 368

DYNAMIC PHYSICAL EDUCATION LESSON PLAN
Fundamental Skills Using Individual Mats
Level I

Supplies and Equipment Needed:
Record player and records
Individual mats—one for each child

MOVEMENT EXPERIENCE—CONTENT	ORGANIZATION AND TEACHING HINTS	EXPECTED STUDENT OBJECTIVES AND OUTCOMES

INTRODUCTORY ACTIVITY (2 – 3 MINUTES)

Locomotor Movements and Freeze

Stop quickly on signal with a wide base of support:
1. Walk
2. Run
3. Jump
4. Hop
5. Skip
6. Gallop
7. Leap
8. Slide

DPE p. 218

Scatter formation.

Have the class try different methods of stopping such as stiff body, flat feet, etc., and have them choose best method.

Explain terms as needed.

PM.—The student will be able to stop the body quickly after moving, using the basic locomotor movements.

Cog.—The student will be able to explain what is necessary to stop quickly.

FITNESS DEVELOPMENT ACTIVITIES (7 – 8 MINUTES)

Movement Challenges

Alternate locomotor movements with strength challenges. Repeat the challenges as necessary.
Locomotor Movement: Walk for 30 seconds.

A. *Trunk Development Challenges*
Bend in different directions.
Stretch slowly and return quickly.
Combine bending and stretching movements.
Sway back and forth.
Twist one body part; add body parts.
Make your body move in a large circle.
In a sitting position, wave your legs at a friend; make circles with your legs.
Locomotor Movement: Skip for 30 seconds.

B. *Shoulder Girdle Challenges*
In a push-up position, do the following challenges:
Lift one foot; the other foot.
Wave at a friend; wave with the other arm.
Scratch your back with one hand; use the other hand.
Walk your feet to your hands.
Turn over and face the ceiling; shake a leg; Crab Walk.
Locomotor Movement: Jog for 30 seconds.

DPE pp. 239 – 242

Scatter formation.

Individual mats can be used as a "home" to keep youngsters spaced properly.

Repeat the various trunk challenges as necessary.

Young children will perform best when locomotor movements are alternated with stationary challenges that allow them to recover aerobically.

Add Animal Walks to replace some of the locomotor movements and to create interest.

Use different qualities of movement such as giant skips, tiny and quick gallops, or slow giant steps to motivate youngsters.

As children become more fit, repeat the entire sequence.

PM.—The student will be able to perform all activities at teacher established level.

PM.—The student will demonstrate the ability to make maximum movements as directed.

Aff.—With regular exercise the heart muscle is strengthened. Encourage student understanding and appreciation of this fact through discussion.

MOVEMENT EXPERIENCE— CONTENT	ORGANIZATION AND TEACHING HINTS	EXPECTED STUDENT OBJECTIVES AND OUTCOMES

C. *Abdominal Development*
From a supine position:
    Lift your head and look at your toes.
    Lift your knees to your chest.
    Wave your legs at a friend.
From a sitting position:
    Slowly lay down with hands on tummy.
    Lift legs and touch toes.
Locomotor Movement: Run and leap for 45 seconds.		

Individual Mats	*DPE* pp. 431 – 432	

A. *Command Movements*
  1. Stretch
    a. Different directions.
    b. Different parts of body.
  2. Curl
  3. Balance
    a. Balance on different parts.
    b. Balance on different number of parts.
    c. Go from one balance to another.
  4. Bridge
    a. Bridge across the short width, long width.
    b. Different parts or number of parts.
    c. Bridge to a full arch.
  5. Reach
    a. Keep toes on mat, reach as far as possible.
    b. Keep hand on mat, reach as far as possible.
    c. Keep hand on mat, reach as far as possible with a foot.
  6. Rock
    a. On different parts.
  7. Roll
    a. Different rolls.
    b. Roll up in the mat.
  8. Twist
    a. Full twist, held.
    b. Moving twists.
    c. Twist and untwist.
  9. Use Other Terms
    a. Straight, curved, narrow, wide, prone, melt, shake, fall, collapse.
  10. Combination Movements
    a. By command (use terms).
    b. By changes (specified number).
	Each child gets a mat and sits (cross-legged) on it.
	
	Emphasize a full stretch.
	
	Try to secure variety. Use levels.
	
	Tightly on different parts.
	
	Hold for a few seconds.
	
	Go 5, 4, 3, 2, 1 parts.
	
	Try to work some nice arches.
	
	Try activities on tummy and back.
	
	Pupil demonstration.
	
	Full stretch out.
	
	Pupil demonstration.
	
	Forward, backward, sideways, log.
	
	Work each movement separately and then combine them.
	
	Get pupil input.
	
	Develop this well. Four or five changes.
		PM.—The student will be able to move the body into various shapes and positions quickly and efficiently.
		
		Cog.—The student will know the shapes and be able to identify the positions by name.
		
		PM.—The student will be able to develop versatility and variation in movement.
		
		Cog.—The student will be able to describe the proper care and use of mats.
		
		PM.—The student will be able to change from one pattern to another smoothly.

B. *On and off the Mats*
  1. Different locomotor movements—hop, jump, leap.
  2. Weight on the hands. Crouch jumps. Forward, backward.
	Use levels. Add turns, shapes, patterns.
	
	Secure suggestions.
		Cog.—The student will be able to differentiate and describe the following movements: hopping, jumping, and leaping.
		
		PM.—The student will be able to perform the hop, jump, and leap.

MOVEMENT EXPERIENCE—CONTENT	ORGANIZATION AND TEACHING HINTS	EXPECTED STUDENT OBJECTIVES AND OUTCOMES
3. Animal imitations: Rabbit, frog, etc.		

C. *Over the Mat*
  1. Locomotor movements: Add turns, secure height.
  2. Weight on the hands.
  3. Combinations: Over one, back another way.
  4. How many mats can you jump over in 10 seconds? Change the movements over the mat.
  5. Hop over five blue mats. Change the movement, number, and color of mats.
	Body shapes.
	
	Stress soft landing—relaxed.
	
	Stress levels.
	
	Allow choice.	

D. *Movements Around the Mat*
  1. Different locomotor movements.
  2. Animal walks: Dog, bear, cat, rabbit.
  3. Keep hands on the mat.
  4. Keep feet on the mat.
	Use both clockwise and counterclockwise directions.
	
	Allow exploration.
	
	Build up variation here.
		Aff.—Discuss the importance of watching out for others while moving. This could initiate a good discussion about concern for the welfare of other people.

E. *Mats as a Base*
  1. Different magic numbers
    a. So many movements out and back.
    b. Different combinations.
    c. Animal imitations.
    d. Others.
	Stress general space.
	
	Use magic numbers.	

F. *Challenge Activities*
  1. Try some individual and partner stunts with the mats as a base.
    a. Coffee Grinder
    b. Chinese Get-Up
    c. Wring the Dishrag
  2. Jump from mat to mat without touching floor. Can you move across the area? Skip from mat to mat.
  3. Play "Ring around the mat." Skip around the mat and all fall down.
  4. Move between five mats and cartwheel over two mats. Use different movements and tumbling activities.
  5. Put your mat together with a partner and make different shapes, numbers, and letters.
  6. Do the same thing in small groups. Magic carpet ride—one person pulls a partner sitting on the mat.
	Encourage students to build new challenges and sequences of movement.
	
	Turn the mat over and drive it like a car. (Push the mat with hands on the mat.)	

MOVEMENT EXPERIENCE— CONTENT	ORGANIZATION AND TEACHING HINTS	EXPECTED STUDENT OBJECTIVES AND OUTCOMES

GAME (5 – 7 MINUTES)

The following are suggested:
1. Mat Game, p. 432
   Like musical chairs, jump over mats. Use different command positions.
2. Red Light, p. 523
3. Sneak Attack, p. 523

Keep all mats on the floor at first, and then turn over one mat.

Students may not stand on the mat that is turned over.

DYNAMIC PHYSICAL EDUCATION LESSON PLAN
Kicking, Trapping, Bowling, and Rolling Skills
Level I

Supplies and Equipment Needed:
  One partially deflated playground or foam training ball for each child
  Cones for marking areas for lead-up activities
  One hoop for each child
  Bowling pins or Indian clubs

MOVEMENT EXPERIENCE— CONTENT	ORGANIZATION AND TEACHING HINTS	EXPECTED STUDENT OBJECTIVES AND OUTCOMES

INTRODUCTORY ACTIVITY (2 – 3 MINUTES)

Hoops—Free Activity

Issue a hoop for each child. Give them 2–3 minutes of free activity.

If students have difficulty thinking of activities, suggest some of the following:
  1. Run or hop with hoop, stop and jump the hoop.
  2. Run and roll the hoop like a tire.
  3. Spin the hoop and see how many times you can run around it.
  4. Roll the hoop and go through it.

DPE p. 386

Scatter formation.

Encourage variety of response by asking individuals to show their activity.

Students should combine some locomotor movement with their hoop activities.

Cog.—Introductory activity is performed in order to warm up the body for more strenuous activity.

PM.—The student will develop an introductory activity that combines two hoop activities with a locomotor movement.

FITNESS DEVELOPMENT ACTIVITIES (7 – 8 MINUTES)

Walk, Trot, and Sprint

Move to the following signals:
  1. One drumbeat - walk.
  2. Two drumbeats - trot.
  3. Three drumbeats - sprint.
  4. Whistle - freeze and perform exercises.

Perform various strength and flexibility exercises between bouts of walk, trot, and sprint. Examples are:
  a. Bend and Twist
  b. Sitting Stretch
  c. Push-Up variations
  d. Sit-Up variations
  e. Trunk Twister
  f. Body Circles

DPE p. 245

Use a tom-tom or tambourine.

Scatter formation.

Emphasize quality of movement and rapid changes

Check heart rate after bouts of sprinting.

Alternate bouts of movement with strength and flexibility exercises.

Cog.—The student will be able to explain why it is necessary to increase the activity work load in order to provide additional stress on the body and increase fitness levels.

Aff.—Physically fit people are rewarded by society. Teachers, parents, and peers respond much more favorably to those fit and attractive. Discuss the social importance of fitness.

LESSON FOCUS (15 – 20 MINUTES)

Kicking and Ball Control Skills

  1. *Inside of Foot Kick*
     Approach at 45° angle; inside of foot meets ball. Place nonkicking foot alongside ball.
  2. *Outside of Foot Kick*
     Short distance kick; keep toe down.
  3. *Long Pass*

DPE pp. 618 – 622

Begin with informal kicking and trapping to get the feel of the ball.

Partner work or triangle formation.

One ball for three children.

Keep head down. Eyes on ball. Follow through.

PM.—The student will be able to pass, kick, and trap the ball successfully at the end of the week.

Cog.—The student will be able to explain why in kicking, accuracy is much preferred over raw power and lack of control.

MOVEMENT EXPERIENCE—CONTENT	ORGANIZATION AND TEACHING HINTS	EXPECTED STUDENT OBJECTIVES AND OUTCOMES

Not accurate; used for distance; approach ball from behind.
4. *Sole of Foot Control*
   Use sole of foot to stop ball; make sure weight is placed on the nonreceiving foot.
5. *Inside of Foot Control*
   Use inside of foot; learn to "give" with leg so ball doesn't ricochet off foot.
	If short supply of gray foam balls, partially deflate 8-1/2-inch playground balls. They will move more slowly and be easier for youngsters to handle.
	
	Make sure students don't handle the balls with their hands. They must retrieve and move the balls with feet only.
		Aff.—Even in basic lead-up games, teamwork is necessary for success and enjoyment by all.

Lead-Up Activities Note: It is possible to teach soccer-related activities at the primary level. However, emphasis must be placed on the individual. Give each child a ball when possible and work in as small groups as possible. Drills have little value as do complicated team games. It might be necessary to play an unrelated game in the middle of the lesson when interest wanes. Emphasize correct movement patterns—it is important that youngsters develop proper motor patterns so they will not have to be changed at a later date. Skill level will vary widely, but if children learn to handle an object with their feet, they will be much more advanced than most American students. 1. *Circle Kickball*—p. 629 For younger children, put them in a circle and let them kick the ball back and forth. Use small circles. 2. *Soccer Touch Ball*—p. 629 – 630 3. *Dribblerama*—p. 630	Teach skills from a stationary position; as students improve, introduce movement. Practice the kicking skills against a wall. Emphasis should be on velocity of the kick rather than accuracy if a correct pattern is to be developed. Practice individual dribbling skills. Students move throughout the area and dodge other students. Foam training balls are excellent for teaching lead-up activities to prevent fear of being hurt. Circle formation, two circles necessary. Emphasize kicking the ball below *waist* level. Two circles. Emphasize short, accurate passes. Pass quickly; don't hold the ball.	Aff.—It is acceptable to make mistakes when learning a skill. Even professional athletes make many performance mistakes. Aff.—Students will learn to appreciate individual differences and show concern for the welfare of others. Take time to discuss this important attitude.
Bowling and Rolling Skills 1. Two-handed roll—between the legs, with wide straddle stance. 2. Roll the ball with one hand. Use both left and right hands. 3. Roll the ball and put spin on the ball so it will curve to the left and right.	When bowling with one hand, the other hand should serve as a guide. Use the opposite rule; when bowling with the right hand, step forward with the left foot. Use beachballs or foam balls for very small children.	PM.—The student will be able to explain the opposition rule in his own words. PM.—The student will be able to roll the ball properly utilizing opposition of body parts and body coordination. PM.—While using human straddle targets, the student will be able to score 7 points from a distance of 15 feet.

MOVEMENT EXPERIENCE—CONTENT	ORGANIZATION AND TEACHING HINTS	EXPECTED STUDENT OBJECTIVES AND OUTCOMES

4. Roll the ball through human straddle targets:
   a. Start rolling at moderate distances and gradually increase as bowlers become more proficient.
   b. Use left and right hands.
   c. Scoring can be done giving two points for a ball that goes through the target without touching and one point for a ball going through, but touching a leg.
5. Use objects such as milk cartons, Indian clubs, or bowling pins for targets. Various bowling games can be developed using the targets.
6. Stand with your back facing your partner. Bend over, look through your legs, and bowl.
7. Play Bowling One Step (p. 531) as a culminating activity.
8. Soccer skills can be practiced by the receiver. For example, the following skills are suggested:
   a. Toe Trap
   b. The Foot Pickup
   c. Bowl with Your Feet

Encourage students to keep their eyes on the target.

Work in groups of three—one on each end and one in the middle.

Some students should retrieve the ball, others reset the pins, and the rest bowl. Rotate responsibilities often.

Emphasize the importance of accuracy over speed.

The playground balls can be deflated somewhat to make them easier to handle.

Aff.—The student will demonstrate a desire to help others by performing all the duties necessary such as retrieving the ball and setting up the pins.

Cog.—The student will be able to explain the difference between a "hook" ball and a "backup" ball.

GAME (5 – 7 MINUTES)

The following are suggested:
1. Back to Back, p. 516
2. Change Sides, p. 520
3. Musical Ball Pass, p. 512

DYNAMIC PHYSICAL EDUCATION LESSON PLAN
Educational Movement (Lesson 1)
Level I

Fundamental Skill: Walking
Manipulative Activity: Beachballs
Educational Movement Themes: Identification of body parts, personal space

Supplies and Equipment Needed:
  One inflated beachball for each child (or use balloons)
  Tom-tom or dance drum
  One jump rope for each child
  Lummi sticks
  Stocking paddles
  One beanbag for each child
  Tape player

MOVEMENT EXPERIENCE—CONTENT	ORGANIZATION AND TEACHING HINTS	EXPECTED STUDENT OBJECTIVES AND OUTCOMES

INTRODUCTORY ACTIVITY (2 – 3 MINUTES)

European Running

1. Run and stop.
2. Run, and on signal make a full turn; continue in same direction. Turn the other way.
3. Run, and on signal run in general space. On next signal, re-form the original pattern.
4. Run and move the upper body up and down in a rhythmic fashion.
5. Run and clap the rhythm.

DPE pp. 217 – 218

Scatter around perimeter of area.

Check on stopping techniques.

Turn is made with four running steps. Lift knees.

PM.—The student will be able to develop a smooth, rhythmic run.

PM.—Students will be able to develop the ability to space themselves while running.

Cog.—The student will be able to describe stopping techniques.

FITNESS DEVELOPMENT ACTIVITIES (7 – 8 MINUTES)

Jump Rope Exercises

1. Place the rope on the floor and perform locomotor movements around and over the rope. Make different shapes and letters with the rope.
2. Hold the folded rope overhead. Sway from side to side. Twist right and left.
3. Lie on back with rope held with outstretched arms toward ceiling. Bring up one leg at a time and touch the rope with toes. Lift both legs together. Sit up and try to hook the rope over the feet. Release and repeat.
4. Jump rope. If not able to jump, practice swinging the rope to the side - 45 seconds.
5. Fold the rope and perform various isometric exercises.
6. Fold the rope and use it as a tail. Try to keep others from pulling the tail.
7. Touch toes with the folded rope.
8. Jump rope - 45 seconds.

DPE p. 245

Place the ropes around the perimeter of the area so they can quickly pick up and return a jump rope.

If youngsters have difficulty jumping the rope, offer alternate challenges.

Use music to motivate children when they are jumping rope.

An alternative is to substitute long-rope jumping. Since not all children are jumping, it is less demanding and easier for children to perform.

PM.—The student will demonstrate the ability to change from slow to fast and vice versa.

Cog.—The student will know the meaning of the terms "slow" and "fast" times.

MOVEMENT EXPERIENCE— CONTENT	ORGANIZATION AND TEACHING HINTS	EXPECTED STUDENT OBJECTIVES AND OUTCOMES

9. Place rope on the floor and do various Animal Walks along or over the rope.
10. Do Push-Up variations with the rope folded and held between the hands.
11. Jump rope - 45 seconds.

LESSON FOCUS (15 – 20 MINUTES)

Educational Movement

Note: A few activities should be chosen from each section and presented alternately so students receive a wide variety of activities. If students are fatigued from the fitness portion of the lesson, start with the manipulative activities.

A. *Fundamental Skill: Walking*
Toes reasonably pointed ahead.
Arms swing naturally.
Head up and eyes focused ahead.
Stride normal.
Avoid up-and-down motion.
Upper body erect, shoulders in good position.

  DPE pp. 292 – 294

  Select from formations on pp. 81 – 85
  Cue by saying:

    "Head up—eyes forward. Point toes straight ahead. Nice, easy, relaxed arm swing.

    Lift chest, stand tall. Shoulders back and easy. Hold tummy in, chest up."

  Cog.—The student will know the meaning of the term "walking."

1. Walk in different directions, changing direction on signal (90°).
2. While walking, bring up the knees and slap with the hands on each step.
3. Walk on heels, toes, side of the foot, Charlie Chaplin fashion (toes pointed way out).
4. Gradually lower the body while walking; gradually raise body.
5. Walk with a smooth gliding step.
6. Walk with a wide base on tiptoes; rock from side to side.

  Drum rhythm can be provided throughout.

  PM.—The student will be able to walk smoothly and rhythmically in good postural position.

7. Clap hands alternately front and back. Clap hands under the thighs (slow walk).
8. Walk slowly. Accelerate. Decelerate.
9. Take long strides. Tiny steps.
10. Change levels on signal.
11. Walk quickly and quietly. Slowly and heavily. Quickly and heavily, etc.
12. Change direction on signal while facing the same way.
13. Walk, angrily, happily; add others.
14. Hold arms in different positions. Try different arm movements as you walk.

  Cog.—The student will understand and react in conformance to the different directives.

  Cue: "Reach with the toes."

  Explain terms.

  Cog.—The student will be able to create unique responses.

MOVEMENT EXPERIENCE— CONTENT	ORGANIZATION AND TEACHING HINTS	EXPECTED STUDENT OBJECTIVES AND OUTCOMES
15. Walk different patterns: circle, square, rectangle, figure eight, etc.	Explain terms as needed.	
16. Walk through heavy mud, on ice or slick floor on a rainy day.		
17. Walk like a soldier, a giant, a robot; add others.		
18. Duck under trees or railings while walking.		
19. Point toes out in different directions while walking—in, forward, and out.		
20. Walk with high knees, stiff knees, one stiff knee, sore ankle.		
21. Walk toward a spot, turn around in four steps. Move in a different direction.		
22. Practice changing steps while walking.		
23. Walk with a military goose step.		
24. Walk a different way.		

B. *Working with Balloons or Beach-balls*

MOVEMENT EXPERIENCE— CONTENT	ORGANIZATION AND TEACHING HINTS	EXPECTED STUDENT OBJECTIVES AND OUTCOMES
1. Keep your balloon in the air by rebounding it from the hand, fist, arm, elbow, knee, shoulder, head, and other body parts. Use one finger. Use the feet to keep balloon in the air.	*DPE* pp. 364 – 365 Scattered formation. Some movement in general space. Begin with specific body parts and move to general areas. Challenge with directives using the terms. Half with sticks, half with paddles.	PM.—The student will develop the ability to track the descending balloon or beachball and control it. Cog.—The student will understand the meaning of contrasting terms as used. Cog.—An object rebounds according to the amount of force applied to it. The student will be able to explain this concept in his own words.
2. Work out combinations of body parts, four different parts in succession.		

3. Add contrasting terms:
    close–far
    in front of–behind
    near–far
    right–left
    high–low
    sudden–smooth		

4. Use Lummi sticks and/or paddles:
  a. Explore keeping balloon or beachball up in the air.
  b. Hit with different parts of stick or paddle. Work out sequences. Alternate a body part with the stick or paddle.
  c. Use contrasting terms.
  d. Work with a partner.
  e. Change sticks with paddles.		

5. Keep one foot in place, control balloon or beachball.	Could use hoops, individual mats, carpet squares, etc.	
6. Play "let's pretend" we are volleyball players. Practice overhand, underhand, dig passes. Show serving.	Explain volleyball terms.	

MOVEMENT EXPERIENCE—CONTENT	ORGANIZATION AND TEACHING HINTS	EXPECTED STUDENT OBJECTIVES AND OUTCOMES
7. Exploratory activity by individuals. Allow choice or partners.		
C. *Identifying Body Parts* 1. Children can be standing or seated. Touch the part or parts with both hands without looking at it. Children should repeat out loud the designated part touched by saying, "I am touching _____." Touch your shoulders Touch your ankles Touch your head Touch your toes Touch your ears Touch your knees Touch your eyes Touch your hips Touch your cheeks Touch your forehead Touch your thighs Touch your elbows	*DPE* pp. 279 – 280 Scatter formation or circle. This is a thinking–doing activity. Give commands briskly. Children hold until the following command is given. Order can be varied.	PM.—The student will be able to demonstrate the ability to touch the designated parts with assurance. Cog.—The student will know the names of the various body parts.
2. *Fun Activity* Teacher touches the incorrect part of the body as commands are given.		
3. As a part is named, form a pose so that this part is the highest position of your body; the lowest.	Add other body parts, such as face, eyebrows, nose, jaw, chin, neck, chest, back, stomach, arms, forearms, wrists, thumbs, waist, feet, arches, heels.	
4. Move about general space in any manner you wish. When I call out a body part, stop and put both hands on the part or parts.	Check for accuracy. Name muscles such as biceps, abdominals, quadriceps, etc.	
5. Toss your beanbag in personal space. When I call out the name of a body part, sit down and put the beanbag on or against the part.	Issue beanbags.	
6. Select some kind of a way you wish to move in general space. The signal to move will be the name of a body part. Move around the room with one hand on the body part. When another body part is called out, change the type of movement and also hold that body part.		
D. *Exploring Personal Space* 1. Each child has a jump rope. Double the rope and grasp it by the handles. In a kneeling position, swing the rope in a full arc along the floor. Use other positions: sitting cross-legged, or others.	*DPE* p. 280 Issue jump ropes. Circle both clockwise and counterclockwise. Ropes do not touch other ropes or children. Put ropes to one side.	Cog.—Each child will be able to grasp the concept and define personal space. PM.—Each student will be able physically to define her personal space.

MOVEMENT EXPERIENCE— CONTENT	ORGANIZATION AND TEACHING HINTS	EXPECTED STUDENT OBJECTIVES AND OUTCOMES
2. Keeping one foot in place on a spot, make a full arc with the other foot. Keep both one foot and one hand touching the spot; arc again with other foot. 3. Keeping your feet in place, sway and reach out as far as you can without losing balance or moving feet. Try with feet together and feet apart. Which is better for balance? Sit down and repeat movements. Do you need more or less space? 4. Here are some of the kinds of movements you can do in personal space: a. Make yourself as wide as possible. Change to narrow. Experiment with narrow, small–large, high–low, etc. Try from other positions—kneeling, sitting, balancing on seat, standing on one foot, lying on stomach, and others. b. In supine position, move arms and legs in different combinations out and back. c. Select one part of the body to keep in place. Make big circles with the rest of the body. Select other parts. d. Explore different positions where one foot is higher than any other body part. e. Pump yourself up like a balloon. Get bigger and bigger until I say "Pop!" f. Let's pretend you are a snowman melting to the ground under a hot sun. g. With your feet in place, twist as far as you can one way and then the other (arms out to sides). Show me how a top spins.	Also identifies personal space. Stretch fully, all directions. Provide choice. Look for unilateral, bilateral, and cross-lateral movements. May need to speed up the melting a bit.	Cog.—Students should find that a wide base is best. Cog.—Students should find that less space is needed when seated. Aff.—The children will have the urge to explore and create.

GAME (5 – 7 MINUTES)

The following are suggested:
1. Jack Frost and Jane Thaw, p. 513
2. Marching Ponies, p. 513
3. Tag Games, p. 518

DYNAMIC PHYSICAL EDUCATION LESSON PLAN
Rhythmic Movement (Lesson 1)
Level I

Supplies and Equipment Needed:
Magic number cards
Record player and records
Parachute
Tom-tom
Balls
Cones
Wands
Hoops
Mats

Dances Taught:
Ach Ja
Let Your Feet Go Tap, Tap, Tap
Did You Ever See a Lassie
Carrousel
Movin' Madness
Jolly Is the Miller

MOVEMENT EXPERIENCE—CONTENT	ORGANIZATION AND TEACHING HINTS	EXPECTED STUDENT OBJECTIVES AND OUTCOMES

INTRODUCTORY ACTIVITY (2 – 3 MINUTES)

Magic Number Challenges

Students put together a series of movements based on the magic numbers given. For example, hold a card with three numbers on it (10, 8, 14). The students must then perform any three movements the specified number of times, respectively.

DPE p. 220

Encourage variety of response.

Scatter formation.

Encourage students to use all the available space.

If difficulty occurs, use only two numbers in the sequence.

PM.—The student will be able to change movements quickly and correctly count the desired number of repetitions.

FITNESS DEVELOPMENT ACTIVITIES (7 – 8 MINUTES)

Mini-Challenge Course

Arrange three or four courses with a group at each course. Students perform the challenges from start to finish and jog back to repeat the course. On signal, groups move to a new course.

Course 1. Crouch jumps; pulls or scooter movements down a bench; through two hoops; and skip to a cone.

Course 2. Weave in and out of four wands held upright by cones; Crab Walk; hang from a climbing rope for 5 seconds; and gallop to a cone.

Course 3. Do a tumbling activity length of mat; agility run through hoops; Frog Jump; and slide to a cone.

Course 4. Move over and under six obstacles; Log Roll length of mat; while jumping, circle around three cones; and run to a cone.

DPE p. 243

Set up four parallel (side-by-side) courses in one-half of the area. Rotate groups to each course after a specified time.

An alternative is to organize the courses into a single circuit around the perimeter of the area.

Movement should be continuous.

Since young children fatigue and recover quickly, stop the class after 30–45 seconds and perform fitness movement challenges.

Cog.—The students will be able to name each of the movements they select.

Cog.—The student will recognize and perform all verbally designated tasks.

PM.—The student will be able to perform the new fitness routine by the end of the week,

Aff.—In most sports, performance falls off when muscular fatigue sets in. Muscular endurance is an important factor in delaying fatigue. Discuss the value of fitness for better athletic performance.

MOVEMENT EXPERIENCE—CONTENT	ORGANIZATION AND TEACHING HINTS	EXPECTED STUDENT OBJECTIVES AND OUTCOMES

LESSON FOCUS (15 – 20 MINUTES)

Rhythms

A. *Marching*
Try the following sequence:
1. Clap hands while standing in place to the beat of a tom-tom or record.
2. Take steps in place; always start with the left foot.
3. March to the music in scatter formation, adding some of the following challenges:
   a. Be as big or small as you can.
   b. Count the rhythm.
   c. Change direction on signal.
   d. March backwards.
   e. March loudly or quietly.
   f. Make up a rhythmic poem like "Sound Off."
4. Try some simple patterns such as the following:
   a. Single-line formation.
   b. Double-line formation (with a partner).
   c. Two lines meet and go up the center.
   d. Two lines meet and split on signal.
   e. Make up your own formation.

DPE pp. 313 – 362

Scatter formation.

Use any piece of music that has a steady rhythm.

Try to keep head up and stay in good posture.

By adding different challenges to the marching, it will force the student to concentrate and remain motivated.

When marching in line, try to maintain even spacing between people.

This activity can be an excellent lead-up for the Grand March.

Wave at the "people" while marching. Pretend you are in a parade.

Try teaching commands such as "mark time," "about face," "forward march," and "halt." Be a drum major.

Pretend to play an instrument in a marching band.

PM.—The student will be able to march in time to the rhythmic beat.

Aff.—Discuss the difficulty of learning to perform two or more skills at the same time: for example, a marching band or ice skating to music.

Cog.—Temperature affects physical performance. Discuss how heat will decrease performance in endurance activities and the need for replenishing body fluids.

B. *Parachute Rhythmic Routine*
Try a rhythmic routine using the parachute. An example might be the following:

Beats 1-8 Eight walking steps to the left. Hold chute in both hands.
9-16 Eight backward steps to the right.
17-20 Raise parachute above head (Up-2-3-4).
21-24 Lower chute to floor (Down-2-3-4).
25-32 Shake the chute (Up and Down).
33-36 Raise the chute overhead.
37-44 Lower chute quickly to floor and form a dome. Hold the dome for eight beats.

DPE pp. 433 – 436

Before trying this routine to music, it might be wise to practice with the beat of a tom-tom.

A good idea for practice might be to first try the routine without the chute.

Offer youngsters an opportunity to develop simple routines and parachute movements.

Cog.—Parachute activities require teamwork. Students must work together to perform the tasks.

PM.—The student will be able to perform the parachute activities to the rhythm of the music.

MOVEMENT EXPERIENCE— CONTENT	ORGANIZATION AND TEACHING HINTS	EXPECTED STUDENT OBJECTIVES AND OUTCOMES

C. *Dances*

1. Ach Ja (p. 327)

2. Let Your Feet Go Tap, Tap, Tap (p. 326)

3. Did You Ever See a Lassie? (p. 324)

4. Carrousel (pp. 331 – 332)

5. Movin' Madness (p. 324)

6. Jolly Is the Miller (p. 332)

When teaching a dance, use the following steps:
1. Tell about the dance and listen to the music.
2. Clap the beat and learn the verse.
3. Practice the dance steps without the music and with verbal cues.
4. Practice the dance with the music.

Make dances easy for students to learn by using some of the following ideas:
1. Teach the dances without partners.
2. Allow youngsters to move in any direction—avoid the left–right orientation.
3. Use scattered formation instead of circles—it helps avoid embarrassment.
4. Emphasize strong movements such as clapping and stomping to encourage involvement.
5. Tape the music at a slower speed when first learning the dance.

Rhythms should be taught like other sport skills. Avoid expecting perfection when teaching rhythms. Teach a variety of dances rather than one or two in depth. Youngsters will enjoy rhythms if they know it is acceptable to make mistakes without being ridiculed.

Cog.—The student will be able to sing the verses of the singing games.

Aff.—Rhythmic activities are a learned skill. Performers need to practice them many times before they are mastered. Discuss the need for understanding individual differences in rates of learning.

GAMES (5 – 7 MINUTES)

1. Squirrel in the Trees, p. 518
2. Stop Ball, p. 519

DYNAMIC PHYSICAL EDUCATION LESSON PLAN
Long-Rope Jumping Skills
Level I

Supplies and Equipment Needed:
  One long-jump rope (16 ft.) for each group of 4–6 children
  Individual jump ropes
  Tom-tom
  Cones
  Circuit training signs
  Balls
  Hula hoops
  Beanbags

MOVEMENT EXPERIENCE—CONTENT	ORGANIZATION AND TEACHING HINTS	EXPECTED STUDENT OBJECTIVES AND OUTCOMES

INTRODUCTORY ACTIVITY (2 – 3 MINUTES)

Crossing the River

A river is designated by two lines about 40 feet apart. Each time the youngsters cross the river they must perform a different movement. For example:
1. Run, walk, hop, skip, leap.
2. Animal Walks such as bear, crab, and puppy dog.
3. Partner run, back to back, side by side.

DPE p. 220

Delineate two lines 40 feet apart with cones.

Divide class with one-half on each side of the river.

Perform movements for 1 minute, rest, and stretch. Perform movements again.

PM.—The student will be able to perform the various movement activities for one minute.

Cog.—The student will understand and be able to explain the need for introductory activities.

FITNESS DEVELOPMENT ACTIVITIES (7 – 8 MINUTES)

Circuit Training

1. Rope jumping
2. Push-Ups
3. Agility run
4. Arm Circling
5. Rowing
6. Crab Walk
7. Hula Hooping

Begin with 20 seconds activity, 10 seconds to change.

Use animal walks or locomotor movements to move between stations.

DPE pp. 259 – 262

Increase the amount of time at each station to 25 seconds and decrease the amount of rest between stations.

The students must be able to perform the exercises well to assure the effectiveness of circuit training.

Have youngsters point to the next station before rotating to avoid confusion.

Perform aerobic activities at the end of the circuit.

PM.—The student will be able to perform all exercises on the circuit.

Cog.—The student will be able to explain how the circuit exercises all areas of the body: arm–shoulder girdle, trunk, and legs.

Aff.—Most fitness gains are made when the body is exercised past the point of initial fatigue. Thus, briefly discuss the value of pushing one's self past the first signs of tiring.

LESSON FOCUS (15 – 20 MINUTES)

Long-Rope Jumping

1. Jump a stationary rope, gradually raise the rope.
2. Ocean Waves—Shake the rope with an up-and-down motion. Students try to jump a "low spot."

DPE pp. 399 – 403

Groups of four to six children.

These are introductory activities that should aid nonjumpers.

Concentrate on *not* touching the rope (body awareness).

Primary-grade children must be taught *how* to start and maintain proper turning of the long rope. Work hard on this step.

PM.—The student will be able to jump the rope a minimum of eight times consecutively without a miss.

Cog.—In terms of physical exercise, 10 minutes of rope jumping is equal to 30 minutes of jogging. The student will be able to explain this fact in his own words.

MOVEMENT EXPERIENCE—CONTENT	ORGANIZATION AND TEACHING HINTS	EXPECTED STUDENT OBJECTIVES AND OUTCOMES

3. Snake in the grass—Wiggle the rope back and forth on the grass. Jump without touching the rope.
4. Pendulum swing—Move the rope back and forth like a pendulum. Jump the rope as it approaches the jumper.
5. Practice turning the rope with a partner. A good lead-up activity is to practice turning with individual jump ropes. The skill of turning *must* precede jumping skills.
6. Practice turning the rope to rhythm. A record with a strong beat or a steady tom-tom beat is useful for developing rhythmic turning. Turning the rope to a steady rhythm *must* precede jumping skills.
7. Stand in the center of the turners and jump the rope as it is turned once.
8. Run through a turning rope.
9. Run in, jump once, and run out.
10. Front door—turn the rope toward the jumper.
11. Try the following variations:
    a. Run in front door and out back door.
    b. Run in back door and out front door.
    c. Run in back door and out back door.
    d. Run in front or back door, jump a specified number of times, and out.
    e. Run in front or back door, jump, and do a quarter, half, and full turn in the air.
    f. Touch the ground while jumping.
    g. Turn around while jumping.
12. Hot Pepper—*gradually* increase the speed of the rope.
13. High Water—*gradually* raise the height of the rope while it is turned.

Tying one end of a rope to a hook on the wall or a chair will make it easier for children to turn long ropes.

Use 9- 12-foot ropes for teaching primary grade rope turning. The shorter ropes are easier for young children to turn.

Cross-age tutoring is excellent. Have older students teach kindergarten children to turn.

Two children turn and the others jump. Make sure that all children get a chance to both turn and jump.

Back door is much more difficult. Approach the rope at a 45° angle.

Girls will probably be much more skilled in this activity.

Make sure the turners maintain a constant rhythm with the rope. Children who have trouble should face one of the turners and key their jumps to both the visual and audio cues (hand movement and sound of the rope hitting the floor).

It might be helpful to review beanbag activity as a change-of-pace activity.

Try to eliminate excessive body movement while jumping, i.e., jumping too high.

Use Hot Pepper verse, p. 402.

Cog.—Rope jumping burns a large number of calories as compared to other activities. The youngster will understand that exercise helps prevent obesity.

Aff.—Rope jumping is neither a masculine nor feminine activity. It is performed by boxers, football players, and dancers for fitness development. Discuss its value for both sexes.

PM.—The student will be able to turn the rope front and back door, hot pepper, and high water.

GAME (5 – 7 MINUTES)

A game that doesn't contain too much activity probably is a good choice due to the active lesson focus. The following are suggested:
1. Ball Passing, p. 519
2. Hot Potatoes, p. 522
3. Aviator, p. 520

DYNAMIC PHYSICAL EDUCATION LESSON PLAN
Manipulative Skills Using Playground Balls
Level I

Supplies and Equipment Needed:
One 8-1/2" playground ball for each student
Tom-tom

MOVEMENT EXPERIENCE—CONTENT	ORGANIZATION AND TEACHING HINTS	EXPECTED STUDENT OBJECTIVES AND OUTCOMES

INTRODUCTORY ACTIVITY (2 – 3 MINUTES)

Combination Movements

1. Hop, turn around, and shake.
2. Jump, make a shape in the air, balance.
3. Skip, collapse, and roll.
4. Curl, roll, jump with a half turn.
5. Whirl, skip, sink slowly.
6. Hop, collapse, creep.
7. Kneel, sway, jump to feet.
8. Lift, grin, and roll.

DPE p. 220

Scatter formation.

Use the tom-tom to signal movement changes.

Challenge students to develop their own sequences.

Repeat the challenges so youngsters can create different movements using the same words.

PM.—The student will be able to perform the various combinations and demonstrate an understanding of the movements' terms.

Cog.—The student will be able to recognize various movements by name.

FITNESS DEVELOPMENT ACTIVITIES (7 – 8 MINUTES)

Movement Challenges

Alternate locomotor movements with strength challenges. Repeat the challenges as necessary.
Locomotor Movement: Walk for 30 seconds.

A. *Trunk Development Challenges*
Bend in different directions.
Stretch slowly and return quickly.
Combine bending and stretching movements.
Sway back and forth.
Twist one body part; add body parts.
Make your body move in a large circle.
In a sitting position, wave your legs at a friend; make circles with your legs.
Locomotor Movement: Skip for 30 seconds.

B. *Shoulder Girdle Challenges*
In a push-up position, do the following challenges:
Lift one foot; the other foot.
Wave at a friend; wave with the other arm.
Scratch your back with one hand; use the other hand.
Walk your feet to your hands.
Turn over and face the ceiling; shake a leg; Crab Walk.
Locomotor Movement: Jog for 30 seconds.

DPE pp. 239 – 242

Scatter formation.

Individual mats can be used as a "home" to keep youngsters spaced properly.

Repeat the various trunk challenges as necessary.

Young children will perform best when locomotor movements are alternated with stationary challenges that allow them to recover aerobically.

Add Animal Walks to replace some of the locomotor movements and to create interest.

Use different qualities of movement such as giant skips, tiny and quick gallops, or slow giant steps to motivate youngsters.

As children become more fit, repeat the entire sequence.

Cog.—The student will be able to recognize the names of the activities and be able to demonstrate each one.

PM.—The student will be able to perform the challenges at an increased dosage level.

MOVEMENT EXPERIENCE—CONTENT	ORGANIZATION AND TEACHING HINTS	EXPECTED STUDENT OBJECTIVES AND OUTCOMES

C. *Abdominal Development*
From a supine position:
Lift your head and look at your toes.
Lift your knees to your chest.
Wave your legs at a friend.
From a sitting position:
Slowly lay down with hands on tummy.
Lift legs and touch toes.
Locomotor Movement: Run and leap for 45 seconds.

Playground Balls

A. *Individual Activities*
1. Bounce and Catch
   a. Two hands, one hand.
   b. Bounce at different levels.
   c. Bounce between legs.
   d. Close eyes and bounce.
   e. Dribble ball in a stationary and/or moving position.
   f. Dribble and follow the commands, such as move forward, back, in a circle, sideways, while walking, galloping, trotting, etc.
   g. Exploratory activity.
2. Toss and Catch
   a. Toss and catch, vary height.
   b. Add various challenges while tossing (i.e., touch floor, clap hands, turn, sit down, lie down).
   c. Toss and let bounce. Also add some challenges as above.
   d. Toss up and catch behind back—toss from behind back and catch in front of body.
   e. Create moving challenges, i.e., toss, run five steps and catch, toss and back up five hops and catch.
   f. Exploratory activity.
3. Foot Skills
   a. Lift the ball up with both feet and catch. Both front and rear of body catch.
   b. From a sitting position, ball between feet, toss up, and catch with hands.
   c. Keep the ball in the air with feet and different body parts.

LESSON FOCUS (15 – 20 MINUTES)

DPE pp. 368 – 372

One 8-1/2" playground ball per child.

Warm up with controlled rolling while sitting. Also practice rolling from standing position.

Emphasize keeping the eyes on the ball and catching with the fingertips.

Make sure children "give" when they catch the ball and make a soft home.

Encourage children to start with a low toss in the air and gradually increase the height of the throw as skill increases.

The purpose of the many variations is to force children to keep their eyes on the moving object while performing another activity with their bodies.

Practice tossing the ball straight up and accurately.

See how many catches can be made in a row.

Strive for quality, good throws, and a high percentage of catches.

PM.—The students will be able to keep their eyes on the ball during all challenges and activities.

PM.—The student will be able to make a good toss to enable a good catch.

Cog.—The student will be able to interpret orally the many uses of the basic ball skills introduced in this lesson.

Aff.—Develop the attitude that mere accomplishment of a skill is not a goal of people who excel. Rather, a person must be able to master the skill many times and with consistency to be a champion.

Cog.—The student will be able to identify the sport in which the various passes are used.

PM.—The student will be able to pass (all variations) and catch the ball without dropping it, three times in succession.

MOVEMENT EXPERIENCE—CONTENT	ORGANIZATION AND TEACHING HINTS	EXPECTED STUDENT OBJECTIVES AND OUTCOMES

B. *Partner Activities: Partner Rolling, Throwing*
  1. Roll ball back and forth
    a. Two-handed, right and left.
    b. Targets, straddle, pins, etc.
  2. Bouncing and throwing
    a. Begin with bouncing skills.
    b. Different tosses first.
    c. Different throws. Two-handed right and left.
  3. Batting
    a. Serve to partner, who catches.
    b. Toss for a volleyball return.
    c. Bat back and forth positions.
  4. Throwing from different positions.
    a. Kneeling, sitting.
  5. Use follow activity, one partner leads and the other follows.
  6. Allow for exploration and creativity.
 	
The following games are suggested:
  1. Teacher Ball, p. 519
  2. The Scarecrow and the Crows, p. 514
	Partner organization.
	
	Distances should be short, then increased.
	
	Keep body low.
	
	Use one-step.
	
	Use underhand first. One bounce to partner.
	
	Keep distances short. Show technique. Use a line or bench.
	
	If possible, have students throw against a wall and catch on the rebound.
	
	Take three turns, then change.
	
	See what they can create.
	
	GAME (5 – 7 MINUTES)
		PM.—The students will be able to demonstrate the ability to control the balls so their partners can handle them successfully.
		
		Aff.—For people to improve throwing and catching skills, they must have the cooperation of a partner. Discuss the importance of helping others improve their skills and how that relates to self-development.
		
		Cog.—Students will understand it is easier to catch larger objects, i.e., the difference between a small sponge ball and a beachball.

DYNAMIC PHYSICAL EDUCATION LESSON PLAN
Educational Movement Using Rope Patterns
Level I

Supplies and Equipment Needed:
Tambourine
Music for rope jumping
One jump rope for each child
One beanbag for each child
Tape player

MOVEMENT EXPERIENCE— CONTENT	ORGANIZATION AND TEACHING HINTS	EXPECTED STUDENT OBJECTIVES AND OUTCOMES

INTRODUCTORY ACTIVITY (2 – 3 MINUTES)

Bend, Stretch, and Shake

1. Bend various body parts individually and then bend various combinations of body parts.
2. Stretch the body in various levels. Encourage stretching from various positions such as standing, sitting, and prone position.
3. Shake the body when the tambourine is shaken. Shake from a stationary as well as a moving position.
4. Bend body parts while doing different locomotor movements. Bend limbs while shaking.

DPE p. 224

Use a tambourine to signal changes.

Encourage smooth bending movements through the full range of joint movement.

Stretch beyond usual limits.

As children learn variations of the movements, increase the speed of change from one movement to the other.

Encourage creative and new responses.

Cog.—The student will recognize the meaning of the word "level" in relation to her body in space.

Cog.—Stretching beyond normal limits is necessary to maintain flexibility and range of motion at the joints.

PM.—The student will be able to perform at least five variations of stretch, bend, and shake.

FITNESS DEVELOPMENT ACTIVITIES (7 – 8 MINUTES)

Fitness Games and Challenges

Stoop Tag - 45 seconds.
Freeze; perform stretching activities.
Back-to-Back Tag - 45 seconds.
Freeze; perform Abdominal Challenges using Curl-Up variations.
Balance Tag - 45 seconds.
Freeze; perform Arm–Shoulder Girdle Challenges using Push-Up variations.
Elbow Swing Tag - 45 seconds.
Freeze; perform Trunk Development Challenges.
Color Tag - 45 seconds.

DPE pp. 242 – 243

Maximize movement by using simple fitness games that require little explanation.

Many Movement Challenges are found in *DPE*, pp. 239 – 242.

Remember that the goal of fitness games is to stimulate movement rather than teach children to follow rules.

Assign many youngsters to be it to increase the amount of movement.

Cog.—The body starts to perspire in an attempt to maintain a constant temperature. The student will verbalize this in his own words.

PM.—The student will be able to perform all challenges of the fitness activities.

Aff.—Regulation of body temperature is essential for comfort and safety. Discuss the many ways we attempt to regulate this temperature: more or fewer clothes, perspiring, swimming, and fires.

LESSON FOCUS (15 – 20 MINUTES)

Educational Movement Using Rope Patterns

Lay rope lengthwise on floor.
1. Walk as on a balance beam.
   a. Forward
   b. Backward
   c. Sideways

DPE pp. 397 – 399

Throughout the lesson use much student choice.

PM.—The student will be able to develop versatility in movement.

Cog.—The student will be able to develop the ability to solve problem situations.

29

MOVEMENT EXPERIENCE— CONTENT	ORGANIZATION AND TEACHING HINTS	EXPECTED STUDENT OBJECTIVES AND OUTCOMES

2. Jump/hop down length and back.
  a. Vary time—slow, fast, accel., decel., even, uneven.
  b. Vary levels and force—light, heavy, high to low.
3. Other locomotor movements.
  a. Crisscross
  b. Jumps with one-half turn
  c. Ask for suggestions
4. Imitate animals.
5. Crouch jumps.
  a. Various combinations: forward, backward, sideward.
  b. Allow exploration.
6. Put rope in shapes, letters, numbers.
  a. Move in and out of figures.
  b. Add motions, keeping the body in figure.
7. Partner work.
  a. Make figure with two ropes. Move in and out of figure.
  b. Using one rope, do follow activity. Take turns.
	Use right and left. When hopping, change feet on reversing, or repeat with the other foot the next time.
	
	Could add—leading with different parts of the body.
	
	Use demonstration.
	
	Use demonstration and have class guess.
	
	Place some of the body weight on hands.
	
	Alternate the rope pattern activities with rope jumping activities. This will give students a needed rest from jumping.
	
	Allow enough time for exploration. Have achievement demonstration.
		Aff.—The student will develop an understanding of movements principles and terms.
		
		PM.—The student will be able to create three movements and teach them to a partner.

Rope Jumping

This lesson should introduce youngsters to rope jumping. It should not be too instructional, but should be used for the purpose of giving them a positive introduction to rope jumping. Instruction will come in a later lesson.

1. Hold rope. Jump in time.
2. Perform the slow-time and fast-time rhythm with the rope held in one hand and turned.
3. Jump the rope and practice slow to fast time.
4. Introduce a few basic steps.
  a. Two-step basic
  b. Alternating basic
  c. Backwards
  d. One foot
	DPE pp. 404 – 410
	
	Use a record that possesses a rhythm that is steady, unchanging, and easy to hear.
	
	Turn up the tape player so the music is loud and easy to hear.
	
	It may be necessary to take a short break and work with something like beanbags or play an inactive game, as children tire easily in this activity.
		PM.—The student will be able to jump rope.
		
		Cog.—The student will be able to recognize the basic underlying beat and clap his hands to the rhythm after listening to a variety of records.
		
		Aff.—The student will learn the value of overlearning a skill. Here is a chance to discuss the overlearning principle and explain that it is hard to listen for the rhythm if you haven't overlearned the skill of rope jumping. If you *have* overlearned rope jumping, you can easily listen to the music *without* thinking about rope jumping.

GAME (5 – 7 MINUTES)

1. Tag Games, p. 518
2. Charlie over the Water, p. 520
3. Flowers and Wind, p. 520

DYNAMIC PHYSICAL EDUCATION LESSON PLAN
Educational Movement (Lesson 2)
Level I

Fundamental Skill: Jumping
Manipulative Activity: Yarn balls
Educational Movement Themes: Moving in general space, use of force (effort)

Supplies and Equipment Needed:
  One yarn ball for each child
  Tom-tom or drum
  Parachute
  Tape player

MOVEMENT EXPERIENCE—CONTENT	ORGANIZATION AND TEACHING HINTS	EXPECTED STUDENT OBJECTIVES AND OUTCOMES

INTRODUCTORY ACTIVITY (2 – 3 MINUTES)

Marking

"Mark" by touching partner. After touch, reverse and the other partner attempts to mark.

Variations:
1. Use the eight basic locomotor movements.
2. Use positions such as Crab Walk, Puppy Dog Walk, etc.
3. Allow a point to be scored only when they touch a specified body part, i.e., knee, elbow, left hand.
4. Use a whistle signal to change partners' roles. (If chasing partner, reverse and attempt to move *away* from the other.)

DPE p. 222

Encourage students to "watch where they are going" so they won't run into each other.

Partners should be somewhat equal in ability.

Change partners once or twice.

PM.—Be able to move with agility and quickness, which would allow students to catch as well as evade their partners.

Cog.—The student will be able to verbalize a simple reason for warm-up prior to strenuous activity.

FITNESS DEVELOPMENT ACTIVITIES (7 – 8 MINUTES)

Parachute Fitness

1. Jog in circle with chute held in left hand.
2. Shake the chute.
3. Slide to the right; Return slide to the left.
4. Sit and perform sit-ups - 30 seconds.
5. Skip for 20 seconds.
6. Freeze, face the center, and stretch the chute tightly. Hold for 8–12 seconds. Repeat five to six times.
7. Run in place while holding the chute taut at different levels.
8. Sit with legs under the chute. Do a seat walk toward the center. Return to the perimeter. Repeat four to six times.
9. Place the chute on the ground. Jog away from the chute and return on signal. Repeat for 30 seconds.

DPE pp. 244 – 245

Evenly space youngsters around the chute.

Use different grips to add variation to the activities.

Develop group morale by encouraging students to move together.

Use music to motivate youngsters.

To cool down, allow youngsters a minute to perform parachute stunts like the Dome or Mushroom.

PM.—The student will be able to perform all the movement challenges.

Cog.—The student will be able to verbalize what body part each of the challenges develops. Cue by saying "Swing your arms forward as fast as possible."

MOVEMENT EXPERIENCE— CONTENT	ORGANIZATION AND TEACHING HINTS	EXPECTED STUDENT OBJECTIVES AND OUTCOMES

10. Shake the chute and jump in place.
11. Lie on back with feet under the chute. Shake the chute with the feet.
12. Hop to the center of the chute and return. Repeat for 20 seconds.
13. Sit with feet under the chute. Stretch by touching the toes with the chute. Relax with other stretches while sitting.

LESSON FOCUS (15 – 20 MINUTES)

Educational Movement

Note: A few activities should be chosen from each section and presented alternately so students receive a wide variety of activities. If students are fatigued from the fitness portion of the lesson, start with the manipulative activities.

A. *Fundamental Skill—Jumping*
Bend the knees and ankles in preliminary motion.

Swing the arms forward and upward to add to the momentum.

Land lightly on the toes, with a cushioned bend of the knees.
  1. Jump upward, trying for height.
  2. Alternate low and high jumps.
  3. Jump in various floor patterns— triangle, circle, square, letters, figure eight, diamond shape.
  4. Over a spot, jump forward, backwards, sideways, criss-cross.
  5. Jump with the body stiff, like a pogo stick. Explore with arms in different positions.
  6. Practice jump turns—quarter, half, three-quarter, full. Add heel clicks with turns.
  7. Increase and decrease the speed of jumping. The height of jumping.
  8. Land with the feet apart sideways and together again. Try it forward and backward (stride).
  9. Jump and land as quietly as possible.
  10. Jump and criss-cross the feet sideways.
  11. See how far you can jump in two, three, or four consecutive jumps.
  12. Pretend you are a bouncing ball.

DPE pp. 295 – 296

Scatter formation.

Cue by saying:
  "Swing your arms forward as fast as possible."
  "Bend your knees."
  "Land lightly, bend knees"
  "On your toes"
  "Jump up and touch the ceiling."

Change activities rapidly.

Concentrate on good landings with the body in good control.

PM.—The student will be able to make a good jump and landing.

Cog.—The student will be able to verbally explain the important stress points that should be followed while jumping.

Cog.—The student will be able to name four sport or recreational activities where the jump is used.

Cog.—The student will understand that strength in relation to body size is an important factor in learning motor skills.

MOVEMENT EXPERIENCE—CONTENT	ORGANIZATION AND TEACHING HINTS	EXPECTED STUDENT OBJECTIVES AND OUTCOMES

13. Clap hands or slap thighs when in the air.
14. Jump so the hands contact the floor.
15. Select a line. Proceed down it by jumping back and forth over the line. Add turns.

B. *Manipulative Activity—Yarn Balls Individual Activity*—Each child has a ball.

DPE pp. 368 – 372

Scatter formation.

Keep eyes on ball, stress "give."

Aff.—The student will appreciate that to become skilled, one must practice.

PM.—The student will be able to improve in the ability to track and catch objects.

PM.—Students will throw yarn balls using the principle of opposition.

   1. Toss and catch to self.
      a. Increase height gradually.
      b. Side to side.
      c. Front to back.
      d. Toss underneath the legs, around the body, etc.
      e. Toss and clap the hands. Clap around the body. Underneath the legs.
      f. Toss and make turns—quarter and half.
      g. Toss, perform the following, catch:
         Heel click
         Touch both elbows, knees, shoulders, and heels.
      h. Use contrasting tosses:
         High and low
         Near and far
         Front and back
         Others
   2. Bat the ball upward as in volleyball, catch. Bat the ball, run forward and catch.
   3. Toss forward, run and catch. Toss sideward and catch. Toss overhead, turn around, run and catch.

Watch out for others. Use these with caution. Be sure of readiness.

   4. Bonk Ball—throw at anyone and say "Bonk" before throwing. Stress opposition of feet and throwing arm. Specify area to be hit.

Partner Activity—One ball for two children.

Keep distances close. Will take some force.

   1. Roll the ball back and forth.
   2. Toss the ball back and forth, various ways.
   3. Throw the ball back and forth.
   4. Exploratory activity—batting, kicking, etc.

Seek ideas.

C. *Moving in General Space*
   Each child has a spot.

DPE pp. 280 – 281

Can use yarn balls for spots. Stress light running under control.

PM.—Children move in general space without interfering with others.

Aff.—Each child will respect the rights of others in general space.

Cog.—Each student will grasp the difference between personal and general space.

   1. Run lightly in the area, changing direction as you wish without bumping or touching anyone. How many were able to do this? Try running zigzag fashion.

MOVEMENT EXPERIENCE—CONTENT	ORGANIZATION AND TEACHING HINTS	EXPECTED STUDENT OBJECTIVES AND OUTCOMES

2. Run again in general space. On whistle signal, change direction abruptly. Try again, only this time change both direction and the type of locomotor movement you are doing.
3. Run lightly and pretend you are dodging another runner. Run directly at another runner and dodge him or her.
4. Use a yarn ball to mark your personal space (spot); run in general space until the signal is given; put the yarn ball on the floor and sit down.

Change the type of locomotor activity.

5. We are going to do orienteering. Point to a spot on a wall, walk directly to the spot in a straight line. You may have to wait for others so as not to bump them. Pick another spot on a different wall and repeat. Return to home base on signal.

Explain orienteering briefly.

6. What happens when general space is decreased? Walk in general space. Now as space is decreased, walk again. Once more we are decreasing the space.

Decrease space by half and then by another half. (One quarter left.)

7. Run around your yarn ball until I say "Bang." Then explode in a straight direction until the stop signal is sounded. Return.
8. From your spot, take three (four or five) jumps (hops, skips, gallops, slides) in one direction, turn around and do the same back to home base. Try with long steps away and tiny steps back.

Remind again about not bumping or interfering with others. Expand this with different number challenges and different movements.

9. Using movement combinations (run-jump-roll, skip-spin-collapse), move out from your spot and back. Set up a combination of three movements of your own.
10. Blow yourself up and pretend you are a soap bubble. Float around in general space. If you touch someone or if I touch you, the bubble bursts and you collapse. Return to your spot and begin again. This time you may say "pop" and break the bubble when you wish.

MOVEMENT EXPERIENCE—CONTENT	ORGANIZATION AND TEACHING HINTS	EXPECTED STUDENT OBJECTIVES AND OUTCOMES
11. I am going to challenge you on right and left movements. First, let's walk in general space. When I say "right" (or "left") you change direction abruptly. Now we'll try some other movements.		PM.—Each child should be able to move right and left without mistakes.
12. This time run rapidly toward another child. Stop and bow. Now stop and shake hands.		
13. From your home spot, run to a selected spot on a wall and return home. Pick spots on two different walls and return.		
D. *Theme: Use of Force*	*DPE* p. 285	
1. Show us how you do some forceful movements, such as chopping, batting, hitting with a sledge, punching the punchbag. Try karate chops and kicks, kicking a soccerball, etc.	Scatter formation. Practice these movements. Use brief discussion of factors. Yell "timber" when chopping. Run the bases after batting.	PM.—The student will be able to develop the ability to create more forceful movement. Cog.—The student will understand that torque is the tendency of force to produce rotation around an axis.
2. Show us a light movement you can make with the arm. Repeat the same movement more forcefully.		
3. Make some movements that are light and sustained, heavy and sudden, heavy and sustained, light and sudden.		Cog.—The student will be able to understand and apply the terms defining light and forceful movement.
4. Make one part of the body move lightly, while another moves heavily.		

GAME (5 – 7 MINUTES)

1. Fire Fighter, p. 513
2. Animal Tag, p. 515
3. Sneak Attack, p. 523

DYNAMIC PHYSICAL EDUCATION LESSON PLAN
Individual Rope Jumping Skills
Level I

Supplies and Equipment Needed:
  Jump rope for each child
  Appropriate music
  Beanbag or hoop for each child
  Tom-tom
  Four cones
  Tape player

MOVEMENT EXPERIENCE— CONTENT	ORGANIZATION AND TEACHING HINTS	EXPECTED STUDENT OBJECTIVES AND OUTCOMES

INTRODUCTORY ACTIVITY (2 – 3 MINUTES)

Individual Movement with Manipulation

Each child is given a beanbag and moves around the area using various basic locomotor movements. Students toss and catch their beanbag while moving. On signal, they drop the beanbags and jump and/or hop over as many bags as possible.

DPE p. 221

Scatter formation.

Hoops can be used instead of beanbags.

Specify the number or color of beanbags they must move, leap over, or around.

Add many challenges while moving to both the locomotor movements and manipulative activities.

PM.—The student will be able to toss and catch an object while moving.

Cog.—The student will be able to recite the fact that it is easier to toss and catch an object while standing stationary than while moving.

FITNESS DEVELOPMENT ACTIVITIES (7 – 8 MINUTES)

Four-Corners Movement

Outline a large rectangle with four cones. Place signs with pictures on both sides of the cones. Youngsters move around the outside of the rectangle and change their movement pattern as they approach a corner sign. The following movement activities are suggested:
  1. Jogging
  2. Skipping/Jumping/Hopping
  3. Sliding/Galloping
  4. Various animal movements
  5. Sport imitation movements
Stop the class after 30–45 seconds of movement and perform various fitness challenges. This will allow students to rest aerobically.

DPE pp. 245 – 246

If signs are not placed at the corners, teachers can specify movements for students to perform.

Increase the demand of the routine by increasing the size of the rectangle.

Faster-moving students can pass on the outside (away from the center) of the rectangle. Also, change directions periodically.

Assure that abdominal and shoulder girdle strength development activities are included.

Cog.—It is interesting to measure the breathing rate at rest and during and after exercise. The student will be able to explain why breathing rate varies.

Aff.—Many experts feel people are overweight due to lack of activity rather than eating too much. Discuss why this might be true.

LESSON FOCUS (15 – 20 MINUTES)

Individual Rope Jumping

A. As a lead-up activity for individual rope jumping, it might be useful to try some of the following activities:
  1. Clap hands to a tom-tom beat.

DPE pp. 404 – 410

Children get tired when learning to jump. It might be wise to split the lesson focus and use a less active activity such as hoops.

PM.—The student will be able to jump the rope at least ten times in succession.

Cog.—The student will be able to recognize the difference between slow and fast time.

MOVEMENT EXPERIENCE— CONTENT	ORGANIZATION AND TEACHING HINTS	EXPECTED STUDENT OBJECTIVES AND OUTCOMES

2. Jump in place to a beat without rope. Jump back and forth over rope on floor.
3. Hold both ends of the jump rope in one hand and turn it so a steady rhythm can be made through a consistent turn. Just before the rope hits the ground, the student should practice jumping.
4. Count the rhythm out loud to cue students when to jump.
5. Start jumping the rope one turn at a time—gradually increase the number of turns.
6. Try jogging and jumping rope. The even rhythm of running often makes it easier for some youngsters to jump the rope.

B. Introduce the two basic jumps:
   1. Slow time
   2. Fast time

C. Introduce some of the basic step variations:
   1. Alternate foot basic step
   2. Swing step forward
   3. Swing step sideward
   4. Backward

D. Add music to the two basic jumps so students can learn to follow a basic underlying beat.

After introducing the basic skills, play music that has a strong beat. (Turn it up so it is easy for children to hear.)

Some students will find it helpful to jump with teacher or another good jumper turning the rope.

Give the children plenty of room so they don't hit someone with their ropes.

Use music to increase interest in rhythmic jumping.

For slow time: Slow rope, slow feet with a rebound.

For fast time: Fast rope, fast feet. Jump the rope every turn.

To offer rest intervals, try making numbers, letters, name, and shapes with the jump rope. Cowboy turns (hold by handle and spin the rope), circling the rope under the legs, and tail tag are good rest activities.

Allow students to progress at their own rate. It is good to show the better jumpers some of the more difficult variations and allow them to practice by themselves.

Aff.—Often, boys think rope jumping is a "sissy" activity. Emphasize the fact that many athletes use it for achieving a high level of fitness. You might also mention that 10 minutes of rope jumping is equal to 30 minutes of jogging.

GAME (5 – 7 MINUTES)

Play an inactive game, as the children will be fatigued by the rope jumping. The following are suggested:
   1. Tommy Tucker's Land, p. 515
   2. Change Sides, p. 520

All of the variations can be done with the turning in a forward or backward direction.

DYNAMIC PHYSICAL EDUCATION LESSON PLAN
Educational Movement (Lesson 3)
Level I

Fundamental Skill: Running
Educational Movement Themes: Over and under, moving in different ways
Manipulative Activity: Paddles and balls

Supplies and Equipment Needed:
  Playground balls (rubber)
  Paddles and balls—one set for each child
  Jump ropes
  Circuit training signs
  Climbing ropes
  Tape player
  Hula hoops

MOVEMENT EXPERIENCE—CONTENT	ORGANIZATION AND TEACHING HINTS	EXPECTED STUDENT OBJECTIVES AND OUTCOMES

INTRODUCTORY ACTIVITY (2 – 3 MINUTES)

Movement Varieties

Move using a basic locomotor movement. Then add variety to the movement by asking students to respond to the following factors:
1. Level—low, high, in between.
2. Direction—straight, zigzag, circular, curved, forward, backward, upward, downward.
3. Size—large, tiny, medium movements.
4. Patterns—forming squares, diamonds, triangles, circles, figure eights.
5. Speed—slow, fast, accelerate.

DPE pp. 218 – 219

Scatter formation.

Emphasize and reinforce creativity.

Change the various factors often and take time to explain the concepts the words describe, if children cannot interpret them.

Cog.—The student will be able to interpret the concepts the words describe by moving the body in a corresponding manner.

PM.—The student will be able to move the body with ease throughout the range of movement varieties.

FITNESS DEVELOPMENT ACTIVITIES (7 – 8 MINUTES)

Circuit Training

1. Tortoise and Hare.
2. Curl-Up variations.
3. Hula Hooping on arms.
4. Jumping Boxes—Step on and off continuously.
5. Agility run—run back and forth between two designated lines.
6. Bench Pulls—pull body along bench.
7. Crab Walk.
8. Bend and Twist.

DPE pp. 259 – 262

Divide class into equal groups at each station.

Have one piece of equipment for each child in the group.

Other activities to try are rope jumping, agility run, swinging on climbing ropes, and arm circles.

Start with 25 seconds of activity at each station with 10 seconds to change stations.

Use timed music segments (25 seconds) to signal when activity should occur. Insert 10 seconds of silence between each bout of music for changing stations.

PM.—The student will be able to perform each activity for a minimum of 25 seconds.

Cog.—The student will be able to identify what part(s) of the body each activity exercises.

MOVEMENT EXPERIENCE—CONTENT	ORGANIZATION AND TEACHING HINTS	EXPECTED STUDENT OBJECTIVES AND OUTCOMES

LESSON FOCUS (15 – 20 MINUTES)

Educational Movement

Note: A few activities should be chosen from each section and presented alternately so students receive a wide variety of activities. If students are fatigued from the fitness portion of the lesson, start with the manipulative activities.

A. *Fundamental Skill: Running*
Run on the balls of the feet. Head is up, eyes forward. Body lean depends upon the speed. In sprinting, use good arm action (opposition).
   1. Run lightly around the area; stop on signal.
   2. Run lightly and change directions on signal.
   3. Run, turn around with running steps on signal and continue in a new direction.
   4. Pick a spot away from you. Run to it and return without bumping anyone.
   5. Run low, gradually increase the height. Reverse.
   6. Run patterns. Run inside and around objects.
   7. Run with high knee action. Add a knee slap with the hand as you run.
   8. Run with different steps—tiny, long, light, heavy, criss-cross, wide, and others.
   9. Run with arms in different positions—circling, overhead, stiff at sides, and others (choice).
   10. Free running. Concentrate on good knee lift.
   11. Run at different speeds.
   12. Touch the ground at times with either hand as you run.
   13. Run backwards, sideways.
   14. Run with exaggerated arm movements and/or high bounce.
   15. Practice running, crossing from one line to another.
      a. Cross your feet as you run.
      b. Touch the ground with one and both hands as you run.
      c. Run forward, looking backward over your right shoulder.
      d. Same, but look over the left shoulder.

DPE pp. 294 – 295

Teaching cues:
   "Run on the balls of the feet."
   "Head up, look ahead."
   "Lift knees."
   "Relax upper body."
   "Breathe naturally."
Scatter formation.

Stress courtesy.

Patterns can be outlined with objects.

Pretend you are a football player (running for a touchdown) or a track star.

Stress body lean for faster running.

Caution to look to avoid possible collisions.

Use appropriate formation for crossing over.

PM.—The students will improve their running form—lightness, and rhythmic pattern.

Cog.—The student will be able to express the mechanics of good running form.

Aff.—The student will show concern for others when moving through general space.

Cog.—Students will be able to express that gravity is always working and always acts in a vertical direction.

Cog.—Students will learn to share space and take turns.

Aff.—The student will work for control rather than just moving across.

Cog.—Students will understand that a fast walk is more difficult than an easy jog. The body is more efficient during the easy jog.

MOVEMENT EXPERIENCE—CONTENT	ORGANIZATION AND TEACHING HINTS	EXPECTED STUDENT OBJECTIVES AND OUTCOMES

e. Change direction every few steps.

f. Run to the center, stop completely, then continue.

g. Make two stops going across—first with the right side forward and then with the left side forward as you stop.

h. Run forward and stop. Come back three steps and stop. Continue in forward direction.

i. Do a two-count stop on the way.
    (Organization) Must be a "one, two" count, slapping the feet.

j. Run sideways across, leading with one side. Next time lead with the other.

k. Run forward halfway and then backward the rest.

l. Run backward halfway and then forward the rest.

m. Make a full turn in the center and continue. Do this right and left.

n. Provide for student choice.

B. *Manipulative Activity*—Paddles and Balls

  1. *Individual Activity*

    a. Place the ball on the paddle face. Roll it around the face.

    b. Hit the ball into the air with the paddle. Retrieve and repeat.

    c. Bounce the ball into the air, using the paddle; specify number.

    d. Bounce the ball into the air, decreasing the height of the bounce until it rests on the face of the paddle.

    e. Bounce the ball on the floor.

    f. Alternate bouncing upward and to the floor.

    g. Dribble the ball and move while dribbling.

    h. Choice activity.

  2. *Partner Activity*

    a. One partner tosses and the other hits it back.

    b. Try batting it back and forth. If using a tennis ball, let it bounce between hits.

    c. Place ball on floor and roll it back and forth.

Organization and Teaching Hints (Section B):

DPE pp. 378 – 380

Scatter formation.

Try for control rather than distance.

Track ball.

Stay with the basics until some progress is made.

Can have show-and-tell demonstration.

Stress easy, controlled tossing (feeding).

Need sufficient room.

Expected Student Objectives and Outcomes (Section B):

PM.—The student will develop the ability to contact the ball solidly and also control it.

PM.—The student will develop better hand-eye coordination, leading to increased automatic play.

Aff.—The student will gain an appreciation that skill in paddle activities comes only from proper practice.

Cog.—The student will be able to explain the best place on the racket to contact the ball.

PM.—The students will improve their object tracking skills.

PM.—The student will be able to make controlled returns to the partner tossing the ball.

PM.—The student will be able to bat the ball back and forth four times without a miss.

PM.—The student will demonstrate the ability to interpret the themes in a variety of responses.

MOVEMENT EXPERIENCE—CONTENT	ORGANIZATION AND TEACHING HINTS	EXPECTED STUDENT OBJECTIVES AND OUTCOMES
C. *Theme: Over and Under* 　1. One partner is an obstacle and the other goes over, under, and around the "obstacle." Reverse positions. 　2. Copying action. One partner takes a position and the other goes over and under the first. Reverse positions, but try to copy the same sequence. 　3. Progressive sequencing. The first child does a movement (over, under, or around). The second child repeats the movement and adds another. The first child repeats the first two movements and adds a third. The second child repeats and adds a fourth.	*DPE* p. 286 Partner activity. Look for unique ideas. This is about the limit for changes.	Aff.—Working cooperatively with a partner is necessary.
D. *Theme: Moving in Different Ways* 　1. Show me different ways to move when your body is in the air part of the time; when your body is always in contact with the floor. 　2. Show me different ways you can progress along the floor without using your hands or feet. Can you "walk" using your seat? 　3. What are the different ways you can roll and move? 　4. What ways can you move sideways? How can you move on all fours? 　5. Move across the floor halfway with one movement and the other half with a decidedly different movement. 　6. Explore the different ways you can move when leading with selected parts of the body.	*DPE* p. 286 Select from formations pp. 81 – 85 Stress not colliding with others. Get pupil demonstration.	Cog.—The student will demonstrate the ability to understand the directions and make broad interpretations.

GAME (5 – 7 MINUTES)

The following are suggested:
1. Rollee Pollee, p. 524
2. Mix and Match, p. 516

DYNAMIC PHYSICAL EDUCATION LESSON PLAN
Fundamental Skills Using Benches
Level I

Supplies and Equipment Needed:
  Six balance-beam benches
  Six tumbling mats
  One jump rope for each child
  Beanbags or fleece balls
  Foam balls, 8-1/2"
  Music
  Tape player
  Plastic jugs

MOVEMENT EXPERIENCE—CONTENT	ORGANIZATION AND TEACHING HINTS	EXPECTED STUDENT OBJECTIVES AND OUTCOMES

INTRODUCTORY ACTIVITY (2 – 3 MINUTES)

New Leader Warm-Up

Groups move around the area, following the leader. As a variation, on signal, the last person can move to the head of the squad and become the leader. Various types of locomotor movements and/or exercises should be used.

In the beginning stages of this activity, it is sometimes helpful to work in pairs or triads.

DPE p. 223

Squad formation.

Encourage students not to stand around. Keep moving unless an exercise or similar activity is being performed.

Assign each squad a specific area if desired. Each area could include a piece of equipment to aid in the activity (beanbag, fleece ball, etc.)

Cog.—Warm-up is necessary to get the blood to the periphery of the body. Always warm up before strenuous exercise.

Aff.—Students will all be capable of leading as well as following. Discuss the necessity of both in our society.

FITNESS DEVELOPMENT ACTIVITIES (7 – 8 MINUTES)

Jump Rope Exercises

1. Place the rope on the floor and perform locomotor movements around and over the rope. Make different shapes and letters with the rope.
2. Hold the folded rope overhead. Sway from side to side. Twist right and left.
3. Lie on back with rope held with outstretched arms toward ceiling. Bring up one leg at a time and touch the rope with toes. Lift both legs together. Sit up and try to hook the rope over the feet. Release and repeat.
4. Jump rope. If not able to jump, practice swinging the rope to the side - 45 seconds.
5. Fold the rope and perform various isometric exercises.
6. Fold the rope and use it as a tail. Try to keep others from pulling the tail.
7. Touch toes with the folded rope.
8. Jump rope - 45 seconds.

DPE p. 245

Place the ropes around the perimeter of the area so they can quickly pickup and return a jump rope.

If youngsters have difficulty jumping the rope, offer alternate challenges.

Use music to motivate children when they are jumping rope.

An alternative is to substitute long-rope jumping. Since not all children are jumping, it is less demanding and easier for children to perform.

Cog.—Rope jumping demands a great deal from all parts of the body. For the conditioning effect to take place, the pulse rate should be elevated above 150 beats per minute for 5 minutes. It might be interesting to use a stop watch and have students check their own pulse rate.

MOVEMENT EXPERIENCE—CONTENT	ORGANIZATION AND TEACHING HINTS	EXPECTED STUDENT OBJECTIVES AND OUTCOMES

9. Place rope on the floor and do various animal walks along or over the rope.
10. Do Push-Up variations with the rope folded and held between the hands.
11. Jump rope - 45 seconds.

LESSON FOCUS (15 – 20 MINUTES)

Benches

DPE pp. 425 – 427

1. Animal walks on the bench
   a. Seal walk
   b. Cat walk
   c. Lame dog walk
   d. Rabbit jump
   e. Choice activity
2. Locomotor movements
   a. Skip on the bench.
   b. Gallop on the bench.
   c. Step on and off the bench.
   d. Jump on and off the bench.
   e. Hop on and off the bench.
   f. Choice activity.
3. Pulls—Pull body along the bench in various positions.
   a. Prone position—head first, feet first.
   b. Supine position—head first, feet first.
   c. Side position—head first, feet first.
4. Pushes—same as above activity except push with the arms in all positions.
5. Movements alongside the benches—proceed alongside the bench in the following positions. (Keep the limbs on the floor as far away as possible from the bench to achieve maximum effort.)
   a. Prone position—hands on bench.
   b. Supine position—hands on bench.
   c. Turn over—proceed along bench changing from prone to supine positions with hands on bench.
   d. All of the above positions performed with the feet on the bench.
6. Scooter movements—sit on bench and proceed along bench without using hands.
   a. Regular scooter—feet leading.
   b. Reverse scooter—legs trailing.
   c. Seat walk—walk on the buttocks.
7. Jump dismounts
   a. Single jump—forward or backward.
   b. Jump with turns—1/2 or 3/4 or full.
   c. Jackknife (Pike).

Six benches—one group behind each bench. Place a mat at end of bench for dismounts.

Use a dismount at the end of each activity. See item 7 for suggestions.

Have the next person in line begin when the person in front of him is halfway across the bench.

Have the youngsters perform a return activity on the way back to their lines.

Differentiate between pulling and pushing movements.

Set up lists of return activities at the end of the gym. After doing the bench activity, students jog to the list and perform a listed activity.

Put hands on head while scooting.

The dismounts should be integrated into all the bench activities.

Encourage variety.

PM.—The student will be able to perform all the animal walks across the bench.

PM.—The student will be able to perform the locomotor movements across the bench.

Cog.—The student will be able to identify which bench activities develop arm and shoulder girdle strength.

Cog.—Quality of movement is necessary on the benches to insure adequate results, and speed is not a goal.

Cog.—Students will understand that force for jumping is increased when extensor muscles of the lower limbs are stretched quickly.

Aff.—Satisfaction results from attaining realistic goals. Discuss the importance of viewing your ability correctly so meaningful goals can be set.

MOVEMENT EXPERIENCE—CONTENT	ORGANIZATION AND TEACHING HINTS	EXPECTED STUDENT OBJECTIVES AND OUTCOMES

d. Jackknife split (straddle).
e. Jump and follow with a log or forward roll.

GAME (5 – 7 MINUTES)

The following are suggested:
1. Hill Dill, p. 522
2. Bottle Kick Ball, p. 521

DYNAMIC PHYSICAL EDUCATION LESSON PLAN
Throwing Skills (Lesson 1)
Level I

Supplies and Equipment Needed:
  Beanbags or fleece balls
  Yarn balls
  Rag balls or tennis balls
  Hoops
  Mats for targets
  Tape player
  Music

MOVEMENT EXPERIENCE—CONTENT	ORGANIZATION AND TEACHING HINTS	EXPECTED STUDENT OBJECTIVES AND OUTCOMES

INTRODUCTORY ACTIVITY (2 – 3 MINUTES)

Group Over and Under One-half of the class is scattered and is in a curled position. The other half of the class leap or jump over the down children. On signal, reverse the groups quickly. In place of a curl, the down children can bridge and the others go under. The down children can also alternate between curl and bridge as well as move around the area while in bridged position.	*DPE* p. 222 Scatter formation. Encourage the students to go over or under a specified number of classmates. Vary the down challenges, i.e., bridge using two body parts, curl face down or on your side. Do various locomotor movements when moving from student to student.	PM.—The student will be able to perform the activities of bridge, curl, leap, jump, and hop at a teacher-acceptable level.

FITNESS DEVELOPMENT ACTIVITIES (7 – 8 MINUTES)

Astronaut Drills 1. Walk. 2. Walk on tiptoes while reaching for the sky. 3. Walk with giant strides. 4. Freeze; perform various stretches. 5. Do a Puppy Dog Walk. 6. Jump like a pogo stick. 7. Freeze; perform Push-Up variations. 8. Walk and swing arms like a helicopter. 9. Trot lightly and silently. 10. Slide like an athlete. 11. Freeze; perform Curl-Up variations. 12. Crab Walk. 13. Skip. 14. Freeze; perform trunk development challenges. 15. Walk and cool down.	*DPE* pp. 262 – 263 Use circle or scatter formation with ample space between youngsters. Children should be in constant movement except when stopped to do strength and flexibility activities. Emphasize quality movement. Taped intervals of music and no music can be used to signal movement and stopping to do exercises. Change direction often. When they are moving on all fours, youngsters should be encouraged to place much of their weight on the hands in order to develop arm-shoulder girdle strength.	Cog.—The training effect occurs when the heart rate is elevated above 150-160 beats per minute. The student will be able to explain why, to achieve this level, one must keep moving without much rest. Aff.—Very little resting time occurs in Astronaut Drills. When one exercises for a long period of time, without rest, muscular and cardiovascular endurance is developed.

LESSON FOCUS (15 – 20 MINUTES)

Throwing
 	
A. *Mimetics*
  1. "Pretend you:
    a. have to throw a rock across a big river!"
	DPE pp. 307 – 308
	
	Mimetics are to be done before every lesson for 1–2 minutes.
	
	Scattered formation teacher modeling.
		PM.—Students will begin to turn their nonthrowing shoulder to the target.

MOVEMENT EXPERIENCE—CONTENT	ORGANIZATION AND TEACHING HINTS	EXPECTED STUDENT OBJECTIVES AND OUTCOMES
b. want to throw a ball over a very tall building!" c. are a javelin thrower and you want to make the longest throw ever!" d. are a baseball pitcher and you are throwing a fast ball!"	Cue if necessary: 1. "Take a big windup!" 2. "Turn your side to the target." etc.	PM.—Students will begin to take a step toward the target with the contralateral foot.
B. *Individual Activities* 1. Throw beanbag or fleece ball against the wall. Concentrate on the following points: a. Feet together b. Contralateral foot forward c. Start with nonthrowing side to the wall 2. Throw from one side of the gym and try to hit the other wall.	At least one beanbag per child. Students should be 4–5 ft. from the wall. Encourage children to throw hard. Redirect children with key points: 1. Start with your throwing hand behind your head. 2. Raise elbow to shoulder level. 3. Turn your side to the wall. 4. Take a big step and throw hard. Have the entire class throw at once if possible, retrieve, and run to wall. Repeat.	Cog.—The student will begin to understand the importance of body rotation to produce force. Cog.—The student will understand the importance of opposition of limbs. PM.—The student will perform the throw by stepping with the contralateral foot. Cog.—The student will understand the importance of the shoulder turn and step in producing a forceful throw.
C. *Mimetics* 1. The teacher should cue students and model a good throw. a. Teacher should use terms such as "wind-up," "turn your nonthrowing side to the target," "step toward the target," "follow through." b. Teacher can also use this time to observe and coach. c. *Encourage* the children to throw *hard.* d. Modeling of good throws by the teacher should be a major objective for this exercise.	These should be done for 1–2 minutes. The teacher should encourage and praise good *form.* The teacher should talk about what the components of a good throw are and how to produce force. The cue of "turn, step, throw" may be useful. The children should be generating maximum force.	Cog.—Students will know what a mature throw looks like. Cog.—Students will know the components of a mature throw. Cog.—Students should begin to realize what parts of the throw result in the greatest force production. Aff.—Students will begin to value throwing hard. PM.—The student should begin every throw from a side-facing position. PM.—The student should take a big step with the contralateral foot.
D. *Individual Activities* 1. Throwing yarn balls a. Throw against wall 1. Throw from a standing position 20 ft. from the wall. 2. Throw five balls, retrieve, and repeat. 2. Throwing rag balls or tennis balls a. Teach the proper grip. b. Throw against mats on the wall. 1. Throw from 20–25 ft. depending on skill level. Student should be able to hit the wall. 2. Student should pick up any ball rolling behind the throwing line and throw again.	Redirect with appropriate cues: 1. "Throw hard!" 2. "Take a big step, then throw!" 3. "Really get your throwing arm behind your head to start the throw!" May need to set up a diagonal throwing line so that all skill levels are challenged to throw hard.	

MOVEMENT EXPERIENCE—CONTENT	ORGANIZATION AND TEACHING HINTS	EXPECTED STUDENT OBJECTIVES AND OUTCOMES
3. Stop and retrieve balls when necessary. c. Throw at hoops leaning against the mats. 1. Throw from a distance so that children can hit the wall, but only with a forceful throw.	The hoops can be used as targets, but the emphasis should still be throwing hard. Teacher comments should emphasize good form rather than hitting the target.	Aff.—The student should value good form more than hitting a target. Discuss the importance of throwing with good form.

GAME (5 – 7 MINUTES)

An active game should be played due to the inactive nature of the above activity. The following are suggested:
1. Red Light, p. 523
2. Sneak Attack, p. 523

DYNAMIC PHYSICAL EDUCATION LESSON PLAN
Stunts and Tumbling Skills (Lesson 1)
Level I

Supplies and Equipment Needed:
   Tumbling mats
   Balls
   Tape player
   Music

MOVEMENT EXPERIENCE— CONTENT	ORGANIZATION AND TEACHING HINTS	EXPECTED STUDENT OBJECTIVES AND OUTCOMES

INTRODUCTORY ACTIVITY (2 – 3 MINUTES)

Countdown

Students and teacher begin a countdown (10, 9, 8, 7, etc.) and gradually crouch with each count. On the words "blast off," they explode and move in different directions.

Vary with challenges such as:
   1. Different locomotor movements
   2. Various animal walks
   3. Change intervals of counting— slow, fast

DPE p. 220

Scatter formation.

Other positions can be used. Students can be challenged to "copy" the teacher's position (curl, stretch, etc.).

Have students run to markers around the area rather than running to the walls.

Try a group countdown where everyone holds hands and moves as a unit.

PM.—The student will be able to move in a controlled fashion during the countdown.

PM.—The student will be able to stop and start rapidly under control.

FITNESS DEVELOPMENT ACTIVITIES (7 – 8 MINUTES)

Animal Movements and Fitness Challenges

Puppy Dog Walk—30 seconds.
Freeze; perform stretching activities.
Measuring Worm Walk—30 seconds.
Freeze; perform abdominal development challenges.
Elephant Walk—30 seconds.
Frog Jump—30 seconds.
Freeze; perform push-up position challenges.
Seal Crawl—30 seconds.
Bear Walk—30 seconds.
Freeze; perform abdominal challenges.
Siamese Twin Walk—30 seconds.
Lame Dog Walk—30 seconds.

DPE p. 242

Emphasize placing the weight on the hands for shoulder girdle development.

Quality of movement should be emphasized rather than speed.

Vary the length of the intervals to match the fitness level of youngsters.

Taped intervals of music and no music can be used to signal movement and stopping to do exercises.

Cog.—The student will be able to perform the fitness activities at the beginning level.

Cog.—The student will be able to react to the different word cues.

Aff.—The student will take pride in being able to perform strenuous physical activity.

Aff.—Smoking shortens the average life span by seven years. Students will understand that choosing *not* to smoke enhances wellness.

48

MOVEMENT EXPERIENCE— CONTENT	ORGANIZATION AND TEACHING HINTS	EXPECTED STUDENT OBJECTIVES AND OUTCOMES

LESSON FOCUS (15 – 20 MINUTES)

Tumbling, Stunts, and Animal Walks

Five groups of activities are found in this lesson to insure that youngsters receive a variety of experiences. Pick a few activities from each group and teach them alternately. For example, teach one or two animal movements, then a tumbling and inverted balance, followed by a balance stunt, etc. Do not place excessive time on one group of activities at the expense of another.

1. Animal Movements
   a. Alligator Crawl
   b. Kangaroo Jump
   c. Puppy Dog Run
   d. Cat Walk
   e. Monkey Run
2. Tumbling and Inverted Balances
   a. Rolling Log
   b. Side Roll
   c. Forward Roll
   d. Back Roller
3. Balance Stunts
   a. One-Leg Balance
   b. Double-Knee Balance
   c. Head Touch
   d. Head Balance
   e. One-Leg Balance Stunts
4. Individual Stunts
   a. Directional Walk
   b. Line Walking
   c. Fluttering Leaf
   d. Elevator
   e. Cross-Legged Stand
   f. Walking in Place
   g. Jump Turns
5. Partner and Group Stunts
   a. Bouncing Ball
   b. Seesaw

DPE pp. 451 – 463

Scatter as many tumbling mats as possible throughout the area in order to avoid waiting lines.

Do not perform many repetitions of tumbling and inverted balances. For most children, limiting the number of forward or backward roll repetitions to four or five will prevent fatigue and injury.

Don't force students to perform tumbling and inverted balances. If they are fearful, gradual encouragement will accomplish more in the long run than intimidation and force.

Demonstrate the activities so students are aware of how they should be performed.

A major concern for safety is the neck and back region. Overweight children are at greater risk and might be allowed to avoid tumbling and inverted balances.

PM.—The student will be able to perform a forward and backward roll.

PM.—The student will be able to balance her body in the balance stunts and manage it easily in the individual stunts.

Cog.—The student will be able to recite the stress points necessary to know in performing the forward and backward roll.

Cog.—The student will be able to identify the activities by name.

PM.—The student will be able to perform the animal movements for a distance of at least 25 feet.

Aff.—Approximately two to three quarts of water are needed for the body to function properly. Students should drink one quart (or four to eight glasses) of water daily and more when exercising strenuously.

GAME (5 – 7 MINUTES)

The following are suggested:
1. Circle Straddle Ball, p. 524
2. Statues, p. 515
3. Soap Bubbles, p. 512

DYNAMIC PHYSICAL EDUCATION LESSON PLAN
Manipulative Ball Skills—Basketball Related
Level I

Supplies and Equipment Needed:
One 8 1/2" playground or foam rubber ball for each student
Hoops
Wastepaper basket or box

MOVEMENT EXPERIENCE—CONTENT	ORGANIZATION AND TEACHING HINTS	EXPECTED STUDENT OBJECTIVES AND OUTCOMES

INTRODUCTORY ACTIVITY (2 – 3 MINUTES)

Free Activity with Playground (Rubber) Balls

Explore as many activities as possible combining locomotor movements with ball skills.

DPE p. 221

Scatter formation. Individual or partner as per choice.

Use efficient way to distribute and collect balls such as placing them at five or six locations in the area.

PM.—The student will be able to combine three ball skills and two locomotor movements into a routine.

FITNESS DEVELOPMENT ACTIVITIES (7 – 8 MINUTES)

Fitness Games and Challenges

Stoop Tag - 45 seconds.
Freeze; perform stretching activities.
Back-to-Back Tag - 45 seconds.
Freeze; perform abdominal Challenges using Curl-Up variations.
Balance Tag - 45 seconds.
Freeze; perform Arm–Shoulder Girdle Challenges using Push-Up variations.
Elbow Swing Tag - 45 seconds.
Freeze; perform Trunk Development Challenges.
Color Tag - 45 seconds.

DPE pp. 242 – 243

Maximize movement by using simple fitness games that require little explanation.

Remember that the goal of fitness games is to stimulate movement rather than teach children to follow rules.

Assign many youngsters to be it to increase the amount of movement.

PM.—The student will be able to perform the various fitness activities.

Aff.—A balanced diet low in saturated fat, cholesterol, and sugar will help reduce the incidence of heart attacks. Discuss the role of diet in maintaining wellness.

Cog.—Stretching allows the body to move with more efficiency. The student will be able to explain why stretching activities are desirable.

Aff.—In order to develop a higher level of physical fitness, it is necessary to exercise to the point of discomfort at times. Discuss the importance of pushing to higher achievement and the need for overloading.

LESSON FOCUS (15 – 20 MINUTES)

Ball Skills—Basketball Related

1. Start with informal passing back and forth between partners.
2. Push (chest) pass—two handed.
   a. Ball at chest level, face partner.
   b. Fingers spread above center of ball.
   c. Step toward partner and extend arms.
   d. Throw to chest level.
   e. Catch with finger tips.
   f. Thumbs together for high pass.

DPE pp. 570 – 575

Organize by partners.

Explain that this is one of the basic passes and must be mastered.

Get the "push" first, then later stress the finger action.

Lower the baskets to encourage development of a "shooting touch." This contrasts with throwing the ball at a basket that is too high.

PM.—The student will be able to adequately perform the following skills:
1. Push and one-handed pass.
2. Dribbling—right and left hands in a stationary position.
3. Shooting—one-handed shot at a target on the floor.
4. Catching—high and low passes.

50

MOVEMENT EXPERIENCE— CONTENT	ORGANIZATION AND TEACHING HINTS	EXPECTED STUDENT OBJECTIVES AND OUTCOMES

    g. Little fingers together for low pass.

    h. Hands relaxed, provide a little "give."

    i. Practice on the fly.

    j. Add the bounce pass—same technique.

    k. Avoid forward spin.

3. One-Handed Pass

    a. Side toward catcher.

    b. Ball back with both hands to side of head or above shoulder. Fingers spread, directly behind the ball.

    c. Release the forward hand and throw with a wrist snap.

    d. Practice both right and left.

4. Birdie in the Cage

    a. Form circles of 7–8 children.

    b. Pass ball among the circle for practice. Be sure everyone handles the ball.

    c. Select "Birdie," put in center until he touches the ball, or there is a loose ball leaving the circle.

5. Dribbling (each has a ball)

    a. Explain technique: wrist action, finger control, eyes ahead.

    b. Dribble in different directions. Use right and left in turn.

    c. Use whistle dribble. Stop on whistle.

6. One-Handed Shot

    a. Raise ball up to eye level, sight, and shoot to a partner (demonstrate).

    b. Shoot from close position around the basket with partners alternating.

7. Add a short dribble and a shot.

ORGANIZATION AND TEACHING HINTS

Bounce the ball just beyond the halfway mark.

Avoid the "hip pocket" windup.

Foam rubber balls bounce in a fashion similar to a basketball and do not create fear of the object.

Let the children call the fault.

Watch for collisions. Loose balls—stop the ball or just return it.

Move through the area and encourage students to look for you. This causes them to take their eyes off the ball from time to time.

Each person takes two shots per turn.

Shoot at wastepaper baskets, boxes, etc. Regulation baskets are much too high and prevent students from developing a proper shooting touch.

Shoot at a hula hoop held by a partner. Dribble and shoot into inverted boxes.

GAME (5 – 7 MINUTES)

EXPECTED STUDENT OBJECTIVES AND OUTCOMES

Aff.—People who live a long time tend to be satisfied. Discuss the importance of self-acceptance. Encourage self-evaluation, rather than comparison to others, as a way of reducing stress and encouraging wellness.

Aff.—Basketball-related skills demand a great deal of fine motor coordination. Discuss the necessity of much repetition and practice over a long period of time before good results appear.

Cog.—Accuracy is relative. All shooters miss more shots than they make.

Play an unrelated game. Primary-level students are not capable of playing basketball. At this level, emphasis should be on developing skills and allowing time to practice them. The following are suggested:

1. Blindfolded Duck, p. 516
2. Cat and Mice, p. 519
3. Freeze, p. 521

DYNAMIC PHYSICAL EDUCATION LESSON PLAN
Educational Movement (Lesson 4)
Level I

Fundamental Skills: Sliding and galloping
Educational Movement Themes: Movement combinations, activities with tires
Manipulative Activity: Yarn balls

Supplies and Equipment Needed:
  Beanbags—one for each child
  Yarn balls—one for each child
  Tires—16–20 (hoops may be substituted)
  Balls
  Parachute
  Tape player
  Music

MOVEMENT EXPERIENCE— CONTENT	ORGANIZATION AND TEACHING HINTS	EXPECTED STUDENT OBJECTIVES AND OUTCOMES

INTRODUCTORY ACTIVITY (2 – 3 MINUTES)

Body Part Identification

Enough beanbags for every child are scattered on the floor. Students are instructed to move over and around the beanbags. When a body part is called, students place that body part on the nearest beanbag.

Variations:
1. Use different movements.
2. Use different equipment such as hoops or jump ropes.
3. Call combinations of body parts.

DPE p. 221

Scatter formation.

Put names of body parts on flash cards.

To encourage fast thinking (after students have learned body parts), scatter one or two fewer beanbags than there are students in the class.

Cog.—The student will be able to identify body parts by name.

PM.—The student will be able to place the proper body parts on the beanbag.

FITNESS DEVELOPMENT ACTIVITY (7 – 8 MINUTES)

Parachute Fitness

1. Jog in circle with chute held in left hand.
2. Shake the chute.
3. Slide to the right; return slide to the left.
4. Sit and perform situps - 30 seconds.
5. Skip for 20 seconds.
6. Freeze, face the center, and stretch the chute tightly. Hold for 8–12 seconds. Repeat five to six times.
7. Run in place while holding the chute taut at different levels.
8. Sit with legs under the chute. Do a seat walk toward the center. Return to the perimeter. Repeat four to six times.
9. Place the chute on the ground. Jog away from the chute and return on signal. Repeat for 30 seconds.
10. Shake the chute and jump in place.

DPE pp. 244 – 245

Evenly space youngsters around the chute.

Use different grips to add variation to the activities.

Develop group morale by encouraging students to move together.

Use music to motivate youngsters.

To cool down, allow youngsters a minute to perform parachute stunts like the Dome or Mushroom.

PM.—The student will be able to perform the grass drill continuously for 60-90 seconds.

Aff.—Grass drills are an old football drill. Discuss the value of this activity in developing endurance and quickness.

MOVEMENT EXPERIENCE— CONTENT	ORGANIZATION AND TEACHING HINTS	EXPECTED STUDENT OBJECTIVES AND OUTCOMES

11. Lie on back with feet under the chute. Shake the chute with the feet.
12. Hop to the center of the chute and return. Repeat for 20 seconds.
13. Sit with feet under the chute. Stretch by touching the toes with the chute. Relax with other stretches while sitting.

LESSON FOCUS (15 – 20 MINUTES)

Educational Movement

Note: A few activities should be chosen from each section and presented alternately so students receive a wide variety of activities. If students are fatigued from the fitness portion of the lesson, start with the manipulative activities.

A. *Fundamental Skill—Sliding*
Move sideways. Light movement on the balls of the feet. Smooth, don't bounce. Slide feet (close to the floor).
   1. Slide in one direction, stop and slide in another.
   2. Begin with short slides, increase slide length. Reverse.
   3. Do a number of slides (3, 4, 5, 6), do a half turn, continue in the same direction, but leading with the other leg.
   4. Slide with a 4-4 pattern.
   5. Slide in a figure-eight pattern.
   6. Change levels while sliding; touch the floor occasionally while sliding.
   7. Slide lightly and noiselessly.
   8. Pretend to be a defensive basketball player, sliding.
   9. Slide with a partner.
   10. Exploratory activity.

DPE pp. 297 – 298

Scatter formation.

Cue by saying:
   "Move sideways."
   "Smooth, light movement."
   "Don't bounce."
   "Slide your feet."

Use a drum to guide the movements.

Basic movement music for sliding is excellent here.

PM.—The student will develop the ability to slide in both directions and make changes at will.

Cog.—The student will be able to explain the difference between sliding techniques and those of galloping.

Aff.—The student will exhibit an appreciation of the fact that sliding has future use in many sport and leisure time activities.

B. *Fundamental Skill—Galloping*
One foot leads. Forward or backward motion. More bounce than sliding. Lift the arms more.
   1. Form a circle. Slide in one direction (clockwise or counterclockwise). Gradually turn the body to face the line of direction; this is galloping.
   2. Practice galloping freely in general space. Gallop backwards.
   3. Gallop in a figure eight and other patterns.
   4. Change gallops (leading foot) on 8, 4, and 2 gallops.
   5. Gallop with a partner.

DPE p. 298

Cue by saying:
   "Lead with one foot."
   "Lead with the other foot."

Use music here. This leads to the polka.

PM.—The student will be able to gallop in various directions.

PM.—The student will demonstrate the ability to gallop backward.

PM.—The student will be able to change the leading foot at will while galloping.

MOVEMENT EXPERIENCE—CONTENT	ORGANIZATION AND TEACHING HINTS	EXPECTED STUDENT OBJECTIVES AND OUTCOMES
6. Ponies in the Stable, p. 219	Use as a fun activity.	
C. *Manipulative Activity—Yarn Balls* This is to be free practice and exploration. Children can work as individuals or as partners. Students should work on needed skills and also come up with activities of their own origin.	*DPE* pp. 368 – 372 Scatter formation. Encourage children to work on skills that need practice. See Educational Movement Lesson 2 for ideas.	PM.—The student will improve skills that need work. Aff.—Students will be stimulated to work on improving skills.
D. *Movement Combinations* 1. Run, leap, roll. 2. Shake (all over), gallop, freeze. 3. Hop, collapse, explode. 4. Whirl, skip, sink (melt) slowly. 5. Creep, pounce, curl. 6. Begin low, lift, grin, roll. 7. Kneel, sway, jump to feet. 8. Shrink, expand, slide. 9. On all fours, run, roll, jump. 10. Do a Jumping Jack (two or three times), slide, jump turn. 11. Hop forward, collapse, creep forward. 12. Jump forward (several jumps), shake yourself, whirl. 13. Rock back and forth on the heels, jump high, sit down quickly. 14. Sink slowly from a high position, roll, do a jump turn. 15. Click heels right and left, jump half turn, run backwards. 16. Twist, skip, sit down, smile. 17. Turn around three times, clap hands behind the back, run, balance on one foot when you stop. 18. Do fast, tiny steps in place; fall forward to the hands; move forward on all fours. 19. Take a deep breath; expel the air, saying "Ah-h-h"; jump forward; spin; sink. 20. Spin on your seat, roll sideward, stand, take five jumps ahead.	Scatter formation. Use of general space. Allow individual response within framework of challenge. Repeat two or three times. Caution to avoid collisions. Ask for student demonstration when a unique or well-done response appears.	PM.—The student will be able to combine the movements together as described. Cog.—Proper diet is necessary if students are to retain optimum wellness. Generally, one serving from each of the following basic food groups is desirable: 1. Leafy green and yellow vegetables. 2. Citrus fruits, tomatoes, and salad greens. 3. Potatoes and other vegetables and fruits. 4. Milk and milk products. 5. Meat, poultry, fish, eggs, dried beans and peas, and nuts. 6. Bread and cereals. 7. Butter and margarine.
21. Allow exploratory activity to put together three or four movements of your choice. 22. From item 21, select one or more unique patterns, have the student verbalize and demonstrate, have all follow the pattern.	Allow sufficient time. Encourage smooth linking of patterns.	Cog.—On the basis of the pattern experiences, the student will be able to put together smooth patterns of his own choosing.
E. *Tire Activities (or Hoops)* Each squad takes four or five tires. Put them in a line on the floor. 1. Walk, hop, and jump through or on the sides of the tires. 2. Leap over the tires from the side.	Squad activity. Tires can be painted and numbered to make them more attractive and to make them useful for color and number challenges.	PM.—The student will be able to move in and out of, on the sides of, and over the tires.

MOVEMENT EXPERIENCE— CONTENT	ORGANIZATION AND TEACHING HINTS	EXPECTED STUDENT OBJECTIVES AND OUTCOMES

3. Run around the tires on the sidewalls.
4. Jump astride the tire and inside it alternately.
5. Jump through each center without touching the tire.
6. Use different animal walks— Bunny Jump, Frog Jump, Crab Walk.
7. Jump off the sidewalls down the line of tires.
8. Using one tire, take a push-up position. Keeping the hands on the tire, circle with the feet. Then put the feet on the tire and circle with the hands.
9. Jog through with high knees.
10. Heel clicks in the center of each hoop.
11. Roll a tire at a partner, who jumps over it as it approaches.
12. Stand the tires upright (two or three tires) and jump in and out of the tires.

If tires are not available, hoops can be substituted.

To make the tires stand up, see the diagram on pp. 715 – 716 for making such tire stands.

Encourage the student not to touch the tires when moving.

Cog.—Tires are often used in football drills to develop good balance and agility. The student will be able to explain how tire activities might accomplish this goal.

GAME (5 – 7 MINUTES)

The following are suggested:
1. Corner Spry, p. 514
2. Hot Potatoes, p. 522
3. Popcorn, p. 514

DYNAMIC PHYSICAL EDUCATION LESSON PLAN
Recreational Activities
Level I

Supplies and Equipment Needed:
  One beanbag or hoop for each child
  Recreational activities equipment
  Tape player
  Music

MOVEMENT EXPERIENCE— CONTENT	ORGANIZATION AND TEACHING HINTS	EXPECTED STUDENT OBJECTIVES AND OUTCOMES

INTRODUCTORY ACTIVITY (2 – 3 MINUTES)

Ponies in the Stable

A beanbag or hoop is used to mark each child's stable. On signal, youngsters gallop around the area and "stables." On a second signal, students return to the nearest stable.

Variations:
1. Use different locomotor movement.
2. Take different positions in the stable such as seated, balanced, collapsed.

DPE p. 219

Place one fewer stable on the floor than children to add challenge.

Have students move in different directions such as northbound, etc.

Place different colors of beanbags (or hoops) on floor. Stipulate that the students must go over (or through) five green bags (or hoops) before returning to their stables.

Cog.—The student will understand that galloping is an uneven rhythmic movement.

PM.—The students will be able to gallop smoothly to and from their stables.

Cog.—Students will understand that it is necessary to warm up the body before doing activities.

FITNESS DEVELOPMENT ACTIVITIES (7 – 8 MINUTES)

Astronaut Drills

1. Walk.
2. Walk on tiptoes while reaching for the sky.
3. Walk with giant strides.
4. Freeze; perform various stretches.
5. Do a Puppy Dog Walk.
6. Jump like a pogo stick.
7. Freeze; perform Push-Up variations.
8. Walk and swing arms like a helicopter.
9. Trot lightly and silently.
10. Slide like an athlete.
11. Freeze; perform Curl-Up variations.
12. Crab Walk.
13. Skip.
14. Freeze; perform trunk development challenges.
15. Walk and cool down.

DPE pp. 262 – 263

Use circle or scatter formation with ample space between youngsters.

Children should be in constant movement except when stopped to do strength and flexibility activities.

Taped intervals of music and no music can be used to signal movement and stopping to do exercises.

Change direction often.

When they are moving on all fours, youngsters should be encouraged to place much of their weight on the hands in order to develop arm–shoulder girdle strength.

PM.—The student will be able to perform all the activies without stopping.

Cog.—Exercise routines, to be effective, must be done regularly. The student will be able to explain the necessity of exercising at least every other day.

LESSON FOCUS (15 – 20 MINUTES)

Recreational Activities

The purpose of the recreation is to teach children activities that they can play during the time when school is not in session. Suggested activities are:

Emphasis should be placed on teaching the rules of the activities so children can enjoy them on their own time.

PM.—The student will be able to play at least four of the given activities.

Cog.—The student will be able to recite the rules for playing four or more of the activities.

MOVEMENT EXPERIENCE—CONTENT	ORGANIZATION AND TEACHING HINTS	EXPECTED STUDENT OBJECTIVES AND OUTCOMES
1. Shuffleboard 2. Two Square 3. Hopscotch 4. Beanbag Horseshoes 5. Jacks 6. Marbles 7. Sidewalk tennis 8. Quoits 9. Rubber Horseshoes 10. Four Square 11. Formulating original, creative games	It might be useful to set up the activities at four or five different stations and then rotate the students from one station to the next. Three or four activities should be available at each station. If you know a traditional game played by children in your area for many years, now is a good time to teach it. Play some background music while children are participating.	Aff.—The recreational unit demands that students be self-directed. Emphasis should be placed on working with others cooperatively. Discuss the need for learning to self-direct oneself as an adult in recreational activities. Aff.—Recreational activities are excellent activities for reducing stress. Constant anxiety and stress increases heart rate, blood pressure, and blood cholesterol. Discuss the importance of playing for the "joy and fun of it."

GAME (5 – 7 MINUTES)

Since the activities above are recreational in nature, the game period is unnecessary.

DYNAMIC PHYSICAL EDUCATION LESSON PLAN
Educational Movement (Lesson 5)
Level I

Fundamental Skill: Skipping
Education Movement Themes: Taking the weight on the hand, leading with different body parts, making bridges
Manipulative Activity: Scoops and balls

Supplies and Equipment Needed:
  Four traffic cones
  Scoops and balls—one for each child

MOVEMENT EXPERIENCE—CONTENT	ORGANIZATION AND TEACHING HINTS	EXPECTED STUDENT OBJECTIVES AND OUTCOMES

INTRODUCTORY ACTIVITY (2 – 3 MINUTES)

Following Activity

One partner leads and performs various kinds of movements. The other partner must move in a similar fashion. This can also be used with squads or small groups, allowing the captain to lead.

DPE p. 222

If the movements seem to be limited, suggest a few ideas for challenges for the students to try.

PM.—The student will be able to lead as well as follow in this activity.

Cog.—The student will be able to create three movement patterns for her partner to follow.

FITNESS DEVELOPMENT ACTIVITIES (7 – 8 MINUTES)

Four-Corners Movement

Outline a large rectangle with four cones. Place signs with pictures on both sides of the cones. Youngsters move around the outside of the rectangle and change their movement pattern as they approach a corner sign. The following movement activities are suggested:
  1. Jogging
  2. Skipping/Jumping/Hopping
  3. Sliding/Galloping
  4. Various animal movements
  5. Sport imitation movements
Stop the class after 30–45 seconds of movement and perform various fitness challenges. This will allow students to rest aerobically.

DPE pp. 245 – 246

If signs are not placed at the corners, teachers can specify movements for students to perform.

Increase the demand of the routine by increasing the size of the rectangle.

Faster-moving students can pass on the outside (away from the center) of the rectangle.

Assure that abdominal and shoulder girdle strength development activities are included.

Cog.—The training effect occurs when the heart rate is elevated above 150-160 beats per minute. Provide a chart listing specific ages and the necessary heart rate (when taken during a 10-second count) to be within the training range. The student will be able to explain that to achieve this level, we must keep moving without much rest.

Aff.—Very little resting time occurs in Four-Corners Movement. When one exercises for a long period of time, without rest, muscular and cardiovascular endurance is developed. Discuss the importance of this type of conditioning.

LESSON FOCUS (15 – 20 MINUTES)

Educational Movement

Note: A few activities should be chosen from each section and presented alternately so students receive a wide variety of activities. If students are fatigued from the fitness portion of the lesson, start with the manipulative activities.

A. *Basic Skill—Skipping*
  Smoothness and rhythm, not speed and distance.
  Weight transferred smoothly.
  Arms swung in opposition to legs.

DPE p. 299

Scatter formation

Use drum beat to stimulate.

PM.—The student will be able to skip in a straight line action.

MOVEMENT EXPERIENCE—CONTENT	ORGANIZATION AND TEACHING HINTS	EXPECTED STUDENT OBJECTIVES AND OUTCOMES
On the balls of the feet. 1. Skip in general space. 2. Vary the skip with exaggerated arm action and lifted knees; side-to-side motion; skip lightly; skip heavily. 3. Skip backward. 4. Clap as you skip. 5. Skip twice on the same side (double skip). Alternate double skips (two on each side). 6. Form a circle. Skip clockwise and counterclockwise. 7. Form by partners or by threes. Skip in general space.	Cue by saying: "Skip high." "Swing your arms." "Skip smoothly." "On your toes." "Be happy." Use the alternative step–hop method for those having trouble.	Cog.—It is a misconception that physical activity is self-defeating because it increases appetite. Decreasing activity does not reduce appetite. Thus, under-exercising rather than overeating is the more important cause of obesity. PM.—The student will be able to skip with a partner.
B. *Manipulative Activities—Scoops and Balls* 1. *Individual Activities* a. Place the ball on the floor, scoop it up with the scoop. b. Toss the ball upward and catch it with the scoop. Change scoop to the other hand and repeat. c. Explore various ways of tossing the ball with the hand and catching in the scoop. d. Throw the ball against a wall and catch with the scoop. e. Throw the ball against the wall with the scoop and catch with the scoop. f. Toss either with the hand or with the scoop and do a stunt before catching. Use heel click, quarter turn, touch scoop to floor. g. Exploratory opportunity.	*DPE* pp. 376 – 377 Scatter with enough personal space. Yarn balls or whiffle balls can be used. Beanbags are a possibility. Eyes on the ball. Some "give" with the scoop. Plastic scoops can be made from 1-gallon jugs. See *DPE*, p. 714 for instructions. Omit if no wall space.	PM.—The student will develop the ability to catch the ball in the scoop. PM.—The student will be able to propel the ball with a toss from the scoop. Cog.—Scoops increase the length of the lever used for throwing. This allows objects to be thrown harder and farther.
2. *Partner Activities* a. Roll the ball and pick up with the scoop. b. Throw the ball back and forth, catching in the scoop. c. Toss the ball on first bounce and catch in the scoop. d. Play One-Step (p. 531). e. Repeat as much of a-d as possible, tossing with the scoop. f. Matching activities—repeat throw of the partner. g. Explore from other positions—sitting, kneeling, back to back, prone position.	One ball for partners. Keep distances relative. Seek variety. Specify different levels. Limit the distance.	PM.—The student will be able to play catch with a partner using only the scoop to both throw and catch.

MOVEMENT EXPERIENCE—CONTENT	ORGANIZATION AND TEACHING HINTS	EXPECTED STUDENT OBJECTIVES AND OUTCOMES

C. *Taking the Weight on the Hands*
  1. Begin in all-fours position, practice taking the weight on the hands by kicking up the feet in a one-two fashion.
  2. From standing position with the arms overhead, bring the hands to the floor and take the weight on the hands.
  3. Take the weight successively on the hands by moving from the side as a preliminary to the cartwheel.
  4. Have a partner hold your knees in a wheelbarrow position. Lift the legs as high as possible. May need to shift hands underneath.
	DPE pp. 288 – 289
	
	Scatter formation.
	
	Try crouch jumps and the mule kick.
	
	Keep elbows straight.
	
	Fingers spread, pointed forward.
	
	Some may be able to do a cartwheel.
		PM.—The student will be able to take the weight momentarily on the hands.
		
		PM.—The student will be able to devise a task where the body weight is placed on the hands.

D. *Theme: Leading with Different Body Parts*
Children move across the space as indicated in the selected movement formation and await the next challenge. Combine walking, running, hopping, jumping, and skipping with the following challenges:
  1. Move across with one arm leading.
  2. Now a different movement with the other arm leading.
  3. Repeat 1 with one foot leading.
  4. Repeat 2 with other foot leading.
  5. Move so one arm and one foot are leading.
  6. Show us a movement where the shoulder leads.
  7. How about a movement where one side leads?
  8. Show a movement along the floor where the foot is leading.
  9. Can you move so your head leads the movement?
  10. What other kinds of leading parts can you show?
	DPE p. 285
	
	Use movement formations, pp. 81 – 85.
	
	Allow variation and choice.
	
	Other factors should be used—light and heavy, soft and loud, tiny and large, slow and fast.
		PM.—The student will be able to move in accordance with the selected body part(s) leading.

E. *Theme: Making Bridges*
  1. Make a bridge using five, four, three, and two parts of the body.
  2. Select the number of body parts you wish to use and see how many different bridges you can make from this base.
  3. Select three different bridges and go from one to the next smoothly in sequence (sustained flow).
  4. Work with a partner and make different kinds of bridges.
  5. Have your partner go under your bridge.
	DPE p. 284
	
	Scatter formation.
	
	Could use achievement demonstration here.
		PM.—The student will be able to show a variety of bridges.
		
		Aff.—The student will demonstrate cooperation with a partner in making bridges.

MOVEMENT EXPERIENCE— CONTENT	ORGANIZATION AND TEACHING HINTS	EXPECTED STUDENT OBJECTIVES AND OUTCOMES

GAME (5 – 7 MINUTES)

The following are suggested:
1. Hill Dill, p. 522
2. Mousetrap, p. 523

DYNAMIC PHYSICAL EDUCATION LESSON PLAN
Stunts and Tumbling Skills (Lesson 2)
Level I

Supplies and Equipment Needed:
  Cones
  Tumbling mats
  Equipment for Mini-Challenge Course

MOVEMENT EXPERIENCE—CONTENT	ORGANIZATION AND TEACHING HINTS	EXPECTED STUDENT OBJECTIVES AND OUTCOMES

INTRODUCTORY ACTIVITY (2 – 3 MINUTES)

Popcorn

Students pair up with one person on the floor in push-up position and the other standing ready to move. On signal, the standing students move over and under the persons on the floor. The person on the floor changes from a raised to a lowered push-up position each time the partner goes over or under her. On signal, reverse positions.

DPE p. 223

Partner formation.

Encourage students to move as quickly as possible.

Challenge them to see how many times they can go over and under each other, or to be the quickest pair to go over, under, and around each other a specified number of times.

For a more difficult activity, the children on the floor can move around the area on all fours.

PM.—The student will be able to move quickly over, under, and around her partner.

Aff.—Warm-up activities only work when an individual motivates himself to move quickly and with quality. Discuss the need for self-motivation.

FITNESS DEVELOPMENT ACTIVITIES (7 – 8 MINUTES)

Mini-Challenge Course

Arrange three or four courses with a group at each course. Students perform the challenges from start to finish and jog back to repeat the course. On signal, groups move to a new course.
Course 1. Crouch jumps; pulls or scooter movements down a bench; through two hoops; and skip to a cone.
Course 2. Weave in and out of four wands held upright by cones; Crab Walk; hang from a climbing rope for 5 seconds; and gallop to a cone.
Course 3. Do a tumbling activity length of mat; agility run through hoops; Frog Jump; and slide to a cone.
Course 4. Move over and under six obstacles; Log Roll length of mat; while jumping, circle around three cones; and run to a cone.

DPE p. 243

Set up four parellel (side-by-side) courses in one-half of the area. Rotate groups to each course after a specified time.

An alternative is to organize the courses into a single circuit around the perimeter of the area.

Movement should be continuous.

Since young children fatigue and recover quickly, stop the class after 30-45 seconds and perform fitness movement challenges.

PM.—The student will be able to perform the various movements offered in the Mini-Challenge Course.

Aff.—Contrary to popular belief, girls can become stronger through exercise and weight training without fear of developing huge, unattractive muscles. Discuss this fact with the class.

It might be helpful to bring pictures of various women athletes as examples of fitness.

MOVEMENT EXPERIENCE—CONTENT	ORGANIZATION AND TEACHING HINTS	EXPECTED STUDENT OBJECTIVES AND OUTCOMES

LESSON FOCUS (15 – 20 MINUTES)

Tumbling, Stunts, and Animal Walks

Five groups of activities are found in this lesson to insure that youngsters receive a variety of experiences. Pick a few activities from each group and teach them alternately. For example, teach one or two animal movements, then a tumbling and inverted balance stunt, etc. Do not place excessive time on one group of activities at the expense of another.

  1. Animal Movements
     a. Bear Walk
     b. Gorilla Walk
     c. Rabbit Jump
     d. Elephant Walk
  2. Tumbling and Inverted Balances
     a. Forward Roll-Straddle
     b. Backward Curl
     c. Backward Roll-Handclasp Position
     d. Climb-Up
  3. Balance Stunts
     a. Kimbo Stand
     b. Knee-Lift Stand
     c. Stork Stand
     d. Balance Touch
     e. Single-Leg Balance
  4. Individual Stunts
     a. Rubber Band
     b. Pumping Up the Balloon
     c. Rising Sun
     d. Heel Click
     e. Lowering the Boom
     f. Turn-Over
     g. Thread the Needle
  5. Partner and Group Stunts
     a. Wring the Dishrag
     b. Partner Toe Toucher

DPE pp. 451 – 463

Scatter as many tumbling mats as possible throughout the area in order to avoid waiting lines.

Do not perform many repetitions of tumbling and inverted balances. For most children, limiting the number of forward or backward roll repetitions to four or five will prevent fatigue and injury.

Don't force students to perform tumbling and inverted balances. If they are fearful, gradual encouragement will accomplish more in the long run than intimidation and force.

Avoid lines to increase activity and avoid the embarrassment of performing in front of others.

A major concern for safety is the neck and back region. Overweight children are at greater risk and might be allowed to avoid tumbling and inverted balances.

Cog.—Momentum needs to be developed and applied when performing rolls. The student will be able to name three ways of developing momentum, i.e., tucking, starting from a higher point, preliminary raising of the arms.

Cog.—The center of weight must be positioned over the center of support in balance stunts. The student will be able to describe and demonstrate this in his own fashion.

PM.—The student will be able to perform at least two of the activities in each of the groups.

Aff.—Tumbling and stunts are activities in which there is a wide range of student ability which is evident to others. Discuss the sensitivity of the situation and the need to understand the shortcomings of others.

GAME (5 – 7 MINUTES)

The following are suggested:
  1. Where's My Partner?, p. 518
  2. Change Sides, p. 520

DYNAMIC PHYSICAL EDUCATION LESSON PLAN
Educational Movement (Lesson 6)
Level I

Fundamental Skill: Hopping
Educational Movement Themes: Body shapes, letters with the body
Manipulative Activity: Hoops

Supplies and Equipment Needed:
  Hoops, one for each child
  Balls

MOVEMENT EXPERIENCE—CONTENT	ORGANIZATION AND TEACHING HINTS	EXPECTED STUDENT OBJECTIVES AND OUTCOMES

INTRODUCTORY ACTIVITY (2 – 3 MINUTES)

Tag Games

Use some of the following tag games to offer children immediate activity.
  1. Skunk
  2. Stork
  3. Stoop
  4. Turtle
  5. Nose and Toe

DPE p. 518

Scatter formation.

Allow many players to be it.

PM.—The student will be able to dodge and evade the person(s) who is it.

FITNESS DEVELOPMENT ACTIVITIES (7 – 8 MINUTES)

Movement Challenges

Alternate locomotor movements with strength challenges. Repeat the challenges as necessary.
Locomotor Movement: Walk for 30 seconds.

A. *Trunk Development Challenges*
  Bend in different directions.
  Stretch slowly and return quickly.
  Combine bending and stretching movements.
  Sway back and forth.
  Twist one body part; add body parts.
  Make your body move in a large circle.
  In a sitting position, wave your legs at a friend; make circles with your legs.
Locomotor Movement: Skip for 30 seconds.

B. *Shoulder Girdle Challenges*
  In a push-up position, do the following challenges:
  Lift one foot; the other foot.
  Wave at a friend; wave with the other arm.
  Scratch your back with one hand; use the other hand.
  Walk your feet to your hands.
  Turn over and face the ceiling; shake a leg; Crab Walk.
Locomotor Movement: Jog for 30 seconds.

DPE pp. 239 – 242

Scatter formation.

Individual mats can be used as a "home" to keep youngsters spaced properly.

Repeat the various trunk challenges as necessary.

Young children will perform best when locomotor movements are alternated with stationary challenges, which allow them to recover aerobically.

Add Animal Walks to replace some of the locomotor movements and to create interest.

Use different qualities of movement such as giant skips, tiny and quick gallops, slow giant steps, to motivate youngsters.

As children become more fit, repeat the entire sequence.

PM.—The student will be able to move around the rectangle using different movements.

Cog.—The student will understand and be able to express verbally the fact that strenuous activity for months will tend to decrease resting heart rate.

MOVEMENT EXPERIENCE—CONTENT	ORGANIZATION AND TEACHING HINTS	EXPECTED STUDENT OBJECTIVES AND OUTCOMES

C. *Abdominal Development*
From a supine position:
 Lift your head and look at your toes.
 Lift your knees to your chest.
 Wave your legs at a friend.
From a sitting position:
 Slowly lay down with hands on tummy.
 Lift legs and touch toes.
Locomotor Movement: Run and leap for 45 seconds.

LESSON FOCUS (15 – 20 MINUTES)

Educational Movement

Note: A few activities should be chosen from each section and presented alternately so students receive a wide variety of activities. If students are fatigued from the fitness portion of the lesson, start with the manipulative activities.

A. *Fundamental Skill—Hopping*
Swing arms up to get height. Begin and land on the balls of the feet. Land lightly with loose knees.
 1. Hopping
  a. Hop in place lightly, changing the feet at will.
  b. Hop numbered sequences, right and left: 1–1, 2–2, 3–3, 4–4, 5–5, 1–2, 2–1, 2–3, 3–2 (hop in place).
  c. Hop, increasing height, reverse.
  d. From your spot, take two, three, or four hops out, turn around and hop back on other foot. How much space can you cover?
  e. Hop on one foot, do a heel and toe pattern with the other. Can you change feet each time doing this?
  f. Pick two spots away from you. Hop in place, then move to one spot. Hop in place, then to the other. Return to spot.
  g. Hop forward, backward, sideward.
  h. Hop different patterns—square, triangle, circle, figure eight, diamond, etc.
  i. Explore different positions in which you can hold the foot while hopping.
  j. Hold the free foot in different positions while hopping.

DPE pp. 296 – 297

Cue by saying: "Hop or jump with good upward arm motion." "Stay on your toes." "Use your arms for balance." "Reach for the sky." "Land lightly."

In hopping, be sure to change feet regularly. Hop 10 to 20 seconds in each sequence.

Stress form more than distance.

Encourage variety. Allow some choice here.

PM.—The student will be able to hop using correct body form and a proper landing.

Cog.—The student will be able to identify the major stress points involved in hopping.

Cog.—The student will be able to name four sports where a hopping movement is used.

PM.—The student will be able to perform a satisfactory hop while performing all the variations.

Aff.—Alcohol allows people to fail and still feel good. This may be why it is habit forming. Discuss the importance of understanding that failure is an important part of learning and must be accepted.

Cog.—The ultimate range of motion at a joint is the distance between absolute flexion and extension. Exercises should involve the full range of motion to maintain flexibility.

MOVEMENT EXPERIENCE—CONTENT	ORGANIZATION AND TEACHING HINTS	EXPECTED STUDENT OBJECTIVES AND OUTCOMES
k. Hop with the body in different leaning positions—forward, sideward, backward. l. Hop lightly, heavily. m. While hopping, touch the floor with either or both hands. n. Hop back and forth over a board or line, moving down the line. o. Trace out letters or numbers. Write your name hopping. p. Do quarter or half turns while hopping.	Try for variety.	

B. *Hoops (Floor Targets) and Hula Hooping*
Take eight or more hoops and form a figure (floor target) for each squad.
  1. Walk, run, hop, or jump through the figures. On the way back, do a movement on all fours (return activity).
  2. Have each squad demonstrate their movements.
  3. Form another figure and repeat.
Hula Hooping
  1. Hula hooping around the waist.
  2. Hula hooping around the hands and arms, the neck, or legs (on back position).
  3. Exploratory activity.
	DPE pp. 386 – 388
	
	Hoops should be placed with dispatch.
	
	Others watch.
	
	Remove extras.
		PM.—The student will be able to do the movements without touching the hoops.
		
		PM.—The student will be able to do simple hula hooping around the waist.

C. *Theme: Body Shapes*
Possibilities include:
  Long or short
  Wide or narrow
  Straight or twisted
  Stretched or curled
  Large or small
  Symmetrical or asymmetrical
  1. Show me a _____ (use terms above) shape.
  2. When I say "change," go from a _____ shape to a _____ shape (vary these).
  3. Explore symmetrical and asymmetrical. Take one of the above and make it symmetrical. Then change the same to an asymetrical shape.
  4. Explore other kinds of shapes.
  5. Contrasting shapes. Do one kind of shape and its contrast. Or name a shape with its contrast or opposite.
	DPE pp. 281 – 282
	
	Scatter formation. Each in personal space.
	
	Go briskly through this. As unique shapes appear, let the child demonstrate.
	
	Explain the terms, expecially the prefix.
	
	Explain this.
		PM.—The student will demonstrate the ability to assume the different named shapes.
		
		Cog.—The student will be able to distinguish between the different kinds of shapes.
		
		Aff.—One of the most important things to achieve in life is a good feeling about one's self. Physical fitness is an important contributing factor to positive feelings. Discuss how physical and mental health are interrelated and necessary to develop total wellness.

D. *Theme: Letters with the Body*
  1. Make letters standing.
  2. Make letters lying on the floor.
	DPE p. 282	

MOVEMENT EXPERIENCE—CONTENT	ORGANIZATION AND TEACHING HINTS	EXPECTED STUDENT OBJECTIVES AND OUTCOMES
3. Divide class into two sets of groups: one group makes a letter and the other names it. Give only one guess. Change groups. 4. Make simple words of two letters or three letters, using one child per letter. 5. Form numbers of two digits.	Can be done individually, but is a fine partner activity. Scatter formation. Demonstrate unique or excellent letters.	Aff.—The student will exhibit a willingness to cooperate with a partner. PM.—The student will be able to form the letters as named. Cog.—The student will be able to mentally visualize how the body is forming the letters.

GAME (5 – 7 MINUTES)

Play an active game as hoops do not require much gross motor activity.
1. Rollee Pollee, p. 524
2. Stop Ball, p. 519

DYNAMIC PHYSICAL EDUCATION LESSON PLAN
Fundamental Skills Using Magic Ropes
Level I

Supplies and Equipment Needed:
  Six to ten magic ropes per class
  Balance-beam benches or jumping boxes (optional)
  Tape player
  Music

MOVEMENT EXPERIENCE—CONTENT	ORGANIZATION AND TEACHING HINTS	EXPECTED STUDENT OBJECTIVES AND OUTCOMES

INTRODUCTORY ACTIVITY (2 – 3 MINUTES)

Run, Stop, and Pivot

Have the children run, and on signal, stop and pivot. Begin teaching a 90° pivot and move gradually to a 180° pivot. Relate the use of the pivot to various sport activities such as basketball.

DPE p. 219

Concentrate on teaching quick reaction and shifting weight to the pivot foot.

Students should be able to bend their knees (to lower the center of gravity) for stability.

Cog.—The student will be able to explain the use of the pivot as a common movement in many sports. For example, football and basketball.

PM.—The student will be able to do a 180° pivot with the body in good control.

FITNESS DEVELOPMENT ACTIVITIES (7 – 8 MINUTES)

Astronaut Drills

  1. Walk.
  2. Walk on tiptoes while reaching for the sky.
  3. Walk with giant strides.
  4. Freeze; perform various stretches.
  5. Do a Puppy Dog Walk.
  6. Jump like a pogo stick.
  7. Freeze; perform Push-Up variations.
  8. Walk and swing arms like a helicopter.
  9. Trot lightly and silently.
  10. Slide like an athlete.
  11. Freeze; perform Curl-Up variations.
  12. Crab Walk.
  13. Skip.
  14. Freeze; perform trunk development challenges.
  15. Walk and cool down.

DPE pp. 262 – 263

Use circle or scatter formation with ample space between youngsters.

Children should be in constant movement except when stopped to do strength and flexibility activities.

Taped intervals of music and no music can be used to signal movement and stopping to do exercises.

Change direction often.

When moving on all fours, encourage youngsters to place much of their weight on the hands in order to develop arm–shoulder girdle strength.

Cog.—Astronaut Drills were a common way of developing fitness in the armed services.

PM.—All students should be able to perform the Astronaut Drills.

Aff.—There is no easy way to fitness. It demands self-discipline. Discuss the importance of possessing a positive attitude toward activity in later life.

LESSON FOCUS (15 – 20 MINUTES)

Magic Ropes

A. *Single-Rope Activities*
  1. Jump back and forth, feet uncrossed.
  2. Jump back and forth, feet crossed.
  3. Jump back and forth, feet crossed and uncrossed alternately.

DPE pp. 429 – 431

Divide the class into small groups of five or six members.

Start activities with the rope at a 6" height and progressively raise it to increase the challenge.

PM.—The students will be able to hop back and forth from one end of the rope to the other without touching the rope at a height of 10".

Cog.—The student will understand and be able to recite why magic ropes are used in the program—to develop body management skills.

MOVEMENT EXPERIENCE—CONTENT	ORGANIZATION AND TEACHING HINTS	EXPECTED STUDENT OBJECTIVES AND OUTCOMES

4. Hop back and forth over rope using right and left feet in turn.
5. Jump the rope and perform various body turns while jumping.
6. Change body shapes and sizes while jumping.
7. Crawl or slide under the rope.
8. Alternate going over and under the rope.
9. Exploratory activity.

B. *Double Ropes*
  1. Ropes parallel to each other:
    a. Jump in one side, out other.
    b. Hop in one side, out other.
    c. Crouch jump in and out.
    d. Perform various animal walks in and out.
    e. Exploratory activity.
  2. Ropes crossed at right angles to each other:
    a. Perform various movements from one to the other.
    b. Jump into one area, crawl out other.

Since the magic ropes are a demanding activity, it might be well to teach the games as an integrated part of the lesson focus. In other words, teach 5-7 minutes of single-rope activities, take a break, and teach a game. Then teach more magic rope activities with double ropes and finish with a game. The following games are suggested:
  1. One, Two, Button My Shoe, p. 517
  2. Mother, May I?, p. 513

ORGANIZATION AND TEACHING HINTS

Emphasize the point that students are *not* supposed to touch the rope. The objective is body management and learning to control the body in space.

Try the activities while holding hands with a partner.

Tie one end of the magic rope to a jumping box or balance-beam bench. This reduces the number of rope holders needed.

Rotate the rope holders.

Students should approach the rope from one end and perform their activities to the other end of the rope.

The child next in turn should begin a movement when the performing child is near the end of the rope.

Try holding one end near the floor and the other end 2–3' high. Children then progress from the low end to the high and more difficult end.

GAME (5 – 7 MINUTES)

EXPECTED STUDENT OBJECTIVES AND OUTCOMES

Aff.—Carbon monoxide in tobacco smoke reduces the physical endurance of the smoker. Discuss the detrimental effects of this habit.

Aff.—Discuss the need for all students to be willing to share rope-holding responsibilities.

Cog.—Readiness for learning a motor skill is necessary for optimal learning. Readiness is individual in nature and occurs at different times.

DYNAMIC PHYSICAL EDUCATION LESSON PLAN
Fundamental Skills Using Balance Beams
Level I

Supplies and Equipment Needed:
  Six balance-beam benches
  24 beanbags
  12 wands
  Equipment for Mini-Challenge Course
  Cones

MOVEMENT EXPERIENCE—CONTENT	ORGANIZATION AND TEACHING HINTS	EXPECTED STUDENT OBJECTIVES AND OUTCOMES

INTRODUCTORY ACTIVITY (2 – 3 MINUTES)

European Running with Variations

Review variations previously used:
1. Clap hands on various beats.
2. On signal, make a complete turn using four running steps.
3. On signal, scatter and run in general space. On next signal, resume circular running.
4. Stamp feet, say "hey!" and do a hop on stipulated beats.

DPE pp. 217 – 218

Try different formations using different leaders.

Have the students move in individual directions and, on signal, have them move into a specified formation.

Work on quality of movement. Students should be able to move to the beat of the tom-tom and maintain proper spacing.

PM.—The student will be able to run to the beat of the tom-tom.

PM.—The student will be able to move into the following formations—circle, triangle, and rectangle—from scatter formation.

FITNESS DEVELOPMENT ACTIVITIES (7 – 8 MINUTES)

Mini-Challenge Course

Arrange three or four courses with a group at each course. Students perform the challenges from start to finish and jog back to repeat the course. On signal, groups move to a new course.
Course 1. Crouch jumps; pull or scooter movements down a bench; through two hoops; and skip to a cone.
Course 2. Weave in and out of four wands held upright by cones; Crab Walk; hang from a climbing rope for 5 seconds; and gallop to a cone.
Course 3. Do a tumbling activity length of mat; agility run through hoops; Frog Jump; and slide to a cone.
Course 4. Move over and under six obstacles; Log Roll length of mat; while jumping, circle around three cones; and run to a cone.

DPE p. 243

Set up four parallel (side-by-side) courses in one-half of the area. Rotate groups to each course after a specified time.

An alternative is to organize the courses into a single circuit around the perimeter of the area.

Movement should be continuous.

Since young children fatigue and recover quickly, stop the class after 30–45 seconds and perform fitness movement challenges.

PM.—The student will be able to perform all the activities by the end of the week.

Cog.—The student will be able to name the immediate changes in body functions that occur when one exercises, i.e., increased heart rate, breathing rate.

MOVEMENT EXPERIENCE—CONTENT	ORGANIZATION AND TEACHING HINTS	EXPECTED STUDENT OBJECTIVES AND OUTCOMES

LESSON FOCUS (15 – 20 MINUTES)

Balance-Beam Activities

1. May want to practice on lines to establish qualities of controlled movement and not looking at feet.
2. Walk length of beam and dismount correctly.
   a. Walk forward.
   b. Walk backward.
   c. Walk sideways—lead with both left and right sides of body.
   d. Try other steps—follow steps, heel and toe, on toes, etc.
   e. Allow for exploratory activity.
3. Walk different directions and vary arm and body positions.
   a. Hands on hips
   b. Hands on head
   c. Hands folded across chest
   d. Lean to one side or the other
   e. Body bent forward or backward
   f. Hands on knees or feet
   g. Student choice
4. Balance objects such as beanbags or wands while walking across beam. (Use exploratory approach.)
5. Pause momentarily in good balance and dismount with a small controlled jump.
6. Allow a few minutes for students' exploration of ideas.

DPE pp. 422 – 424

Use at least six beams with equal number of students behind each beam.

Use a mat at the finishing end of the beam for students to perform their dismounts.

Assign a return activity for students so they are busy off as well as on the beam.

Place return activity signs on cones. Students perform one of activities after dismounting from the beam. Return activities should be done for the length of area to assure students don't stand in line.

Stress quality of the movement across the beam as well as during the dismount.

If a child falls, have her step back on the beam and continue. This will assure her of the same amount of practice as the gifted child.

Place a target on the wall in front of the beams for students to focus their eyes.

Make sure student performs a dismount. Pause first.

Encourage a variety of dismounts such as:
   a. Jumps
   b. Quarter and half turns
   c. Pike and Straddle Jumps

Encourage a broad variety of activities.

PM.—The student will be able to balance self while walking across beam. A desirable goal would be for the child to walk across the beam without falling.

Cog.—Balance is a learned activity. The student will be able to state that practice and concentration are necessary for improvement.

Cog.—Changing arm and leg positions or direction of movement creates a new task for the body and it must compensate to maintain balance. The student will be able to explain this in her own words.

Aff.—Awareness of the status and prestige given to a skilled performer. Discuss the payoff when one is skilled such as friends, money, prizes, etc.

Cog.—Muscle size is determined by gender (testosterone in male) and exercise. The student will understand the physical differences between males and females in terms of musculature.

GAME (5 – 7 MINUTES)

Play a game that is active. Try to introduce new games rather than falling back on a few that both you and the class know well. Have you tried the following?
1. Back to Back, p. 516
2. Mousetrap, p. 523
3. Red Light, p. 523

DYNAMIC PHYSICAL EDUCATION LESSON PLAN
Manipulative Skills Using Hoops
Level I

Supplies and Equipment Needed:
  One hoop per child
  Tom-tom
  Balls
  Plastic jugs

MOVEMENT EXPERIENCE—CONTENT	ORGANIZATION AND TEACHING HINTS	EXPECTED STUDENT OBJECTIVES AND OUTCOMES

INTRODUCTORY ACTIVITY (2 – 3 MINUTES)

Marking

One partner moves in any fashion he wishes and the other partner attempts to tag him. Once tagged, the partners change roles and the other attempts to tag. A variation is to have one of the partners move in a desired fashion and the other attempts to stay with him (marking). On signal, both partners freeze. The following partner attempts to touch (mark) the partner.

DPE p. 222

Partners in general space.

Can use various locomotor movements.

Challenges can be made by marking certain body parts.

PM.—The student will be able to demonstrate the ability to mark his partner, to stay with him so when the whistle sounds he is within one yard of his partner.

FITNESS DEVELOPMENT ACTIVITIES (7 – 8 MINUTES)

Walk, Trot, and Sprint

Move to the following signals:
  1. One drumbeat - walk.
  2. Two drumbeat - trot.
  3. Three drumbeat - sprint.
  4. Whistle - freeze and perform exercises.
Perform various strength and flexibility exercises between bouts of walk, trot, and sprint. Examples are:
  a. Bend and Twist
  b. Sitting Stretch
  c. Push-Up variations
  d. Sit-Up variations
  e. Trunk Twister
  f. Body Circles

DPE p. 245

Use a tom-tom or tambourine.

Scatter formation.

Emphasize quality of movement and rapid changes.

Check heart rate after bouts of sprinting.

Alternate bouts of movement with strength and flexibility exercises.

PM.—The student will be able to perform the activity at an increased pace.

Cog.—One method often used to measure fitness is to count the pulse rate after exercise within 2 or 3 minutes. It might be interesting to measure pulse rate at various intervals after exercise. The more fit one is, the faster pulse rate returns to normal.

Cog.—A well-balanced diet provides fuel for physical activity. Discuss the basics of a good diet and the need for such.

LESSON FOCUS (15 – 20 MINUTES)

Hoops

  1. Place the hoops on the floor to create various patterns. Have the children perform various fundamental locomotor movements and animal walks in, out of, and between the hoops. Create different challenges by having students go in and out of various color hoops and specify a certain number of hoops they must enter.

DPE pp. 386 – 388

Scatter formation.

Hula hooping demands that body part is moved back and forth, *not* in a circle.

Have the class drop their hoops when you desire their attention.

When jumping through hoops, encourage children to hold them loosely to prevent falls.

PM.—The student will be able to hula-hoop on at least one part of their body.

PM.—The student will be able to place a reverse spin on the hoop, causing it to return to them.

Aff.—Many students will not immediately be able to hula-hoop or apply the reverse spin. Discuss the value of continued practice versus the alternative of quitting and never learning the skill.

MOVEMENT EXPERIENCE— CONTENT	ORGANIZATION AND TEACHING HINTS	EXPECTED STUDENT OBJECTIVES AND OUTCOMES

2. Hula-hoop using various body parts such as waist, neck, knees, arms, and fingers.
  a. While hula-hooping on the arms, try to change the hoop from one arm to the other.
  b. Change hoop from one partner to another while hula-hooping.
  c. Try leg skippers—hula-hoop with one leg and jump the hoop with the other leg.
  d. On back, circle hoop around one leg; both legs.
  e. Hula-hoop around waist while on knees. While hooping, try to stand up and go back to knees.
  f. Thread the needle. Balance the hoop on head and try to step through the hoop. Do it forward, backward, and sideways.
  g. Exploratory activity.
	Use the hoops as a home area for children. This will keep them in a designated area.	Cog.—Spin reduces the amount of force available for forward projection. Discuss the effect reverse spin of the hoop has on forward movement of the hoop.
		
		Cog.—Fiber is an important part of a healthy diet. Vegetables and fruit play significant roles in the health of the digestive tract.
		
		Cog.—Muscular strength is an important defense against joint injury. Discuss how professional athletes lift weights in an attempt to lessen potential injury.

3. Jump rope with the hoop—forward and backward. Begin with a back-and-forth swing. Also sideways jumping.		
4. Roll hoop and run alongside it. Run ahead of it. Cross in front of it.		
5. Spin the hoop like a top. How many times can you make it spin? How many times can you run around the spinning hoop before it falls?		
6. Balance the hoop and then go through it before it falls.		
7. For a change-of-pace activity, put hoops on floor. Perform various locomotor movements around many hoops. On signal, curl up inside a hoop. For challenge, have fewer hoops than students.		
8. Roll hoop with a reverse spin to make it return to the thrower.	The reverse spin must be taught and practiced. Many students find it to be a difficult skill.	
9. Reverse spin, catch on arm, and hula-hoop it. Try catching on foot.		
10. Partner Activities—roll hoops back and forth. Play catch with the hoops.	When throwing and catching two hoops, each partner should throw one and then progress to both hoops being thrown at the same time by one partner.	
11. Roll with a reverse spin and see how many times partner can go through with it.		
12. Exploratory activity.		

MOVEMENT EXPERIENCE— CONTENT	ORGANIZATION AND TEACHING HINTS	EXPECTED STUDENT OBJECTIVES AND OUTCOMES

GAME (5 – 7 MINUTES)

The following are suggested:
1. Animal Tag, p. 515
2. Bottle Bat Ball, p. 524

DYNAMIC PHYSICAL EDUCATION LESSON PLAN
Educational Movement (Lesson 7)
Level I

Fundamental Skill: Leaping
Educational Movement Themes: Levels and speed, partner; jump ropes as floor targets, partner; supporting the weight wholly or in part; acceleration and deceleration

Supplies and Equipment Needed:
  Jump ropes—one for each child
  Benches and other obstacles to leap over
  Tom-tom

MOVEMENT EXPERIENCE—CONTENT	ORGANIZATION AND TEACHING HINTS	EXPECTED STUDENT OBJECTIVES AND OUTCOMES

INTRODUCTORY ACTIVITY (2 – 3 MINUTES)

Locomotor Movement Variations

Using the basic locomotor movements (walking, running, skipping, hopping, etc.), try the following variations:
1. Changes in speed
2. Weight bearing on different parts of foot (toes, heels, sides of feet)
3. Change directions
4. Making different patterns (triangles, squares, etc.)
5. Putting together sequences of various locomotor movements

DPE p. 219

Try to encourage children to move with quality.

The tom-tom can be used to offer different qualities to the movement.

Cog.—The student will be able to verbalize the importance of locomotor movements and their variations in sports activities.

PM.—The student will be able to originate his sequence of locomotor movements and variations.

FITNESS DEVELOPMENT ACTIVITIES (7 – 8 MINUTES)

Animal Movements and Fitness Challenges

Puppy Dog Walk - 30 seconds.
Freeze; perform stretching activities.
Measuring Worm Walk - 30 seconds.
Freeze; perform abdominal development challenges.
Elephant Walk - 30 seconds.
Frog Jump - 30 seconds.
Freeze; perform push-up position challenges.
Seal Crawl - 30 seconds.
Bear Walk - 30 seconds.
Freeze; perform abdominal challenges.
Siamese Twin Walk - 30 seconds.
Lame Dog Walk - 30 seconds.

DPE p. 242

Emphasize placing the weight on the hands for shoulder girdle development.

Quality of movement should be emphasized rather than speed.

Vary the length of the intervals to match the fitness level of youngsters

Taped intervals of music and no music can be used to signal movement and stopping to do exercises.

Cog.—It is interesting to measure the breathing rate at rest and during and after exercise. The student will be able to explain why breathing rate varies.

Aff.—Many experts feel people are overweight due to lack of activity rather than eating too much. Discuss why this might be true.

Cog.—Flexor muscles decrease the angle of a joint. Extensors return the movement from flexion. Identify flexors and extensors among students.

LESSON FOCUS (15 – 20 MINUTES)

Educational Movement

Note: A few activities should be chosen from each section and presented alternately so students receive a wide variety of activities. If students are fatigued from the fitness portion of the lesson, start with the manipulative activities.

MOVEMENT EXPERIENCE— CONTENT	ORGANIZATION AND TEACHING HINTS	EXPECTED STUDENT OBJECTIVES AND OUTCOMES
A. *Leaping* Strive for graceful flight. 1. Run in different directions and practice your leaping. Alternate the leading foot. 2. As you run, try a leap for good height; for distance; for both. 3. Explore the different arm positions you can use in leaping. Which is best? Try sailing through the air like an airplane. 4. Leap with a quarter or half turn. 5. If there are benches or other obstacles present, leap over these. Put several in succession for consecutive leaps. 6. Put one-half the children down scattered in curled position, face to the floor. The others leap over as many as possible. 7. Run and leap from an inclined bench. 8. Practice making two or three leaps in succession. 9. Practice Leap the Brook.	*DPE* pp. 298 – 299 Scatter formation. Stress "soft" landing. Alternate leading foot. Cues: "Up and over." "Push off and reach." "Use your arms to help." Change groups. Use a mat for landing.	M.—The student will be able to secure good height in leaping. PM.—The student will be able to land lightly. Cog.—The student will be able to explain how force is applied to result in an effective leap. Cog.—The number and size of muscles used for a movement will determine the amount of force generated. Identify the size and number of muscles used when leaping.
B. *Theme: Levels and Speed* Each set of partners has a line on the floor. Each partner goes down the line and explores the following: 1. Show me a slow, low level movement down and back. 2. What other ways can you go down and back at a slow, low level? 3. Change to a high level, fast movement. 4. What other ways can you do a high level, fast movement? 5. Combine a low, fast movement down with a high, slow movement back. 6. Explore other ways to move at different levels and speeds.	*DPE* pp. 282 – 283 By partners. Each takes a turn. Encourage student-developed ideas and responses. Students should be given a chance to share their ideas with each other.	PM.—The student will demonstrate the ability to react to the level and speed as challenged. Cog.—The student will be able to explain the concepts of levels and speed. Aff.—Emotional health is impossible unless individuals can acknowledge and express their feelings. Discuss the importance of accepting our own and others' feelings in a gentle and empathetic fashion.
C. *Theme: Partner Activity Based on a Jump Rope Floor Target* Begin with the rope laid in a straight line along the floor. Various movements down the rope: 1. Jumping, hopping, cross steps, scissors steps, heel clicks, etc. 2. Add quarter and half-turns, levels. 3. Take the weight partially on the hands; crouch jumps, bunny jump, cartwheel, etc. 4. Form a selected shape with the rope. Repeat 1, 2, 3. Form the same shape with your body.	*DPE* pp. 397 – 399 Partners scattered around the space. Go down the rope one way only. Develop this well. Each takes a turn. Challenge for variety. Low, in-between, high levels.	PM.—The student will be able to move down the rope with a variety of movements.

MOVEMENT EXPERIENCE—CONTENT	ORGANIZATION AND TEACHING HINTS	EXPECTED STUDENT OBJECTIVES AND OUTCOMES
5. Matching activity. One partner performs and the other matches the movement. 6. Partner activity. Join hands in some way; hop, jump, or use other movements down the rope or figure. Wheelbarrow or use partner-support activities and move down the rope. *Other factors that can be used are*: Light and heavy movement; time variations. Angry, happy, and other expressive movements leading with different parts of the body.		PM.—The student will be able to respond in a proper physical expression when given expressive words, depicting moods. Cog.—Muscle fibers in a motor unit contract in an all-or-none fashion. The strength of a contraction depends on the number of muscle fibers that contract. Discuss the difference in maximum contractions compared to generating less force.
D. *Theme: Supporting the Weight Wholly or in Part (Partners)* 1. Support with partner's feet on floor; with one foot on the floor. 2. Support with partner's hands on the floor. 3. Support with partner completely off the floor. 4. Support and turn the partner in a full circle.	*DPE* pp. 278 – 279 Scatter formation with partners. This should be flexible, with emphasis on variety of response. Use half-and-half achievement, demonstration. One-half the class watches the other half.	PM.—The student will be able to create a variety of responses. Cog.—Aerobic endurance is important for long-term, low-intensity activities. Discuss how aerobic endurance can be improved.
E. *Acceleration and Deceleration* 1. Begin a movement and accelerate. 2. Begin with a fast movement and decelerate. 3. Accelerate to a fast speed and decelerate the same movement. 4. Accelerate with one movement to fast speed, shift to another movement, and decelerate. 5. Can you accelerate one movement of the body while decelerating another at the same time? *Suggested movements*: Stepping in place, running in place, circling body parts, arm thrust movements, jumping, hopping, changing stride, arm and leg movement while lying on back, pretending to be a locomotive engine of a railroad train.	*DPE* pp. 282 – 283 Scatter formation. Explain prefixes. Get other suggestions from the children.	PM.—The student will demonstrate the ability to interpret acceleration and deceleration in selected movements. Cog.—The student will be able to verbally explain the terms "acceleration" and "deceleration." Cog.—Strength is an important factor for learning motor skills. Exercises designed to develop strength are not effective in developing endurance. Discuss the need for separate conditioning activities that will develop fitness in endurance and strength activities.

GAME (5 – 7 MINUTES)

The following are suggested:
1. Mix and Match, p. 516
2. Colors, p. 512

DYNAMIC PHYSICAL EDUCATION LESSON PLAN
Stunts and Tumbling Skills (Lesson 3)
Level I

Supplies and Equipment Needed:
  Tumbling mats
  Cones
  Balls

MOVEMENT EXPERIENCE—CONTENT	ORGANIZATION AND TEACHING HINTS	EXPECTED STUDENT OBJECTIVES AND OUTCOMES

INTRODUCTORY ACTIVITY (2 – 3 MINUTES)

Move, Perform Task on Signal

Do a locomotor movement; on signal, stop and perform a task such as an exercise or stunt.
  1. Seat Circles
  2. Balances—foot, seat, and knee
  3. Crab Kicks
  4. Coffee Grinder
  5. Wring the Dishrag
  6. Partner Hopping
  7. Twister

DPE p. 219

Many individual stunts such as the heel click, heel slap, or jump turn can be performed. These add challenge and excitement to the activity.

Vary the locomotor movements by adding quality words, i.e., slow–fast, high–low.

PM.—The student will be able to perform the basic locomotor movement variations as well as the designated stunts or exercises.

Aff.—The body should be gradually warmed up, rather than moving into demanding activity immediately. Discuss with the class a need to self-pace and gradually work toward maximum output. Incorporate this principle into your teaching by demanding more as the introductory and fitness work progress.

FITNESS DEVELOPMENT ACTIVITIES (7 – 8 MINUTES)

Four-Corners Movement

Outline a large rectangle with four cones. Place signs with pictures on both sides of the cones. Youngsters move around the outside of the rectangle and change their movement pattern as they approach a corner sign. The following movement activities are suggested:
  1. Jogging
  2. Skipping/Jumping/Hopping
  3. Sliding/Galloping
  4. Various animal movements
  5. Sport imitation movements
Stop the class after 30–45 seconds of movement and perform various fitness challenges. This will allow students to rest aerobically.

DPE pp. 245 – 246

If signs are not placed at the corners, teachers can specify movements for students to perform.

Increase the demand of the routine by increasing the size of the rectangle.

Faster-moving students can pass on the outside (away from the center) of the rectangle.

Assure that abdominal and shoulder girdle strength development activities are included.

PM.—The student will be able to perform the activities on all sides of the rectangle.

Cog.—The students will be able to explain in their own words how exercise, if demanding enough, will cause the training effect to occur in a short period of time.

MOVEMENT EXPERIENCE—CONTENT	ORGANIZATION AND TEACHING HINTS	EXPECTED STUDENT OBJECTIVES AND OUTCOMES

LESSON FOCUS (15 – 20 MINUTES)

Tumbling, Stunts, and Animal Walks

Five groups of activities are found in this lesson to insure that youngsters receive a variety of experiences. Pick a few activities from each group and teach them alternately. For example, teach one or two animal movements, then a tumbling and inverted balance, followed by a balance stunt, etc. Do not place excessive time on one group of activities at the expense of another.

1. Animal Movements
   a. Siamese Twin Walk
   b. Tightrope Walk
   c. Lame Dog Walk
   d. Crab Walk
2. Tumbling and Inverted Balances
   a. Forward and Backward Roll Review
   b. Three Point Tip-Up
   c. Mountain Climber
   d. Switcheroo
3. Balance Stunts
   a. Forward Balance
   b. Backward Balance
   c. Side Balance
   d. Hand and Knee Balance
   e. Single-Knee Balance
4. Individual Stunts
   a. Heel Slap
   b. Pogo Stick
   c. Top
   d. Turk Stand
   e. Crazy Walk
   f. Seat Circle.
5. Partner and Group Stunts
   a. Double Top
   b. Rollee Pollee

DPE pp. 451 – 463

Scatter as many tumbling mats as possible throughout the area in order to avoid waiting lines.

Present students with two or three activities and allow them to choose one they feel able to perform.

Review activities from previous lessons and allow less gifted students to practice less difficult challenges.

Don't force students to perform tumbling and inverted balances. If they are fearful, gradual encouragement will accomplish more in the long run than intimidation and force.

Demonstrate the activities so students are aware of how they should be performed.

A major concern for safety is the neck and back region. Overweight children are at greater risk and might be allowed to avoid tumbling and inverted balances.

PM.—The student will be able to perform a forward and backward roll with at least two variations.

PM.—The student will be able to perform at least two activities from each of the categories.

Cog.—The student will be able to describe positioning of the hands and knees in partner support activities.

Cog.—The student will be able to name at least three safety principles that are important in tumbling and inverted balance activities.

Aff.—Tumbling is an excellent activity for overcoming personal fear of harm from the activities. Discuss how many athletes must conquer fears and take risks in order to succeed.

Cog.—Regular aerobic exercise lowers blood pressure. Discuss the importance of regular exercise and blood pressure monitoring.

Cog.—Regular exercise keeps the bones from demineralizing. When bones demineralize, they become brittle and less resistant to breakage.

GAME (5 – 7 MINUTES)

The following are suggested:
1. Charlie over the Water (ball version), p. 520
2. Red Light, p. 523
3. Flowers and Wind, p. 520

DYNAMIC PHYSICAL EDUCATION LESSON PLAN
Rhythmic Movement (Lesson 2)
Level I

Supplies and Equipment Needed:
Tom-tom and beater
Tape player and selected music
Cones
Equipment for Mini-Challenge Course

Dances Taught:
How D'Ye Do, My Partner
Jump Jim Jo
Children's Polka
Chimes of Dunkirk
Turn the Glasses Over
Shortnin' Bread
Bombay Bounce
Jingle Bells, Var. 1

MOVEMENT EXPERIENCE— CONTENT	ORGANIZATION AND TEACHING HINTS	EXPECTED STUDENT OBJECTIVES AND OUTCOMES

INTRODUCTORY ACTIVITY (2 – 3 MINUTES)

Drill Sergeant

Designate a student in each squad to be a drill sergeant. The sergeant then gives commands to the squad such as:
1. Walk, jump twice, and roll
2. Lean, jump twice, and freeze (pose)
3. Shake, leap, and roll
4. Seal Walk, forward roll, and jump
The sergeant can call the squad or group to attention, give them directions, and command them to move.

DPE p. 223

Teacher may want to act out the drill sergeant role with the entire class first, then appoint student leaders.

Squad formation.

Commands can be written on note cards to prompt the leaders.

Allow students to act out the role of soldiers.

A "military drumbeat" on the tom–tom may be used with this activity.

PM.—The student will be able to change quickly from one movement to the next.

Cog.—When a person exercises, breathing becomes deeper and more frequent. Discuss the reason why—working muscles need more oxygen.

FITNESS DEVELOPMENT ACTIVITIES (7 – 8 MINUTES)

Mini-Challenge Course

Arrange three or four courses with a group at each course. Students perform the challenges from start to finish and jog back to repeat the course. On signal, groups move to a new course.
Course 1. Crouch jumps; pulls or scooter movements down a bench; through two hoops; and skip to a cone.
Course 2. Weave in and out of four wands held upright by cones; Crab Walk; hand from a climbing rope for 5 seconds; and gallop to a cone.
Course 3. Do a tumbling activity length of mat; agility run through hoops; Frog Jump; and slide to a cone.
Course 4. Move over and under six obstacles; Log Roll length of mat; while jumping, circle around three cones; and run to a cone.

DPE p. 243

Set up four parallel (side-by-side) courses in one-half of the area. Rotate groups to each course after a specified time.

Set up four parallel (side-by-side) courses in one-half of the area. Rotate groups to each course after a specified time.

An alternative is to organize the courses into a single circuit around the perimeter of the area.

Movement should be continuous.

Since young children fatigue and recover quickly, stop the class after 30–45 seconds and perform fitness movement challenges.

Cog.—When a person exercises regularly, additional capillaries form in the muscle tissue so that the muscle cells are better supplied with blood. The student will be able to describe this occurrence in her own words.

Aff.—Lack of exercise is one of the key factors in heart disease. Symptoms of heart disease are often found in young people, and thus fitness activities may help retard this health problem. Discuss heart disease and the role of exercise.

MOVEMENT EXPERIENCE—CONTENT	ORGANIZATION AND TEACHING HINTS	EXPECTED STUDENT OBJECTIVES AND OUTCOMES

LESSON FOCUS (15 – 20 MINUTES)

Rhythms

Fundamental movement: Creative identification. Cross-floor movement exchange or halfway.

A. *Locomotor Movements*
1. Walk, run, skip, hop, jump, gallop, slide, draw steps, leap.
2. Gallop in different directions.
   a. Change on 8, 4, 2.
3. Jump patterns. Hopping practice.
   a. Back and forth over a spot (board, line, or jump rope).
   b. Circle or other form.
   c. Use numbers and letters.
   d. Exploratory opportunity.
4. Crab Kick and Walk.
   a. Alternate kicking.
   b. Together kicking.
   c. Walk to slow beat.
5. Sprinter (Treadmill)
   a. Change feet. Try together.
6. Combinations
   a. Walk and run (4 and 8).
   b. Walk-walk-hop-hop-hop.
   c. Run 4 and jump 3.
   d. Draw steps 2 and walk 4.
   e. Slide 4 and skip 4.
   f. Gallop 4 and jump 3.
   g. Others (exploratory).

B. *Nonlocomotor Movements*
1. Elevator, piston machine (use arms).
2. Clock, rubber band, balloon.
3. Exploratory opportunity.

C. *Dances*
1. How D'Ye Do, My Partner? (pp. 326 – 327)
2. Hokey Pokey (p. 325)
3. Jump Jim Jo (p. 329)
4. Children's Polka (p. 328)
5. Chimes of Dunkirk (Var. 1) (p. 328)
6. Turn the Glasses Over (p. 333)
7. Shortnin' Bread (p. 328)
8. Bombay Bounce (p. 331)
9. Jingle Bells (Var. 1) (p. 334)

DPE pp. 313 – 318

Selected movement formations.

Change hopping foot in center (can use loud beat).

Signal with loud beat.

Use right and left in hopping.

Can use rope for different patterns on the floor.

Add turns.

Stimulate different tempos, qualities, and intensities of movement by varying the beat.

This is a somewhat creative lesson and you should allow yourself and students a great amount of freedom of movement and exploration.

A heavy drum beat can be used to signal changes.

Let children develop others.

Discuss these objects and their movements and have children mimic them in their own way.

When teaching a dance, use the following steps:
1. Tell about the dance and listen to the music.
2. Clap the beat and learn the verse.
3. Practice the dance steps without the music and with verbal cues.
4. Practice the dance with the music.

Make dances easy for students to learn by using some of the following ideas:
1. Teach the dances without partners.
2. Allow youngsters to move in any direction—avoid the left–right orientation.
3. Use scattered formation instead of circles—it helps avoid embarrassment.

PM.—The student will be able to move rhythmically (keep time).

Cog.—The student will be able to recognize the various tom-tom rhythms, i.e., slow, fast, gallop, skip, walk.

Cog.—To minimize muscle soreness, static stretching exercises should be performed. Significant soreness occurs when exercise work load is increased too rapidly. Discuss the importance of progression when developing higher levels of fitness.

PM.—The student will be able to move using combinations of basic locomotor movements.

Cog.—Rhythm and timing are important elements in motor skill performance. Discuss the need for learning rhythmic activities through correct practice and repetition.

Cog.—The student will be able to sing the verses of the singing games.

Aff.—Rhythmic activities are a learned skill. Performers need to practice them many times before they are mastered. Discuss the need for understanding individual differences in rates of learning.

MOVEMENT EXPERIENCE— CONTENT	ORGANIZATION AND TEACHING HINTS	EXPECTED STUDENT OBJECTIVES AND OUTCOMES

4. Emphasize strong movements such as clapping and stomping to encourage involvement.
5. Tape the music at a slower speed when first learning the dance.

Rhythms should be taught like other sport skills. Avoid expecting perfection when teaching rhythms. Teach a variety of dances rather than one or two in depth. Youngsters will enjoy rhythms if they know it is acceptable to make mistakes without being ridiculed.

GAME (5 – 7 MINUTES)

The following are suggested:
1. Skunk Tag, p. 518
2. Red Light, p. 523
3. Right Angle, p. 522

DYNAMIC PHYSICAL EDUCATION LESSON PLAN
Fundamental Skills Using Jumping Boxes
Level I

Supplies and Equipment Needed:
  Jumping boxes
  Tumbling mats
  Cones and lists of return activities
  Secret movement cards
  Tom-tom
  Balls
  Beanbag
  Hula hoop
  Wand

MOVEMENT EXPERIENCE—CONTENT	ORGANIZATION AND TEACHING HINTS	EXPECTED STUDENT OBJECTIVES AND OUTCOMES

INTRODUCTORY ACTIVITY (2 – 3 MINUTES)

Secret Movement

Many different movements and/or combinations of movements are written on large flash cards. Without looking, the teacher or a student selects a card and directs the class to "show me" the secret movement. Youngsters select a movement and peform it until signaled to stop. The card is then revealed to the class to see which youngsters, by chance, guessed the secret movement.

DPE p. 220

Scatter formation.

Use demanding movements (locomotor movements, animal walks, stunts, exercises, sports imitation activities) so youngsters will move and warm up quickly.

Challenge the students to see who can correctly guess the most movements.

Cog.—When a person exercises, the muscular action aids in returning the venous blood to the heart. The student will be able to explain why this occurs. (One-way valves and pressure of muscular contraction.)

PM.—The student will be able to form four different curls and bridges.

FITNESS DEVELOPMENT ACTIVITIES (7 – 8 MINUTES)

Fitness Games and Challenges

Stoop Tag - 45 seconds.
Freeze; perform stretching activities.
Back-to-Back Tag - 45 seconds.
Freeze; perform Abdominal challenges using Curl-Up variations.
Balance Tag - 45 seconds.
Freeze; perform Arm–Shoulder Girdle challenges using Push-Up variations.
Elbow Swing Tag - 45 seconds.
Freeze; perform Trunk Development challenges.
Color Tag - 45 seconds.

DPE pp. 242 – 243

Maximize movement by using simple fitness games that require little explanation.

Many movement challenges are found in *DPE* pp. 239 – 242.

Remember that the goal of fitness games is to stimulate movement rather than teach children to follow rules.

Assign many youngsters to be it to increase the amount of movement.

PM.—The student will be able to perform the movement combinations and create three new patterns.

Cog.—The student will be able to distinguish between a nonlocomotor movement and a locomotor movement.

LESSON FOCUS (15 – 20 MINUTES)

Jumping Boxes

Activities fall into three basic categories: approaching the box, mounting the box, and dismounting the box. A wide range of activities can be developed by combining these variables and making many different routines.

DPE pp. 428 – 429

Squad formation—one squad per box with tumbling mats used in front of the boxes to cushion landings.

List return activities on signs so that students are busy and doing some activity on their way back to the end of the line.

PM.—The student will be able to dismount from the box with a controlled landing.

PM.—The student will be able to manage her body in the air and perform different stunts in the air.

MOVEMENT EXPERIENCE— CONTENT	ORGANIZATION AND TEACHING HINTS	EXPECTED STUDENT OBJECTIVES AND OUTCOMES
A. *Approaches to the Boxes* 1. Basic movements such as skip, hop, jump, etc. 2. Various animal walks. 3. Stunts like heel clicks, half turns, and scooter movements can be used to approach the box.	Emphasize landing softly so that students "meet the ground." Stress lightness, bending the knees, balance, and body controlling. Students should not fall to the ground upon landing. Encourage students to be creative and think of their own activities.	
B. *Mounting the Box* 1. Step, jump, leap, or hop onto the box. 2. Rabbit jump or leap frog onto the box.		Aff.—Jumping boxes are used for learning body management skills. Discuss the need for learning to control the body in the air and prepare it for the landing. Cog.—Students will understand that limbs must be bent and "give" in order to absorb force.
C. *Dismounting* 1. Jump off with a quarter, half, and full turn. 2. Jump off forward, backward, and sideways. 3. Jump off with different body shapes, i.e., stretch, curl, jack-knife. 4. Jump off followed by a forward or backward roll. 5. Change the above dismounts by substituting a hop or leap in place of the jump. 6. Hold a hoop in front of the box. Have the rest of the squad jump through the hoop.	Use the larger boxes for the upper grades, as well as combinations of both large and small. Combine the approach, mount, and dismount in a smooth, skillful manner. To encourage landing with knees bent, ask students to touch the floor with the hands.	
D. *Challenge Activities* 1. Crouch jump over the boxes. 2. Use a beanbag, toss in air, dismount, and catch. 3. Dribble a playground ball while mounting and dismounting boxes. 4. Hula-hoop to the box, mount and dismount without losing control of hoop. 5. Jump over a wand on the dismount. 6. Jump-rope to the box. Mount and dismount maintaining jumping rope.	Challenge students to think of other activities for their squad. Tape signs to cones listing return activities to perform on the return to line. The leader of the squad can raise a hand on returning so the teacher knows when to introduce a new activity.	Cog.—The student will be able to describe the proper technique of landing from a jump off the box.

GAME (5 – 7 MINUTES)

The following games are suggested:
 1. Squirrel in the Trees, p. 518
 2. Stop Ball, p. 519

DYNAMIC PHYSICAL EDUCATION LESSON PLAN
Educational Movement (Lesson 8)
Level I

Fundamental Skills: Pushing and pulling
Educational Movement Themes: Balancing the body
Manipulative Activity: Rope jumping
Parallel Sequence Building: Circles in the body—planes of movement
Creative Activity: Sports imitation activities

Supplies and Equipment Needed:
  Objects to push—jumping boxes, cardboard boxes (filled), sacks of balls, etc.
  Beanbags—one for each child
  Individual tug-of-war ropes—one for each two children
  Tape player and tapes for rope jumping to music
  Cones
  Jump rope—one for each student
  Balls
  Tom-tom
  Plastic jugs
  Pictures of athletes (optional)

MOVEMENT EXPERIENCE—CONTENT	ORGANIZATION AND TEACHING HINTS	EXPECTED STUDENT OBJECTIVES AND OUTCOMES

INTRODUCTORY ACTIVITY (2 – 3 MINUTES)

Run and Assume Shape

Run and go to a prone (one drumbeat) or supine (two drumbeats) position on signal.

Run and go to some kind of balance position.

Run and freeze in various shapes.

DPE p. 219

Scatter formation.

If outside and wet, use only the balances.

Other challenges such as curl, stretch, rock can be used.

PM.—The student will be able to respond to a signal and quickly change movements.

FITNESS DEVELOPMENT ACTIVITIES (7 – 8 MINUTES)

Walk, Trot, and Sprint

Move to the following signals:
  1. One drumbeat - walk.
  2. Two drumbeats - trot.
  3. Three drumbeats - sprint.
  4. Whistle - freeze and perform exercises.
Perform various strength and flexibility exercises between bouts of walk, trot, and sprint. Examples are:
  a. Bend and Twist
  b. Sitting Stretch
  c. Push-Up variations
  d. Sit-Up variations
  e. Trunk Twister
  f. Body Circles

DPE p. 245

Use a tom-tom or tambourine.

Scatter formation.

Emphasize quality of movement and rapid changes.

Check heart rate after bouts of sprinting.

Alternate bouts of movement with strength and flexibility exercises.

PM.—The student will demonstrate proper form in the following movements:
  1. Walk
  2. Trot
  3. Sprint

Cog.—Walk, trot, and sprint only develops the leg region and cardiovascular endurance. The student will be able to explain this in his own words.

MOVEMENT EXPERIENCE— CONTENT	ORGANIZATION AND TEACHING HINTS	EXPECTED STUDENT OBJECTIVES AND OUTCOMES

LESSON FOCUS (15 – 20 MINUTES)

Educational Movement

Note: A few activities should be chosen from each section and presented alternately so students receive a wide variety of activities. If students are fatigued from the fitness portion of the lesson, start with the manipulative activities.

A. *Fundamental Skill: Pushing*
Base of support broadened. Center of gravity lowered. Line of force directed against (toward) the object. Push is controlled and steady.
  1. Push against a wall first in an erect position and then with knees bent and one foot braced behind the other. Which is better?
  2. Push an imaginary object that is very light. Now try pushing a very heavy object.
  3. Try to push a partner who is sitting on a jumping box. Then try to push your partner sitting on a gym scooter. What changes are made?
  4. Can you push an object with your feet without using your arms and hands? Try with the hands braced behind you.
  5. Put your back against an object and push with your feet.
  6. Explore different ways to push your object.
  7. Find a friend to explore different ways to push him or her over a line.
  8. Sit down back to back with your partner and see whether you can move him or her.
  9. Lie on the floor and push yourself backward, forward, sidewards. Which is easiest?
  10. Lie on the floor and push yourself forward with one hand and one foot. Which hand-foot combination is best?
  11. Put a beanbag on the floor and push it with the elbow, shoulder, nose, and other selected body parts.
  12. Show how you can push a ball to a friend. Push slowly and steadily.
  13. Push something toward the ceiling—a ball or other object.

DPE pp. 304 – 305

Cues:
  "Widen your feet."
  "Lower your body."
  "Get body in line with push."
  "Push steadily and evenly."

Make the comparison.

What changes occur?

Show differences. Discuss friction.

Partner uses passive resistance.

Partner resists.

Opposition probably works best.

Cog.—The student will learn the most effective pushing techniques.

PM.—The student will learn to execute forceful pushing.

Aff.—Students will work together cooperatively to explore pushing movements.

Cog.—To improve performance, feedback is necessary. Students need to identify and use feedback about the outcome of the performance and feedback about how the skill was performed. In pushing activities, they can easily gauge outcome and the effect that modifications of pushing technique have on the outcome.

Cog.—Static stretching is the best means for increasing flexibility. This means holding the stretch for 15–30 seconds. Help students understand the difference between ballistic and static stretching.

MOVEMENT EXPERIENCE—CONTENT	ORGANIZATION AND TEACHING HINTS	EXPECTED STUDENT OBJECTIVES AND OUTCOMES

B. *Fundamental Skill: Pulling*
Base of support broadened. Center of gravity lowered. Vertical axis away from object. Pull steadily—avoid jerks and tugs.
1. Reach for an imaginary object near the ceiling and pull the object toward you quickly. Now slowly and smoothly.
2. Use an individual tug-of-war rope and practice pulling at different levels against a partner.
3. With the rope, pull from a kneeling position.
4. With the rope on your feet, pull from a sitting position.
5. Clasp your hands together and pull against each hand as hard as you can. Vary the positions of the arms.
6. Hold hands with your partner and try to pull against each other balancing on one foot.
7. Hold hands with partner, drop low, and pull hard against each other.
8. Have partner sit down. Pull partner slowly by the feet.
9. Pretend to pull a heavy object while you are lying on the floor.
10. With partner seated on the floor, pull him or her to his or her feet.
	DPE pp. 305 – 306
	Cues:
	  "Widen base."
	  "Lower body."
	  "Lean away from object."
	  "Take a good grip."
	Practice a variety of pulling movements.
	Use one-hand and two-hand grips. Practice pulling but avoid contests.
	Pull like a water skier.
		Cog.—The student will learn how best to exert force in pulling.
		PM.—The student will be able to execute forceful pulling movements.
		Cog.—Weak abdominal muscles are a major cause of low back pain. Discuss the importance of exercises to strengthen abdominal muscles and maintain proper posture.
		Cog.—Not practicing at all is better than practicing incorrect motor patterns. Discuss the importance of seeking feedback in developing correct motor patterns.

C. *Manipulative Activity: Rope Jumping* Encourage children to work on needed skill areas. Suggest working first without music and then with music.	*DPE* pp. 404 – 410 The progress of the children will determine the approach. See what they can do and then provide necessary coaching.	PM.—The student will improve in rope jumping skills. Aff.—The student will be stimulated to work on areas needing improvement.
D. *Theme: Circles in the Body-Planes of Movement* 1. How many joints of the body can do circular motion (circles)? 2. How many different ways can you make the arms circle, using both arms at once? 3. Lie on your back, lift your legs. Can you make the arms and legs go in circles? Can you make them go in different circles? 4. In a standing position, show arm circles in horizontal, vertical, and diagonal planes using one arm at a time. 5. Repeat item 4, using both arms in bilateral movements.	*DPE* p. 284 Scatter formation. When a child comes up with a suggestion, have all practice that movement. Show examples and then all practice. Explain terms. Bilateral means that the arms move the same way.	PM.—The student will be able to make circles with five different body parts. Cog.—The student will be able to differentiate among the various planes of movement—horizontal, vertical, and diagonal.

MOVEMENT EXPERIENCE—CONTENT	ORGANIZATION AND TEACHING HINTS	EXPECTED STUDENT OBJECTIVES AND OUTCOMES
6. Lie on back and lift the legs. Make the feet describe the three planes of movement first singly and then together.		Cog.—Rotation occurs when force is applied off-center. To make a ball spin, the force must be applied away from the center of gravity.
7. Explore different ways where two different body parts illustrate two different planes of movement.		
8. Make a large circle with one part of the body and a small one with another. Explore with different planes of movement.		
9. With which part of the body can you make the biggest circle?		
10. What joints can also twist as well as circle? Explore.	Come up with some answers.	
E. *Balancing the Body* Put the youngsters through a variety of balancing movements, varying the challenges.	*DPE* p. 283 Scatter or circle formation. Hold balance poses for 3–5 seconds.	PM.—The student will be able to form and hold a variety of balance poses.
1. On different parts of the body.		
2. On different number of body parts, varying from one through five. Different combinations.		
3. Balancing on different levels.		
4. Work out a sequence of three or four balance poses. Move from one to the next (sustained flow).	Utilize pupil demonstration.	
5. Try to balance on both hands.		
6. With a partner, form different balances.		
F. *Sports Imitation Activities*	This is a "let's pretend" activity. Scatter in general space.	PM.—The student will be able to imitate the movements found in the various sport activities.
1. Pretend you are a football player—kicking the ball, passing the ball, making a tackle, centering the ball.	Allow students to imitate various movements and have others guess what sport it is.	Cog.—The student will be able to identify the sport when other students imitate various movements.
2. Pretend you are a basketball player—shooting a basket, dribbling, guarding, jump ball, a free throw shot.	It might be useful to show pictures of various athletes if students have not seen the sport activity previously.	
3. Let's pretend you are a track and field star performing at: the shotput, the javelin throw, discus.		
4. Pretend you are a baseball player—pitching, catching a fly ball, fielding a grounder and throwing to first, batting, bunting, sliding into a base.		

GAME (5 – 7 MINUTES)

The following are suggested:
1. Change Sides, p. 520
2. Bottle Bat Ball, p. 524

DYNAMIC PHYSICAL EDUCATION LESSON PLAN
Jogging Skills
Level I

Supplies and Equipment Needed:
  One parachute

MOVEMENT EXPERIENCE—CONTENT	ORGANIZATION AND TEACHING HINTS	EXPECTED STUDENT OBJECTIVES AND OUTCOMES

INTRODUCTORY ACTIVITY (2 – 3 MINUTES)

Simple Games

Use a game that requires little teaching and much gross motor activity. The following might be good selections:
1. Back to Back, p. 516
2. Twins, p. 514

DPE p. 224

Tag games require only a light tag, not a push or shove.

Emphasize the importance of admitting when you were tagged and thus the need for sportsmanship.

PM.—The student will be able to evade the tagger through effective use of dodging.

Aff.—All games that are competitive demand cooperation as well. Discuss the value of sportsmanship as well as self-officiating.

FITNESS DEVELOPMENT ACTIVITIES (7 – 8 MINUTES)

Parachute Fitness

1. Jog in circle with chute held in left hand.
2. Shake the chute
3. Slide to the right; return slide to the left.
4. Sit and perform situps - 30 seconds.
5. Skip for 20 seconds.
6. Freeze; face the center, and stretch the chute tightly. Hold for 8–12 seconds. Repeat five to six times.
7. Run in place while holding the chute taut at different levels.
8. Sit with legs under the chute. Do a seat walk toward the center. Return to the perimeter. Repeat four to six times.
9. Place the chute on the ground. Jog away from the chute and return on signal. Repeat for 30 seconds.
10. Shake the chute and jump in place.
11. Lie on back with feet under the chute. Shake the chute with the feet.
12. Hop to the center of the chute and return. Repeat for 20 seconds.
13. Sit with feet under the chute. Stretch by touching the toes with the chute. Relax with other stretches while sitting.

DPE pp. 244 – 245

Evenly space youngsters around the chute.

Use different grips to add variation to the activities.

Develop group morale by encouraging students to move together.

Use music to motivate youngsters.

To cool down, allow youngsters a minute to perform parachute stunts like the Dome or Mushroom.

Cog.—Muscles grow when exercised regularly. To support the stronger muscles, larger bones are developed.

PM.—The student will be able to perform the parachute exercises using three different grips.

MOVEMENT EXPERIENCE— CONTENT	ORGANIZATION AND TEACHING HINTS	EXPECTED STUDENT OBJECTIVES AND OUTCOMES

LESSON FOCUS (15 – 20 MINUTES)

Jogging

Three types of jogging programs can be used:

1. *Jog-Walk-Jog*—In this method, the student jogs until he feels the need to rest, walks until somewhat rested, and then jogs again.
2. *Jog a Set Distance*—The pace is varied depending on the body's reaction to the demands.
3. *Increase the Distance*—The pace is maintained, but the distance is increased.

 Encourage students to do jogging at a realistic pace. A good idea is to have them jog with a friend and talk while running. They should be able to run and talk comfortably—if not, they are running too fast. *Pace*, not *Race*.

 It is sometimes motivating for youngsters if they run with a piece of equipment, i.e., beanbag or jump rope. They can play catch with a beanbag while jogging or roll a hoop while jogging.

Take the students through jogging practice. Have them:

1. Jog 50 steps, walk 50 steps, etc.
2. Run for a specific time in a random fashion to wherever one desires but try to keep running. The advantage here is that students won't race as they do on a track.

DPE pp. 268 – 269

Teach the children the proper style of running.

Start students at a short distance so they will not become discouraged.

Concentrate on teaching the values of jogging and encouraging students to start their own jogging program.

A good motivating technique is to jog across the state or United States. The distance each student runs could be added together for a class total. This total is then the distance the class has progressed across the country.

Praise students running with pace, not the first few people coming back from their run, if you are working on pace.

Bring in a high school track or cross-country runner to talk about their running.

"Train, don't strain."

"Pace, not race."

PM.—The student will be able to demonstrate proper jogging style.

PM.—The student will be able to jog 220 yards nonstop.

Aff.—Jogging is one of the best activities for developing cardiovascular endurance. Discuss the value of jogging for personal health.

Cog.—The student will be able to list three chronic effects jogging has on the body.

Cog.—Fast walking is less efficient than a slow jog due to internal resistance created by the body. Discuss the importance of jogging rather than walking at a pace that is comfortable. (Be able to talk with a friend while jogging.)

Cog.—Jogging strengthens the back, in relation to the abdominal muscles. Discuss the importance of choosing exercises to strengthen the abdominal muscles and stretch the back muscles.

GAME (5 – 7 MINUTES)

Low Organization Games

When the jogging is finished, students may be somewhat fatigued. Play games that they enjoy. It is an opportune time to allow them to choose their favorite games.

Another good idea is to allow youngsters free time with various types of equipment and apparatus. Since they will not finish jogging at the same time, they can work with the equipment when finished. Recreational activities are also excellent activities.

DYNAMIC PHYSICAL EDUCATION LESSON PLAN
Throwing Skills (Lesson 2)
Level I

Supplies and Equipment Needed:
  Tumbling mats for targets
  Tires, hoops, or jump ropes
  Cones
  Tennis balls, rag balls, fleece balls, beanbags
  Tape player
  Music

MOVEMENT EXPERIENCE—CONTENT	ORGANIZATION AND TEACHING HINTS	EXPECTED STUDENT OBJECTIVES AND OUTCOMES

INTRODUCTORY ACTIVITY (2 – 3 MINUTES)

Hoop Activities

Each child is given a hoop. For a short time, the children may work with the hoops as they wish.

On signal, drop the hoops and move in and out of as many hoops as possible. Then, on signal, pick up a hoop and resume exploration.

DPE p. 221

Scatter formation.

Encourage using the hoops as jump ropes or to hula-hoop.

Use different locomotor movements to move in and out of the hoops.

PM.—The student will be able to change quickly from one movement to the next.

Cog.—When a person exercises, breathing becomes deeper and more frequent. Discuss the reason that working muscles need more oxygen.

FITNESS DEVELOPMENT ACTIVITIES (7 – 8 MINUTES)

Circuit Training

1. Rope jumping or Tortoise and Hare
2. Push-Ups
3. Agility run
4. Arm circling
5. Rowing
6. Crab Walk
7. Add a recreational station, i.e., beanbag toss, basket shoot, bench pull, rope climb, or hula hoop

DPE pp. 259 – 262

Establish "starting stations" and maintain them throughout the unit.

Start with 25 seconds of exercise at each station with 10 seconds rest between stations. Gradually decrease rest periods and increase exercise periods.

Use signals such as "start," "stop," and "move up" to ensure quick and effective movement from station to station. An effective method is to use timed music segments recorded on tape. Children exercise when the music plays and move to the next station when it stops.

Cog.—The student will be able to explain why circuit training should work all parts of the body, but no two similar parts in succession.

Cog.—The student will be able to explain how overload is achieved by increasing the length of activity at each station and decreasing the rest between stations.

Cog.—In order that circuit training be effective, *quality* exercise must be performed at each station. The student will be able to verbalize this concept.

LESSON FOCUS (15 – 20 MINUTES)

Throwing

A. Mimetics
  1. The teacher should cue students and model a good throw.
     a. Teacher should use terms such as "wind-up," "turn your nonthrowing side to the target," "step toward the target, follow through."
     b. Teacher can also use this time to observe and coach.

DPE pp. 307 – 308

These should be done for 1–2 minutes.

The teacher should encourage and praise good *form*.

The teacher should talk about what the components of a good throw are and how to produce force.

The cue of "turn, step, throw" may be useful.

Cog.—Students will know what a mature throw looks like.

Cog.—Students will know the components of a mature throw.

Cog.—Students should begin to realize what parts of the throw result in the greatest force production.

Aff.—Students will begin to value throwing hard.

MOVEMENT EXPERIENCE—CONTENT	ORGANIZATION AND TEACHING HINTS	EXPECTED STUDENT OBJECTIVES AND OUTCOMES
c. *Encourage* the children to throw *hard*. d. Modeling of good throws by the teacher should be a major objective for this exercise.	The children should be generating maximum force.	PM.—The students should begin every throw from a side facing position. PM.—The student should take a big step with the contralateral foot.

B. Station Format
  1. Activities emphasizing form.
    a. Mats 5–6" thick.
      1. The student stands on the edge of the mat and steps to the floor with her contralateral foot as she throws toward the wall. (The other foot remains on the mat.)
    b. Both feet in tire or hoop.
      1. The student begins in side-facing position to the target, with both feet inside the tire (or hoop); she then steps outside of the tire with the contralateral foot and throws to the wall.
    c. Cone behind the student.
      1. The student must touch the cone with the throwing hand on the backswing, then throw to the wall.
	All students should do these activities a minimum of two days.
	
	All throws are made to the wall and with force.
	
	This activity forces the student to take a long stride toward the target.
	
	If tires or hoops are not available, use jump ropes. The circle should be large enough to encourage the student to take a long stride.
	
	This activity should encourage the student to rotate and take a wind-up before throwing.
	
	The cone should be directly behind the student and about an arm's length distance.
		Aff.—The student should understand that a lot of practice is necessary to master the skill of throwing.
		
		PM.—The student should begin to take a long stride with the throw.
		
		Cog.—The student should understand that a longer stride helps increase force production.

C. Activities using large targets so students will throw forcefully.
  1. Throw at mats on the wall.
    a. Throw tennis or rag balls hard from 15–20 ft.
    b. Retrieve only if the balls roll behind the throwing line.
  2. Mats laid over tables.
    a. If tables are on rollers, see if forceful throws can move the table.
  3. Throw at hoops leaning against mats against the wall.
  4. Large target throw.
    a. A circle or square 4 ft. in diameter should be placed on the wall.
    b. Students should throw from 20–25 ft.
	Everyone should do the stations under C a minimum of two days.
	
	Each student should start with five balls.
	
	The teacher should continue to give feedback to the students that will help them improve their form.
	
	The mats should be placed on the table so they hang to the floor.
	
	Put hoops touching one another for easier targets; spread apart for more difficult target.
	
	Another excellent large target is a 4-ft. cage ball.	

GAME (5 – 7 MINUTES)

1. Animal Tag, p. 515
2. Forest Ranger, p. 521

DYNAMIC PHYSICAL EDUCATION LESSON PLAN
Educational Movement (Lesson 9)
Level I

Fundamental Skill: Bending and Stretching
Educational Movement Themes: Receiving and transferring weight, partner matching movements,
    partner obstacle movements
Manipulative Activity: Parachute

Supplies and Equipment Needed:
  Jumping boxes or benches
  Parachute
  Cones

MOVEMENT EXPERIENCE—CONTENT	ORGANIZATION AND TEACHING HINTS	EXPECTED STUDENT OBJECTIVES AND OUTCOMES

INTRODUCTORY ACTIVITY (2 – 3 MINUTES)

Bridges by Three

Children work in groups of three, with two of the children making bridges and the third moving under them. As soon as the third person has moved under the others, he makes a bridge. Each child in turn goes under the bridges of the other two students.

DPE p. 223

Groups of three.

Different challenges can be tried by specifying different types of bridges or having the moving child perform different movements and tasks.

To increase challenges, increase distance between bridging youngsters.

PM.—The student will be able to make at least five different bridges.

Cog.—The student will identify the isometric exercises (bridging) as well as the isotonic exercises (moving).

FITNESS DEVELOPMENT ACTIVITY (7 – 8 MINUTES)

Four-Corners Movement

Outline a large rectangle with four cones. Place signs with pictures on both sides of the cones. Youngsters move around the outside of the rectangle and change their movement pattern as they approach a corner sign. The following movement activities are suggested:
  1. Jogging
  2. Skipping/Jumping/Hopping
  3. Sliding/Galloping
  4. Various animal movements
  5. Sport imitation movements
Stop the class after 30–45 seconds of movement and perform various fitness challenges. This will allow students to rest aerobically.

DPE pp. 245 – 246

If signs are not placed at the corners, teachers can specify movements for students to perform.

Increase the demand of the routine by increasing the size of the rectangle.

Faster-moving students can pass on the outside (away from the center) of the rectangle.

Assure that abdominal and shoulder girdle strength development activities are included.

PM.—The student will be able to perform the grass drills and challenge activities.

Cog.—Sweating occurs when the body is overheated due to stress in an attempt to maintain a constant body temperature. The student will be able to explain why the body sweats.

LESSON FOCUS (15 – 20 MINUTES)

Educational Movement

Note: A few activities should be chosen from each section and presented alternately so students receive a wide variety of activities. If students are fatigued from the fitness portion of the lesson, start with the manipulative activities.

MOVEMENT EXPERIENCE—CONTENT	ORGANIZATION AND TEACHING HINTS	EXPECTED STUDENT OBJECTIVES AND OUTCOMES
A. *Fundamental Skill: Bending* Bend to limits. Bend as many joints as possible. 1. Can you bend forward and up? 2. Show how far you can bend backward. Can you see behind you on your backward bend? 3. Combine a forward bend with a backward bend. 4. Bend right and left. Try with your hands out to the sides. Overhead. 5. Explore different ways the body can bend in a standing position. 6. Sit down. How does this affect the bending possibilities of the body? Can you bend forward so your chin touches the floor? 7. How many body parts (joints) can you bend below the waist? Above the waist? 8. Who can lie down and bend two, three, four, five, six parts? 9. Pick two similar parts. Bend one while unbending the other. 10. Pick two body parts (joints). Beginning at the same time, bend one quickly and one slowly. Bend one smoothly and one with jerks. 11. Make a familiar shape by bending two body parts. 12. Think of a toy that bends, and you bend the same way. 13. Working with a partner, do matching bending movements. Try having one partner make big bends while the other makes small bends at corresponding joints. 14. Show how you can bend to look funny, happy, sad, slow, and quick.	*DPE* p. 300 Cues: "Bend as far as possible." "Bend one part while holding other fixed." Repeat movements several times. Learn names of body joints that bend. In straightening (unbending), straighten completely. Begin with two parts. Matching movements can begin with one joint and then add multiple movements. Seek other terms.	Cog.—The student will learn what bending means and what parts of the body do this. PM.—The student will be able to bend joints independently of others as specified. Cog.—There are many ways to evaluate performance and improvement. For example, accuracy, distance, speed, and time are commonly used. Students should begin to learn different ways to measure their performance. Aff.—Competency in physical skill increases a youngster's desire to participate. Discuss the importance of practicing skills that are difficult to master in order to increase the range of activities one is willing to participate in regularly. PM.—The student will be able to match single and double bending movements with a partner.
B. *Fundamental Skill: Stretching* Stretching means to make the body parts as long or wide as possible. Stretch over full range of movement. Involve many body parts. Do from many different positions. Stretching can be combined with the opposite movement, curling. 1. Stretch as many body parts as you can. 2. Stretch your arms, legs, and feet in as many ways as possible. 3. At the same time stretch your feet in one direction and your arms in another.	*DPE* pp. 303 – 304 Cues: "Stretch as far as you can." "Make it hurt a little." "Keep it smooth, don't jerk." "Involve as many parts (joints) as you can." Much emphasis on exploratory movement. Look to stimulate wide application to many body parts. Stress smoothness. Stress the fun aspect, as this needs spicing up.	PM.—The student will be able to stretch many parts of the body to full range. Cog.—The student will understand the meaning of the word "stretch" and be able to apply this to her movement vocabulary. Aff.—The student will apply herself fully to the movement challenges. Discuss the importance of effort and intensity when performing motor tasks. Use the illustration of outstanding athletes practicing with intensity so they will be able to perform well in games.

MOVEMENT EXPERIENCE—CONTENT	ORGANIZATION AND TEACHING HINTS	EXPECTED STUDENT OBJECTIVES AND OUTCOMES
4. Stretch one body part quickly, slowly, smoothly. Try another. Repeat.	Repeat movements several times for S-R bonds. Keep this nontechnical.	
5. Bend a body part and tell me which muscles or muscle groups are being stretched.		Cog.—Stretching to increase the range of motion at a joint should be done slowly and under control. Stretches should be held for 15–30 seconds. Encourage smooth sustained movements in stretching activities.
6. How many ways can you stretch while sitting on the floor?		
7. Lie on the floor (prone or supine) and stretch two parts at once. Add others up to five.		Aff.—Nonsmokers who are in residence with smokers suffer many of the same effects. For example, a nonsmoker inhales 11 cigarettes when living with a person who smokes a pack a day. Discuss the effects of smoking on wellness.
8. From any position you like, see if you can at the same time stretch one part quickly (but smoothly) and one part slowly. Try one part quickly and two parts slowly.		
9. From a kneeling position set a mark on the floor where you can reach (stretch) without losing balance. Increase the distance.	Use a spot, line, or beanbag.	
10. Stretch your one arm while your other curls (bends). Reverse.		
11. Find a partner and show how many different ways you can help each other stretch.		
12. Can you stretch as tall as a giraffe? As wide as an elephant? As long as a snake?	Add other animals.	
13. Stretch and make a wide bridge. Have a partner go under, around, and over the bridge.	Show that some body parts are more difficult to stretch than others.	
14. Try bending forward slowly and touch your toes without bending your knees. Try to keep the knees straight. Can you touch the floor?		
15. Can you stretch the muscles in your chest, back, ankles, wrist, and fingers? Is this easy?	Use small–tall, wide–thin, stretched–curled. Make up other verses.	Cog.—Children will be able to interpret stretching movements as incorporated in the action song.
C. *Manipulative Activity: Parachute Activity Practice* Use mostly locomotor activities with the parachute as the prior activities (bending and stretching) are mostly in-place activities. 1. Shake the Rug. 2. Making Waves. 3. Walk, run, skip, slide, hop, jump CW or CCW as the parachute rotates.	*DPE* pp. 433 – 436 Make this mostly locomotor movements. The drum beat can direct the movements.	
D. *Theme: Receiving and Transferring Weight* Receiving means handling the weight after flight from either jumping, hopping, or leaping. Emphasis should be on a relaxed, controlled landing.	*DPE* pp. 287 – 288 Cues: "Be relaxed." "Keep knees slightly bent on landing." "Provide 'give' on landing."	Cog.—The student will learn correct landing techniques. PM.—The student will be able to control his landing from a jump into the air to a jump from a height of 24 to 30 in.

MOVEMENT EXPERIENCE— CONTENT	ORGANIZATION AND TEACHING HINTS	EXPECTED STUDENT OBJECTIVES AND OUTCOMES
1. Project yourself high into the air and land. Try to land now with as little noise as possible. 2. Practice projecting yourself into the air and landing in different fashions. 3. Experiment with different landings where one or both hands touch the floor at the completion of the landing. 4. Experiment with turns as you land. 5. Begin your movement through the air with a short run and practice landings. 6. Jumping boxes and inclined benches can project you higher. Practice some types of landings. Begin low and increase the height. 7. Swinging and landing from climbing ropes also can be a part. 8. Take a position with the body balanced on two different parts. Transfer the weight to another two parts. Go from three to three. 9. Transfer the weight from a rounded part of the body to the hands and/or the feet. Go back to the rounded part. 10. Jump and land under control. Transfer the weight to another two body parts. 11. Explore different combinations of transferring the weight from various parts to others.	No noise means soft landing. Crouching helps take the landing shock. Use whatever you have—chairs, tables, benches (inclined)—to provide height for jumping and landing. Landing over benches; through hoops. Weight transfer to be made smoothly.	Cog.—To absorb force from a jump upon landing, as many joints as possible should be flexed. Discuss the importance of "giving" with the knees, hips, and ankles in order to land softly.
E. *Theme: Partner Obstacle Movements* With one partner acting as an obstacle, the other partner goes over, under, and around the partner posing as the obstacle. Explore different ways this can be accomplished.	*DPE* pp. 278 – 279 Exploratory emphasis. Show-and-tell demonstration.	

GAME (5 – 7 MINUTES)

The following are suggested:
1. Marching Ponies, p. 513
2. Cat and Mice, p. 519

DYNAMIC PHYSICAL EDUCATION LESSON PLAN
Fundamental Skills Using Parachute Activity
Level I

Supplies and Equipment Needed:
Six jump ropes
Beanbags or playground balls, one for each child
Parachute
Six to ten beanbags
Two basketballs or cageballs
Tom-tom

MOVEMENT EXPERIENCE—CONTENT	ORGANIZATION AND TEACHING HINTS	EXPECTED STUDENT OBJECTIVES AND OUTCOMES

INTRODUCTORY ACTIVITY (2 – 3 MINUTES)

European Running with Equipment

Review European Running and emphasize the following points:
1. Move to the rhythm.
2. Lift the knees and prance.
3. Maintain proper spacing between each other.

After the review, have each child get a beanbag or playground ball. Every fourth step, they can toss up the bag or bounce the ball. Other variations can be tried using different beats of the rhythm.

DPE pp. 217 – 218

Since the parachute will be used in the fitness development activity, it might be enjoyable to do European Running while holding the chute.

Encourage the students to try different challenges with their beanbag or ball.

PM.—The student will be able to toss the beanbag into the air and catch it while doing European Running.

PM.—The student will be able to create three activities with the beanbag or ball while doing European Running.

FITNESS DEVELOPMENT ACTIVITIES (7 – 8 MINUTES)

Walk, Trot, and Sprint

Move to the following signals:
1. One drumbeat - walk.
2. Two drumbeats - trot.
3. Three drumbeats - sprint.
4. Whistle - freeze and perform exercises.

Perform various strength and flexibility exercises between bouts of walk, trot, and sprint. Examples are:
a. Bend and Twist
b. Sitting Stretch
c. Push-Up variations
d. Sit-Up variations
e. Trunk Twister
f. Body Circles

DPE p. 245

Use a tom-tom or tambourine.

Scatter formation.

Emphasize quality of movement and rapid changes.

Check heart rate after bouts of sprinting.

Altenate bouts of movement with strength and flexibility exercises.

PM.—The student will be able to perform the activity at an increased pace.

Cog.—One measure often used to measure fitness is to count the pulse rate after exercise within 2 or 3 minutes. It might be interesting to measure pulse rate at various intervals after exercise. The more fit one is, the faster pulse rate returns to normal.

Cog.—A well-balanced diet provides fuel for physical activity. Discuss the basics of a good diet and the need for such.

LESSON FOCUS (15 – 20 MINUTES)

Parachute Activities

1. Circular movements.
   Move utilizing locomotor movements and holding the chute at various levels—walk, run, hop, jump, skip, slide, draw steps.

DPE pp. 433 – 436

Teach the proper terminology so students can identify the various activities.

Perform the activities with different grips.

Cog.—The student will be able to identify the various parachute activities by name.

MOVEMENT EXPERIENCE— CONTENT	ORGANIZATION AND TEACHING HINTS	EXPECTED STUDENT OBJECTIVES AND OUTCOMES

2. Shaking the Rug and Making Waves.
   Shaking the Rug should involve small, rapid movements, whereas Making Waves is large movements.
3. Making a Dome.
   Parachute should be on the floor and held with both hands. Make a dome by standing up and rapidly lifting the chute overhead.
4. Mushroom.
   Similar to the Dome except three or four steps toward the center are taken by each student.
   a. Mushroom Release—all students release the chute at its peak of inflation.
   b. Mushroom Run—Make a mushroom, move into center, release grip, and run around the inside of the chute back to place.
5. Activities with Balls and Beanbags.
   a. Ball Circle—Use a basketball or cageball and make it circle around the outside of the chute. Add a second ball.
   b. Popcorn—Place six to ten beanbags on the chute and shake them into the air.
   c. Poison Snake—Place six to ten jump ropes on the chute. Divide the players in half. Try to shake the ropes so they touch a player on the opposing team.
   d. Cannonball—Use a 24" cageball on the chute. On the command "load," place the chute on the floor. On "fire," lift the chute and fire the cageball into the air.
6. Kite Run.
   Half the class holds the chute on one side. They run in any direction together and as fast as possible. The parachute should trail like a kite.
7. Tug-of-War.
   Divide the class into two equal halves. On signal, they pull and try to move each other.
8. Hole in One.
   Use six or eight small balls of two different colors. The object is to get the other team's balls to fall through the hole in the center.

Various patterns can be made by having the class work in small groups around the chute.

Try making a dome while moving in a circle.

Teach the proper technique of standing and lifting the parachute to avoid back strain.

Work for precision so that all students are together in their movement.

Proper care of the chutes should be taught so that they are not ripped.

Many routines to music can be developed and incorporated with the various chute activities. Many singing games can be done utilizing parachute activities, which increases motivation for students.

Aff.—The parachute requires group cooperation for successful implementation of the activities. Discuss the importance of working together to improve everybody's welfare.

PM.—The student will be able to cooperatively perform the following activities:
1. Making Waves
2. Making a Dome
3. Popcorn
4. Ball Circles

Cog.—Air resistance has an effect on athletic performances. When using the parachute, the effect of air resistance is obvious. Discuss the difference between a slow parachute movement and a fast one. Which is more difficult? Why?

Cog.—Stability is increased by lowering the center of gravity and widening the base of support in the direction of the force. Discuss how youngsters automatically do this in the Tug-of-War activity.

MOVEMENT EXPERIENCE—CONTENT	ORGANIZATION AND TEACHING HINTS	EXPECTED STUDENT OBJECTIVES AND OUTCOMES

9. Ocean Walk.
   The class is on their knees, making waves with the chute. Three or four youngsters are selected to walk "in the ocean" without falling.

GAME (5 – 7 MINUTES)

The following games are suggested:
1. May I Chase You? p. 523
2. Tommy Tucker's Land, p. 515
3. Colors, p. 512

DYNAMIC PHYSICAL EDUCATION LESSON PLAN
Rhythmic Movement (Lesson 3)
Level I

Supplies and Equipment Needed:
One playground ball per student
Parachute
Appropriate music for dances
Tape player

Dances Taught:
Muffin Man
Danish Dance of Greeting
Seven Jumps
Yankee Doodle
Eins Zwie Drei
Bleking
Pease Porridge Hot
Nixie Polka
Chimes of Dunkirk

MOVEMENT EXPERIENCE— CONTENT	ORGANIZATION AND TEACHING HINTS	EXPECTED STUDENT OBJECTIVES AND OUTCOMES

INTRODUCTORY ACTIVITY (2 – 3 MINUTES)

Ball Activities

Each child dribble his or her ball around the area. On signal:
1. Stop and freeze.
2. Balance on different body parts.
3. Handle the ball—around back, over head, under leg, etc.
Variation: Use different poses and different objects.

DPE p. 221

Dribble both as a basketball and soccer player.

Dribble under control—slowly without running into other students.

Encourage variety.

PM.—The student will be able to dribble the ball for 10 seconds without losing control.

Cog.—The student will be able to describe the relationships between the height and speed of the dribble.

FITNESS DEVELOPMENT ACTIVITIES (7 – 8 MINUTES)

Parachute Fitness

1. Jog in circle with chute held in left hand.
2. Shake the chute
3. Slide to the right; return slide to the left.
4. Sit and perform situps - 30 seconds.
5. Skip for 20 seconds.
6. Freeze; face the center, and stretch the chute tightly. Hold for 8–12 seconds. Repeat five to six times.
7. Run in place while holding the chute taut at different levels.
8. Sit with legs under the chute. Do a seat walk toward the center. Return to the perimeter. Repeat four to six times.
9. Place the chute on the ground. Jog away from the chute and return on signal. Repeat for 30 seconds.
10. Shake the chute and jump in place.
11. Lie on back with feet under the chute. Shake the chute with the feet.
12. Hop to the center of the chute and return. Repeat for 20 seconds.

DPE, pp. 244 – 245

Evenly space youngsters around the chute.

Use different grips to add variation to the activities.

Develop group morale by encouraging students to move together.

Use music to motivate youngsters.

To cool down, allow youngsters a minute to perform parachute stunts like the Dome or Mushroom.

Cog.—Muscles grow when exercised regularly. To support the stronger muscles, larger bones are developed.

PM.—The student will be able to perform the parachute exercises using three different grips.

MOVEMENT EXPERIENCE—CONTENT	ORGANIZATION AND TEACHING HINTS	EXPECTED STUDENT OBJECTIVES AND OUTCOMES

13. Sit with feet under the chute. Stretch by touching the toes with the chute. Relax with other stretches while sitting.

LESSON FOCUS (15 – 20 MINUTES)

Dances

1. Muffin Man (pp. 325 – 326)
2. Danish Dance of Greeting (p. 327)
3. Seven Jumps (pp. 327 – 328)
4. Yankee Doodle (p. 330)
5. Eins Zwie Drei (pp. 330 – 331)
6. Bleking (p. 332)
7. Pease Porridge Hot (pp. 329 – 330)
8. Nixie Polka (p. 333)
9. Chimes of Dunkirk, Var. 2 (p. 331)

When teaching a dance, use the following steps:
1. Tell about the dance and listen to the music.
2. Clap the beat and learn the verse.
3. Practice the dance steps without the music and with verbal cues.
4. Practice the dance with the music.

Make dances easy for students to learn by using some of the following ideas:
1. Teach the dances without partners.
2. Allow youngsters to move in any direction—avoid the left–right orientation.
3. Use scattered formation instead of circles—it helps avoid embarassment.
4. Emphasize strong movements such as clapping and stomping to encourage involvement.
5. Tape the music at a slower speed when first learning the dance.

Rhythms should be taught like other sport skills. Avoid expecting perfection when teaching rhythms. Teach a variety of dances rather than one or two in depth. Youngsters will enjoy rhythms if they know it is acceptable to make mistakes without being ridiculed.

Cog.—The student will be able to sing the verses of the singing games.

Aff.—Rhythmic activities are a learned skill. Performers need to practice them many times before they are mastered. Discuss the need for understanding individual differences in rates of learning.

GAME (5 – 7 MINUTES)

1. Circle Stoop, p. 517
2. Blindfolded Duck, p. 516

DYNAMIC PHYSICAL EDUCATION LESSON PLAN
Educational Movement (Lesson 10)
Level I

Fundamental Movements: Twisting, turning, and rocking
Educational Movement Themes: Stretching and curling, contrasting movements, tension and relaxation
Manipulative Activities: Teacher's choice

Supplies and Equipment Needed:
  Tambourine, scoops and balls, or beanbags
  Tape player
  Music

MOVEMENT EXPERIENCE—CONTENT	ORGANIZATION AND TEACHING HINTS	EXPECTED STUDENT OBJECTIVES AND OUTCOMES

INTRODUCTORY ACTIVITY (2 – 3 MINUTES)

Creative and Exploratory Opportunities

1. Put out enough equipment for all children to have a piece. Allow them to explore and create activities while moving.
2. Work with a piece of equipment with a partner or small group.

DPE pp. 223 – 224

Use hoops, balls, or beanbags.

Use different locomotor movements.

Rotate on signal.

PM.—The student will be able to manipulate his or her piece of equipment while moving.

Aff.—Partner activity is more enjoyable for youngsters. Discuss the need for gracefully selecting a partner.

FITNESS DEVELOPMENT ACTIVITIES (7 – 8 MINUTES)

Animal Movements and Fitness Challenges

Puppy Dog Walk - 30 seconds.
Freeze; perform stretching activities.
Measuring Worm Walk - 30 seconds.
Freeze; perform abdominal development challenges.
Elephant Walk - 30 seconds.
Frog Jump - 30 seconds.
Freeze; perform push-up position challenges.
Seal Crawl - 30 seconds.
Bear Walk - 30 seconds.
Freeze; perform abdominal challenges.
Siamese Twin Walk - 30 seconds.
Lame Dog Walk - 30 seconds.

DPE p. 242

Emphasize placing the weight on the hands for shoulder girdle development.

Quality of movement should be emphasized rather than speed.

Vary the length of the intervals to match the fitness level of youngsters.

Taped intervals of music and no music can be used to signal movement and stopping to do exercises.

Cog.—The student will recognize the animal movements by name.

PM.—The student will be able to perform each of the animal movements over a distance of 25 feet.

LESSON FOCUS (15 – 20 MINUTES)

Educational Movement

Note: A few activities should be chosen from each section and presented alternately so students receive a wide variety of activities. If students are fatigued from the fitness portion of the lesson, start with the manipulative activities.

MOVEMENT EXPERIENCE— CONTENT	ORGANIZATION AND TEACHING HINTS	EXPECTED STUDENT OBJECTIVES AND OUTCOMES

A. *Fundamental Skill: Twisting*
Twisting should be done as far as possible. Fix or stabilize a part of the body so twisting can be done on this base. Twist one way and then reverse.

1. Glue your feet to the floor. Can you twist your body to the right and to the left? Can you twist slowly, quickly? Can you bend and twist at the same time? How far can you twist your hands back and forth?
2. Twist two parts of the body at the same time. Try three. More?
3. Can you twist one part of the body in one direction and another in a different direction?
4. Is it possible to twist the upper half of your body without twisting the lower part? How about the reverse?
5. Seated on the floor, what parts of the body can you twist?
6. Can you twist one part of the body around another? Why or why not?
7. Balance on one foot and twist your body. Can you bend and twist in this position?
8. Show different shapes that can be made using twisted body parts.
9. Can you twist like a spring?

B. *Fundamental Skill: Turning*
Turning involves the body as a whole, around the long axis of the body. Maintain good control and balance. Turn right and left; also learn clockwise and counterclockwise.

1. Turn your body left and right with quarter and half turns. Turn clockwise and counterclockwise.
2. Post compass directions on the walls—north, south, east, and west. Have children face the correct direction on call. Introduce some in-between directions—northwest, southeast, etc.
3. Can you stand on one foot and turn around slowly, quickly, with a series of small hops?
4. Show me how you can cross your legs with a turn and then sit down. Can you get up without moving your feet too much?

DPE p. 303

Cue by saying:
   "Twist far (fully)."
   "Hold supporting parts firm."
   "Twist the other way."

Seek full exploration.

DPE pp. 302 – 303

Cue by saying:
   "Keep your balance."
   "Turn smoothly."
   "Make turns definite—1/4, 1/2, or full turns."

Turn right and left.

Expand these activities.

PM.—The student will be able to isolate different parts of the body for twisting.

Cog.—Students will give meaning to the term to be added to their movement vocabularies.

PM.—The student will be able to turn right and left on signal.

Cog.—The student will understand the differences between twisting and turning.

MOVEMENT EXPERIENCE— CONTENT	ORGANIZATION AND TEACHING HINTS	EXPECTED STUDENT OBJECTIVES AND OUTCOMES

5. When you hear the signal, turn completely around once. Next time turn the other way. Now try with two full turns; three.
6. Lie on your tummy and turn yourself around in an arc. Try seated position.
7. Find a friend and see how many different ways one can turn the other.
8. Play follow-the-leader activities with your friend.

C. *Fundamental Skill: Rocking*
Rocking movements are probably best described as movements like a rocking chair. Rocking is best done on a rounded body part. Arm, leg, and body movements can help gain momentum. Rocking should be done smoothly in good rhythm. Rocking should be done to good limits—full range of motion.

1. How many different ways can you rock? Which part of the body is used to rock the highest?
2. Select a part of the body and show me how you can rock smoothly and slowly. How about quickly and smoothly?
3. Can you rock like a rocking chair?
4. Lie on your back and rock. Point both hands and feet toward the ceiling and rock on the back.
5. Lie on your tummy and rock. Rock as high as you can. Can you hold your ankles and make giant rocks?
6. Can you rock in a standing position? Try forward, sideward, and diagonal rocking directions.
7. Select a position where you can rock and twist at the same time.
8. Who can lie on his or her back, with knees up and rock side to side?
9. From a standing position, sway back and forth, right and left. Experiment with different foot positions. Sway slowly and as far as you can without losing your balance.
10. Repeat swaying movements from a kneeling position.
11. Show three different ways you can rock with a partner.

DPE pp. 300 – 301

Cue by saying:
"Rock smoothly."
"Rock higher (farther)."
"Rock in different directions."
"Use your arms (legs) to help you rock."

Emphasize exploration.

Arms and feet can aid the tummy rock.

Swaying maintains a stable base.

PM.—The student will be able to do rocking movements smoothly and rhythmically on several parts of the body.

Cog.—The student will learn the ways to apply force with arms and legs to increase momentum in rocking.

MOVEMENT EXPERIENCE—CONTENT	ORGANIZATION AND TEACHING HINTS	EXPECTED STUDENT OBJECTIVES AND OUTCOMES
D. *Manipulative Activity: Teacher's Choice* Select one or more manipulative activities that need additional developing with respect to the children's needs and progress. During the week's work, a different activity might be scheduled each individual day.	*DPE* pp. 363 – 391 Use balls, beanbags, jump ropes, scoops and balls, etc.	
E. *Theme: Stretching and Curling* 1. While on your feet, show us a stretched position. A curled position. 2. Go very slowly from your stretched position to the curled one you select. Go rapidly. 3. Keeping one foot in place (on a spot), show how far you can stretch in different directions. 4. Show us a straight (regular) curled position. A twisted curled position. A tight curled position. 5. Select three different curled positions. On signal, go from one to the other rapidly. Repeat with stretch positions. 6. Explore and show the different ways that the body can support itself in curled positions.	*DPE* p. 288 Emphasize personal space. Scatter formation. Have a show-and-tell demonstration.	Cog.—The meaning of "curled" and "stretched" will be clarified and reinforced through activity and discussion. PM.—The student will demonstrate the ability to make changes as defined.
F. *Theme: Contrasting Movements* The focus is the use of contrasting terms, which can be applied to a variety of movement patterns. In the lesson one suggestion is given. The teacher should reinforce with other movement patterns. 1. Above—below, beneath, under. Make arm circles above your head. Below. With your partner, you make a bridge above him or her. Beneath (under). 2. Across—around, under. Jump across your partner. Move under your partner. 3. Around clockwise—around counterclockwise. Jump around your partner in a clockwise direction, and skip around your partner counterclockwise. 4. Between—beside. Crawl between your partner's legs. Stand beside your partner. 5. Make different shapes to illustrate: a. Big—little, small b. Crooked—straight c. Curved—flat, straight d. Large—small e. Round—straight, flat	*DPE* pp. 284 – 285 Begin by showing the contrasting movements first. Later, stress the opposite movement. In the latter, the teacher gives the one term and the children move to the opposite term. For example: the teacher says "reach high." The children will reach low. Emphasize exploration. Stress: "Do it a different way." Some of the activities are best illustrated with partners. With partners, repeat actions, so roles change.	Cog.—The student will understand and be able to employ the majority of these contrasting terms in her movement patterns.

MOVEMENT EXPERIENCE—CONTENT	ORGANIZATION AND TEACHING HINTS	EXPECTED STUDENT OBJECTIVES AND OUTCOMES

    f. Short—long, tall
    g. Tiny—big, large
    h. Wide—narrow, thin
6. Using locomotor movements, illustrate:
    a. Zig-zag—straight
    b. Fast—slow
    c. Forward—backward, back
    d. Graceful—awkward
    e. Heavy—light
    f. Right—left
    g. Sideways—forward, backward
    g. High—low

G. *Theme: Tension and Relaxation*
With tension and relaxation, dwell on the distinction between tightness and looseness.
1. Make yourself as tense as possible. Now relax.
2. Take a deep breath, hold it tight. Expel the air and relax.
3. Reach as high as you can tensed, slowly relax and droop to the floor.
4. Show how you can tense different parts of the body.
5. Tense one part of the body and relax another. Shift the tenseness to the relaxed part and vice versa.
6. Press your fingers hard against your tensed abdominal muscles. Take your fists and beat lightly against the tensed position. Relax. Repeat.
7. Run forward, stop suddenly in a tensed position. Relax. Repeat.
8. Run in a tensed position, change direction on signal, and run relaxed.

DPE p. 289

Scatter formation.

Emphasize exploration.

Illustrate this with the basketball free-throw shooter, who does this to relax.

Cog.—Physical activity is an excellent outlet for stress and tension.

GAME (5 – 7 MINUTES)

Teacher has choice of using the lead-up activities as games or teaching an unrelated game as a change of pace. The following are suggested:
1. Midnight, p. 516
2. Twins and Triplets, p. 514

DYNAMIC PHYSICAL EDUCATION LESSON PLAN
Balance Beam Activities with Manipulative Equipment
Level I

Supplies and Equipment Needed:
  Balance beams
  Mats (placed at ends of beams)
  Playground balls
  Hoops
  Beanbags
  Tape player
  Music

MOVEMENT EXPERIENCE—CONTENT	ORGANIZATION AND TEACHING HINTS	EXPECTED STUDENT OBJECTIVES AND OUTCOMES

INTRODUCTORY ACTIVITY (2 – 3 MINUTES)

Airplanes

Children pretend to be airplanes. They take off, zoom with arms out, swoop, turn, and glide. On signal, they drop to the floor in prone position. To begin again, they must "refuel" their engines by doing a series of Push-Ups while making a "vroom, vroom" engine sound.

DPE p. 220

Utilize different locomotor movements.

Repeat the pattern.

Imitate different types of airplanes.

Substitute a rocket or helicopter for an airplane and allow students to create a new pattern.

PM.—The student will be able to effectively imitate an airplane and a rocket.

FITNESS DEVELOPMENT ACTIVITIES (7 – 8 MINUTES)

Astronaut Drills

  1. Walk.
  2. Walk on tiptoes while reaching for the sky.
  3. Walk with giant strides.
  4. Freeze; perform various stretches.
  5. Do a Puppy Dog Walk.
  6. Jump like a pogo stick.
  7. Freeze; perform Push-Up variations.
  8. Walk and swing arms like a helicopter.
  9. Trot lightly and silently.
  10. Slide like an athlete.
  11. Freeze; perform Curl-Up variations.
  12. Crab Walk.
  13. Skip.
  14. Freeze; perform trunk development challenges.
  15. Walk and cool down.

DPE, pp. 262 – 263

Use circle or scatter formation with ample space between youngsters.

Children should be in constant movement except when stopped to do strength and flexibility activities.

Taped intervals of music and no music can be used to signal movement and stopping to do exercises.

Change direction often.

When they are moving on all fours, youngsters should be encouraged to place much of their weight on the hands in order to develop arm–shoulder girdle strength.

Cog.—Astronaut Drills were a common way of developing fitness in the armed services.

PM.—All students should be able to perform the Astronaut Drills.

Aff.—There is no easy way to fitness. It demands self-discipline. Discuss the importance of possessing a positive attitude toward activity in later life.

MOVEMENT EXPERIENCE—CONTENT	ORGANIZATION AND TEACHING HINTS	EXPECTED STUDENT OBJECTIVES AND OUTCOMES

LESSON FOCUS (15 – 20 MINUTES)

Balance Beam Activities with Manipulative Equipment

A. *Moving Across the Beam*
  1. Try some of the following steps forward, backward, and sideways:
     a. Walk
     b. Follow steps
     c. Heel and Toe
     d. Side or Draw Step
     e. Tip Toes
     f. Grapevine
  2. Try different arm positions:
     a. On hips
     b. On head
     c. Behind back
     d. Folded across chest
     e. Pointing toward ceiling
  3. Move across the beam using animal walks.

B. *Activities to Self*
  1. Use one or two beanbags and toss to self in various fashions—around the body, under the legs, etc.
  2. Use a playground ball and toss to self.
  3. Bounce the ball on the floor and on the beam. Dribble the ball.
  4. Play catch with a partner.
  5. Balance a beanbag on various body parts. Use more than one bag.

C. *Activities with Hoops*
  1. Carry a hoop. Step through the hoop in various fashions—forward, sideways, backward.
  2. Step through hoops held by a partner.
  3. Hula-hoop on various body parts while moving across the beam.
  4. Carry a hoop on various body parts while moving across the beam.
  5. Twirl a hoop and proceed across the beam.

DPE pp. 422 – 424

Move deliberately, catching balance after each step. Quality, not speed, is the goal.

Mats should be placed at the end of each beam to cushion the dismount and allow selected rolls and stunts.

Encourage a wide variety of dismounts. Students should pause at the end of the beam before dismounting.

Both sides of the body should receive equal treatment. If students walk with the left side leading, they should also walk with the right side leading.

If the student steps off the beam, he should step back on at that point and continue to the end of the beam.

Place visual targets in front of the beams (on the wall at eye level). Those students with competency can look at the targets instead of the beam.

Allow each student to determine the degree of challenge desired.

PM.—The student will be able to walk the beam forward and backward while manipulating a piece of equipment.

Cog.—The student will be able to name five activities where balance is the major factor.

Aff.—Balance is affected a great deal by the auditory and visual senses. Experiment by trying various balance activities and eliminating some of the senses.

Cog.—Walking and moving across balance beams involves dynamic balance. Dynamic balance involves balancing while moving. Static balance involves a minimal amount of movement. Students can learn to combine static and dynamic balance when performing on the beam.

GAME (5 – 7 MINUTES)

The following games are suggested:
  1. Stork Tag, p. 518
  2. Flowers and Wind, p. 520

DYNAMIC PHYSICAL EDUCATION LESSON PLAN
Fundamental Skills Using Climbing Ropes
Level I

Supplies and Equipment Needed:
  Climbing ropes
  Mats (placed under ropes)
  Bench, box, or stool

MOVEMENT EXPERIENCE— CONTENT	ORGANIZATION AND TEACHING HINTS	EXPECTED STUDENT OBJECTIVES AND OUTCOMES

INTRODUCTORY AND FITNESS DEVELOPMENT ACTIVITIES

This lesson may be substituted for any of the previous lessons. Use the introductory and fitness development activities given in the sequenced lesson plans.

LESSON FOCUS (15 – 20 MINUTES)

Climbing Ropes

A. *Supported Pull-Ups*
  1. Knee and pull to feet, return.
  2. Sit, pull to feet and back to seat.
  3. Stand, keep body straight while lowering body to the floor.

B. *Hangs*
  1. Sit, pull body off floor except for feet, and hold.
  2. Jump up, grasp the rope, and hang and perform the following movements:
    a. One or both knees up
    b. Bicycling movement
    c. Half-lever
    d. Choice of movement
  3. Hang upside down with the rope hanging and looking like a "monkey's tail."

C. *Pull-Ups*
  Repeat all the activities suggested under Hangs, except substitute the pull-up for the hang.

D. *Swinging and Jumping*
  Use a bench, box, or stool for a take-off point. The student should reach high and jump to a bent-arm position while swinging.
  1. Swing and jump. Add one-half and full turns.
  2. Swing and return to perch.
  3. Jump for distance or land on a target. (Place a chalk mark on the floor.)
  4. Swing and pick up an Indian club and return to perch.
  5. Play Tarzan—take a running start, jump up, and swing as far as possible.

DPE pp. 414 – 418

Place tumbling mats under all the climbing apparatus.

Caution students not to slide quickly down the rope to prevent rope burns.

The pull-up and hang activities are excellent lead-ups for students who are not strong enough to climb the rope.

Students should be encouraged to learn the various techniques of climbing and descending.

If there are only a few climbing ropes, it would be a good teaching technique to have the nonclimbing students work on another unit. Some good units are beanbags, hoops, wands, and playground balls.

Rope climbing is a very intense and demanding activity. A good idea is to break up the lesson focus with a game or relay. This will also offer leg development activities.

If other climbing equipment is available such as a horizontal ladder and/or exercise bar, many activities are offered in *DPE* (see Chapter 19).

P.M.—The student will be able to demonstrate proper techniques in the following activities:
  1. Supported pull-ups
  2. Hangs
  3. Swinging and jumping
  4. Climbing and descending with the scissors grip

Cog.—The student will be able to describe the safety rules necessary when climbing ropes.

Aff.—Strength development activities do not significantly increase cardiovascular efficiency. Discuss the need for both strength and endurance activities when developing total fitness.

MOVEMENT EXPERIENCE—CONTENT	ORGANIZATION AND TEACHING HINTS	EXPECTED STUDENT OBJECTIVES AND OUTCOMES

E. *Climbing the Rope*
  1. Scissors grip—Place the rope inside of the knee and outside the foot. Climb halfway up and practice descending using the reverse scissors grip before climbing to the top of the rope.

Create a bulletin board with a theme such as the "Tarzan or Spider Man Club." The names of those youngsters who climb halfway up the rope could be listed on one chart. Another chart could be made for those reaching the top of the rope.

GAME (5 – 7 MINUTES)

1. Change Sides, p. 520
2. Where's My Partner?, p. 518

LESSON PLANS FOR THE SCHOOL YEAR
Developmental Level II

WEEK	INTRODUCTORY ACTIVITY	FITNESS DEVELOPMENT ACTIVITY	LESSON FOCUS ACTIVITY	GAME ACTIVITY	PAGE
1	Orientation and Class Management Games				114
2	Fundamental Movements and Stopping	Teacher Leader Exercises	Manipulative Skills Using Beanbags	Galloping Lizzie Crows and Cranes	116
3	Move and Assume Pose	Teacher Leader Exercises	Throwing Skills (1)	Whistle Mixer Couple Tag Partner Stoop	119
4	Walk, Trot, and Sprint	Teacher Leader Exercises	Soccer-Related Activities (1)	Circle Kickball Soccer Touch Ball Diagonal Soccer Soccer Take-Away	122
5	Partner Over and Under	Teacher Leader Exercises	Soccer-Related Activities (2)	Diagonal Soccer Soccer Touch Ball Dribblerama Bull's Eye	124
6	Run, Stop, and Pivot	Circuit Training	Fundamental Skills Through Playground Games	Playground Games	126
7	European Running	Circuit Training	Long-Rope Jumping Skills	Fly Trap Trades	128
8	Magic Number Challenge	Circuit Training	Manipulative Skills Using Playground Balls	Fox Hunt Bounce Ball One-Step	130
9	Fastest Tag in the West	Walk, Trot, and Sprint	Throwing Skills (2)	In the Prison Snowball Center Target Throw Target Ball Throw	133
10	Group Tag	Walk, Trot, and Sprint	Jogging Skills	Recreational Activity	136
11	Locomotor and Manipulative Activity	Exercises to Music	Rhythmic Movement (1)	Whistle March Arches Home Base	138
12	Movement Varieties	Exercises to Music	Hockey-Related Activities (1)	Circle Keep-Away Star Wars Hockey Lane Hockey Circle Straddleball	141
13	New Leader	Astronaut Drills	Hockey-Related Activities (2)	Modified Hockey Lane Hockey	143
14	Group Over and Under	Astronaut Drills	Individual Rope Jumping Skills	Follow Me Trades Beachball Bat Ball	145

WEEK	INTRODUCTORY ACTIVITY	FITNESS DEVELOPMENT ACTIVITY	LESSON FOCUS ACTIVITY	GAME ACTIVITY	PAGE
15	Low Organization Games	Continuity Drills	Stunts and Tumbling Skills (1)	Whistle Mixer Competitive Circle Contests Alaska Baseball	147
16	Following Activity	Continuity Drills	Rhythmic Movement (2)	Fox Hunt Steal the Treasure Addition Tag	149
17	Leapfrog	Aerobic Fitness and Partner Resistance Exercises	Fundamental Skills Using Benches	Cageball Kick-Over Squad Tag	153
18	Bridges by Three	Aerobic Fitness and Partner Resistance Exercises	Basketball-Related Activities (1)	Birdie in the Cage Dribblerama Captain Ball Basketball Tag	156
19	Jumping and Hopping Patterns	Challenge Course Fitness	Basketball-Related Activities (2)	Captain Ball Five Passes Around the Key	159
20	Fleece Ball Fun	Challenge Course Fitness	Recreational Activities	Recreational Activities	161
21	Ball Activities	Challenge Course Fitness	Fundamental Skills Using Balance Beams	Fly Trap Nonda's Car Lot	163
22	Moving to Music	Aerobic Fitness	Stunts and Tumbling Skills (2)	Partner Stoop Crows and Cranes	166
23	European Running with Variations	Aerobic Fitness	Manipulative Skills Using Wands	Home Base Indianapolis 500 Nine Lives	168
24	Tortoise and Hare	Aerobic Fitness	Rhythmic Movement (3)	Jump the Shot Beachball Bat Ball Club Guard	171
25	Bend, Stretch, and Shake	Astronaut Drills	Volleyball-Related Skills	Beachball and Informal Volleyball Shower Service Ball	175
26	Move, Perform Task	Astronaut Drills	Manipulative Skills Using Hoops	Hand Hockey Cageball Kickover	178
27	Tag Games	Continuity Drills	Manipulative Skills Using Paddles and Balls	Steal the Treasure Trees	180
28	Combination Movement Patterns	Continuity Drills	Stunts and Tumbling Skills (3)	Trades Beachball Bat Ball	183
29	European Running with Equipment	Exercises to Music	Fundamental Skills Using Tug-of-War Ropes	Relays	185
30	Marking	Exercises to Music	Rhythmic Movement with Equipment (4)	Alaska Baseball Addition Tag	188

WEEK	INTRODUCTORY ACTIVITY	FITNESS DEVELOPMENT ACTIVITY	LESSON FOCUS ACTIVITY	GAME ACTIVITY	PAGE
31	Stretching	Jogging	Track and Field-Related Activities (1)	Potato Shuttle Relay	191
32	Stretching	Jogging	Track and Field-Related Activities (2)	Relays	194
33	Creative Routine	Hexagon Hustle	Fundamental Skills Using Parachute Activity	Nonda's Car Lot Box Ball	196
34	Four-Corner Movement	Hexagon Hustle	Manipulative Skills Using Frisbees	Frisbee Keep-Away Frisbee Through-the Legs Target Throw Frisbee Golf	198
35	Long-Rope Routine	Parachute Fitness	Softball-Related Activities (1)	Throw It and Run Two-Pitch Softball Hit and Run	200
36	Squad Leader Movement	Parachute Fitness	Softball-Related Activities (2)	In a Pickle Beat Ball Kick Softball	203

Alternate Lessons

WEEK	INTRODUCTORY ACTIVITY	FITNESS DEVELOPMENT ACTIVITY	LESSON FOCUS ACTIVITY	GAME ACTIVITY	PAGE
A	Substitute	Substitute	Football-Related Activities (1)	Football End Ball Five Passes	205
B	Substitute	Substitute	Football-Related Activities (2)	Football Box Ball Speed Football	207
C	Substitute	Substitute	Softball-Related Activities (3)	Beat Ball Kick Softball Two-Pitch Softball	209
D	Substitute	Substitute	Fundamental Skills Using Balance Beams and Manipulative Equipment	Hand Hockey Nine Lives	210
E	Substitute	Substitute	Fundamental Skills Using Climbing Ropes	Nonda's Car Lot Indianapolis 500	212
F	Substitute	Substitute	Fundamental Skills Using Magic Ropes	Busy Bee Box Ball	214

DYNAMIC PHYSICAL EDUCATION LESSON PLAN
Orientation and Class Management Games
Level II

Note: See Chapter 7 in *Dynamic Physical Education for Elementary School Children,* Tenth Edition

ORIENTATION LESSON PLAN

This week should be used to get students involved in the system you are going to use throughout the year. The following are reminders you might find useful in establishing your organizational schemes.

1. Tell the class what is expected with regard to entry and exit behavior. If you are using the squad method, it might be helpful to place four cones (one per squad) in the same area each day and ask the squads to get into line behind the cones.
2. If you organize the class into squads, get a class list and divide the class ahead of time. Try to equalize the number of boys and girls in each squad. If the squads are somewhat unequal in ability, changes can be made later. Name a captain for each squad and tell the class how often you are going to change captains (2–3 weeks is recommended). Give the captains various responsibilities so they have a chance to be a leader. An alternate can be designated to act as squad leader if the regular leader is absent.
3. Explain briefly the lesson plan format to the class. Each lesson will contain an introductory activity, fitness activity, lesson focus, and game activity. They will know what to expect and won't have to ask if "we're going to play a game today," etc.
4. When classes come to the activity area, explain briefly what you are going to do in the day's lesson. It should be short and concise, but they should know what you have planned for them.
5. Establish rules and expectations. Usually, basic rules state that students must listen when you are speaking and vice versa, and they must act in a socially sound manner, respecting the rights of other students.
6. If you are going to test, let the students know the reason for the test and exactly what it will involve on their behalf.
7. Emphasize the value of fitness and take them through a fitness routine. Set expectations high—it is easier to lower them later. Practice various formations such as open-squad and closed-squad, so they know what to do when you ask them to assume these positions. Try formations such as squares, triangles, and rectangles.
8. Discuss issuance, distribution, and care of equipment and where and how it is to be stored. Students should play an integral part in handling equipment and should understand what is expected of them.
9. Decide how excuses for nonparticipation should be handled. Children should know where they go to be excused and where they go after they are excused.
10. Establish a signal to stop the class and gain attention. Usually a whistle and a hand signal are effective. Practice gaining the attention of the class with the signal during this orientation period. Activity should be started by verbal command.
11. Select activities for this week in which you know all students will be successful. This is one of the best ways to develop enthusiasm for a program in its early stages. The corollary of this rule is to teach a few games and activities you enjoy.
12. The orientation week usually requires more explanation than is normal. After the first week, keep talking to a minimum and activity to a maximum. Remember that when you are talking or children are standing in line, there is no way they can learn and practice new physical skills.
13. Circulate among students as you develop movement experiences and skills. This allows for individualized instruction and attention to the lesser skilled. Avoid spending the majority of teacher time "at the podium," in front of the class.
14. In each of the lessons, read the reference areas in *Dynamic Physical Education* to provide an in-depth discussion of the activity.

15. Frequent reference should be made as needed to Chapter 7, "Effective Class Management," in *Dynamic Physical Education for Elementary School Children*. This chapter applies to all activities taught and offers strategies and techniques to enhance the teaching process.

16. Safety is an important issue to be covered in the first week. Children should receive safety rules to be followed when using large apparatus as well as similar rules for playground and gymnasium conduct. Rules should be posted in the gymnasium and throughout the school. See Chapter 9 in *Dynamic Physical Education* for an in-depth discussion on safety and liability.

17. It is crucial to the success of the teacher that good student management skills be developed early in the school year. During the first week, students should practice getting into various formations quickly and without talking, getting into groups of different sizes, and stopping on signal quickly (within 5 seconds). Games, such as those that follow, are excellent for teaching class management skills.

18. Express interest in your students and that you are anxious to learn their names. Inform them that you are going to ask them their names many times to expedite learning them. It also might be helpful to ask classroom teachers to put name tags on students before they come to physical education class. Having students write their names on a piece of masking tape is a quick and easy way to make name tags.

ACTIVITY

Play a few favorite games after a fitness routine has been introduced. The following games are excellent management activities and offer the students a chance to get to know each other.

1. Whistle Mixer, p. 536
2. Change Sides, p. 520
3. Couple Tag, p. 526
4. Squad Tag, p. 535
5. Whistle March, p. 531

DYNAMIC PHYSICAL EDUCATION LESSON PLAN
Manipulative Skills Using Beanbags
Level II

Supplies and Equipment Needed:
  Two beanbags per child
  Tom-tom or tambourine
  Jump ropes

MOVEMENT EXPERIENCE— CONTENT	ORGANIZATION AND TEACHING HINTS	EXPECTED STUDENT OBJECTIVES AND OUTCOMES

INTRODUCTORY ACTIVITY (2 – 3 MINUTES)

Fundamental Movements and Stopping

1. Teach the run, walk, hop, jump, leap, slide, gallop, and skip with proper stopping.
2. Practice moving the stopping correctly—emphasize basics of proper movement.

DPE p. 219

Scatter formation.

A tom-tom can be used. Otherwise use a whistle to signal the stop.

PM.—The student will be able to stop quickly under control.

Cog.—Know the elements involved in stopping quickly.

PM.—The student will be able to execute the various locomotor movements.

FITNESS DEVELOPMENT ACTIVITIES (7 – 8 MINUTES)

Teacher Leader Exercises

Arm Circles	25 seconds
Bend and Stretch	25 seconds
Treadmill	25 seconds
Sit-Up	35 seconds
Single-Leg Crab Kick	25 seconds
Knee to Chest Curl	35 seconds
Run in Place	30 seconds
Trunk Twister	25 seconds

Conclude the routine with 2 to 4 minutes of jogging, rope jumping, or other continuous activity.

DPE p. 258

Scatter formation.

Allow students to adjust the work load to their ability and fitness level. This implies that some students will perform more repetitions in the same amount of time.

Emphasize proper form and technique.

Rotate to different parts of the teaching area and help motivate students.

Cog.—Know why it is necessary to increase the number of repetitions (overload principle).

PM.—The student will be able to perform all activities at teacher-established level.

Aff.—A positive attitude toward exercise and its value to man.

LESSON FOCUS (15 – 20 MINUTES)

Beanbag Activities

A. *In place, tossing to self*
   1. Toss and catch with both hands—right hand, left hand.
   2. Toss and catch with the back of hands. (This will force children to give and thus develop "soft hands.")
   3. Toss the beanbag to higher levels *emphasizing* a good straight throw. (To force the child to throw the beanbag directly overhead, have him or her sit down.)
   4. Exploratory activity.

B. *In place, adding stunts*
   1. Toss overhead and perform the following stunts and catch bag.

DPE pp. 365 – 368

Scatter formation.

Stress soft catch. Keep eyes on the bag.

Students should practice the activities with both the left and right hands.

Emphasize keeping eyes on object while performing stunts.

PM.—The student will develop the necessary visual concentration to follow a moving object.

PM.—The student will be able to "give" with the body to create a soft home for the beanbag.

Cog.—The student will be able to recite the necessary ingredients for successful catching.

MOVEMENT EXPERIENCE—CONTENT	ORGANIZATION AND TEACHING HINTS	EXPECTED STUDENT OBJECTIVES AND OUTCOMES

a. Half turn
b. Full turn
c. Touch floor
d. Clap hands
e. Clap hands around different parts of body
f. Heel click
g. Student choice

C. *In place, kicking to self*
 1. Place beanbag on foot, kick up and catch—right foot, left foot.
 2. Try above activity from sitting and lying positions.
 3. Kick up and catch behind back.
 4. Kick up overhead, make 1/2 turn, and catch.
 5. Put beanbag between feet, jump up, and catch beanbag.
 6. Toss beanbag with one foot and catch with the other foot.

D. *Locomotor movements*
 (Toss, Move, and Catch)
 1. Toss overhead, move to another spot, and catch.
 2. Toss, do a locomotor movement, and catch.
 3. Move from side to side.
 4. Toss overhead behind self, move, and catch.
 5. Exploratory movements.

E. *Balance the beanbag*
 1. Balance on the following body parts:
  a. Head
  b. Back of hand
  c. Shoulder
  d. Knee
  e. Foot
  f. Elbow
  g. Others (choice)
 2. Balance and move as follows:
  a. Walk
  b. Run
  c. Skip
  d. Gallop
  e. Sit down
  f. Lie down
  g. Turn around
  h. Balance beanbag on body part and move on all fours
  i. Play Beanbag Balance Tag
  j. Others (choice)

F. *Partner activities*
 1. Toss back and forth using the following throws:
  a. Two-handed throws—overhead, underhand, side, and over shoulder.

ORGANIZATION AND TEACHING HINTS

Give them two or three activities to attempt so that you have time to move around and help children in need.

Catching is more important than the stunt. Make sure that they are making good throws and catching the bag.

Encourage the class to look where they are moving. This will force them to take their eyes off the object, relocate it, and catch it, which is a more advanced skill.

Look for new and exciting ways of balancing the bags. Allow students to show their ideas to the rest of the class.

See who can balance a bag the longest on various body parts while moving.

If time allows, go back and polish some of the activities performed earlier in the week.

Those students balancing red beanbags are it, or those with blue beanbags are it, etc.

Start partners close together and gradually increase distance to increase challenge.

Polish the activities at this level. Fourth and 5th graders should be expected to throw and catch with few misses. *Demand* and expect quality.

EXPECTED STUDENT OBJECTIVES AND OUTCOMES

Cog.—The length of the lever determines the amount of force that can be generated when propelling an object. Discuss how the length of the lever is shortened when making accurate tosses.

Cog.—The student will be able to state why catching is more difficult when the person is moving.

PM.—The student will be able to propel the body and balance an object simultaneously.

Cog.—Proper nutrition is important for ensuring strong physical performance. Studies show that Americans eat too much salt, sugar, and fat. Discuss the types of foods that can be eaten to reduce these areas of excessive intake.

Aff.—Most sport activities require teamwork (working with a partner) for success to occur. Discuss with the students the need for working closely with their partner in the beanbag activities.

MOVEMENT EXPERIENCE—CONTENT	ORGANIZATION AND TEACHING HINTS	EXPECTED STUDENT OBJECTIVES AND OUTCOMES

b. One-handed throws and catches.

c. Throw at different levels and targets such as high, low, left, right.

d. Throw under leg, around body, from behind back, center, as in football, etc.

e. Sit down and play catch—try different throws and catches.

f. Toss in various directions to make partner move and catch. Have one partner move around other in a circle while catching and throwing.

g. Propel more than one beanbag back and forth. Toss both beanbags together as well as at opposite times.

A motivating idea is to challenge students by asking them to perform an activity a certain number of times in a row without missing.

Also, try to follow activities where one partner throws or catches exactly as the lead thrower does.

PM.—The student will be able to throw and catch at various distances and levels.

PM.—The student will be able to throw and catch the beanbag while moving in circular formation.

GAME (5 – 7 MINUTES)

Teacher's choice—make this an active game in order to ensure that the class receives enough running. The following are suggested:
1. Galloping Lizzie, p. 528
2. Crows and Cranes, p. 527

DYNAMIC PHYSICAL EDUCATION LESSON PLAN
Throwing Skills (Lesson 1)
Level II

Supplies and Equipment Needed:
  Beanbags or fleece balls
  Yarn balls
  Rag balls or tennis balls
  Hoops
  Mats for targets
  Jump ropes (optional)

MOVEMENT EXPERIENCE— CONTENT	ORGANIZATION AND TEACHING HINTS	EXPECTED STUDENT OBJECTIVES AND OUTCOMES

INTRODUCTORY ACTIVITY (2 – 3 MINUTES)

Move and Assume Pose

1. Have the child move using a variation of a basic movement. Freeze on signal; assume a pose using the following commands.
   a. Balance
   b. Stretch
   c. Curl
   d. Bridge
   e. Push-up position
   f. Make shape with a partner (double bridge, arch)
   g. Choice

DPE p. 219

Scatter formation.

Emphasize proper method of stopping quickly.

Discourage falling and lack of body control.

Encourage creativity in various poses.

Stretching exercises should be slow and sustained movements.

PM.—The student will be able to perform the basic poses on command.

Cog.—The student will recognize the basic command names and non-locomotor movements.

PM.—The student will be able to stop quickly with good balance.

FITNESS DEVELOPMENT ACTIVITIES (7 – 8 MINUTES)

Teacher Leader Exercises

Arm Circles	35 seconds
Sitting Stretch	35 seconds
Treadmill	35 seconds
Sit-Up	45 seconds
Single-Leg Crab Kick	35 seconds
Knee to Chest Curl	45 seconds
Power Jumper	40 seconds
Trunk Twister	35 seconds

Conclude the routine with 2 to 4 minutes of jogging, rope jumping, or other continuous activity.

Increase the duration of exercises by 10 to 20% over the previous week.

DPE p. 258

Scatter formation.

Allow students to adjust the work load to their ability and fitness level. This implies that some students will perform more repetitions in the same amount of time.

Emphasize proper form and technique.

Rotate to different parts of the teaching area and help motivate students.

Cog.—The student will be able to explain verbally why correct form is important when performing fitness activities.

PM.—The student will be able to perform all activities at the teacher-established level.

Aff.—One of the reasons for fitness activities now is to establish patterns for later life. Establish the need for fitness throughout life through example and brief comments.

LESSON FOCUS (15 – 20 MINUTES)

Throwing

A. *Individual activities*
   1. Throw beanbag or fleece ball against the wall. Emphasize the following points:
      a. Feet together
      b. Contralateral foot forward
      c. Start with nonthrowing side to the wall

DPE pp. 307 – 308

At least one beanbag per child.

Students should be 4–5 ft from the wall.

Encourage children to throw hard.

Cog.—The student will begin to understand the importance of body rotation to produce force.

Cog.—The student will understand the importance of opposition of limbs.

119

MOVEMENT EXPERIENCE— CONTENT	ORGANIZATION AND TEACHING HINTS	EXPECTED STUDENT OBJECTIVES AND OUTCOMES
2. Throw from one side of the gym and try to hit the other wall.	Redirect children with key points: 1. Start with your throwing hand behind your head. 2. Turn your side to the wall. 3. Take a big step and throw hard. Have the entire class throw at once if possible, retrieve, and run to wall. Repeat.	PM.—The student will perform the throw by stepping with the contralateral foot. Cog.—Student will understand the importance of the shoulder turn and step in producing a forceful throw.

B. *Station format*
   1. Activities emphasizing form
     a. Mats 5–6" thick.
       1. The student stands on the edge of the mat and steps to the floor with his contralateral foot as he throws toward the wall. (The other foot remains on the mat.)
 	
     b. Both feet in tire or hoop.
       1. The student begins in side-facing position to the target, with both feet inside the tire (or hoop); she then steps outside the tire with the contralateral foot and throws to the wall.
     c. Cone behind the student.
       1. The student must touch the cone with the throwing hand on the backswing, then throw to the wall.
	All students should do these activities a minimum of two days.
	
	 All throws are made to the wall and with force.
	
	 This activity forces the student to take a long stride toward the target.
	
	 If tires or hoops are not available, use jump ropes. The circle should be large enough to encourage the student to take a long stride.
	
	 This activity should encourage the student to rotate and take a wind-up before throwing.
	
	 The cone should be directly behind the student and about at arm's length–distance.
		Aff.—The student should understand that a lot of practice is necessary to master the skill of throwing.
		
		 PM.—The student should begin to take a long stride with the throw.
		
		 Cog.—The student should understand that a longer stride helps increase force production.

C. *Activities using large targets so students will throw forcefully*
   1. Throw at mats on the wall
     a. Throw tennis or rag balls hard from 15 to 20 ft.
     b. Retrieve only if the balls roll behind the throwing line.
   2. Mats laid over tables
     a. If tables are on rollers, see if forceful throws can move the table.
   3. Throw at hoops leaning against mats against the wall.
   4. Large target throw
     a. A circle or square 4 ft. in diameter should be placed on the wall.
     b. Students should throw from 20 to 25 ft.
	Everyone should do the stations under C for a minimum of two days.
	
	 Each student should start with five balls.
	
	 The teacher should continue to give feedback to the students that will help them improve their form.
	
	 The mats should be placed on the table so they hang to the floor.
	
	 Put hoops touching one another for easier targets; spread apart for more difficult target.
	
	 Another excellent large target is a 4-ft. cage ball.	

MOVEMENT EXPERIENCE—CONTENT	ORGANIZATION AND TEACHING HINTS	EXPECTED STUDENT OBJECTIVES AND OUTCOMES

GAME (5 – 7 MINUTES)

An active game should be played due to the inactive nature of the above activity. The following are suggested:
1. Whistle Mixer, p. 536
2. Couple Tag, p. 526
3. Partner Stoop, p. 534

DYNAMIC PHYSICAL EDUCATION LESSON PLAN
Soccer-Related Activities (Lesson 1)
Level II

Supplies and Equipment Needed:
8 1/2" foam rubber balls (8 1/2" playground balls may be substituted)
Cones for marking areas for lead-up activities
Tom-tom
Jump ropes (optional)

MOVEMENT EXPERIENCE— CONTENT	ORGANIZATION AND TEACHING HINTS	EXPECTED STUDENT OBJECTIVES AND OUTCOMES

INTRODUCTORY ACTIVITY (2 – 3 MINUTES)

Walk, Trot, and Sprint

Move to the following signals:
1. One signal—walk
2. Two signals—trot
3. Three signals—run
4. Whistle—freeze

DPE p. 245

Scatter formation.

Work on quality of movements and quick changes.

Try to "fool" the class by changing signals and catching them "off guard."

May vary this activity by adding a fourth tom-tom beat to signal an exercise.

Cog.—Introductory activity is performed in order to warm up the body for more strenuous activity.

FITNESS DEVELOPMENT ACTIVITIES (7 – 8 MINUTES)

Teacher Leader Exercises

Arm Circles	30 seconds
Bend and Stretch	30 seconds
Treadmill	30 seconds
Sit-Up	40 seconds
Single-Leg Crab Kick	30 seconds
Knee to Chest Curl	40 seconds
Run in Place	35 seconds
Standing Hip Bend	30 seconds

Conclude the routine with 2 to 4 minutes of jogging, rope jumping, or other continuous activity.

Increase the duration of exercises by 10 to 20% over the previous week.

DPE p. 258

Scatter formation.

Allow students to adjust the work load to their ability and fitness level. This implies that some students will perform more repetitions in the same amount of time.

Emphasize proper form and technique.

Rotate to different parts of the teaching area and help motivate students.

Cog.—It is necessary to increase the number of repetitions of activity to provide additional stress on the body and increase fitness levels.

PM.—The student will be able to perform one to two more repetitions of each exercise than he was capable of two weeks ago.

Aff.—Physically fit people are rewarded by society. Teachers, parents, and peers respond much more favorably to those fit and attractive.

LESSON FOCUS (15 – 20 MINUTES)

Soccer

Discuss basic rules necessary for soccer lead-up games.

A. *Skills*
   1. The long pass:
      Approach at 45° angle, top of instep meets ball. Place non-kicking foot alongside ball.
   2. Side of foot pass (short pass):
      Short distance kick, keep toe down. Use both the inside and outside of the foot.

DPE pp. 617 – 637

Partner or triangle formation, one ball for two or three children.

Keep head down, eyes on ball, follow through.

8 1/2" foam rubber training balls should be used as they remove the fear of being hurt by a kicked soccer ball.

PM.—The student will be able to pass, kick, and trap the ball successfully at the end of the week.

Cog.—The student will be able to state two reasons why, in soccer activities, accuracy is much preferred over raw power and lack of control.

MOVEMENT EXPERIENCE— CONTENT	ORGANIZATION AND TEACHING HINTS	EXPECTED STUDENT OBJECTIVES AND OUTCOMES
3. Sole of the foot control: Use sole of foot to stop ball, make sure weight is placed on the nonreceiving foot.	If short supply of foam rubber balls, use 8 1/2" playground balls. Partially deflate them and they will move more slowly and offer children more success.	
4. Foot control: Use inside of foot, learn to "give" with leg so ball doesn't ricochet off foot.	Make sure students handle the ball with their feet, not the hands. They should retrieve and move the balls with feet only.	
5. Dribbling: Practice moving the ball with a series of controlled taps. Practice dribbling with the left and the right foot.		
B. *Drills* (optional) Each student should practice dribbling and handling the ball individually. Partner or triplet work is excellent for practicing kicking, passing, and trapping skills.	Teach skills from a stationary position; as students improve, introduce movement.	
1. Circle formation: Useful for kicking, trapping, and passing.	Drills should be used after students' individual skills have improved to enable them to participate successfully. Progress from *individual* work to group drills.	
2. Circle and leader: Useful for emphasizing accuracy and allowing all a chance to lead.		
C. *Lead-Up activities* 1. Circle Kickball (p. 629) Try playing this game with a beachball.	Circle formation, two circles necessary. Emphasize kicking the ball below *waist* level.	Aff.—Even in basic lead-up games, teamwork is necessary for success and enjoyment by all. Cog.—The student will be able to state the basic rules necessary for soccer lead-up games.
2. Soccer Touch Ball (pp. 629 – 630)	Two circles. Emphasize short, accurate passes. Pass quickly; don't hold the ball. This is a good chance to learn to trap the ball with various body parts.	Aff.—The student will learn to appreciate individual differences and show concern for the welfare of others. Aff.—Cooperation needs to be learned before students can compete with others. Discuss how it is impossible to have a competitive game if others choose not to cooperate and follow rules.
3. Diagonal Soccer (p. 630)	It is a good time to emphasize the necessary ingredients for boys and girls learning to participate together.	
4. Soccer Take-Away	All but four or five students dribble their soccer ball in the gym. The remaining students attempt to successfully "steal" another student's soccer ball and then dribble the ball.	

GAME (5 – 7 MINUTES)

Generally, the aforementioned lead-up games can be used as the game activity. In the early stages of learning, skills are not developed enough, and an unrelated game can be played.

DYNAMIC PHYSICAL EDUCATION LESSON PLAN
Soccer-Related Activities (Lesson 2)
Level II

Supplies and Equipment Needed:
  One foam rubber or playground ball per two or three children
  Cones for marking playing areas
  Tape player
  Music
  Jump ropes (optional)

MOVEMENT EXPERIENCE—CONTENT	ORGANIZATION AND TEACHING HINTS	EXPECTED STUDENT OBJECTIVES AND OUTCOMES

INTRODUCTORY ACTIVITY (2 – 3 MINUTES)

Partner Over and Under

Students pair up with one person on the floor and the other standing ready to move. On signal, the standing students move over, under and/or around the persons on the floor. On signal, reverse positions. Students on the floor can also alternate between positions such as curl, stretch, and bridge.

DPE p. 222

Partner formation.

Encourage students to move as quickly as possible.

Challenge them to see how many times they can go over and under each other.

PM.—The student will be able to move quickly over, under, and around his or her partner.

Aff.—Warm-up activities work only when an individual motivates himself to move quickly and with intensity.

FITNESS DEVELOPMENT ACTIVITIES (7 – 8 MINUTES)

Teacher Leader Exercises

Sitting Stretch	40 seconds
Power Jumper	40 seconds
Jumping Jacks	40 seconds
Sit-Up	50 seconds
Single-Leg Crab Kick	40 seconds
Knee to Chest Curl	50 seconds
Windmill	45 seconds
Trunk Twister	40 seconds

Conclude the routine with 2 to 4 minutes of jogging, rope jumping, or other continuous activity.

Increase the duration of exercises by 10 to 20% over the previous week.

DPE p. 258

Scatter formation.

Allow students to adjust the work load to their ability and fitness level. This implies that some students will perform more repetitions in the same amount of time.

Taped intervals of music and no music can be used to signal time for each exercise.

Rotate to different parts of the teaching area and help motivate students.

Cog.—The student will be able to identify the activities by name.

Aff.—Compare performances occurring three weeks ago with present performances. Discuss the attitude that self-improvement is self-rewarding and motivates the learner to continue the effort.

LESSON FOCUS (15 – 20 MINUTES)

The soccer lesson works well in a circuit of instructional stations. Divide the skills into four to six stations and place the necessary equipment and instructions at each.

Soccer

A. *Skills*
  1. Review long pass and short pass.
  2. Outside foot pass: Use the outside of the foot. More of a push than a kick.
  3. Dribbling: Move the ball with a series of taps. Start slowly and don't kick the ball too far away from the player.

DPE pp. 617 – 637

One ball per two children or triangle formation; one ball for each group of three children.

8 1/2" foam rubber training balls are best for learning proper form in soccer activities.

Start expecting quality and accuracy in the kicks, passes, and traps.

PM.—The student will be able to kick, dribble, trap, and pass the soccer ball by the end of the week.

Cog.—The student will be able to describe the situations in which the heel and outside foot kicks should be used.

Aff.—When soccer is taught in a co-ed situation, students must appreciate individual differences.

124

MOVEMENT EXPERIENCE—CONTENT	ORGANIZATION AND TEACHING HINTS	EXPECTED STUDENT OBJECTIVES AND OUTCOMES
4. Passing: Start passing the ball from a stationary position and then progress to moving while passing.	Heel kick and outside foot kick are used for short distances only.	Aff.—Good passes can be easily handled by a teammate. Praise passes and teamwork.
B. *Drills* 1. Shuttle turnback: Use this drill to practice passing for accuracy. 2. Shuttle dribbling: Use to practice dribbling and short passes. 3. Three-man shuttle dribble drill. A good drill to use to encourage well-controlled dribbling. 4. Passing drill: Use a double shuttle formation. Two players progress down the field. 5. Dribbling Keep-Away: Half of class has a ball for each player. The other half of the class tries to take away a ball and retain control while dribbling. Activity is continuous.	Review the skills taught last lesson and integrate them into this lesson. Proper motor patterns can be learned only when they are reviewed and practiced many times. Keep the lines short in the drill activities. Use a series of cones as objects to dribble around. Use short lines with an emphasis on passing accuracy. Emphasis should be placed on controlled, accurate dribbling.	Cog.—Flexibility is the range of motion at a joint. Flexibility is important in kicking activities as more force can be generated over a greater range of motion. Discuss the importance of stretching in order to lengthen connective tissue.
C. *Lead-Up activities* 1. Diagonal Soccer (p. 630) 2. Soccer Touch Ball (pp. 629–630) 3. Dribblerama (p. 630) 4. Bull's-Eye (p. 630)	Use cones for marking the corners. Emphasize kicking the ball below *waist* level. Encourage students to move the ball under control. Delineate a large area. Use more than one bull's-eye. Use foam training balls.	PM.—The student will practice and use the soccer skills learned previously. Cog.—The student will be able to recite the basic rules of soccer. Cog.—Muscle soreness may occur from the breakdown of connective tissue. Excessive exercise (in relation to the amount of activity a person normally performs) may cause an imbalance in the breakdown–buildup process, and soreness will result. Students should understand the need for progressively increasing work load to minimize soreness.

GAME (5 – 7 MINUTES)

An unrelated game can be played, if desired. However, it is more effective to use the lead-up games and mini-soccer for this part of the lesson.

DYNAMIC PHYSICAL EDUCATION LESSON PLAN
Fundamental Skills Through Playground Games
Level II

Supplies and Equipment Needed:
  Jump ropes
  Signs for circuit training stations
  Cones
  Balls
  Hula hoops

MOVEMENT EXPERIENCE—CONTENT	ORGANIZATION AND TEACHING HINTS	EXPECTED STUDENT OBJECTIVES AND OUTCOMES

INTRODUCTORY ACTIVITY (2 – 3 MINUTES)

Run, Stop, and Pivot

The class should run, stop on signal, and pivot. Vary the activity by having the class pivot on the left or right foot and increase the circumference of the pivot.

Movement should be continuous. Students should continue running after the pivot.

DPE p. 219

Emphasize correct form in stopping and absorbing force.

Make sure students do not cross legs or lose balance while pivoting.

Allow a few moments of free practice.

Cog.—The pivot is used in many sports such as basketball and baseball.

PM.—The student will be able to stop, pivot, and move by the end of the week.

FITNESS DEVELOPMENT ACTIVITIES (7 – 8 MINUTES)

Circuit Training

Rope Jumping
Triceps Push-Ups
Agility Run
Body Circles
Hula Hoop
Partial Sit-Ups
Crab Walk
Tortoise and Hare
Bend and Stretch

Conclude circuit training with 2–4 minutes of walking, jogging, rope jumping, or other aerobic activity.

DPE pp. 259 – 262

Start with 25 seconds of exercise followed by 10 seconds of time to move and prepare for the next station.

Use signals such as "start," "stop," "move up" to ensure rapid movement to the next station.

Move randomly from station to station to offer help for students who are not using correct technique.

Cog.—Circuit training should work all parts of the body, but no two similar parts in succession.

Cog.—The student will be able to describe how overload is achieved (by increasing the length of activity at each station and decreasing the rest between stations).

Cog.—In order that circuit training be effective, *quality* exercise must be performed at each station.

LESSON FOCUS (15 – 20 MINUTES)

Playground Games

The objective of this lesson should be to teach youngsters the rules and methods for playing games during their free time. Emphasis should be on self-direction so students do not need supervision.
  1. Tetherball, p. 545
  2. Four Square, p. 544
  3. Two Square, p. 544
  4. Volley Tennis, p. 546
  5. Basketball
    a. Around the Key, p. 585

Emphasis should be placed on teaching the rules of the activities so children can enjoy them on their own time.

It might be useful to set up the activities at four or five different stations and then rotate the students from one activity to the next.

If you know a traditional game played by children in your area for many years, now is a good time to teach it.

PM.—The student will be able to play at least four of the given activities.

Cog.—The student will be able to recite the rules for playing four or more of the activities.

Aff.—Recreational activities can be an excellent release for reducing stress. Relaxation demands playing for enjoyment and personal pleasure. Adults spend millions of dollars searching for activities that are relaxing and rewarding.

MOVEMENT EXPERIENCE—CONTENT	ORGANIZATION AND TEACHING HINTS	EXPECTED STUDENT OBJECTIVES AND OUTCOMES

    b. Twenty One, p. 587
    c. Freeze Out, p. 588
  6. Hopscotch
  7. Jump Rope, pp. 399 – 410
  8. Soccer (2 on 2), pp. 624 – 625
  9. Frisbee, pp. 380 – 382
10. Wall Handball
11. Softball - Five hundred, p. 652

GAME (5 – 7 MINUTES)

All the activities above are games and should be continued throughout this time.

DYNAMIC PHYSICAL EDUCATION LESSON PLAN
Long-Rope Jumping Skills
Level II

Supplies and Equipment Needed:
Two long-jump ropes (16 ft.) for a group of four to six children
Individual jump ropes
Tom-tom
Cones
Circuit training signs
Balls or beanbags
Cageball
Tape player
Music
Hula hoops

MOVEMENT EXPERIENCE—CONTENT	ORGANIZATION AND TEACHING HINTS	EXPECTED STUDENT OBJECTIVES AND OUTCOMES

INTRODUCTORY ACTIVITY (2 – 3 MINUTES)

European Running

Develop the ability to follow the leader, maintain proper spacing, and move to the rhythm of the tom-tom.

Variation: Have leader move in different shapes and designs. Have class freeze and see if they can identify the shape or formation.

DPE pp. 217 – 218

Single-file formation with a leader.

Start the class by moving feet, in place, to the beat of the tom-tom at a slow pace and gradually speed up. Add clapping hands. Add movement after the above is accomplished. The beat must be fast enough so students move at a fast trot with knees up.

Cog.—The student will describe six sport and recreational activities in which the body moves rhythmically.

PM.—The student will be able to move rhythmically with the beat of the tom-tom by the end of the week.

FITNESS DEVELOPMENT ACTIVITIES (7 – 8 MINUTES)

Circuit Training

Rope Jumping
Triceps Push-Ups
Agility Run
Body Circles
Hula Hoop
Partial Sit-Ups
Crab Walk
Tortoise and Hare
Bend and Stretch

Conclude circuit training with 2–4 minutes of walking, jogging, rope jumping, or other aerobic activity.

DPE pp. 259 – 262

Increase to 30 seconds of exercise followed by 10 seconds of time to move and prepare for the next station.

Emphasize quality of movement rather than quantity and lack of technique.

Taped intervals of music and no music can be used to signal duration of exercise at each station and time to move to the next station.

PM.—The student will be able to perform all exercises.

Cog.—The student will be able to state which circuit exercises develop the various areas of the body.

Aff.—Most fitness gains are made when the body is exercised past the point of initial fatigue. Thus, briefly discuss the value of pushing one's self past the first signs of tiring.

LESSON FOCUS (15 – 20 MINUTES)

Long–Rope Jumping

1. Run through turning rope, front door.
2. Run in front door, jump once, run out.
3. Run through turning rope, back door.
4. Run in back door, jump once, run out.

DPE pp. 399 – 403

Groups of 4 or 5 children.

Change turners frequently. Make sure that all children get a chance to both turn and jump.

PM.—The student will be able to jump the rope a minimum of 15 times consecutively without a miss.

Cog.—In terms of physical exertion, 10 minutes of rope jumping is equal to 30 minutes of jogging.

MOVEMENT EXPERIENCE—CONTENT	ORGANIZATION AND TEACHING HINTS	EXPECTED STUDENT OBJECTIVES AND OUTCOMES

5. Try the following variations:
   a. Run in front door, out back door.
   b. Run in front door and out front door.
   c. Run in back door and out back door.
   d. Run in front or back door, jump a specified number of times, and out.
   e. Run in front or back door, jump and do a quarter, half, and full turn in the air.
   f. Add individual rope.
   g. Individual choice or with a partner.
6. Hot Pepper: *Gradually* increase the speed of the rope. Use the verse, p. 402.
7. High Water: *Gradually* raise the height of the rope while it is turned.
8. Have more than one child jump at a time. Students can enter in pairs or any other combination. Have jumpers change positions while jumping.
9. Have jumper attempt to jump while holding beanbag or playground ball between knees.
10. Have one of the turners jump the long rope.
11. Play catch with a partner while jumping the rope.
12. Egg Beater: Two long ropes are turned simultaneously with four turners.
13. Double Dutch: Requires two long ropes turned alternately. Rope near jumper is turned back door and far rope front door.
14. Combination movements: three or four ropes in sequence.

When jumping front door, the rope is turned toward the jumper, as compared to back door where the rope is turned away from the jumper.

Back door is much more difficult. Approach the rope at a 45° angle.

Girls will probably be much more skilled in this activity.

Turners maintain a constant rhythm with the rope.

Children who have trouble jumping should face one of the turners and key their jumps to both the visual and audio cues (hand movement and sound of the rope hitting the floor).

It might be helpful to review beanbag activities briefly as a change of pace (rest) activity.

Try to eliminate excessive body movement while jumping, i.e., jumping too high, knees too high, or excessive arm movement.

Double Dutch contests for speed and endurance may be motivating.

The jumper must jump twice as fast as each rope is turning to succeed (Double Dutch).

Students can be challenged to perform a different activity as they pass through each rope.

Aff.—Rope jumping is neither a male nor a female activity. It is performed by boxers, football players, and dancers for fitness development.

Cog.—The student will learn to react to rope jumping terms: front door, back door, hot pepper, high water, etc.

Cog.—Two misconceptions prevail in regard to weight control. One is that exercise burns a small amount of calories and thus has no impact on weight, and the other is that exercise increases appetite. This ignores the fact that if a mile were run every day, the person would burn 12 lbs. of fat in a year. Activity does not appear to significantly increase appetite.

Cog.—Aerobic endurance is usually measured by speed or distance in a given time frame. Allow students to devise some informal methods of evaluating their aerobic fitness.

GAME (5 – 7 MINUTES)

A game that doesn't contain too much activity is probably a good choice. The following are suggested:
1. Fly Trap, p. 527
2. Trades, p. 535

DYNAMIC PHYSICAL EDUCATION LESSON PLAN
Manipulative Skills Using Playground Balls
Level II

Supplies and Equipment Needed:
One 8 1/2" playground ball for each student
Tambourine
Eight cones
Magic number cards
Circuit training signs
Balls
Tape player
Music
Jump ropes
Hula hoops and scarves

MOVEMENT EXPERIENCE—CONTENT	ORGANIZATION AND TEACHING HINTS	EXPECTED STUDENT OBJECTIVES AND OUTCOMES

INTRODUCTORY ACTIVITY (2 – 3 MINUTES)

Magic Number Challenge

Students are challenged to put together a combination of movements corresponding to the magic numbers designated (e.g., 10, 8, and 7). Students would have to do three different movements 10, 8, and 7 times, respectively. The number of movements, the repetitions, and the types of movements can be changed to offer a wide variety of challenges.

DPE p. 220

Scatter formation.

Movements can be locomotor, non-locomotor, and specialized sport skills.

Challenge students to develop new sequences.

PM.—The student will be able to perform the challenges rapidly and with concise changes from one movement to the next.

Cog.—The student will be able to immediately identify the total number of repetitions as well as movements.

FITNESS DEVELOPMENT ACTIVITIES (7 – 8 MINUTES)

Circuit Training

Rope Jumping
Push-Ups
Agility Run
Lower Leg Stretch
Juggling Scarves
Sit-Ups
Alternate Leg Extension
Tortoise and Hare
Bear Hug
Conclude circuit training with 2–4 minutes of walking, jogging, rope jumping, or other aerobic activity.

DPE pp. 259 – 262

Increase to 35 seconds of exercise followed by 10 seconds of time to move and prepare for the next station.

Hula hoops and juggling scarves placed at a station allow youngsters a chance to rest and are motivating activities.

This is the last week of circuit training. Encourage improvement of performance and technique.

Cog.—Muscles atrophy without exercise and grow stronger with use. The student will be able to describe in his own words the need for exercise.

PM.—All students will be able to move and exercise through the circuit within 6 minutes.

LESSON FOCUS (15 – 20 MINUTES)

Playground Balls

Individual Activities

A. *Controlled rolling and handling*
   1. Sit, stand, or on back—roll ball around and handle it between legs, behind back to develop a proper "feel" of the ball.

DPE pp. 368 – 372

Emphasize keeping the eyes on the ball and catching with the fingertips.

One 8 1/2" playground ball is needed for each child.

PM.—The students will be able to catch the balls on their fingertips.

MOVEMENT EXPERIENCE—CONTENT	ORGANIZATION AND TEACHING HINTS	EXPECTED STUDENT OBJECTIVES AND OUTCOMES
B. *Bounce and catch* 　1. Two hands, one hand. 　2. Bounce at different levels. 　3. Bounce between legs. 　4. Close eyes and bounce. 　5. Dribble ball in a stationary and/or moving position. 　6. Dribble and follow the commands, such as: move forward, backward, in a circle, sideways, while walking, galloping, trotting, etc. 　7. Exploratory activity.	Make sure children "give" when they catch the ball and make a soft home. Encourage children to start with a low toss in the air and gradually increase the height of the throw as skill increases. The purpose of the many variations is to force children to keep their eyes on the moving object while performing other activities with their bodies.	PM.—The student will be able to keep her eyes on the ball during all challenges and activities. PM.—The student will be able to make a toss that enables her to make a catch. Cog.—The student will be able to interpret orally the many uses of the basic ball skills introduced in this lesson.
C. *Toss and catch* 　1. Toss and catch, vary height. 　2. Add various challenges while tossing (i.e., touch floor, clap hands, turn, make body turns, sit down, lie down). 　3. Toss and let bounce. Also add some challenges as above. 　4. Toss up and catch behind back—toss from behind back and catch in front of body. 　5. Create moving challenges (i.e., toss, run five steps, catch, toss, back up five hops, and catch). 　6. Exploratory activity.	Strive for quality, good throws, and a high percentage of catches. Watch for proper challenges. Change activities rapidly. The music "Sweet Georgia Brown" may stimulate special ball-handling skills.	Aff.—Develop the attitude that mere accomplishment of a skill is not a goal of people who excel. Rather, a person must be able to master the skill many times and with consistency to be a champion.
D. *Bat the ball (as in volleyball) to self* (teach a low-controlled bat). 　1. Bat the ball—use palm, back, and side of hand. 　2. Bat the ball using different body parts. E. *Foot skills* 　1. Pick the ball up with both feet and catch. Both front and rear of body catch. 　2. From a sitting position, ball between feet, toss ball up and catch with hands. 　3. While sitting, toss ball up with hands and catch with feet. 　4. Put ball between feet or knees and play tag games. 　5. Keep ball in air by using feet, knees, head. How many times can you bounce it in succession? 　6. Exploratory activity.	Allow student choice.	Cog.—A study in England classified 2.5 million people by occupation (sedentary and nonsedentary). Findings revealed that people engaged in occupations requiring only light physical work had a higher rate of death due to coronary heart disease compared with people engaged in heavy physical work. Discuss the need for exercise to ensure cardiovascular health.
Partner Activities A. *Practice various kinds of passes* 　1. Two-handed, right, and left. 　2. Throw to various targets—high, low, right, and left. 　3. Odd throws—under leg, around body, football center, shotput, windmill, discus. Off floor.	Partner formation. Distance about 15 feet. Chest target first. Stress passing and catching skills. Seek variety.	Cog.—The student will be able to identify the sport in which various passes are used.

MOVEMENT EXPERIENCE— CONTENT	ORGANIZATION AND TEACHING HINTS	EXPECTED STUDENT OBJECTIVES AND OUTCOMES
4. Push-shot types. Straight push, arch. 5. Roll the ball to partner. Flick it in the air with foot and catch. 6. Exploratory activity. 7. Have one partner dribble and the other attempt to take it away without fouling.	Watch finger position.	PM.—The student will be able to pass (all variations) and catch the ball without dropping it, three times in a row. Cog.—"Giving" at the elbow and shoulder joint when catching a ball increases the distance over which the force is absorbed. This lessens rebound and makes catching easier.
B. *Volleyball and handball-type skills* 1. Serve. Toss and return. Overhand serve. 2. Bat back and forth like hand tennis. Bat over a line. C. *Use follow activity* One partner try something, other follows. 1. Specify number of turns; then reverse.	Use care on control. Experiment with hand positions. Stress control. Seek variety. Could set up sequences.	Aff.—Ask students to keep an activity diary for 24 hours. At the next meeting, the amounts of time involved in activity can be compared. The amount of calories expended can be evaluated.

GAME (5 – 7 MINUTES)

Teacher's choice—Good opportunity to use the playground balls in a follow-up game. The following are suggested:
1. Fox Hunt, p. 525
2. Bounce Ball, p. 530
3. One-Step, p. 531

DYNAMIC PHYSICAL EDUCATION LESSON PLAN
Throwing Skills (Lesson 2)
Level II

Supplies and Equipment Needed:
Tumbling mats for targets
Tires, hoops, or jump ropes
Cones
Yarn balls, beanbags, and beach balls
Scooters
Tom-tom or tambourine
Tennis or rug balls
Blocks or bottles

MOVEMENT EXPERIENCE— CONTENT	ORGANIZATION AND TEACHING HINTS	EXPECTED STUDENT OBJECTIVES AND OUTCOMES

INTRODUCTORY ACTIVITY (2 – 3 MINUTES)

Fastest Tag in the West

All students are it. On signal, they try to tag each other. If they are tagged, they must freeze, but they are eligible to tag other students who pass near them.

DPE p. 222

Avoid playing the game when only one or two players are left untagged. Start the game over a number of times to assure all students will have the opportunity to be active.

FITNESS DEVELOPMENT ACTIVITIES (7 – 8 MINUTES)

Walk, Trot, and Sprint

Move to the following signals:
1. One drumbeat - walk.
2. Two drumbeats - trot.
3. Three drumbeats - sprint.
4. Whistle - freeze and perform exercises.

Perform various strength and flexibility exercises between bouts of walk, trot, and sprint. Examples are:
   a. Bend and Twist
   b. Sitting Stretch
   c. Push-Ups
   d. Sit-Ups
   e. Trunk Twister
   f. Body Circles
   g. Crab Walk

Alternate walk, trot, and sprint for 30 seconds with 30 seconds for each exercise.

DPE p. 245

Use a tom-tom or tambourine.

Scatter formation.

Emphasize quality of movement and rapid changes.

Check heart rate after bouts of sprinting.

Assure that sprinting is done under control to avoid collisions.

Encourage students to change directions sharply, even to the point of pivoting at each turn.

Cog.—Static stretching involves stretching without bouncing. Stretches should be held for 15–30 seconds for maximum benefit.

Cog.—The student will be able to explain why stretching exercises and warm-ups are essential to track and field work.

PM.—The student will demonstrate the ability to put proper stress on muscles in stretching.

LESSON FOCUS (15 – 20 MINUTES)

Throwing

A. *Individual Activities*
   1. Throwing yarn balls
      a. Throw against wall
         1. Throw from a standing position 20 ft. from the wall.

DPE pp. 307 – 308

Redirect with appropriate cues:
   1. Throw hard!
   2. Take a big step, then throw!
   3. Really get your throwing arm behind your head to start the throw!

Cog.—Students will know what a mature throw looks like.

Cog.—Students will know the components of a mature throw.

Cog.—Students should begin to realize what parts of the throw result in the greatest force production.

MOVEMENT EXPERIENCE— CONTENT	ORGANIZATION AND TEACHING HINTS	EXPECTED STUDENT OBJECTIVES AND OUTCOMES

2. Throw five balls, retrieve, and repeat.
2. Throwing rag balls or tennis balls:
  a. Teach the proper grip.
  b. Throw against mats on the wall.
    1. Throw from 20 to 25 ft. depending on skill level. Student should be able to hit the wall.
	May need to set up a diagonal throwing line so that all skill levels are challenged to throw hard.	Aff.—Students will begin to value throwing hard.
		
		PM.—The students should begin every throw from a side-facing position.
		
		PM.—The student should take a big step with the contralateral foot.

B. *Station Format*
1. Activities using large targets so students will throw forcefully.
  a. Throw at mats on the wall.
    1. Throw tennis balls hard from 15 to 20 ft.
    2. Retrieve only if the balls roll behind the throwing line.
  b. Throw at hoops leaning against mats against the wall.
  c. Large target throw.
    1. A circle or square 4 ft in diameter should be placed on the wall.
    2. Students should throw from 20 to 25 ft.
	Everyone should do the stations a minimum of two days.
	
	Each student should start with five balls.
	
	The teacher should continue to give feedback to the students that will help them improve their form.
	
	Put hoops touching one another for easier targets; spread apart for more difficult target.	

C. *Advanced Station Format*
1. Intermediate-level target activities.
  a. Hoops suspended from goals.
  b. Partner holds hoop.
  c. Use large boxes for targets.
    1. Throw inside the box.
    2. Throw at the side of the box.
  d. Cageball throw. Throwers try to move it into the corner by throwing at it.
  e. Upright hoops set on floor.
  f. Graduated-size target throw. Use a large concentric circle (or square) with 4 ft, 3 ft, and 2 ft diameter circles.
	The teacher should make a special effort to encourage throwing with force and good form, rather than hitting a target.
	
	Use firm yarn balls.
	
	Washer/dryer or refrigerator boxes.
	
	Two types of targets:
	a. Cut the side out of the box so that the opening faces the student. Use beanbags.
	b. Paint targets on the side of the box and throw at the target. Use yarn balls or beanbags.
	
	Use small playground balls.
	
	Place the cageball 15 ft. from the wall, in a corner.
	
	Student should be encouraged to hit the target anywhere.
	
	Student should be encouraged to set goals as his skill increases.
		Aff.—Students should value throwing with good form more than hitting a target.
		
		Aff.—Students should feel comfortable choosing any task.

MOVEMENT EXPERIENCE— CONTENT	ORGANIZATION AND TEACHING HINTS	EXPECTED STUDENT OBJECTIVES AND OUTCOMES

GAMES (5 – 7 MINUTES)

Throwing Games

1. In the Prison—Two teams each on half of gym. 15–20 balls are placed on the center line. On the signal, each team throws the balls to the other side of the gym. The object of the game is to get all the balls into the other team's back-court area (or prison), which extends 10 ft from the wall. The teacher stops play by blowing a whistle, then counting the number of balls in the "prison."

2. Snowball—Two teams each on half of gym. Ten balls per team. Players can be hit three times. Each time they are hit they just call out the number—1, 2, or 3. After the third hit they must go to the side, count to 25, then come back in the game. Teams must stay on their half of the gym. Variation: Nerf dodgeball—Same rules but with Nerf balls.

3. Center Target Throw—The gym floor is divided into quadrants. Two teams compete, and each team has its own set of targets (blocks or bottles) set on a center line running lengthwise. Team A, on the left half of the area, has players on both sides of the center line behind restraining lines 15 to 20 ft. away from the center target line. Team B is positioned the same way on the right half of the area. Each team tries to knock all of its targets down or off the center line. The team sits down immediately when this is done.

4. Target Ball Throw—Beach balls are placed on the center line of the gym. There are two teams and each must stay on its half of the gym. Players have yarn balls. The object of the game is to roll the beach balls into the other team's court by hitting them with the yarn balls. The team that has the least number of beach balls on its side when the teacher blows the whistle is the winner.

This game should be used early in the unit because it encourages forceful throws with no emphasis on a target.

Use small balls (e.g., fleece balls) that children can grip easily, but that will not hurt if someone is hit.

Encourage overhand throws.

The teacher may need to adjust the size of the play area.

The teacher should encourage forceful throws.

Use small baseball-size sponge balls.

Restraining line should be far enough away to encourage forceful throws.

Everyone should have a ball or bean-bag.

```
_____

        Team A      Team B
_____

_____15–20'

_____

        Team A      Team B
_____
```

PM.—The student will throw with force.

Cog.—The student will understand that using good form will produce more forceful throws.

Aff.—The student can play a throwing game where no pressure is placed on hitting a target.

Aff.—The student should understand that it is okay to get hit, and get back into the game as quickly as possible.

DYNAMIC PHYSICAL EDUCATION LESSON PLAN
Jogging Skills
Level II

Supplies and Equipment Needed:
  Recreational and individual equipment as desired
  Tom-tom or tambourine

MOVEMENT EXPERIENCE— CONTENT	ORGANIZATION AND TEACHING HINTS	EXPECTED STUDENT OBJECTIVES AND OUTCOMES

INTRODUCTORY ACTIVITIES (2 – 3 MINUTES)

Group Tag

A number of players are designated to be it. On signal, they try to tag other players. If a player is tagged, that player becomes it and must try to tag another. In other words, each person who is it tags only one player. If players want to be "safe," they must hold hands in a group of three or more students.

DPE p. 518

This should be a continuous-movement tag game. Players who are it should simultaneously tag and verbalize "you're it" to avoid confusion.

FITNESS DEVELOPMENT ACTIVITIES (7 – 8 MINUTES)

Walk, Trot, and Sprint

Move to the following signals:
  1. One drumbeat - walk.
  2. Two drumbeats - trot.
  3. Three drumbeats - sprint.
  4. Whistle - freeze and perform exercises.

Perform various strength and flexibility exercises between bouts of walk, trot, and sprint. Examples are:
  a. Bend and Twist
  b. Sitting Stretch
  c. Push-Ups
  d. Sit-Ups
  e. Trunk Twister
  f. Body Circles
  g. Crab Walk

Alternate walk, trot, and sprint for 35 seconds with 35 seconds for each exercise.

DPE p. 245

Use a tom-tom or tambourine.

Scatter formation.

Emphasize quality of movement and rapid changes.

Check heart rate after bouts of sprinting.

Assure that sprinting is done under control to avoid collisions.

Encourage students to change directions sharply, even to the point of pivoting at each turn.

Cog.—The student will be able to explain why stretching exercises and warm-ups are essential to track and field work.

PM.—The student will demonstrate the ability to put proper stress on muscles in stretching.

Cog.—Flexors decrease the angle of a joint, and extensors cause the return from flexion. Identify different flexor and extensor muscle groups and the joint they affect.

LESSON FOCUS (15 – 20 MINUTES)

Jogging

A. Three types of jogging programs that can be used:
  1. *Jog-walk-jog*
     In this method, the student jogs until he feels the need to rest, walks until somewhat rested, and then jogs again.

DPE pp. 268 – 269

Teach children the proper style of running.

Start students at a short distance so they will not become discouraged.

Concentrate on teaching the values of jogging and encourage students to start their own jogging program.

PM.—The student will be able to demonstrate proper jogging style.

PM.—The student will be able to jog 220 yd nonstop.

Aff.—Jogging is one of the best activities for developing cardiovascular endurance. Discuss the value of jogging for personal health.

MOVEMENT EXPERIENCE— CONTENT	ORGANIZATION AND TEACHING HINTS	EXPECTED STUDENT OBJECTIVES AND OUTCOMES
2. *Jog a set distance* The pace is varied depending on the body's reaction to the demands. 3. *Increase the distance* The pace is maintained, but the distance is increased.		
B. Take the students through jogging practice. Have them: 1. Jog 100 steps, walk 50 steps, etc. 2. Run a specific distance without stopping. 3. Run for a specific time in a random direction. A student may run in any direction, but should try to keep running. The advantage to this approach is that students won't race as they tend to do on a track.	A good motivating technique is to jog across the state or United States. The distance each student runs could be added together for a class total. "Train, don't strain."	Cog.—The student will be able to list three chronic effects jogging has on the body.
C. Encourage students to jog at a realistic pace. A good idea is to have them jog with a friend and talk while running. They should be able to run and talk comfortably. If not, they are running too fast. D. It is sometimes motivating for youngsters if they run with a piece of equipment (i.e., beanbag or jump rope). They can play catch with a ball or roll a hoop while jogging.	"Pace, not race." Reinforce students who work on pacing. The praise will encourage students to run with pace rather than running all-out and then fading. Bring in high school track or cross-country runners to talk about their training.	Cog.—For exercise to have the most impact on the cardiovascular system, heart rate should reach the training state. This amounts to 70 to 85% of one's maximum heart rate. Maximum heart rate is 220 minus your age. Thus, if one is 10 years old, the training state will require a heart rate of 147 to 179. Compute the training rate for yourself. The student will learn to measure pulse rate and move the heart rate into the training state.

GAME

Individual or Recreational Activity

Since youngsters will finish at different times, individual equipment can be placed out so those youngsters who have completed the course and are warming down can be actively involved. Another good choice would be a recreational activity, such as Four Square, Beanbag, Horseshoes, and Sidewalk Tennis.

DYNAMIC PHYSICAL EDUCATION LESSON PLAN
Rhythmic Movement (Lesson 1)
Level II

Supplies and Equipment Needed:
- One beanbag for each child
- Exercise-to-music tape
- One jump rope for each child
- One 8 1/2" playground ball per child
- Hoops or yarn balls
- Tape player
- Music for rhythms

Dances Taught:
- The Bird Dance
- La Raspa
- Csebogar
- Teddy Bear Mixer
- Pop Goes the Weasel
- Crested Hen
- Greensleeves
- Grand March

MOVEMENT EXPERIENCE— CONTENT	ORGANIZATION AND TEACHING HINTS	EXPECTED STUDENT OBJECTIVES AND OUTCOMES

INTRODUCTORY ACTIVITIES (2 – 3 MINUTES)

Locomotor and Manipulative Activity

Each child is given a beanbag and moves around the area using various basic locomotor movements. Students toss and catch their beanbags while moving. On signal, they drop the beanbags and jump and/or hop over as many bags as possible.

DPE p. 221

Scatter formation.

Hoops or yarn balls can be used instead of beanbags.

Specify the number or color of beanbags they must move, leap over, or around.

Add many challenges while moving to both the locomotor movements and the manipulative activities.

PM.—The student will be able to toss and catch an object while moving.

Cog.—The student will recite the fact that it is easier to toss and catch an object while standing stationary than while moving.

FITNESS DEVELOPMENT ACTIVITIES (7 – 8 MINUTES)

Exercises to Music

Side Flex (switch sides)	40 seconds
Trunk Twister	25 seconds
Rhythmic Sit-Ups	35 seconds
Slide/Skip	20 seconds
Jumping Jack variations	30 seconds
Triceps Push-Ups	25 seconds
Partial Curl-Ups	45 seconds
Gallop	15 seconds
Push-Ups	25 seconds
Aerobic Bouncing and Clapping	35 seconds
Leg Extensions	40 seconds
Walking to cool down	45 seconds

DPE p. 259

Student should know the exercises before trying to do them rhythmically.

Rhythmic sit-ups are four counts - knees, toes, knees, and down.

The exercise music should be taped prior to the routine. This frees the teacher to move and help students.

Voice instructions can be dubbed onto the tape to tell students when to change to a new exercise.

Cog.—The student will recognize the names of the activities and be able to demonstrate each one.

PM.—The student will be able to perform the exercises to the beat of the music on the tape.

LESSON FOCUS (15 – 20 MINUTES)

Rhythms

When teaching a dance, use the following steps:
- a. Tell about the dance and listen to the music.
- b. Clap the beat and learn the verse.
- c. Practice the dance steps without the music and with verbal cues.
- d. Practice the dance with the music.

Make dances easy for students to learn by using some of the following ideas:
1. Teach the dances without partners.
2. Allow youngsters to move in any direction—avoid the left–right orientation.

MOVEMENT EXPERIENCE— CONTENT	ORGANIZATION AND TEACHING HINTS	EXPECTED STUDENT OBJECTIVES AND OUTCOMES
	3. Use scattered formation instead of circles—it helps avoid embarrassment. 4. Emphasize strong movements such as clapping and stomping to encourage involvement. 5. Tape the music at a slower speed when first learning the dance. Rhythms should be taught like other sport skills. Avoid expecting perfection when teaching rhythms. Teach a variety of dances rather than one or two in depth. Youngsters will enjoy rhythms if they know it is acceptable to make mistakes without being ridiculed.	
1. The Bird Dance (also called the Chicken Dance) (pp. 334 – 335)	Basic dance skills: 1. Skipping or walking 2. Elbow swing or star 3. Grand right and left 4. Click, flap, twist, and clap pattern Scattered or circle formation.	PM.—The student will participate in the dance successfully with others.
2. La Raspa (pp. 336 – 337)	A Mexican dance. Basic dance skills: 1. Bleking step 2. Elbow turn As a variation, this dance may begin with students scattered individually around the room, finding different partners for the elbow turn. Change partners each time the dance starts over.	Aff.—The student will gain some appreciation of the Mexican culture. PM.—The student will do the bleking step well enough to employ it in this dance and in other dances.
3. Csebogar (p. 335)	A Hungarian dance. Basic dance skills: 1. Skipping and sliding 2. Draw step 3. Elbow swing Single circle of partners facing center.	Aff.—The student will gain an appreciation of the Hungarian culture. PM.—The student will be able to go through the entire dance without difficulty.
4. Teddy Bear Mixer (p. 336)	An American dance. Basic dance skill: 1. Walking, with changing directions Double circle of couples facing counterclockwise.	PM.—The student will develop the proper rhythm to do this dance successfully.
5. Pop Goes the Weasel (p. 335)	An American dance. Basic dance skills: 1. Walking, skipping 2. "Popping" under This dance may be done in circles or sets of either three or four. Try the jump rope version of Pop Goes the Weasel. Ball routines may be performed to the song, with students dribbling during the verse and passing the ball during the chorus.	PM.—The student will develop enough skill to perform this dance successfully. Cog.—The student will recognize the name of this dance and be able to demonstrate the major step in the dance.

MOVEMENT EXPERIENCE— CONTENT	ORGANIZATION AND TEACHING HINTS	EXPECTED STUDENT OBJECTIVES AND OUTCOMES

6. Crested Hen (pp. 342 – 343)	A Danish dance.
	
	Basic dance skills:
	  1. Step-hop
	  2. Turning under
	Circles of three, either in one large circle or scattered in the gym. This dance may also be done in a single circle of partners.
	
	There are many variations of this dance.
		Aff.—The student will gain some appreciation of the Danish culture.
		
		Aff.—The student will recognize the importance of cooperation when performing dances.

7. Greensleeves (p. 340)	An English dance.
	
	Basic dance steps:
	  1. Walking
	  2. Star formation
	  3. Over and under (arches)
	Circle of couples.
	
	Couples are numbered one and two. Two couples form a set.
		PM.—The student will be able to go through the entire dance without difficulty.

8. Grand March (pp. 339 – 340)	An American dance.
	
	Any good marching music may be used.
	
	May want to use pinnies on the students on one-half of the gym.
	
	Various Grand March formation and terms:
	  1. "Head" and "foot" of the hall
	  2. Down the center by fours
	  3. Form arches
	  4. Couples arch
	  5. Over and under
	  6. Down the center by eights
		PM.—The student will be able to go through various formations in the Grand March without difficulty.
		
		Cog.—Failing to learn an activity is not necessarily a negative outcome. Focus on the importance of learning to make failure a positive and necessary experience in the total learning process.

GAME (5 – 7 MINUTES)

1. Whistle March, p. 531
2. Arches, p. 529
3. Home Base, p. 526

DYNAMIC PHYSICAL EDUCATION LESSON PLAN
Hockey-Related Activities (Lesson 1)
Level II

Supplies and Equipment Needed:
  Exercise tape
  One puck or whiffle ball and stick for each student
  Tumbling mats for goals
  Tape player
  Music

MOVEMENT EXPERIENCE—CONTENT	ORGANIZATION AND TEACHING HINTS	EXPECTED STUDENT OBJECTIVES AND OUTCOMES

INTRODUCTORY ACTIVITY (2 – 3 MINUTES)

Movement Varieties

Move using a basic locomotor movement. Then add some variety to the movement by asking students to respond to the following factors:
1. Level—low, high, in-between.
2. Direction—straight, zigzag, circular, curved, forward, backward, upward, downward.
3. Size—large, tiny, medium movements.
4. Patterns—forming squares, diamonds, triangles, circles, figure eights.

DPE pp. 218 – 219

Scatter formation.

Emphasize and reinforce creativity.

Change the various factors often and take time to explain the concepts the words describe if children cannot interpret them.

Cog.—The student will be able to interpret the concepts the words describe by moving the body in a corresponding manner.

PM.—The student will be able to move the body with ease throughout the range of movement varieties.

FITNESS DEVELOPMENT ACTIVITIES (7 – 8 MINUTES)

Exercises to Music

Side Flex (switch sides)	40 seconds
Trunk Twister	25 seconds
Rhythmic Sit-Ups	35 seconds
Slide/Skip	20 seconds
Jumping Jack variations	30 seconds
Triceps Push-Ups	25 seconds
Partial Curl-Ups	45 seconds
Gallop	15 seconds
Push-Ups	25 seconds
Aerobic Bouncing and Clapping	35 seconds
Leg Extensions	40 seconds
Walking to cool down	45 seconds

DPE p. 259

Students should know the exercises before trying to do them rhythmically.

Rhythmic sit-ups are four counts - knees, toes, knees, and down.

Students can lead the exercise to music routine while the instructor monitors student progress.

Voice instructions can be dubbed onto the tape to tell students when to change to a new exercise.

Cog.—The overload principle dictates that to increase strength, one must perform progressively larger work loads. Duration, frequency, and intensity can be modified to progressively overload the system. Students should be able to develop work loads that are meaningful to their fitness levels.

LESSON FOCUS (15 – 20 MINUTES)

Hockey

A. *Skills*
  1. Gripping and carrying of stick.
  2. Controlled Dribble: Ball controlled by individual. Keep the ball in front of stick while moving.

DPE pp. 607 – 616

Individual or partner work.

Use a plastic puck indoors and a whiffle ball outdoors.

Keep stick below waist level to ensure accuracy and safety.

Cog.—The student will be able to describe the meaning of the following terms: grip, carry, dribble, field, dodge, tackle, and drive.

PM.—The student will be able to perform each of the skills listed.

141

MOVEMENT EXPERIENCE— CONTENT	ORGANIZATION AND TEACHING HINTS	EXPECTED STUDENT OBJECTIVES AND OUTCOMES

3. Front Field: This is catching the puck or ball with the stick. As the ball approaches, get in line with the ball and extend the flat side of the stick forward to meet it.
4. Hit: Short pass which usually occurs from the dribble.
5. Dodging: Maintaining control of the ball while evading a tackler. Hold the ball as long as possible until one can determine which direction the tackler is going to move—then pass the puck or ball.
6. Driving: Hitting the ball or puck for distance or trying to score a goal.

B. *Drills*
1. Dribbling
   a. Each student has a stick and ball. On signal, change directions while maintaining control of the ball.
   b. Dribble and dodge imaginary tacklers or dodge around a set of cones. Partners may act as tacklers.
   c. Students in pairs–20 ft apart. One partner dribbles toward the other, goes around him or her, and returns to starting point. The first student then drives the ball to the second, who completes the same sequence.
2. Driving and Fielding
   a. Partners drive the ball back and forth to each other both from moving and stationary positions.
   b. Partners 20 ft apart—players pass the ball back and forth with emphasis on *fielding* and *immediately* hitting the ball back.

The ball is pushed with the flat side of the stick in front of the body.

Good fielding requires learning to "give" with the stick.

Practice with a partner—field in front of the body.

Do not lift the stick too high and hit through the ball. Strive for accuracy.

Pass the ball to one side of the tackler and move self around the opposite side.

The stick is raised higher (waist level) and the hands are brought together to give the player a longer level.

Scatter formation.

Stress control.

Allow students time to learn hockey skills before placing them in competitive situations. Competition before skills are learned will lower performance.

Partner formation.

Students should also practice their driving and fielding in this drill.

Passes should be fielded from all angles and sides of the body.

Call words might be "field," "set feet," and "pass."

Aff.—Safety and concern for others is important. Others can be hurt by wild swinging of the stick. Discuss the need for rules in all sports in order to protect the participants.

Cog.—The distance over which a muscle contracts determines, in part, the amount of force to be generated. Various backswings and wind-ups are performed to increase the range of motion prior to contraction. Students will understand why preliminary movements are carried out in sports activities.

PM.—The student will be able to control the ball while moving.

Cog.—Hockey is a team game and passing is a needed skill. The student will be able to describe what factors make up a good hit.

Aff.—In fine motor control skills, much practice is needed to approach a desirable level. Discuss the need for drills and repeated practice.

LEAD-UP GAMES (6 – 7 MINUTES)

These will suffice as the game activities:
1. Circle Keep-Away, p. 613
2. Star Wars Hockey, p. 613
3. Lane Hockey, p. 613
4. Circle Straddleball "Hockey Style," p. 524.

Students stand straddle style in circle. Use five or six pucks. Players inside circle attempt to hit puck through circle players' legs. Only hockey sticks may be used to stop the puck.

DYNAMIC PHYSICAL EDUCATION LESSON PLAN
Hockey-Related Activities (Lesson 2)
Level II

Supplies and Equipment Needed:
  Hockey sticks and pucks
  Tumbling mats for goals
  Cones
  Tape player
  Music

MOVEMENT EXPERIENCE—CONTENT	ORGANIZATION AND TEACHING HINTS	EXPECTED STUDENT OBJECTIVES AND OUTCOMES

INTRODUCTORY ACTIVITY (2 – 3 MINUTES)

New Leader

Squads move around the area, following the squad leader. On signal, the last person can move to the head of the squad and become the leader. Various types of locomotor movements and/or exercises should be used.

DPE p. 223

Squad formation. Encourage students to keep moving unless an exercise or similar activity is being performed.

Assign each squad a specific area if desired. Each area could include a piece of equipment to aid in the activity (beanbag, fleece ball, etc.).

Cog.—The student will be able to give two reasons why warm-up is necessary prior to strenuous exercises.

Aff.—The student will be capable of leading as well as following. Discuss the necessity of both in our society.

FITNESS DEVELOPMENT ACTIVITIES (7 – 8 MINUTES)

Astronaut Drills

Perform the following activities, stopping only to do the exercises.

Walk while doing	
Arm Circles	20 seconds
Crab Alternate-	
Leg Extension	20 seconds
Skip	15 seconds
Body Twist	25 seconds
Slide	15 seconds
Jumping Jack variations	25 seconds
Crab Walk to center	
and back	20 seconds
Sit-Ups	25 seconds
Hop to center and back	20 seconds
Push-Ups	20 seconds
Gallop	25 seconds
Bear Hugs	25 seconds
Pogo Stick Jump	20 seconds
Trot	15 seconds
Power Jumper	20 seconds

Cool down with stretching and walking or jogging for 2–3 minutes.

DPE pp. 262 – 263

Use circle or scatter formation with ample space between youngsters. If a circle formation is used, establish a "passing lane" to the outside for faster students.

Change directions occasionally to keep students spread out.

Taped intervals of music and no music can be used to signal movement and stopping to do exercises.

Emphasize quality movement over quantity. Allow students to adjust the work load pace. They should be able to move at a pace that is consistent with their fitness level.

Cog.—The student will be able to explain the need to exercise on "all fours" to increase arm and shoulder girdle strength.

PM.—The student will be able to perform the fitness activities at the beginning level.

Aff.—This routine is used by astronauts. They need to be fit, as fitness is extremely useful when unexpected demands are made on the body. Discuss some of these unexpected demands.

LESSON FOCUS (15 – 20 MINUTES)

Hockey

A. *Review skills taught in previous lesson:*
   1. Controlled dribble
   2. Front field
   3. Quick hit

DPE pp. 606 – 616

See previous hockey lesson plan for description and teaching hints.

PM.—The student will be able to perform the basic skills in hockey.

Cog.—The student will be able to recite the proper time to tackle.

MOVEMENT EXPERIENCE— CONTENT	ORGANIZATION AND TEACHING HINTS	EXPECTED STUDENT OBJECTIVES AND OUTCOMES

4. Dodging
5. Driving
 	
B. *Introduce:*
  1. Tackling—tackling is an attempt to intercept the ball from an opponent.
  2. Goalkeeping—the goalie should practice moving in front of the ball and bringing the feet together. Turn the stick sideways and stop the puck or ball.
 	
C. *Review the following drills:*
  1. Dribble around a set of cones.
  2. Students dribbling in pairs.
  3. Partner driving and fielding drill—stationary and moving.
 	
D. *Introduce:*
  1. Tackling and dribbling drill—one partner dribbles toward the other player, who attempts to make a tackle.
  2. Three-on-three drill—Many goals can be set up, and six students can work in small groups of three offensive and three defensive players.
  3. Shooting Drill—Mats are set up as goals (three or four on each end of the floor). Half of class on each half of the floor. Each team attempts to hit pucks into opponents' goals without crossing center line of gym. Use a large number of pucks.
	The proper time to tackle is when the ball is *off* the opponent's stick.
	
	Assure students that it is impossible to make a successful tackle every time.
	
	The goalie may kick the puck, stop it with any body part, or allow it to rebound off any body part.
	
	An 8-ft folding tumbling mat set on end makes an excellent goal.
	
	See previous hockey lesson plan for description of the drills reviewed.
	
	Emphasize the importance of proper timing to facilitate a "clean" tackle. Tripping with the stick is illegal and should be avoided.
	
	In the three-on-three drill, the offensive team should concentrate on passing, dribbling, and dodging, and the defense on tackling and good body position.
		Cog.—Wellness demands learning to cope with stressful situations. A study demonstrated that a 15-minute walk reduced tension more effectively than a tranquilizer. Students will understand the importance of exercise for stress reduction.
		
		PM.—The student will be able to demonstrate the proper manner of blocking a shot on goal.
		
		PM.—The student will be able to successfully participate in the three-on-three drill.
		
		Cog.—The student will be able to explain the importance of practicing and developing basic hockey skills before playing a regulation game.
		
		Aff.—Violence in sport is evident, particularly in hockey. Discuss the need for ethics in sport including self-discipline, accepting one's own and others' feelings, and the immorality of physical violence.

LEAD-UP GAMES (5 – 7 MINUTES)

These are adequate for game activities if so desired:
  1. Modified Hockey, pp. 613 – 614. This is an excellent lead-up game for regulation hockey.
  2. Lane Hockey, p. 613
	Emphasize position play rather than everyone chasing the puck.
	
	Teach the basic rules first and then play the game. As the game progresses, the more subtle rules can be introduced. In other words, don't sit the class down and discuss rules for 5–10 minutes. Play the game and introduce them as necessary.
		PM.—The student will be able to play all positions in Regulation Elementary Hockey.
		
		Cog.—The student will be able to recite the basic rules of Regulation Elementary Hockey.
		
		Aff.—Teamwork and cooperation are important for a successful game of hockey. Discuss the importance of these two elements in all team sport activities.

DYNAMIC PHYSICAL EDUCATION LESSON PLAN
Individual Rope Jumping Skills
Level II

Supplies and Equipment Needed:
Jump rope for each student
Appropriate music
Tape player
Balls
Beach balls
Tom-tom
Wands
Hoops (optional)

MOVEMENT EXPERIENCE— CONTENT	ORGANIZATION AND TEACHING HINTS	EXPECTED STUDENT OBJECTIVES AND OUTCOMES

INTRODUCTORY ACTIVITY (2 – 3 MINUTES)

Group over and Under

One half of the class is scattered. Each is in a curled position. The other half of the class leap or jump over the down children. On signal, reverse the group quickly. In place of a curl, the down children can bridge and the others go under. The down children can also alternate between curl and bridge as well as move around the area while in a bridged position.

DPE p. 222

Scatter formation.

Encourage the students to go over or under a specified number of classmates.

Vary the down challenges (i.e., bridge using two body parts, curl face down or on your side).

PM.—The student will be able to perform the activities of bridge, curl, leap, jump, and hop at a teacher-acceptable level.

Cog.—Warm-up loosens the muscles, tendons, and ligaments, decreasing the risk of injury. It also increases the flow of blood to the heart muscle.

FITNESS DEVELOPMENT ACTIVITIES (7 – 8 MINUTES)

Astronaut Drills

Perform the following activities, stopping only to do the exercises.

Walk while doing
Arm Circles	20 seconds
Crab Alternate- Leg Extension	25 seconds
Skip	20 seconds
Body Twist	30 seconds
Slide	20 seconds
Jumping Jack variations	30 seconds
Crab Walk to center and back	25 seconds
Sit-Ups	30 seconds
Hop to center and back	25 seconds
Push-Ups	25 seconds
Gallop	30 seconds
Bear Hugs	30 seconds
Pogo Stick Jump	25 seconds
Trot	20 seconds
Power Jumper	25 seconds

Cool down with stretching and walking or jogging for 1–2 minutes.

DPE pp. 262 – 263

Use circle or scatter formation with ample space between youngsters. If a circle formation is used, establish a "passing lane" to the outside for faster students.

Change directions occasionally to keep students spread out.

Taped intervals of music and no music can be used to signal movement and stopping to do exercises.

Emphasize quality movement over quantity. Allow students to adjust the work load pace. They should be able to move at a pace that is consistent with their fitness level.

Cog.—The training effect occurs when the heart rate is elevated above 150–160 beats per minute. To achieve this level, we keep moving without much rest.

Aff.—Very little resting time occurs in Astronaut Drills. When one exercises for a long period of time without rest, muscular and cardiovascular endurance is developed.

MOVEMENT EXPERIENCE— CONTENT	ORGANIZATION AND TEACHING HINTS	EXPECTED STUDENT OBJECTIVES AND OUTCOMES

LESSON FOCUS (15 – 20 MINUTES)

Individual Rope Jumping

1. As a lead-up activity for individual rope jumping, it might be useful to try some of the following activities:
   a. Clap hands to a tom-tom beat.
   b. Jump in place to a beat without rope.
   c. Hold both ends of the jump rope in one hand and turn it to the side so a steady rhythm can be made through a consistent turn. Just before the rope hits the ground, the student should practice jumping.
   d. Start jumping the rope one turn at a time—gradually increase the number of turns.
2. Introduce the two basic jumps:
   a. Slow time
   b. Fast time
3. Introduce some of the basic step variations:
   a. Alternate foot basic step
   b. Swing step forward
   c. Swing step sideways
   d. Rocker step
   e. Spread legs, forward and backward
   f. Toe touch, forward and backward
   g. Shuffle step
   h. Cross arms, forward and backward
   i. Double jump
4. Teach how to go from rope turning forward to rope turning backward without stopping the rope.
5. Using an individual rope with one partner holding each end: Each partner turns, partners take turns jumping in while turning.
6. One partner holds and turns rope. Second partner jumps with partner.

DPE pp. 404 – 410

Children get tired easily when learning to jump. It might be wise to split the lesson focus and use a less strenuous activity such as wands or hoops.

After introducing the basic skills, play some music that has a good strong beat. (Turn it up so it is easy for children to hear.)

Give the children plenty of room so they don't hit someone with their rope.

For slow time: Slow rope, slow feet with a rebound.

For fast time: Fast rope, fast feet. Jump the rope every turn.

Allow students to progress at their own rate. It is good to show the better jumpers some of the more difficult variations and allow them to practice by themselves.

All of the variations can be done with the turning in a forward or backward direction.

PM.—Youngsters will be able to jump rope to slow and fast time rhythm for 30 to 60 seconds.

Cog.—High-density lipoproteins (HDL) can slow the deposit of fat on arteries. The ratio of HDL to low-density lipoproteins (LDL) can be enhanced through exercise. Aerobic activity performed 30–45 minutes four times a week increases HDL levels in 7 to 10 weeks.

Aff.—Stress can be detrimental to a person's health. Discuss various situations that create stress among students. Discuss ways of coping with the stress.

Cog.—Some doctors estimate that young people eat 150–200 pounds of sugar per year. Sugar offers "empty calories"—calories, but no nutritional value. Eating too much sugar releases insulin to handle the extra sugar and soon depresses the blood sugar level to make you feel sluggish. Discuss the importance of reducing raw sugar intake.

GAME (5 – 7 MINUTES)

Play a less active game. The following are suggested:
1. Follow Me, p. 527
2. Trades, p. 535
3. Beach ball Bat Ball, p. 525

DYNAMIC PHYSICAL EDUCATION LESSON PLAN
Stunts and Tumbling Skills (Lesson 1)
Level II

Supplies and Equipment Needed:
  Tumbling mats
  Jump ropes
  Tape player
  Music
  Playground ball

MOVEMENT EXPERIENCE—CONTENT	ORGANIZATION AND TEACHING HINTS	EXPECTED STUDENT OBJECTIVES AND OUTCOMES

INTRODUCTORY ACTIVITY (2 – 3 MINUTES)

Low Organization Games

Play a game such as:
  1. Addition Tag, p. 532
  2. Squad Tag, p. 535
  3. Couple Tag, p. 526

Students should know the game so that immediate activity occurs.

Make sure the games are active enough so *all* students are warmed up simultaneously.

Bridge Tag is played like Frozen Tag except that when student is tagged, he must assume a bridged position.

PM.—The student will be active in the games to ensure physiological warm-up.

FITNESS DEVELOPMENT ACTIVITY (7 – 8 MINUTES)

Continuity Drills

Students alternate jump rope activity with exercises done in two-count fashion. Exercises are done with the teacher saying "Ready"; the class answers "One-two" and performs a repetition of the exercise. Teachers or students can lead.

Rope Jumping - Forward	20 seconds
Double Crab Kick	30 seconds
Rope Jumping - Backward	20 seconds
Partial Bent-Knee Sit-Up	45 seconds
Jump and Slowly Turn Body	20 seconds
Push-Ups	45 seconds
Rocker Step	20 seconds
Sit and Twist	30 seconds
Swing-Step Forward	20 seconds
Side Flex	30 seconds
Free Jumping	30 seconds
Sit and Stretch	45 seconds

DPE p. 262

Use scatter formation.

Taped intervals of music and no music can be used to signal rope jumping (with music) and performing exercises (without music).

A number of enjoyable chants can be used (e.g., "Physical Education" followed by a two-count response and repetition "is fun!").

Allow students to adjust the work load to their fitness level. This implies resting if the rope jumping is too strenuous.

PM.—The student will be able to perform all activities at the increased load level.

Cog.—The student will be able to verbalize in her own words the fact that regular exercise strengthens muscles and helps prevent joint and muscle injury.

LESSON FOCUS (15 – 20 MINUTES)

Stunts and Tumbling

Six groups of activities are found in this lesson to insure that youngsters receive a variety of experiences. Pick a few activities from each group and teach them alternately. For example, teach one or two tumbling and inverted balances, then one or two balance stunts, followed by individual stunts, etc. Do not place excessive time on one group of activities at the expense of another.

  1. Animal Movements
     a. Cricket Walk
     b. Frog Jump

DPE pp. 463 – 481

MOVEMENT EXPERIENCE— CONTENT	ORGANIZATION AND TEACHING HINTS	EXPECTED STUDENT OBJECTIVES AND OUTCOMES

c. Seal Crawl
 d. Reverse Seal Crawl
 2. Tumbling and Inverted Balances
   a. Forward Roll to a Walkout
   b. Backward Roll (Inclined)
   c. Backward Roll
   d. Headstand
   e. Climb Up
 3. Balance Stunts
   a. One-Leg Balance Reverse
   b. Tummy Balance
   c. Leg Dip
 4. Individual Stunts
   a. Reach Under
   b. Stiff Person Bend
   c. Coffee Grinder
   d. Scooter
   e. Hip Walk
   f. Long Bridge
 5. Partner and Group Stunts
   a. Partner Hopping
   b. Partner Twisting
   c. Partner Pull-Up
   d. Chinese Get-Up
 6. Partner Support Stunts
   a. Double Bear
   b. Table
	Scatter as many tumbling mats as possible throughout the area in order to avoid waiting lines.
	
	 Do not perform many repetitions of tumbling and inverted balances. For most children, limiting the number of forward or backward roll repetitions to four or five will prevent fatigue and injury.
	
	 There is usually a wide range of ability among youngsters in this lesson. If necessary, start at a lower level than listed here to assure students find success.
	
	 A major concern for safety is the neck and back region. Overweight children are at greater risk and might be allowed to avoid tumbling and inverted balances.
	
	 Teach youngsters to stand on the hips and shoulders when doing partner-support stunts.
		PM.—The student will be able to perform a forward and a backward roll.
		
		 PM.—The student will be able to perform the basic headstand.
		
		 PM.—The student will be able to balance her body in the balance stunts and manage it easily in the individual stunts.
		
		 Cog.—The student will be able to state the key points necessary to spot the headstand.
		
		 Aff.—Tumbling is an excellent activity as it teaches children to control their bodies in various situations. Discuss the courage and perseverance gymnasts must have to meet success.
		
		 Cog.—Wellness refers to taking care of one's self for better health. It places the responsibility for good health on the individual rather than a doctor. Discuss various facets of wellness and making responsible decisions for better health.
		
		 Cog.—The student will be able to recite the stress points necessary to know in performing the forward and backward rolls.
		
		 Cog.—Stability and balance can be increased by (1) keeping the body weight over the base of support, (2) increasing the size of the base of support, and (3) lowering the center of gravity. Identify this process being performed in the stunts and tumbling exercises.
		
		 Aff.—Combatives are a good example of "one-on-one" competition. Discuss the need for self-control and good sportsmanship.

GAME (5 – 7 MINUTES)

1. Whistle Mixer, p. 536
2. Competitive Circle Contests, p. 531
3. Alaska Baseball, p. 532

DYNAMIC PHYSICAL EDUCATION LESSON PLAN
Rhythmic Movement (Lesson 2)
Level II

Supplies and Equipment Needed:
  Tape player
  Jump ropes
  Music for rhythms

Dances Taught:
  Wild Turkey Mixer
  Bingo
  Oh Susanna
  Patty Cake Polka
  Polly Wolly Doodle
  Ve David
  Troika
  Jingle Bells (Var. 2)

MOVEMENT EXPERIENCE— CONTENT	ORGANIZATION AND TEACHING HINTS	EXPECTED STUDENT OBJECTIVES AND OUTCOMES

INTRODUCTORY ACTIVITY (2 – 3 MINUTES)

Following Activity

One partner leads and performs various kinds of movements. The other partner follows and performs the same movements. This can also be used with squad organization with the squad following a leader.

DPE p. 222

The leaders should be changed often. Use a whistle to signal the change of roles.

Partner or squad formation.

Encourage good reproduction of the leader's movements.

PM.—Be able to follow and accurately reproduce the movements of the leader.

Aff.—People must be able to lead as well as follow at times. Briefly discuss the need for cooperation between people.

FITNESS DEVELOPMENT ACTIVITY (7 – 8 MINUTES)

Continuity Drills

Students alternate jump rope activity with exercises done in two-count fashion. Exercises are done with the teacher saying "Ready"; the class answers "One-two" and performs a repetition of the exercise. Teachers or students can lead.

Rope Jumping - Forward	25 seconds
Double Crab Kick	30 seconds
Rope Jumping - Backward	25 seconds
Partial Bent-Knee Sit-Up	45 seconds
Jump and Slowly Turn Body	25 seconds
Push-Ups	45 seconds
Rocker Step	25 seconds
Sit and Twist	30 seconds
Swing-Step Forward	25 seconds
Side Flex	30 seconds
Free Jumping	35 seconds
Sit and Stretch	45 seconds

DPE p. 262

Use scatter formation.

Taped intervals of music and no music can be used to signal rope jumping (with music) and performing exercises (without music).

A number of enjoyable chants can be used (e.g., "Physical Education" followed by a two-count response and repetition "is fun").

Allow students to adjust the work load to their fitness level. This implies resting if the rope jumping is too strenuous.

Cog.—Continuity Drills are a balanced routine that exercises all parts of the body. For the conditioning effect to take place, the pulse rate should be elevated above 150 beats per minute for 5 minutes. Use a stop watch and have students check their pulse rate.

Cog.—A study showed that regular cigarette smoking reduced average life spans by 7 years. Discuss how smoking is not a responsible choice on the pathway to wellness.

MOVEMENT EXPERIENCE— CONTENT	ORGANIZATION AND TEACHING HINTS	EXPECTED STUDENT OBJECTIVES AND OUTCOMES

LESSON FOCUS (15 – 20 MINUTES)

Rhythms

Usually begin each lesson with a dance the children know and enjoy. Then brush up on (review) dances from the unit as needed before going on.

When teaching a dance, use the following steps:
1. Tell about the dance and listen to the music.
2. Clap the beat and learn the verse.
3. Practice the dance steps without the music and with verbal cues.
4. Practice the dance with the music.

1. Listen to the music, clapping the rhythms and pointing out where changes occur.
2. Teach the basic skills used in the dance.

Make dances easy for students to learn by using some of the following ideas:
1. Teach the dances without partners.
2. Allow youngsters to move in any direction—avoid the left-right orientation.
3. Use scattered formation instead of circles—it helps avoid embarrassment.
4. Emphasize strong movements such as clapping and stomping to encourage involvement.
5. Tape the music at a slower speed when first learning the dance.

Rhythms should be taught like other sport skills. Avoid expecting perfection when teaching rhythms. Teach a variety of dances rather than one or two in depth. Youngsters will enjoy rhythms if they know it is acceptable to make mistakes without being ridiculed.

1. Wild Turkey Mixer (p. 336)

An American dance.

Basic dance skills:
1. Walking
2. Elbow swing
In lines of three facing CCW.

The center person is the "Wild Turkey."

As a mixer, the "Wild Turkey" moves forward to join the next group.

Aff.—The student will be courteous when accepting a new partner.

2. Bingo (pp. 338 – 339)

An American dance.

Basic dance skills:
1. Walking
2. Grand right and left
This dance may be performed using a parachute.

Cog.—The student will learn what a right-and-left grand is.

MOVEMENT EXPERIENCE—CONTENT	ORGANIZATION AND TEACHING HINTS	EXPECTED STUDENT OBJECTIVES AND OUTCOMES
3. Oh Susanna (p. 342)	An American dance. Basic dance skills: 1. Walking 2. Right-and-left grand 3. Skater's position (while walking) Any two students may be partners. Boy–girl partners are not necessary. Students may be identified as "pinnie" and "nonpinnie." Students continue the right-and-left grand until they reach the seventh person, who then becomes their new partner.	Cog.—Students will learn the right-and-left grand, and will be able to state it in their own words. PM.—The student will learn the right-and-left grand for this dance, and be able to apply the learning to other dances.
4. Patty Cake Polka (Heel and Toe Polka) (p. 337)	This is an international dance. Basic dance skills: 1. Heel and toe step 2. Slide 3. Elbow swing Double circle, partners facing, boy in inner circle with back to the center. Boy begins with the left foot free, girl with the right foot free. Practice the partner change until the class is able to perform it smoothly before adding the music.	PM.—The students will learn the heel and toe step and be able to transfer the step to other dances. PM.—The student will participate in the dance successfully with others. Aff.—The student will accept a new partner graciously.
5. Polly Wolly Doodle (pp. 337–338)	An American dance. Basic dance skills: 1. Slide 2. Turn solo 3. Walk 4. Swing 5. "Polly" stamp Double circle of dancers, partners facing, boys with back to center of circle. This dance involves a change of partners. It may be helpful to teach the dance without the partner change, practice it with the music, and then add the partner change as a progression.	PM.—The student will be able to perform the "Polly" stamp in time to the music.
6. Ve David (pp. 341–342)	An Israeli dance. Basic dance skills: 1. Walk 2. Pivot 3. Buzz-step turn Circle of couples facing counterclockwise.	Aff.—The student will gain some appreciation for the culture of Israel. PM.—The student will be able to successfully perform the "buzz" step.

MOVEMENT EXPERIENCE—CONTENT	ORGANIZATION AND TEACHING HINTS	EXPECTED STUDENT OBJECTIVES AND OUTCOMES
7. Troika (p. 343)	A Russian dance. Basic dance skills: 1. Running step 2. Turning under Trios in lines, facing counterclockwise. This dance may also be done with the groups of threes scattered in the gym. As a mixer, the center dancer releases joined hands and moves to a new pair to begin the dance again.	Aff.—The student will gain an appreciation of the Russian culture. PM.—The student will have sufficient endurance to perform this dance without becoming fatigued.
8. Jingle Bells (var. 2) (pp. 340 – 341)	Basic dance skills: 1. Skipping 2. Skater's position 3. Sliding 4. Elbow swing Circle of partners facing CCW. Begin with slow tempo and gradually increase to normal tempo.	PM.—The student will be able to go through the entire dance without difficulty.

GAME (5 – 7 MINUTES)

1. Fox Hunt, p. 525
2. Steal the Treasure, p. 529
3. Addition Tag, p. 532

DYNAMIC PHYSICAL EDUCATION LESSON PLAN
Fundamental Skills Using Benches
Level II

Supplies and Equipment Needed:
Balance-beam benches
Tumbling mats
Cageball
Cones

MOVEMENT EXPERIENCE— CONTENT	ORGANIZATION AND TEACHING HINTS	EXPECTED STUDENT OBJECTIVES AND OUTCOMES

INTRODUCTORY ACTIVITY (2 – 3 MINUTES)

Leapfrog

Two, three, or four children are used for this group activity. They form a straight or curved line, with all except the last child in line taking the low leapfrog position. The last child moves or leaps over the other children in turn and, after going over the last child, gets down in position so that the others can leap him or her. Variations:

1. Increase the distance between the youngsters in the leapfrog position.
2. Add some locomotor movements or stunts that the youngster on the move must perform between leaps over each child.

DPE p. 223

Lines should curve to avoid running into other jumpers.

Stress good form on the jump.

Encourage, but don't force, youngsters to try the jump. If they are reticent, allow them to be in the down position and run around each student when it is their turn to jump.

PM.—The student will be able to crouch jump over the students in the down position.

Cog.—The student will be able to identify the elements necessary to land softly after jumping over another student.

Cog.—Reciprocal innervation is a dual set of messages to the muscles which tells one set to contract and the opposing set to relax. Discuss the importance of this process for efficient movement.

FITNESS DEVELOPMENT ACTIVITY (7 – 8 MINUTES)

Aerobic Fitness and Partner Resistance Exercises

Bounce and Clap	25 seconds
Arm Curl-Up	45 seconds
Jumping Jack variations	25 seconds
Camelback	45 seconds
Lunge variations	25 seconds
Fist Pull Apart	45 seconds
Directional Runs	25 seconds
Scissors	45 seconds
Rhythmic Running	25 seconds
Butterfly	45 seconds
Bounce with Body Twist	25 seconds
Resistance Push-Up	45 seconds
Bounce with Kick variations	25 seconds
Knee Bender	45 seconds

Walk, stretch, and relax for a minute or two.

DPE pp. 263 – 266 lists aerobic fitness activities.

DPE pp. 256 – 258 describes partner resistance exercises.

During the time allowed for partner resistance exercises, both students should have the opportunity to exercise.

Exercises should be done through the full range of motion.

Youngsters should take 6–10 seconds to move through the full range of motion while their partner applies resistance.

PM.—The student will be able to perform the grass drill continuously for 60–90 seconds.

Cog.—The grass drill is primarily an endurance activity and thus it is necessary to perform partner resistance exercises to develop strength.

Aff.—Grass drills are an old football drill. Discuss the value of this activity in developing endurance and quickness.

PM.—The student will be able to perform all the exercises.

Cog.—The student will be able to recite the fact that resistance should be offered throughout the full range of motion for maximum benefit.

MOVEMENT EXPERIENCE— CONTENT	ORGANIZATION AND TEACHING HINTS	EXPECTED STUDENT OBJECTIVES AND OUTCOMES

LESSON FOCUS (15 – 20 MINUTES)

Benches

1. Animal walks on bench.
   a. Seal Crawl.
   b. Cat Walk.
   c. Lame Dog Walk.
   d. Rabbit Jump.
2. Locomotor movements.
   a. Skip on the bench.
   b. Gallop on the bench.
   c. Step on and off the bench.
   d. Jump on and off the bench.
   e. Hop on and off the bench.
   f. Jump or hop over the bench.
   g. Jump on and off the bench. (Jump down with legs in a straddle position.)
3. Pulls—pull body along the bench in various positions.
   a. Prone position—head first, feet first.
   b. Supine position—head first, feet first.
   c. Side position—head first, feet first.
4. Pushes—same as above activity except push with the arms in all positions.
5. Movements alongside the benches—proceed alongside the bench in the following positions.
   a. Prone position—hands on bench.
   b. Supine position—hands on bench.
   c. Turn over—proceed along bench changing from prone to supine positions with hands on bench.
   d. All of the above positions performed with the feet on the bench.
6. Scooter movements—sit on bench and proceed along bench without using hands.
   a. Regular scooter—feet leading.
   b. Reverse scooter—legs trailing.
   c. Seat walk—walk on the buttocks.
7. Crouch jumps.
   a. Straddle jump.
   b. Regular jump.
   c. One hand, two feet.
   d. One hand, one foot.

DPE pp. 425 – 427

Six benches, one group behind each bench.

Place a mat at end of bench for dismounts.

Use a dismount at the end of each activity. See items 8 and 9 for suggestions.

Have the next person in line begin when the person in front of him is halfway across the bench.

Have the youngsters perform a return activity on the way back to their line. Place return activity signs on cones to stimulate and signal movements.

Speed is not the goal. Move deliberately across the bench.

Keep the limbs on the floor as far away as possible from the bench to achieve maximum developmental effect.

Allow students time to develop their own routines on the benches including dismounts and return activities.

PM.—The student will be able to perform all the animal walks across the bench.

PM.—The student will be able to perform the locomotor movements across the bench.

Cog.—The student will be able to identify which bench activities develop arm and shoulder girdle strength.

Cog.—The student will be able to describe why quality of movement is necessary on the benches to ensure beneficial results.

Cog.—Increased fat causes the heart to have to work harder. The resting pulse rate of an obese person is often 10 beats per minute faster than a normal-weight individual. This amounts to approximately 14,000 extra beats per day due to excessive fat.

Aff.—Satisfaction is increased from attaining goals that are realistic. Discuss the importance of setting goals based upon individual characteristics and abilities.

MOVEMENT EXPERIENCE—CONTENT	ORGANIZATION AND TEACHING HINTS	EXPECTED STUDENT OBJECTIVES AND OUTCOMES

8. Jump dismounts.
   a. Single jump—forward or backward.
   b. Jump with turns—1/2, 3/4, or full.
   c. Pike.
   d. Straddle.
   e. Heel or knee slap.
9. Jump followed by a stunt.
   a. Jump, forward roll.
   b. Back jump, back roll.
   c. Side jump, side roll.
   d. Shoulder roll.
   e. Cartwheel.
	Use the dismounts to add variety to each of the previous activities. Proper dismounting should be encouraged and can be associated with gymnastic routines.	Cog.—Flexing at the ankles, knees, and hips is important when landing after a dismount. This increases the time over which the force is absorbed. Students should understand the importance of absorbing force for a stable landing and minimizing the risk of injury.

GAME (5 – 7 MINUTES)

1. Cageball Kick-Over, p. 533
2. Squad Tag, p. 535

DYNAMIC PHYSICAL EDUCATION LESSON PLAN
Basketball-Related Activities (Lesson 1)
Level II

Supplies and Equipment Needed:
  One junior basketball or playground ball per student
  Hoops or chalk to make circles for Captain Ball
  Hoops or individual mats

MOVEMENT EXPERIENCE—CONTENT	ORGANIZATION AND TEACHING HINTS	EXPECTED STUDENT OBJECTIVES AND OUTCOMES

INTRODUCTORY ACTIVITY (2 – 3 MINUTES)

Bridges by Three

Children work in groups of three, with two of the children making bridges and the third moving under them. As soon as the third person has moved under the others, she makes a bridge. Each child in turn goes under the bridge of the other two students.

DPE p. 223

Groups of three.

Different challenges can be tried by specifying different types of bridges, having the moving child perform different movements and tasks, or increasing the distance between bridges.

PM.—The student will be able to make at least five different bridges.

Cog.—The student will identify the isometric exercises (bridging) as well as the isotonic exercises (moving).

FITNESS DEVELOPMENT ACTIVITY (7 – 8 MINUTES)

Aerobic Fitness and Partner Resistance Exercises

Bounce and Clap	30 seconds
Arm Curl-Up	45 seconds
Jumping Jack variations	30 seconds
Camelback	45 seconds
Lunge variations	30 seconds
Fist Pull Apart	45 seconds
Directional Runs	30 seconds
Scissors	45 seconds
Rhythmic Running	30 seconds
Butterfly	45 seconds
Bounce with Body Twist	30 seconds
Resistance Push-Up	45 seconds
Bounce with Kick variations	30 seconds
Knee Bender	45 seconds

Walk, stretch, and relax for a minute or two.

DPE pp. 263 – 266 lists aerobic fitness activities.

DPE pp. 256 – 258 describes partner resistance exercises.

During the time allowed for partner resistance exercises, both students should have the opportunity to exercise.

Exercises should be done through the full range of motion.

Youngsters should take 6–10 seconds to move through the full range of motion while their partner applies resistance.

PM.—The student will be able to perform the grass drill continuously for 75–105 seconds.

Cog.—Sweating occurs when the body is overheated due to stress in an attempt to maintain a constant body temperature. The student will be able to explain why the body sweats.

Cog.—The student will be able to explain that maximum effort must be exerted if the exercise is going to be of any value.

PM.—The student will be able to demonstrate one new partner resistance exercise to the class.

LESSON FOCUS (15 – 20 MINUTES)

Basketball

A. *Chest (Push) Pass* (two-handed)
  1. Ball at chest level, face partner.
  2. Fingers spread above center of ball.
  3. Step toward partner and extend arms.
  4. Throw to chest level.
  5. Catching.
  6. Thumbs together for high pass.
  7. Little fingers together for low pass.
  8. Hands relaxed, provide a little "give."

DPE pp. 569 – 591

Organize by partners.

Explain that this is one of the basic passes and must be mastered.

Get the "push" first, then later stress the finger action.

Encourage the students to throw at different levels in order to challenge their catching skills as well as throwing accuracy.

Bounce the ball just beyond the halfway mark.

PM.—The student will be able to perform the following skills adequately:
  1. Push, baseball, underhand, and one-hand passes
  2. Dribbling—right and left hands while moving
  3. Shooting—one-handed shot
  4. Catching—high and low passes

MOVEMENT EXPERIENCE—CONTENT	ORGANIZATION AND TEACHING HINTS	EXPECTED STUDENT OBJECTIVES AND OUTCOMES

9. Practice on the fly.
10. Add the bounce pass—same technique.
11. Avoid forward spin.
		Cog.—The student will be able to recite the basic rules of basketball in the following areas:
		  1. Dribbling
		  2. Traveling
		  3. Out of bounds
		  4. Jump ball

B. *Basketball (One Hand) Pass*
  1. Side toward catcher.
  2. Ball back with both hands to side of head or above shoulder. Fingers spread, one hand directly behind the ball.
  3. Release the forward hand and throw with a wrist snap.
  4. Practice both right and left.
	Try "Keep-away" drills in groups of three using basketball passes and dribbling.
	
	Avoid the "hip pocket" wind-up.	

C. *Underhand Pass* (two-handed)
  1. Use both hands.
  2. Side toward catcher, arms almost fully extended with the ball between the hands, fingers spread, and little fingers fairly close.
  3. Step with the forward foot and deliver the ball. Practice both right and left.
  4. Mix up the passes in the practice session.
	This is a personal choice.
	
	Step is short.
		Cog.—A spinning object will rebound from the floor in the direction of its spin. Discuss how spin can be applied to a basketball (by applying force off-center) and be used to advantage.

D. *Birdie in the Cage* (p. 584)
  1. Form circles of 7 or 8 children.
  2. Pass ball among the circle for practice. Be sure everyone handles the ball.
  3. Select "Birdie," put in center. Must stay in center until he touches the ball, or there is a loose ball leaving the circle.
	Encourage short quick passes. Try not to "telegraph" the pass by looking at the target.
	
	Let children call the fault.
		PM.—The student will be able to play Birdie in the Cage successfully both as a passer and as "Birdie."
		
		Cog.—Ligaments are inelastic and do not contract. Joint injuries usually damage ligaments. When ligaments are stretched, they do not grow back to their regular length. Discuss the need for surgery to repair ligament damage.

E. *Dribbling* (each has a ball)
  1. Explain rules: traveling, double dribbles.
  2. Explain technique: wrist action, finger control, eyes ahead.
  3. Dribble in different directions. Use right and left in turn.
  4. Use whistle dribble. Stop on whistle.
  5. Dribble under leg, or around back.
  6. Dribble with eyes closed (in place).
	Watch for collisions. Loose balls—stop the ball or just return it.	Cog.—Many backaches occur from weak abdominal muscles. This occurs due to the strength of psoas tilting the pelvis forward and creating excessive back arch. Discuss how back muscles are developed by walking and running, whereas the abdominal muscles must be strengthened using curl-ups, rowing, and partial curl-ups.

F. *Shuttle Dribbling* (two sets of partners):
 	
  X X   X X
  3 1   2 4
 	
  1. Use right and left. Have a race.
	1 dribbles to 2, who returns the ball by dribbling to 3, who dribbles to 4, and so on back to 1. This can also be done with three players.	Aff.—Basketball is a team sport demanding contribution from all members of the team. Discuss the importance of using all players without prejudice when developing plays and strategy.

MOVEMENT EXPERIENCE—CONTENT	ORGANIZATION AND TEACHING HINTS	EXPECTED STUDENT OBJECTIVES AND OUTCOMES

G. *One-Handed Passing* (by partners)
  1. Left hand in front, right hand in back.
  2. Push to partner with one hand.
  3. Raise the ball in an arc.
	Start passing with partners 10–15 ft apart and gradually increase the distance.	Cog.—The student will be able to explain the rules of Captain Ball.
		
		PM.—The student will be able to play all positions in Captain Ball.

H. *One-Handed Shot*
  1. Raise ball up to eye level, sight and shoot (demonstrate).
  2. Shoot from close position around the basket with partners alternating.
  3. Add a short dribble and a shot.
	If too many balls, alternate with dribbling or reduce the number of balls.
	
	Each can take two shots.
	
	This is preliminary to lay-up practice later.
		Cog.—Skill can be improved with practice. However, readiness will determine when the fastest improvement will occur. This indicates that students will develop their skills at different times, regardless of chronological age. Discuss the need to understand individual growth patterns.

I. *Dribblerama* (p. 584)

J. *Play Captain Ball* (p. 584)
  1. Lay out the court(s).
  2. Select teams (seven on a side).
  3. Put one team in place and show scoring.
  4. Put second team in and practice scoring:
    a. One point from forward to captain.
    b. Two points for circuit and then captain.
  5. Explain center jump, free throw, fouling the captain scores a point.
  6. Show how to get the ball in to the forwards.

```
        O       O
 ───────────────────────
   X       X       X
```

  7. Play and then rotate the other teams or the substitutes.

K. *Play Basketball Tag* (p. 583)
Play without defenders so students can concentrate on passing.

GAME (5 – 7 MINUTES)

These are included in the lesson focus above.

DYNAMIC PHYSICAL EDUCATION LESSON PLAN
Basketball-Related Activities (Lesson 2)
Level II

Supplies and Equipment Needed:
  One basketball or playground ball per student
  Apparatus for the Challenge Course
  Hoops or individual mats
  Balance-beam bench
  Jumping box

MOVEMENT EXPERIENCE—CONTENT	ORGANIZATION AND TEACHING HINTS	EXPECTED STUDENT OBJECTIVES AND OUTCOMES

INTRODUCTORY ACTIVITY (2 – 3 MINUTES)

Jumping and Hopping Patterns

Many combinations can be devised with the basic idea being to work combinations so one returns to home place. An example is: Jump in all directions and hop back to place; or three jumps forward and a half twist, three jumps back to place and a half twist.

DPE p. 220

Students should devise their own combinations of movement.

Pick out a few students and have them demonstrate their ideas to the rest of the class.

PM.—The student will be able to create and perform five different movement combinations utilizing jumping and hopping.

FITNESS DEVELOPMENT ACTIVITY (7 – 8 MINUTES)

Challenge Course Fitness

Design a course around the perimeter of the area using the following ideas:
1. Step on jumping box, dismount to tumbling mat, and do a forward roll.
2. Run and weave through four wands held upright by cones.
3. Handwalk across a horizontal ladder or do a flexed-arm hang from a climbing rope for 5 seconds.
4. Step on and off three jumping boxes (small-large-small).
5. Agility run through hoops.
6. Perform jump turns.
7. Leap over a magic rope held taut with two chairs or jumping boxes.
8. Hop on one foot.
9. Do a Log Roll across a tumbling mat.
10. Alternate going over and under six obstacles (cones and wands or hoops).
11. Crouch jump or scooter movements the length of a balance-beam bench.
12. Slide through a parallel tumbling mat maze (mats stood on their sides).

DPE p. 263

Design a Challenge Course that exercises all body parts.

Emphasize moving through the Challenge Course with quality movements. The goal is fitness, not how fast youngsters can move through the course.

Distribute youngsters throughout the course rather than lining them up to start at one point. Faster moving youngsters can pass a station one time only.

Stop the class at regular intervals to perform flexibility and strength development activities for the shoulder girdle and abdominal region.

Change directions periodically. This will help prevent a build-up of students at slower moving stations.

Cog.—The student will be able to design a Challenge Course that exercises all parts of the body.

PM.—The student will be able to accomplish all the challenges successfully.

Aff.—Many different methods for developing and maintaining physical fitness are used in this curriculum. Discuss the importance of people analyzing their likes and dislikes as they find an approach to fitness that best suits them.

MOVEMENT EXPERIENCE— CONTENT	ORGANIZATION AND TEACHING HINTS	EXPECTED STUDENT OBJECTIVES AND OUTCOMES

LESSON FOCUS (15 – 20 MINUTES)

Basketball

1. Review and use different drills to practice prior skills. Skills that should be reviewed are:
   a. Chest pass
   b. One-handed and under-handed passes
   c. Dribbling
   d. One-hand set shot
   Use some different drills such as figure-eight drill, file dribbling drill, dribble and pass drill, and set-shot formations.
2. Introduce the lay-up shot. Use the lay-up drill to practice. Practice without a ball so that children can practice taking off on the correct foot and using the proper number of steps.
3. Introduce guarding. Emphasis should be placed on the following points:
   a. Slide feet, don't cross them.
   b. Keep one or both hands up.
   c. Stay loose, not flat-footed.
4. Integrate the following lead-up games into each day's lesson focus:
   a. Captain Ball, p. 584
   b. Five Passes, p. 586
   c. Around the Key, p. 585

DPE pp. 569 – 591

Try to organize the lesson focus period so that half of the time is spent practicing skills and half playing lead-up or skill-related games.

Don't turn every drill into a relay. Competition will force children to think more about winning than polishing their skills.

It takes a long time to learn basic skills. Don't be in a hurry to teach all activities, and allow plenty of review time.

Stress:
1. Take off on the left foot when shooting with the right hand, and vice versa.
2. Carry the ball in both hands until just before shooting.
3. Aim at a spot on the backboard above the basket.
4. Shoot with right hand when approaching the basket from the right side, and vice versa.

When playing lead-up games, encourage person-to-person guarding so that youngsters learn to stay with their opponent, rather than chasing the ball.

Cog.—Blood pressure measurements are recorded using two numbers. When your heart contracts, the pressure in the arteries is called systolic pressure. When the heart is relaxed and filling with blood, the diastolic pressure is recorded. Discuss how blood pressure is measured and what constitutes high blood pressure.

Cog.—The reason backspin is put on a basketball when it is shot is that the spin opposite to the direction of flight will cause the ball to remain closer to the backboard and increase the possibility of its dropping in. Discuss the effects of spin in the direction of flight and when it is used to advantage.

Cog.—Muscle fatigue occurs when muscles will no longer contract. Training will delay the onset and severity of fatigue. Discuss the effects of fatigue on athletic play and the importance of maintaining a high level of fitness.

GAME (5 – 7 MINUTES)

The games are included in the lesson focus.

DYNAMIC PHYSICAL EDUCATION LESSON PLAN
Recreational Activities
Level II

Supplies and Equipment Needed:
Fleece balls—one for each child
Apparatus for Challenge Course
Equipment for recreational activities

MOVEMENT EXPERIENCE—CONTENT	ORGANIZATION AND TEACHING HINTS	EXPECTED STUDENT OBJECTIVES AND OUTCOMES

INTRODUCTORY ACTIVITY (2 – 3 MINUTES)

Fleece Ball Fun

Each child has a fleece ball. Allow students to kick, throw, or move with the ball for a designated time (e.g., 1 minute).

On signal, place the balls on the floor and perform movements around, between, and over the balls.

DPE p. 221

This activity works best when students have enough room to move freely.

Movement patterns can be designated, such as rectangular, circular, and figure eight.

Beanbags may be substituted for fleece balls.

PM.—The students will be able to demonstrate the ability to kick and throw their fleece balls without running into other people.

FITNESS DEVELOPMENT ACTIVITIES (7 – 8 MINUTES)

Challenge Course Fitness

Design a course around the perimeter of the area using the following ideas:
1. Step on jumping box, dismount to tumbling mat, and do a forward roll.
2. Run and weave through four wands held upright by cones.
3. Handwalk across a horizontal ladder or do a flexed-arm hang from a climbing rope for 5 seconds.
4. Step on and off three jumping boxes (small-large-small).
5. Agility run through hoops.
6. Perform jump turns.
7. Leap over a magic rope held taut with two chairs or jumping boxes.
8. Hop on one foot.
9. Do a Log Roll across a tumbling mat.
10. Move through a tunnel made with jumping boxes covered by a tumbling mat.
11. Crouch jump or scooter movements the length of a balance-beam bench.
12. Slide through a parallel tumbling mat maze (mats stood on their sides).

DPE p. 263

Design a Challenge Course that exercises all body parts. Allow students an opportunity to develop new challenge ideas.

Emphasize moving through the Challenge Course with quality movements. The goal is fitness, not how fast youngsters can move through the course.

Distribute youngsters throughout the course rather than lining them up to start at one point. Faster moving youngsters can pass a station one time only.

Stop the class at regular intervals to perform flexibility and strength development activities for the shoulder girdle and abdominal region.

Change directions periodically. This will help prevent a build-up of students at slower moving stations.

Cog.—Challenge Courses were a common way of developing fitness in the armed services.

PM.—All students should be able to run the Challenge Course three times.

Aff.—There is no easy way to fitness. It demands self-discipline. Discuss the importance of possessing a positive attitude toward activity in later life.

MOVEMENT EXPERIENCE—CONTENT	ORGANIZATION AND TEACHING HINTS	EXPECTED STUDENT OBJECTIVES AND OUTCOMES

LESSON FOCUS (15 – 20 MINUTES)

Recreational Activities

The purpose of the recreation is to teach children activities that they can play during time when school is not in session.

Suggested activities are:
1. Shuffleboard
2. Four Square
3. Hopscotch
4. Beanbag Horseshoes
5. Jacks
6. Marbles
7. Sidewalk Tennis
8. Rope Quoits
9. Deck Tennis
10. Kick Shuffle
11. Tetherball
12. Tennis Volleyball

Emphasis should be placed on teaching the rules of the activities so children can enjoy them on their own time.

Three or four activities may be set up in each of four quadrants. Students work on any activity in their quadrant until signaled to move to the next quadrant.

If you know a traditional game played by children in your area for many years, now is a good time to teach it.

PM.—The student will be able to play at least four of the given activities.

Cog.—The student will be able to recite the rules for playing four or more of the activities.

Aff.—Recreational activities can be an excellent release for reducing stress. Relaxation demands playing for enjoyment and personal pleasure. Adults spend millions of dollars searching for activities that are relaxing and rewarding.

GAME (5 – 7 MINUTES)

Since the activities above are recreational in nature, the game period is unnecessary.

DYNAMIC PHYSICAL EDUCATION LESSON PLAN
Fundamental Skills Using Balance Beams
Level II

Supplies and Equipment Needed:
  Beanbags, wands, hoops, and jump ropes
  Balance-beam benches
  Apparatus for Challenge Course
  Cones
  Playground ball for each student
  Targets

MOVEMENT EXPERIENCE— CONTENT	ORGANIZATION AND TEACHING HINTS	EXPECTED STUDENT OBJECTIVES AND OUTCOMES

INTRODUCTORY ACTIVITY (2 – 3 MINUTES)

Ball Activities

Each student has an 8 1/2" playground ball. The balls can be dribbled as in basketball or as in soccer. On signal, students stop, balance on one leg, pass the ball under other leg and around back and overhead, maintaining control and balance.

Variations:
1. Toss ball up in place or dribble.
2. Play catch with a friend while moving.
3. Have a leader challenge the class to try different stunts and manipulative actions.

DPE p. 221

Emphasis should be on movement rather than ball skill activities.

Spread the playground balls throughout the area so the time needed to secure and put away equipment is minimized.

Cog.—The student will explain the concept of making a toss that leads the catcher so she can move into the path of the ball.

PM.—The students will be able to toss the balls in front of themselves so movements are not interrupted.

FITNESS DEVELOPMENT ACTIVITIES (7 – 8 MINUTES)

Challenge Course Fitness

Design a course around the perimeter of the area using the following ideas:
1. Step on jumping box, dismount to tumbling mat, and do a forward roll.
2. Run and weave through four wands held upright by cones.
3. Handwalk across a horizontal ladder or do a flexed-arm hang from a climbing rope for 5 seconds.
4. Step on and off three jumping boxes (small-large-small).
5. Agility run through hoops.
6. Perform jump turns.
7. Leap over a magic rope held taut with two chairs or jumping boxes.
8. Hop on one foot.
9. Do a Log Roll across a tumbling mat.

DPE p. 263

Change some of the challenges and add new ones designed by students.

Emphasize moving through the Challenge Course with quality movements. The goal is fitness, not how fast youngsters can move through the course.

Distribute youngsters throughout the course rather than lining them up to start at one point. Faster moving youngsters can pass a station one time only.

Stop the class at regular intervals to perform flexibility and strength development activities for the shoulder girdle and abdominal region.

Change directions periodically. This will help prevent a build-up of students at slower moving stations.

Cog.—The student will be able to explain that in order to support stronger muscles, larger bones are developed. Muscles grow when exercised regularly and bones become stronger in response to the increased stress.

PM.—The student will be able to go through the Challenge Course four times.

MOVEMENT EXPERIENCE—CONTENT	ORGANIZATION AND TEACHING HINTS	EXPECTED STUDENT OBJECTIVES AND OUTCOMES

10. Alternate going over and under six obstacles (cones and wands or hoops).
11. Crouch jump or scooter movements the length of a balance-beam bench.
12. Slide through a parallel tumbling mat maze (mats stood on their sides).

LESSON FOCUS (15 – 20 MINUTES)

Balance-Beam Activities

May want to practice on lines to establish qualities of controlled movement and not looking at feet.
1. Walk length of beam and dismount correctly.
   a. Walk forward.
   b. Walk backward.
   c. Walk sideways—lead with both left and right sides of body.
2. Walk different directions and vary arm and body positions.
   a. Hands on hips.
   b. Hands on head.
   c. Hands folded across chest.
   d. Lean to one side or the other.
   e. Body bent forward or backward.
   f. Hands on knees or feet.
   g. Exploratory activity.
3. Balance objects such as beanbags, erasers, or wands while walking across beam. (Exploratory approach.)
4. Move across the beam in various directions using the following movements:
   a. Slide
   b. Heel and toe
   c. Tiptoes
   d. Grapevine
   e. Dip step
   f. Student choice
5. Use various equipment:
   a. Play catch with beanbags. Try different throws and movements.
   b. Bounce a playground ball and catch it, dribble it, play catch with a partner.
   c. Step over a wand, go under a wand, change directions.
   d. Go through a hoop.
   e. Jump-rope with an individual jump rope.
6. Allow a few minutes for student's exploration of ideas.

DPE pp. 422 – 424

Use at least six beams with equal number of students at each beam.

Use a mat at the finishing end of the beam for students to perform their dismounts.

Assign a return activity for students so they are busy off as well as on the beam.

Stress quality of movement across the beam as well as during the dismount.

If a child falls, have him step back on the beam and continue. This will ensure him of the same amount of practice that the gifted child receives.

Make sure each student performs a dismount. The dismount will discourage the student from running across the beam and will closely simulate the competitive balance-beam event.

Stress student choice and exploration.

Place a target on the wall in front of the beams. Ask students to visually focus on the targets while walking on the beams.

PM.—The students will be able to balance themselves while walking across beam. A desirable goal would be for the child to walk across the beam without falling.

Cog.—Balance is a learned activity. The student will be able to explain that balance and concentration are necessary for improvement.

Cog.—The student will be able to explain how changing arm and leg positions or direction of movement creates a new balance task for the body.

Aff.—Awareness of the status and prestige given to a skilled performer. Discuss the payoff when one is skilled, such as friends, money, prizes, etc.

Cog.—Balance activities are best performed when performers are relaxed. Increased leg strength also plays an important part in balance. Encourage practice at home where there is little fear of falling and embarrassment.

Cog.—For increased balance control, widen the base of support and lower the center of gravity. Discuss the impact of the narrow base of support found on balance beams.

MOVEMENT EXPERIENCE—CONTENT	ORGANIZATION AND TEACHING HINTS	EXPECTED STUDENT OBJECTIVES AND OUTCOMES

GAME (5 – 7 MINUTES)

Play a game that is active. Try to introduce new games rather than falling back on a few that both you and the class know well. The following are suggested:
1. Fly Trap, p. 527
2. Nonda's Car Lot, p. 528

DYNAMIC PHYSICAL EDUCATION LESSON PLAN
Stunts and Tumbling Skills (Lesson 2)
Level II

Supplies and Equipment Needed:
  Tape player and tapes
  Tumbling mats

MOVEMENT EXPERIENCE—CONTENT	ORGANIZATION AND TEACHING HINTS	EXPECTED STUDENT OBJECTIVES AND OUTCOMES

INTRODUCTORY ACTIVITY (2 – 3 MINUTES)

Moving to Music

Use different music to stimulate various locomotor and nonlocomotor movements. Different dance steps such as polka, two-step, and schottische could be practiced.

DPE p. 221

Emphasis should be placed on creating a movement that is synchronized to the music.

If youngsters have difficulty sensing the rhythm, use a tom-tom to aid them.

PM.—The student will be able to move, in time with the music, to five different rhythms.

Cog.—The student will be able to identify the difference between 3/4 and 4/4 rhythm.

FITNESS DEVELOPMENT ACTIVITIES (7 – 8 MINUTES)

Aerobic Fitness (suggested routine)

 1. Rhythmic run with clap—24 counts.
 2. Bounce turn and clap—24 counts.
 3. Rhythmic 4-count sit-ups (knees, toes, knees, back)—24 counts.
 4. Rhythmic Crab Kicks (slow time)—24 counts.
Repeat steps 1–4 three times.
 5. Jumping Jack combination—24 counts.
 6. Double knee lifts—24 counts.
 7. Lunges (right, left, forward) with single-arm circles (on the side lunges) and double-arm circles (on the forward lunge)—24 counts.
 8. Rhythmic trunk twists—24 counts.
Repeat steps 5–8 three times.
 9. Directional run (forward, backward, sides, turning)—24 counts.
10. Rock side to side with clap—24 counts.
11. Side leg raises (alternate legs)—24 counts.
12. Rhythmic 4-count push-ups—24 counts. (If these are too difficult for students, substitute single-arm circles in the push-up position.)
Repeat steps 9–12 three times.

Directional run, jump, and say "HEY!" to finish.

DPE pp. 263 – 266

Perform the routine for 7 minutes. Increase by 30 seconds per week.

Emphasis should be placed on continuous movement rather than on specific dance steps and routines.

Alternate bouncing and running movements with flexibility and strength development movements.

Do not use confusing steps and combinations.

Make the routine easy to follow.

Select music that has a definite beat.

A poster may be used to list the steps as an aid for students.

Help students become interested in aerobic dance and in fitness activities by making the routine enjoyable.

Monitor heart rate to check to see how this activity raises the heart rate into the training zone.

Try adding rhythmic bounces or jogging between steps to allow students to regroup.

Don't stress or expect perfection. The routine should be for fitness development.

Cog.—It is interesting to measure the breathing rate at rest as well as during and after exercise. Why does breathing rate vary?

Aff.—Many experts feel people are overweight due to lack of activity rather than eating too much. Discuss why this might be true.

MOVEMENT EXPERIENCE—CONTENT	ORGANIZATION AND TEACHING HINTS	EXPECTED STUDENT OBJECTIVES AND OUTCOMES

LESSON FOCUS (15 – 20 MINUTES)

Stunts and Tumbling

Six groups of activities are found in this lesson to insure that youngsters receive a variety of experiences. Pick a few activities from each group and teach them alternately. For example, teach one or two tumbling and inverted balances, then one or two balance stunts, followed by individual stunts, etc. Do not place excessive time on one group of activities at the expense of another.

1. Animal Movements
   a. Elbow Crawl
   b. Measuring Worm
   c. Mule Kick
   d. Walrus Walk
2. Tumbling and Inverted Balances
   a. Headstand Kick-Up
   b. Frog Handstand
   c. Half Teeter-Totter
   d. Cartwheel
   e. Forward Roll - Pike Position
3. Balance Stunts
   a. Leg Dip
   b. Balance Jump
   c. Seat Balance
4. Individual Stunts
   a. Heelstand
   b. Wicket Walk
   c. Knee Jump to Standing
   d. Knee Drop
   e. Forward Drop
5. Partner and Group Stunts
   a. Rowboat
   b. Leapfrog
   c. Wheelbarrow
   d. Wheelbarrow Lifting
6. Partner Support Stunts
   a. Table
   b. Statue

DPE pp. 463 – 481

Scatter as many tumbling mats as possible throughout the area in order to avoid waiting lines.

Do not perform many repetitions of tumbling and inverted balances. For most children, limiting the number of forward or backward roll repetitions to four or five will prevent fatigue and injury.

If necessary, start at a lower level than listed here to assure students find success.

After students learn the basic activities, emphasize three phases of correct performance:
1. Starting position
2. Execution
3. Finishing position

Teach youngsters to stand on the hips and shoulders when doing partner support stunts.

Cog.—Momentum needs to be developed and applied when performing rolls. The student will be able to name three ways of developing momentum (i.e., tucking, starting from a higher point, preliminary raising of the arms).

Cog.—The center of weight must be positioned over the center of support in balance stunts. The student will be able to describe and demonstrate this in his own fashion.

P.M.—The student will be able to perform at least two of the activities in each of the groups.

Aff.—Tumbling and stunts are activities in which there is a wide range of student ability which is evident to others. Discuss the sensitivity of the situation and the need to understand the shortcomings of others.

Cog.—Certain sports and activities offer a greater degree of aerobic conditioning. Contrast activities such as basketball, jogging, bicycling, rope jumping, and swimming with bowling, golf, softball, and football.

Aff.—Many people take drugs to help them handle stress. Unfortunately, they avoid dealing with the cause of stress. Drugs are short-term solutions and ultimately cause more problems than they solve. Discuss how drugs can cause physiological and psychological changes and addiction.

GAME (5 – 7 MINUTES)

Try the following games:
1. Partner Stoop, p. 534
2. Crows and Cranes, p. 527

DYNAMIC PHYSICAL EDUCATION LESSON PLAN
Manipulative Skills Using Wands
Level II

Supplies and Equipment Needed:
  One wand per child
  Tom-tom
  Record player and records
  Poster for aerobic routines
  Deck tennis rings

MOVEMENT EXPERIENCE— CONTENT	ORGANIZATION AND TEACHING HINTS	EXPECTED STUDENT OBJECTIVES AND OUTCOMES

INTRODUCTORY ACTIVITY (2 – 3 MINUTES)

European Running with Variations

1. Run lightly counterclockwise.
2. Clap hands on every fourth beat.
3. Stamp foot on every second beat.
4. Stamp every second beat and clap every fourth.
5. On signal, make a complete turn, using four running steps.
6. On signal, stop, pivot, and move in the opposite direction.
7. Appoint a student to lead the class through various formations.

DPE pp. 217 – 218

Variations should be tried after the class has mastered the quality requirements of rhythm, spacing, and staying in line.

At times, stop the drum beat and have the class continue running. The patter of their feet is a good measure of their success in this activity.

Cog.—Skilled runners do not need the beat of the tom-tom, but can keep time with a leader.

PM.—The student will be able to perform the variation and maintain the proper rhythm at the same time.

FITNESS DEVELOPMENT ACTIVITY (7 – 8 MINUTES)

Aerobic Fitness (suggested routine)

1. Rhythmic run with kicks—24 counts.
2. Bounce forward and backward with clap—24 counts.
3. Rhythmic 4-count sit-ups—24 counts.
4. Crab Kick combinations—24 counts.
Repeat steps 1–4 three times.
5. Jumping Jack variations—24 counts.
6. Knee lifts, turning—24 counts.
7. Side bends—24 counts.
8. Leg extensions (seated)—24 counts.
Repeat steps 5–8 three times.
9. Directional run (changing formations)—24 counts.
10. Bounce with body twist—24 counts.
11. Side leg raises (alternate legs)—24 counts.
12. Rhythmic push-ups—24 counts.
Repeat steps 9–12 three times.

Run randomly, jump turn, and say "YEA!" to finish.

DPE pp. 263 – 266

Perform the routine for 7 1/2 minutes.

May be done in scattered formation or in a circle.

A follow-the-leader approach is excellent.

Use music that stimulates students to exercise.

Alternate bouncing and running movements with flexibility and strength development movements.

While performing rhythmic running movements, students can move into different formations.

Place poster with cues on the wall that list steps, number of repetitions, and "cue words."

Smile and have a good time—students will believe you enjoy fitness activity.

Variations may be made in the suggested routines.

PM.—The student will be able to perform all of the exercises in time to the music by the end of the week.

Cog.—The student will be able to recognize all of the exercises by name by the end of the week.

Cog.—The blood is transported back to the lungs in the veins. This system is called the circulatory system.

MOVEMENT EXPERIENCE—CONTENT	ORGANIZATION AND TEACHING HINTS	EXPECTED STUDENT OBJECTIVES AND OUTCOMES

LESSON FOCUS (15 – 20 MINUTES)

Wands

Select some activities from each of the three groups: Exercises, Stunts, and Partner Activities.

A. *Exercises Using Wands*
   1. Standing isometrics
      a. Push hands together; chest high, overhead, behind seat.
      b. Pull hands apart; chest high, overhead, behind seat.
   2. Wand overhead, with straight arms
      a. Bend right, left, forward.
   3. Body twist
      a. Twist right, left.
      b. Bend right, left.
   4. Long sitting, wand overhead
      a. Touch toes with wand.

B. *Wand Stunts*
   1. Wand catch
      a. Practice different combinations.
      b. Do four-way routine.
   2. Thread needle—V-Seat
      a. Legs crossed.
      b. Legs together.
      c. Combination.
   3. Thread needle—standing
      a. Front–back, reverse, side to side.
      b. Add shoulder dislocate.
   4. Grapevine
      a. 1st stage.
      b. 2nd stage—stepout.
      c. Reverse.
   5. Back Scratcher
      a. 1st stage—down back.
      b. 2nd stage—down over seat.
   6. Wand whirl
      a. Practice standing wand.
      b. Grab with hand, grab with one finger.
      c. Do right and left turns.
   7. Twist under
      a. Right hand, left hand.
      b. Twist right, left. Reverse.
   8. Jump stick
   9. Wand balances
      a. Student choice—back of hand, shift back to front, change hands, sit, lie. Get up. Try balances on foot.
   10. Crab Leap
      a. Alternating feet.
   11. Long reach
      a. Perform with the wand in both the left and right hand in turn.

DPE pp. 382 – 386

Watch posture. Stress good effort. Hold for 8 seconds.

Stress full bends. Reach beyond toes.

Do one each way. Keep balance.

Stress not touching.

Hold wand in fingertips.

Allow kneeling, may be better for some. Use demonstration.

Crossed-hands position, palms up. Use demonstration.

Secure some skill in standing wand.

Stick will slip. Must control.

Do not reverse jump. Get height. Practice without stick.

Aff.—Wand stunts demand a great deal of flexibility. Often, girls are more successful at flexibility activities than boys. This is an opportune time to discuss individual differences as well as ability differences between sexes.

Cog.—The students will be able to explain in their own words that frequent stretching makes possible a wider range of motion and conserves energy.

Cog.—It appears to be impossible to improve reaction time. Reaction time is the time it takes to initiate a response to a signal. However, movement time can be improved through increasing strength, shortening the length of a lever, and decreasing the distance to be moved. Movement time is the time it takes to move a certain distance. Discuss a skill and what could be modified to improve movement time.

Cog.—Knowledge of results is important when learning motor skills. Performers can evaluate their movements and make modifications for improvement. Discuss various aspects of a skill students should analyze to improve their skills.

Cog.—Teaching a skill in parts is effective when the skill is complex and contains many individual skills, and the learner has limited memory span. Explain and demonstrate to youngsters how skills can be taught in parts and then put together as a complete task.

PM.—The student will be able to perform 6 of the 11 wand stunts.

Cog.—Practice sessions should be short when tasks are difficult and performers young. Also, when excessive repetition is demanded, sessions should be kept short. Students will understand the need for short practice sessions, distributed evenly over a long period of time.

MOVEMENT EXPERIENCE—CONTENT	ORGANIZATION AND TEACHING HINTS	EXPECTED STUDENT OBJECTIVES AND OUTCOMES
C. *Partner Activities*		Aff.—Goals should be set based on a person's capability. Discuss some types of goals students might set to maintain physical fitness. Some examples might be:
1. Partner Catch	Keep distances short.	
a. One wand, two wands.		
2. Partner Change	Distances short, use one step.	1. Jog 1 mile daily.
a. Simple exercise.		2. Do 10 pull-ups daily.
b. Spin.		3. Jump-rope for 10 minutes daily.
3. Partner Rowing		4. Play basketball every day for 30 minutes.
a. Seated, legs spread, feet against feet.	Hold wand instead of hands.	5. Jog 25 miles in a month.
b. Overhand grip, row back and forth.		6. Do 25 sit-ups daily.
4. Stick Twist		
a. Face, arms overhead, overhand grip.	Try to get opponent to shift grip.	
5. Wand Wrestle	Try to wrestle stick away.	
a. One hand outside.		
6. Chinese Pull-Up	Stress equal start.	
a. Sit, facing, knees straight, soles against soles.		
b. Bend forward, grasp wand.	Both hands either inside or out.	
7. Wring the Dishrag		
8. Ring toss with deck tennis rings	Keep distances short at first.	
a. Alternate back and forth.		

GAME (5 – 7 MINUTES)

Play an active game as wands do not require much aerobic activity. The following are suggested:
1. Home Base, p. 526
2. Indianapolis 500, p. 525
3. Nine Lives, p. 534

DYNAMIC PHYSICAL EDUCATION LESSON PLAN
Rhythmic Movement (Lesson 3)
Level II

Supplies and Equipment Needed:
  Tape player
  Music
  Tinikling poles
  Indian clubs
  Beach balls

Dances Taught:
  E-Z Mixer
  Irish Washerwoman
  Gustaf's Skoal
  Tinikling

MOVEMENT EXPERIENCE— CONTENT	ORGANIZATION AND TEACHING HINTS	EXPECTED STUDENT OBJECTIVES AND OUTCOMES

INTRODUCTORY ACTIVITY (2 – 3 MINUTES)

Tortoise and Hare

When the leader calls out the word "tortoise," students run in place slowly. On the word "hare," they change to a rapid run.

Variations:
  1. Perform to music.
  2. Move throughout the area.
  3. Perform various stretching activities on command.
  4. Move in different directions.

DPE p. 219

Encourage good knee lift.

Scatter formation.

Have students lift their knees to their hands, which are held in front of the body at waist level.

PM.—The student will be able to maintain a steady rhythm at both slow and fast speeds.

Cog.—People need to psychologically warm up so they "feel" like moving. Discuss the importance of movement in setting the right frame of mind for fitness development activity.

FITNESS DEVELOPMENT ACTIVITY (7 – 8 MINUTES)

Aerobic Fitness (suggested routine)

  1. Bounce and do arm circles—24 counts.
  2. Grapevine step with clap—24 counts.
  3. Curl-Up variations—24 counts.
  4. Treadmill combinations—24 counts.
Repeat steps 1–4 three times.
  5. Forward and side stride hops—24 counts.
  6. Knee lift and kick combinations— 24 counts.
  7. Rhythmic windmills—24 counts.
  8. Leg extensions (seated)—24 counts.
Repeat steps 5–8 three times.
  9. Rhythmic run with knee lift on every 4th beat—24 counts.
10. Rock side to side with double bounce on each side—24 counts.
11. Rhythmic push-ups (try them in the reverse position!)—24 counts.
12. Bear hugs—24 counts.
Repeat steps 9–12 three times.

Bounce turn and clap, jump up, and say "HEY!" to finish.

DPE pp. 263 – 266

Perform the routine for 8 minutes.

This is the final week of aerobic dance.

Students should be given the opportunity to lead.

Groups of four to six may be formed to create aerobic dance routines.

Use music that stimulates students to exercise.

Smile and have a good time—students will get a positive feeling about fitness activities.

Aff.—Leadership demands an increase in responsibility. Leaders must be concerned for the welfare of others as well as themselves. Discuss how the leaders determine the work load for the rest of the group.

PM.—The student will be able to perform the exercises at an increased work load (longer duration) than the previous week.

Cog.—One method often used to measure fitness is to count the pulse rate after exercise within 2 or 3 minutes. It might be interesting to measure pulse rate at various intervals after exercise. The more fit one is, the faster pulse rate returns to normal.

Aff.—A well-balanced diet provides fuel for physical activity. Discuss the basics of a good diet and the need for such.

PM.—The students will be able to work in small groups and create aerobic dance routines by the end of the week.

MOVEMENT EXPERIENCE— CONTENT	ORGANIZATION AND TEACHING HINTS	EXPECTED STUDENT OBJECTIVES AND OUTCOMES

LESSON FOCUS (15 – 20 MINUTES)

Rhythms

When teaching a dance, use the following steps:
   a. Tell about the dance and listen to the music.
   b. Clap the beat and learn the verse.
   c. Practice the dance steps without the music and with verbal cues.
   d. Practice the dance with the music.

Make dances easy for students to learn by using some of the following ideas:
   1. Teach the dances without partners.
   2. Allow youngsters to move in any direction—avoid the left–right orientation.
   3. Use scattered formation instead of circles—it helps avoid embarrassment.
   4. Emphasize strong movements such as clapping and stomping to encourage involvement.
   5. Tape the music at a slower speed when first learning the dance.

Rhythms should be taught like other sport skills. Avoid expecting perfection when teaching rhythms. Teach a variety of dances rather than one or two in depth. Youngsters will enjoy rhythms if they know it is acceptable to make mistakes without being ridiculed.

1. E-Z Mixer (p. 341)

An American dance.

Circle of partners facing CCW.

Basic dance skills:
   1. Walking
   2. Elbow swing
   3. Pivot (and move to new partner)

PM.—The student will develop the proper rhythm needed to perform this dance successfully.

Aff.—The student will accept new partners graciously.

2. Irish Washerwoman (p. 342)

Basic dance steps:
   1. Walk
   2. Swing
   3. Promenade
Review the terms:
   1. Partner
   2. Corner
Single circle, couples facing center, girl (or "pinnie" person) to the right side of partner.

Spend some time practicing moving smoothly from a swing into a promenade position.

Aff.—The student will be courteous when accepting a new partner.

PM.—The student will be able to go through the entire dance without difficulty.

3. Gustaf's Skoal (pp. 343 – 344)

A Swedish dance.

Basic dance skills:
   1. Stately walking
   2. Skipping
   3. Turning
   4. Forming arches

Review the terms:
   1. Head couples
   2. Side couples

Aff.—The student will appreciate that this dance begins in a stately, dignified manner.

PM.—The student will be able to master the maneuvers in this dance without difficulty.

MOVEMENT EXPERIENCE—CONTENT	ORGANIZATION AND TEACHING HINTS	EXPECTED STUDENT OBJECTIVES AND OUTCOMES
	Set of four couples, each facing center (as with square dancing). Designate two head couples and two side couples. During part one, the music is slow and stately. Encourage students to perform with dignity. Part two is light and fun.	

MOVEMENT EXPERIENCE—CONTENT	ORGANIZATION AND TEACHING HINTS	EXPECTED STUDENT OBJECTIVES AND OUTCOMES

4. Tinikling (pp. 345 – 348)
 1. Teach the Dance Rhythm
   a. Teach the basic step rhythms using two parallel chalked lines or jump ropes.
   b. Practice a two-count weight transfer rocking sideways on the left and right feet.
   c. When students can shift the weight from side to side, introduce the uneven rhythm. This is a similar rocking motion where one hop is done on the left foot and two on the right.
   d. Practice the uneven rhythm moving in and out of the ropes, lines on the floor, or stationary poles.
 2. Teach the Pole Rhythm
   a. Teach the pole rhythm by practicing a three-count clapping rhythm cued by the teacher with a tom-tom. The rhythm is clap (hands together); down (slap top of legs); down (same as previous).
   b. Clap the rhythm to the record. Slow the music down in the early learning stages.
   c. Allow everyone to practice the rhythm with the poles and no dancers.
   d. Add dancers doing the basic step.
 3. Practice other steps and the circling movement:
   a. Crossover step
   b. Rocker step
   c. Circle the poles
   d. Cross step
 4. Formation dancing
   a. Line of poles, individually or with a partner
   b. Square formation
	Small-group formations.
	
	 Make sure the sticks go together on the *down* beat, as this is an auditory cue for the dancer.
	
	 This dance takes some time to learn. Don't be impatient, and allow class enough time to practice.
	
	 Make sure that the people handling the sticks are rotated often.
	
	 The sticks should be kept low or the dancer's legs may be caught.
	
	 The initial step is used only to get the dance under way.
	
	 Eyes should be up, not looking at feet or poles.
	
	 Partners face, holding hands with the side to the poles. Begin with the foot nearest the poles.
	
	 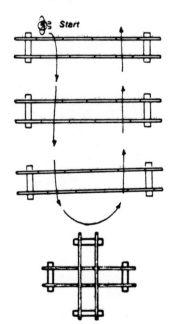
		Cog.—The student will know the origin of the dance.
		
		 PM.—The student will be able to perform the basic tinikling step as well as move the sticks to the proper rhythm.
		
		 Aff.—Dancing is an activity that has been done for many years, in many cultures. Discuss the possibilities as to why this occurs.
		
		 Aff.—One of the important facets to positive social adjustment is accepting individual differences. Discuss the importance of accepting others as they are and avoiding comparing, judging, and disapproving of others' performances.

MOVEMENT EXPERIENCE—CONTENT	ORGANIZATION AND TEACHING HINTS	EXPECTED STUDENT OBJECTIVES AND OUTCOMES

GAME (5 – 7 MINUTES)

1. Jump the Shot, p. 528
2. Beach ball Bat Ball, p. 525
3. Club Guard, p. 530

DYNAMIC PHYSICAL EDUCATION LESSON PLAN
Volleyball-Related Skills
Level II

Supplies and Equipment Needed:
Tambourine
Beach ball for each child
Hoops
Volleyball net (6 ft height)
Tape player
Music

MOVEMENT EXPERIENCE— CONTENT	ORGANIZATION AND TEACHING HINTS	EXPECTED STUDENT OBJECTIVES AND OUTCOMES

INTRODUCTORY ACTIVITY (2 – 3 MINUTES)

Bend, Stretch, and Shake

Students should alternate between various bending and stretching activities. On signal, students shake and relax various body parts. Teach a wide variety of bending and stretching activities.

DPE p. 224

Strike a tambourine to signal changes in bending and stretching and then shake it to signal shaking movements.

Encourage shaking of all body parts. If necessary, start by shaking and adding one body part at a time.

PM.—The student will be able to demonstrate five or more styles of bending and stretching.

Aff.—Warming up the body before exercise is an important step in preparation for activity as it prepares all the body systems for stress. Discuss how the need for warm-up becomes more important as one grows older.

FITNESS DEVELOPMENT ACTIVITY (7 – 8 MINUTES)

Astronaut Drills

Perform the following activities, stopping only to do the exercises.

Walk while doing	
Arm Circles	20 seconds
Crab Alternate- Leg Extension	30 seconds
Skip	25 seconds
Body Twist	35 seconds
Slide	25 seconds
Jumping Jack variations	35 seconds
Flying Angel	30 seconds
Sit-Ups	35 seconds
Hop to center and back	30 seconds
Push-Ups	30 seconds
Gallop	35 seconds
Bear Hugs	35 seconds
Pogo Stick Jump	30 seconds
Trot	25 seconds
Power Jumper	30 seconds

Cool down with stretching for 1–2 minutes.

DPE pp. 262 – 263

Use circle or scatter formation with ample space between youngsters. If a circle formation is used, establish a "passing lane" to the outside for faster students.

Change directions occasionally to keep students spread out.

Taped intervals of music and no music can be used to signal movement and stopping to do exercises.

To vary the work load while moving, less able students can move toward the center of the area if a circle is being used.

PM.—The student will be able to perform the exercises with rhythm and in unison with the rest of the class.

Cog.—Exercise, if demanding enough, will cause the training effect to occur in a short period of time. Discuss the fact that 10 minutes of rope jumping is equal to 30 minutes of jogging.

Aff.—With the class moving together and "sounding like a team," it is a good time to discuss pride in group accomplishment.

LESSON FOCUS (15–20 MINUTES)

Volleyball-Related Skills

A. *Individual Skills*
 1. Practice wall rebounding: Stand 6 ft away from a wall. Pass the ball against the wall and catch it.

DPE pp. 671 – 682

PM.—The student will be able to perform the following skills adequately:
 1. Underhand serve
 2. Overhand pass

MOVEMENT EXPERIENCE— CONTENT	ORGANIZATION AND TEACHING HINTS	EXPECTED STUDENT OBJECTIVES AND OUTCOMES
2. From a spot 6 ft from the wall, throw the ball against the wall and alternate an overhand pass with a forearm pass. 3. Throw the ball to one side (right or left) and move to the side to pass the ball to the wall. Catch the rebound. 4. Pass the ball directly overhead and catch it. Try making two passes before catching the ball. Later, alternate an overhand pass with a forearm pass and catch the ball. This is a basic drill and should be mastered before proceeding to others. 5. Pass the ball 3 ft or so to one side, move under the ball, and pass it back to the original spot. The next pass should be to the other side. 6. Pass the ball directly overhead. On the return, jump as high as possible and make a second pass. Continue. 7. Stand with one foot in a hoop. Pass the ball overhead and attempt to continue passing while keeping one foot in the hoop. Try with both feet in the hoop. B. *Partner Work (Passing)* 1. Players are about 10 ft apart. Player A tosses the ball (controlled toss) to player B, who passes the ball back to A, who catches the ball. Continue for several exchanges and then change throwers. 2. Two players are about 15 ft apart. Player A passes to herself first and then makes a second pass to player B, who catches the ball and repeats. Follow with a return by B. 3. Players A and B try to keep the ball in the air continuously. 4. Players are about 15 ft apart. Player A remains stationary and passes in such a fashion that player B must move from side to side. An option is to have player B move forward and backward. 5. Players are about 10 ft apart. Both have hoops and attempt to keep one foot in the hoop while passing. Try keeping both feet in the hoop. 6. Player A passes to player B and does a complete turnaround. B passes back to A and also does a full turn. Other stunts can be used.	Beach balls are preferred for learning volleyball skills at this age. The slow-moving beach ball allows youngsters to learn proper footwork by moving into position instead of reaching for the ball. If beach balls are not available, 8" foam gray balls can be substituted. Volleyball trainer balls are also on the market, but are quite expensive. They are larger and lighter than regulation volleyballs and will prevent youngsters from injury. If wall space is not available, work in partners and have one player toss the ball to the passer. Emphasis should be placed on correctly volleying the ball rather than seeing how high it can be hit. Discourage striking the ball with one hand. This practice leads to uncontrolled swinging at the ball. If the ball can be reached with only one hand, youngsters should be encouraged to start over. Partner drills are effective only if the set-up toss is accurate. It might be useful to have students practice tossing to each other before proceeding to the tossing and passing drill. Rule out passing the volleyball with a fist. This is always a result of students' being out of position. Emphasize moving the feet and keeping the body weight on the balls of the feet. If students are not doing well with footwork, place the balls on the floor and practice moving the feet in different directions. Hoops or individual mats can be used to restrict movement and emphasize accuracy. If students are having difficulty with accuracy, reduce the distance between them.	Cog.—The student will be able to explain the importance of moving the feet into proper position before passing the ball. Cog.—The student will be able to explain why the fist should not be used for passing the ball. Cog.—The student will be able to explain the most basic rules of volleyball, including: 1. Only the serving team scores. 2. The ball may not be caught. 3. Passing is actually a batting of the ball, not a throw. 4. Only three volleys are allowed before the ball is returned over the net. Aff.—Cooperation is necessary if students are going to learn volleyball skills. Review the need for helping others in practice situations. PM.—The student will be able to accurately toss the ball to a partner. PM.—The student will be able to accurately pass the ball to a partner.

MOVEMENT EXPERIENCE—CONTENT	ORGANIZATION AND TEACHING HINTS	EXPECTED STUDENT OBJECTIVES AND OUTCOMES

C. *Partner Work (Serving)*
1. Partners are about 20 ft apart. Partner A serves to partner B, who catches the ball and returns the serve to A.
2. Partner A serves to partner B, who makes a pass back to A. Change roles.
3. Play Service One-Step. Partners begin about 10 ft apart. Partner A serves to partner B, who catches the serve. B now serves to A, who must catch the serve. Each time the serve is caught, both players take one step back. If a serve is not caught, the players revert to the original distance of 10 ft and start over.

Develop proper serving form rather than concern for how far the serve travels. If youngsters do not have to worry about getting the ball over a net, they will be less concerned with how much power they generate on the serve.

Cog.—The student will be able to explain the importance of passing the ball with accuracy rather than hitting it for distance.

Emphasize process rather than product. Students should be encouraged to help each other learn proper technique rather than worry about the product (distance, height, etc.).

Cog.—The student will be able to describe the importance of proper form rather than the outcome of the skill.

GAMES (5 – 7 MINUTES)

Volleyball Lead-Up Games
1. Beach ball Volleyball, p. 678
2. Informal Volleyball, p. 678
3. Shower Service Ball, p. 679

Use beach balls (or 8-in. foam rubber balls) for all the game activities.

DYNAMIC PHYSICAL EDUCATION LESSON PLAN
Manipulative Skills Using Hoops
Level II

Supplies and Equipment Needed:
 One hoop per child
 Cageball
 Tape player
 Music

MOVEMENT EXPERIENCE—CONTENT	ORGANIZATION AND TEACHING HINTS	EXPECTED STUDENT OBJECTIVES AND OUTCOMES

INTRODUCTORY ACTIVITY (2 – 3 MINUTES)

Move, Perform Task

Do a locomotor movement; on signal, stop and perform a task such as an exercise or stunt.

Suggested activities:
1. Heel Click
2. Push-Up
3. Turnover
4. Top
5. Stork Stand
6. Coffee Grinder

DPE p. 219

Many individual stunts, such as the heel click, heel slap, or jump turn, can be performed. These add challenge and excitement to the activity.

Vary the locomotor movements by adding quality words (i.e., slow–fast, high–low).

PM.—The student will be able to perform the basic locomotor movement variations as well as the designated stunts or exercises.

Aff.—The body should be gradually warmed up, rather than moving into demanding activity immediately. Discuss this with the class with regard to a need to self-pace and gradually work toward maximum output. Incorporate this principle into your teaching by demanding more as the introductory and fitness work progress.

FITNESS DEVELOPMENT ACTIVITY (7 – 8 MINUTES)

Astronaut Drills

Perform the following activities, stopping only to do the exercises.

Walk while doing Arm Circles	20 seconds
Crab Alternate-Leg Extension	30 seconds
Skip	25 seconds
Body Twist	35 seconds
Slide	25 seconds
Jumping Jack variations	35 seconds
Flying Angel	30 seconds
Sit-Ups	35 seconds
Hop to center and back	30 seconds
Push-Ups	30 seconds
Gallop	35 seconds
Bear Hugs	35 seconds
Pogo Stick Jump	30 seconds
Trot	25 seconds
Power Jumper	30 seconds

Cool down with stretching for 1–2 minutes.

DPE pp. 262 – 263

Use circle or scatter formation with ample space between youngsters. If a circle formation is used, establish a "passing lane" to the outside for faster students.

Change directions occasionally to keep students spread out.

Taped intervals of music and no music can be used to signal movement and stopping to do exercises.

To vary the work load while moving, less able students can move toward the center of the area if a circle is being used.

Cog.—When a person exercises regularly, additional capillaries form in the muscle tissue so that the muscle cells are better supplied with blood. The student will be able to describe this occurrence in his or her own words.

MOVEMENT EXPERIENCE—CONTENT	ORGANIZATION AND TEACHING HINTS	EXPECTED STUDENT OBJECTIVES AND OUTCOMES

LESSON FOCUS (15 – 20 MINUTES)

Hoops

1. Hula-hoop using various body parts such as waist, neck, knees, arms, and fingers.
    a. While hula-hooping on the arms, try to change the hoop from one arm to the other.
    b. Change hoop from one partner to another while hula-hooping.
    c. Try leg-skippers—hula-hoop with one leg and jump the hoop with the other leg.
2. Jump-rope with the hoop—forward, sideways, and backward. Begin with a back-and-forth swing.
3. Roll hoop and run alongside it. Run in front of it.
4. Roll hoop with a reverse spin to make it return to the thrower.
5. Roll with a reverse spin and see how many times partner can go through it.
6. Roll with a reverse spin, jump the hoop, and catch it as it returns.
7. Roll with a reverse spin, kick into the air, and catch.
8. Balance the hoop on your head, try to walk through it ("thread the needle") forward, backward, and sideward.
9. Use the hoop as a cowboy lasso, standing, sitting, or lying down.
10. Try partner activities:
    a. Play catch with hoop.
    b. Hula-hoop on one arm, toss to partner who catches it on one arm.
    c. Use two hoops for catching.
    d. Hoop with one hoop and play catch with other.
    e. Move through a hoop held by a partner.

DPE pp. 386 – 388

Scatter formation.

Hula-hooping demands that body parts are moved back and forth, *not* in a circle.

Have the class drop their hoops when you desire their attention.

When they jump through hoops, children should be encouraged to hold them loosely to prevent falls.

Use the hoops as a home area for children. This will keep them in a designated area.

The reverse spin must be taught and practiced. Many students find it to be a difficult skill.

When throwing and catching two hoops, each partner should throw one and then progress to both hoops being thrown at the same time by one partner.

PM.—The students will be able to hula-hoop on at least one part of their bodies.

PM.—The student will be able to jump rope for 20 seconds without missing in at least one of the sessions.

PM.—The students will be able to place a reverse spin on the hoop, causing it to return to them.

Aff.—Many students will not immediately be able to hula-hoop or apply the reverse spin. Discuss the value of continued practice versus the alternative of quitting and never learning the skill.

Aff.—Discuss the value of learning a skill simply for one's own enjoyment and satisfaction.

Cog.—The body adapts rapidly to hot, humid conditions. Within two weeks of practice and training in heat, the body will adapt and become more efficient. Primarily, the body sweats more rapidly and to a greater extent. The evaporation of sweat effectively cools the body. Discuss adaptation and the important role of sweating to maintain a constant body temperature.

Cog.—Aerobic training increases maximal oxygen uptake. A large part of the increase is due to increased stroke volume of the heart. More blood is pumped per heart beat due to increased capacity of the heart and stronger contractions. How is the heart strengthened?

GAME (5 – 7 MINUTES)

Play an active game. The following are suggested:
1. Hand Hockey, p. 533
2. Cageball Kickover, p. 533

DYNAMIC PHYSICAL EDUCATION LESSON PLAN
Manipulative Skills Using Paddles and Balls
Level II

Supplies and Equipment Needed:
  One paddle and ball per child
  One individual jump rope per child
  Fleece balls (optional)
  Tape player
  Music

MOVEMENT EXPERIENCE— CONTENT	ORGANIZATION AND TEACHING HINTS	EXPECTED STUDENT OBJECTIVES AND OUTCOMES

INTRODUCTORY ACTIVITY (2 – 3 MINUTES)

Tag Games

1. Addition Tag, p. 532
2. Squad Tag, p. 535
3. Couple Tag, p. 526

Children should know the games so that little instruction is needed.

Vary the type of locomotor movement the class can use to chase or flee.

PM.—The student will be able to dodge or evade quickly and without falling.

FITNESS DEVELOPMENT ACTIVITY (7 – 8 MINUTES)

Continuity Drills

Students alternate jump rope activity with exercises done in two-count fashion. Exercises are done with the teacher saying "Ready" and the class answers "One-two" and performs a repetition of the exercise. Teachers or students can lead.

Rope Jumping - Forward	30 seconds
Double Crab Kick	30 seconds
Rope Jumping - Backward	30 seconds
Partial Bent-Knee Sit-Up	45 seconds
Jump and Slowly Turn	
Body	30 seconds
Push-Ups	45 seconds
Rocker Step	30 seconds
Sit and Twist	30 seconds
Swing-Step Forward	30 seconds
Side Flex	30 seconds
Free Jumping	40 seconds
Sit and Stretch	45 seconds

DPE p. 262

Use scatter formation.

Taped intervals of music and no music can be used to signal rope jumping (with music) and performing exercises (without music).

Other exercises can be substituted to add variation to the activity.

Allow students to adjust the work load to their fitness level. This implies resting if the rope jumping is too strenuous.

PM.—The student will be able to jump-rope for 20 seconds without missing.

Aff.—Lack of exercise is one of the key factors in heart disease. Symptoms of heart disease are often found in young people, and thus fitness activities may help retard this health problem. Discuss heart disease and the role of exercise.

LESSON FOCUS (15 – 20 MINUTES)

Paddles and Balls

1. Introduce proper method of holding paddle: forehand and backhand grip.
2. Place ball on paddle and attempt to roll it around the edge of the paddle without allowing it to fall off the paddle. Flip the paddle over and roll ball.

DPE pp. 378 – 380

Scatter formation.

Ping pong paddles and old tennis balls with holes punched in them work well. Also, one can use the children's hands as paddles and a fleece ball can be used.

Cog.—The student will be able to name five sports in which paddle skills are used.

PM.—The student will be able to control the paddle and ball in a variety of situations.

MOVEMENT EXPERIENCE— CONTENT	ORGANIZATION AND TEACHING HINTS	EXPECTED STUDENT OBJECTIVES AND OUTCOMES

3. Balance the ball on the paddle using both right and left hands as well as both grips while trying the following challenges:
  a. Touch the floor with hand.
  b. Move to knees and back to feet.
  c. Sit down and back to feet.
  d. Lie down and get back on feet.
  e. Skip, gallop, or any other locomotor movement.
  f. Choice activity.
4. Bounce the ball in the air using the paddle.
  a. See how many times it can be bounced without touching the floor.
  b. Bounce it off the paddle into the air and catch it with the other hand.
  c. Increase the height of the bounce.
  d. Kneel, sit down, other positions (student choice).
  e. Bounce ball off paddle, do a full turn, and continue bouncing, or balance ball on paddle.
  f. Bounce ball in the air, switch paddle to the other hand.
5. Dribble ball with the paddle.
  a. From a kneeling position.
  b. From a sitting position.
  c. From a standing position.
  d. Move in different directions—forward, sideways, circle.
  e. Move using different locomotor movements.
  f. Exploratory activity.
6. Alternate bouncing the ball in the air and on the floor.
7. Bounce ball off the paddle into the air and "catch" it with the paddle.
  a. Increase the height of the bounce.
  b. Perform a heel click, full turn, or similar activity and catch the ball.
8. Bounce the ball continuously off the paddle into the air.
  a. Bounce the ball on the side of the paddle.
  b. Alternate sides of the paddle.
9. Place ball on the floor.
  a. Scoop it up with the paddle.
  b. Roll the ball and scoop it up with the paddle.
	This is a limited-movement activity; thus, break the activity into two parts separated by some running, rope-jumping, or similarly physically demanding activity.
	
	Concentrate on control of the ball and quality of movement. Take your time going through activities.
	
	Use left hands as well as right in developing the paddle skills.
	
	If students have a difficult time controlling the ball, it might be helpful to use fleece balls.
	
	Allow time for student choice.
	
	"Give" with the paddle.
	
	Change the paddle from hand to hand while the ball is in the air.
		Aff.—One way to improve skills is to experiment with different ways of performing them. Discuss the value of trying new activities rather than always practicing areas in which we are already skilled.
		
		Cog.—The length of a lever determines, in part, the amount of force that can be developed in a striking implement. Understand how paddles are an extension of the arm and increase the force generated for striking.
		
		Cog.—Firmness of the grip on a paddle is important when generating force. Force can be lost upon impact if the racket slips.
		
		Cog.—The angle of the paddle when the ball is struck will determine the direction that the ball will travel.
		
		Cog.—A paddle will give the student a longer lever with which to strike the ball, and thus more force can be applied to the ball, which in turn will increase its speed.

MOVEMENT EXPERIENCE— CONTENT	ORGANIZATION AND TEACHING HINTS	EXPECTED STUDENT OBJECTIVES AND OUTCOMES
c. Start dribbling the ball without touching it with hands. 10. Partner Activities. a. Begin partner activities with controlled throwing (feeding) by one partner and the designated stroke return by the other. b. Bounce ball back and forth. How many times can you bounce it back and forth to your partner without missing it? c. Increase the distance between partners and the height of the ball. d. Catch the ball on your paddle after throw from your partner, then return throw. e. Perform stunts while ball is in the air, such as catch ball behind back, under leg, above head, clap hands, heel clicks, full turns, etc. f. Use two balls. g. Move and keep the balls going; try skipping, hopping, jumping, sliding. h. Play Volley Tennis.	Stress the importance of accurate throws.	PM.—The student will be able to perform three partner activities. Aff.—People practice activities in which they are rewarded and praised. Discuss the importance of praising others and encouraging them to practice. Cog.—A balanced diet is important for good nutrition. Foods should be regularly selected from the following four groups: 1. Milk and milk products 2. Meat and protein 3. Fruits and vegetables 4. Breads and cereals Discuss the need for a balanced diet when one is involved in strenuous and demanding activity.

GAME (5 – 7 MINUTES)

Choice:
1. Steal the Treasure, p. 529
2. Trees, p. 535

DYNAMIC PHYSICAL EDUCATION LESSON PLAN
Stunts and Tumbling Skills (Lesson 3)
Level II

Supplies and Equipment Needed:
  One jump rope for each student
  Tumbling mats
  Beach balls
  Tape player
  Music

MOVEMENT EXPERIENCE—CONTENT	ORGANIZATION AND TEACHING HINTS	EXPECTED STUDENT OBJECTIVES AND OUTCOMES

INTRODUCTORY ACTIVITY (2 – 3 MINUTES)

Combination Movement Patterns

Explore some of the following combinations:
1. Run, leap, and roll.
2. Run, collapse, and roll.
3. Hop, turn around, and shake.
4. Run, change direction, and collapse.
5. Kneel and balance.
6. Hop, make a shape in the air, and balance.
7. Twist and untwist.
8. Click heels in different ways.
9. Students' choice.

DPE p. 224

Encourage variety of responses.

Praise children who attempt new and different movements.

Try having students work in pairs and critique each other's movements.

PM.—The student will be able to perform the movement combinations and create three new patterns.

Cog.—The student will be able to distinguish between a nonlocomotor and a locomotor movement.

FITNESS DEVELOPMENT ACTIVITY (7 – 8 MINUTES)

Continuity Drills

Students alternate jump rope activity with exercises done in two-count fashion. Exercises are done with the teacher saying "Ready"; the class answers "One-two" and performs a repetition of the exercise. Teachers or students can lead.

Rope Jumping - Forward	30 seconds
Double Crab Kick	30 seconds
Rope Jumping - Backward	30 seconds
Partial Bent-Knee Sit-Up	45 seconds
Jump and Slowly Turn Body	30 seconds
Push-Ups	45 seconds
Rocker Step	30 seconds
Sit and Twist	30 seconds
Swing-Step Forward	30 seconds
Side Flex	30 seconds
Free Jumping	40 seconds
Sit and Stretch	45 seconds

DPE p. 262

Use scatter formation.

Taped intervals of music and no music can be used to signal rope jumping (with music) and performing exercises (without music).

Other exercises can be substituted to add variation to the activity.

Allow students to adjust the work load to their fitness level. This implies resting if the rope jumping is too strenuous.

PM.—The student will be able to jump-rope continuously without a miss for 30 seconds.

Aff.—Contrary to popular belief, girls can become stronger through exercise and weight training without fear of developing huge, unattractive muscles. Discuss testosterone and the impact it has on muscle development. It might be helpful to bring pictures of various girls as examples of fitness.

MOVEMENT EXPERIENCE—CONTENT	ORGANIZATION AND TEACHING HINTS	EXPECTED STUDENT OBJECTIVES AND OUTCOMES

LESSON FOCUS (15 – 20 MINUTES)

Stunts and Tumbling

Six groups of activities are found in this lesson to insure that youngsters receive a variety of experiences. Pick a few activities from each group and teach them alternately. For example, teach one or two tumbling and inverted balances, then one or two balance stunts, followed by individual stunts, etc. Do not place excessive time on one group of activities at the expense of another.

1. Animal Movements
   a. Double Lame Dog
   b. Turtle
   c. Walrus Slap
   d. Reverse Walrus Slap
2. Tumbling and Inverted Balances
   a. Forward Roll Combinations
   b. Backward Roll Combinations
   c. Headstand Variations
   d. Teeter-Totter
   e. Handstand
3. Balance Stunts
   a. Seat Balance
   b. Face-to-Knee Touch
   c. Finger Touch
4. Individual Stunts
   a. Dead Body Fall
   b. Stoop and Stretch
   c. Tanglefoot
   d. Egg Roll
   e. Toe Touch Nose
   f. Toe Tug Walk
5. Partner and Group Stunts
   a. Camel Lift and Walk
   b. Dump the Wheelbarrow
   c. Dromedary Walk
   d. Centipede
   e. Double Wheelbarrow
6. Partner Support Stunts
   a. Lighthouse
   b. Hip–Shoulder Stand

DPE pp. 463 – 481

Scatter as many tumbling mats as possible throughout the area in order to avoid waiting lines.

Do not perform many repetitions of tumbling and inverted balances. For most children, limiting the number of forward or backward roll repetitions to four or five will prevent fatigue and injury.

As activities become more difficult, the range of skill ability becomes obvious. Allow for individual differences and offer more personalized help.

A major concern for safety is the neck and back region. Overweight children are at greater risk and might be allowed to avoid tumbling and inverted balances.

Whenever youngsters have difficulty, review previously learned activities.

Teach youngsters to stand on the hips and shoulders when doing partner support stunts.

PM.—The student will be able to perform at least two activities from each of the categories.

Cog.—The student will be able to describe proper positioning of the hands and knees in partner support and pyramid activities.

Cog.—The student will be able to name at least three safety principles that are important in tumbling and inverted balance activities.

Aff.—Tumbling is an excellent activity for overcoming personal fear of harm from the activities. Discuss how many athletes must conquer various fears and take risks in order to succeed.

Cog.—When a forward roll is started, the center of gravity is moved outside the base of support. This causes momentum to be developed in the direction of the roll. What skills demand that the performer move into an unstable position?

PM.—The student and his partner will be able to originate and demonstrate two partner support activities.

GAME (5 – 7 MINUTES)

1. Trades, p. 535
2. Beach ball Bat Ball, p. 525

DYNAMIC PHYSICAL EDUCATION LESSON PLAN
Fundamental Skills Using Tug-of-War Ropes and Relays
Level II

Supplies and Equipment Needed:
 15–18 individual tug-of-war ropes
 Relay supplies
 Exercise-to-music tape and tape player
 Tom-tom
 Beanbags or balls
 Relay equipment
 Jump ropes

MOVEMENT EXPERIENCE— CONTENT	ORGANIZATION AND TEACHING HINTS	EXPECTED STUDENT OBJECTIVES AND OUTCOMES

INTRODUCTORY ACTIVITY (2 – 3 MINUTES)

European Running with Equipment

Review European Running and emphasize the following points:
 1. Move to the rhythm.
 2. Lift the knees and prance.
 3. Maintain proper spacing between each other.
After the review, give each child a beanbag or playground ball. Every fourth step, they can toss up the bag or bounce the ball. Other variations can be tried using different beats of the rhythm.

DPE pp. 217 – 218

Use tom-tom to accentuate the rhythm.

Encourage the students to try different challenges with their beanbag or ball.

PM.—The student will be able to toss the beanbag into the air and catch it while doing European Running.

PM.—The student will be able to create three activities with the beanbag or ball while doing European Running.

FITNESS DEVELOPMENT ACTIVITIES (7 – 8 MINUTES)

Exercises to Music

Side Flex (switch sides)	40 seconds
Trunk Twister	25 seconds
Rhythmic Sit-Ups	35 seconds
Slide/Skip	20 seconds
Jumping Jack variations	30 seconds
Triceps Push-Ups	25 seconds
Partial Curl-Ups	45 seconds
Gallop	15 seconds
Push-Ups	25 seconds
Aerobic Bouncing and Clapping	35 seconds
Leg Extensions	40 seconds
Walking to cool down	45 seconds

DPE p. 259

Student should know the exercises before trying to do them rhythmically.

Rhythmic sit-ups are four counts - knees, toes, knees, and down.

The exercise music should be taped prior to the routine. This frees the teacher to move and help students.

Voice instructions can be dubbed onto the tape to tell students when to change to a new exercise.

Aff.—Regular exercise strengthens muscles, thus minimizing the tendency for joint and muscular injury. Discuss that one of the major reasons for the conditioning of athletes is to prevent any injury.

LESSON FOCUS (15 – 20 MINUTES)

Tug-of-War Rope Activities

Alternate tug-of-war rope activities with relays for complete physical development. The relays stimulate the cardiovascular system while the tug-of-war activities develop the muscular system.

DPE pp. 388 – 391

Make sure they hold their *maximum* effort for 8–10 seconds.

Encourage gradual pulling to maximum effort rather than jerking.

PM.—The student will develop sufficient strength to hold her own with partner of equal size.

Cog.—The student will be able to recite what tug-of-war ropes do for body development.

MOVEMENT EXPERIENCE— CONTENT	ORGANIZATION AND TEACHING HINTS	EXPECTED STUDENT OBJECTIVES AND OUTCOMES

A. *Isometric Exercises*
Make sure joints are bent and students aren't leaning.
  1. Standing—use ends of ropes only and try to stretch the handle apart.
    a. Use different hand positions and arm positions.
  2. Partner Resistance Exercises—start and stop on signal.
    a. Standing—sides facing each other and use both arms as well as right and left individually.
    b. Standing facing—use arms at various levels: above, below head, etc.
    c. Seated—sides facing, back to back, facing, legs elevated, etc. Also, hook on feet, knees; tug.
    d. Prone position—feet touching, heads toward each other, pull on ankle, push-up position pull, etc.
    e. On back—pull with feet, knees, arms.
    f. Develop other areas. Pupil choice.
	When signal is given, place tug-of-war ropes on floor, ready for the next activity.
	
	Pull through full range of motion.
		Aff.—Even though tug-of-war ropes are competitive, cooperation is necessary to ensure an equal start and contest. Discuss the necessity of cooperation in all major sports.
		
		Cog.—The student will explain that maximum effort is required for best results in strength development.
		
		Cog.—Oxygen debt occurs when the muscles need more oxygen than is being supplied. Anaerobic exercise usually creates an oxygen debt. Students should be able to distinguish anaerobic from aerobic activities.

B. *Tug-of-War Activities*
  1. Right, left, and both hands.
  2. Leg pulls, elbows, pull between legs.
  3. Tug with three body parts, on all fours.
  4. Crab position, seal walk pull.
  5. Line touch tug (pull until you can touch the line behind you).
  6. Partners facing; on signal, pick up partner's end of rope and pull.
    a. Begin in a push-up position.
    b. Start sitting crossed-leg fashion with hands on head.
    c. Touch a specified line before grabbing partner's end of rope.
	Establish goals to cross in order to win.
	
	Start and stop on signal.
	
	If grip is slipping—stop, renew grip, and proceed.
	
	Rotate partners often.
	
	Place partners on two parallel lines. When one partner is pulled across the opponent's line, the contest is immediately stopped.
		Aff.—A sense of fairness should be encouraged during this highly competitive activity. Take time to discuss the importance of fair play.
		
		Cog.—Arteries, arterioles, and capillaries carry oxygenated blood to the muscles. Capillaries are so small and thin that oxygen passes right through the walls. At the same time, carbon dioxide is transferred from the body cells to the blood cells and carried back to the lungs to be expelled. The blood is transported back to the lungs in the veins. This system is called the circulatory system.

C. *Tug-of-War Games*
  1. Four-way pull.
  2. Two against two pull.
  3. Japanese Tug-of-War.
  4. Hawaiian Tug-of-War.
 	
Relays
 	
Introduce a variety of relays. The following are listed in sequence from easy to difficult.
 	
Partner Relays, p. 551
Carry and Fetch Relay, p. 550
Attention Relay, p. 557
Corner Fly Relay, p. 555
	It might be a good idea to try a change-of-pace activity in the middle of the tug-of-war activities to pick up the tempo of the lesson. Suggested activities are jogging, beanbags, hoops, or jump ropes.
	
	Teach relays with learning to understand the concept of cooperation, competition, playing under stress, and abiding by certain rules in mind, rather than teaching various skills.
	
	Teams should contain four to eight members. Change leaders often.
		PM.—The student will be able to participate in the relays at an adequate level.

MOVEMENT EXPERIENCE— CONTENT	ORGANIZATION AND TEACHING HINTS	EXPECTED STUDENT OBJECTIVES AND OUTCOMES
Pass and Squat Relay, p. 555 Rescue Relay, p. 556 Circular Attention Relay, p. 557 Potato Relays, p. 552 Tadpole Relay, p. 555 Three Spot Relay, pp. 551 – 552 Jack Rabbit Relay, p. 554	Rotate students into different squads so the makeup of each squad changes. Have the children sit down when they are finished. Put the least talented students in the middle of the squad so they do not stand out. Emphasis should be on student enjoyment rather than winning at all costs.	Aff.—Relays involve performing under stress. Explain what happens to athletic performance when stress is too great. Mention the fear of looking stupid and being embarrassed. Cog.—The importance of winning sometimes supersedes the reasons for participating in competitive activities. Discuss participating for enjoyment, skill development, and fitness maintenance.

GAME (5 – 7 MINUTES)

Since relays are spirited and competitive, it might be a good idea to spend a few minutes doing something restful and relaxing.

DYNAMIC PHYSICAL EDUCATION LESSON PLAN
Rhythmic Movement with Equipment (Lesson 4)
Level II

Supplies and Equipment Needed:
  Playground balls or equivalent
  Jump ropes (individual)
  Tape player and music
  Exercise-to-music tape
  Lummi sticks
  Hoops
  Cageball

MOVEMENT EXPERIENCE— CONTENT	ORGANIZATION AND TEACHING HINTS	EXPECTED STUDENT OBJECTIVES AND OUTCOMES

INTRODUCTORY ACTIVITY (2 – 3 MINUTES)

Marking

"Mark" by touching partner. After touch, reverse and the other partner attempts to mark.

Variations:
1. Use the eight basic locomotor movements.
2. Use positions such as Crab Walk, Puppy Dog Walk, etc.
3. Allow a point to be scored only when they touch a specified body part (i.e., knee, elbow, left hand).
4. Use signal to freeze, then student attempts to "mark" (or tag) partner. Reverse roles.
5. Use a whistle signal to change partners' roles. (If chasing partner, reverse and attempt to move *away* from the other.)

DPE p. 222

Encourage students to "watch where they are going" so they won't run into each other.

Partners should be somewhat equal in ability.

Change partners once or twice.

PM.—The students will be able to move with enough agility and quickness to allow them to catch as well as evade their partners.

Cog.—The student will be able to verbalize a simple reason for warm-up prior to strenuous activity.

FITNESS DEVELOPMENT ACTIVITIES (7 – 8 MINUTES)

Exercises to Music

Side Flex (switch sides)	40 seconds
Trunk Twister	25 seconds
Rhythmic Sit-Ups	35 seconds
Slide/Skip	20 seconds
Jumping Jack variations	30 seconds
Triceps Push-Ups	25 seconds
Partial Curl-Ups	45 seconds
Gallop	15 seconds
Push-Ups	25 seconds
Aerobic Bouncing and Clapping	35 seconds
Leg Extensions	40 seconds
Walking to cool down	45 seconds

DPE p. 259

Student should know the exercises before trying to do them rhythmically.

Rhythmic sit-ups are four counts - knees, toes, knees, and down.

The exercise music should be taped prior to the routine. This frees the teacher to move and help students.

Voice instructions can be dubbed onto the tape to tell students when to change to a new exercise.

Cog.—The body starts to perspire in an attempt to maintain a constant temperature. The student will verbalize this in his own words.

PM—The student will be able to perform all repetitions of the fitness activities.

Aff.—Regulation of body temperature is essential for comfort and safety. Discuss the many ways we attempt to regulate this temperature—more or fewer clothes, perspiring, swimming, fires.

MOVEMENT EXPERIENCE—CONTENT	ORGANIZATION AND TEACHING HINTS	EXPECTED STUDENT OBJECTIVES AND OUTCOMES

LESSON FOCUS (15 – 20 MINUTES)

Rhythms with Equipment and Lummi Stick Activities

A. *Rope Jumping to Music*
1. Perform the slow-time and fast-time rhythm with the rope held in one hand and turned.
2. Jump the rope and practice changing back and forth from slow to fast time.
3. Introduce a few basic steps that you plan to use in your routine, for instance, two-foot basic step, swing step forward and sideward, and crossing arms forward.
4. Try a rope jumping routine. The following routine is based on a schottische record and can serve the dual purpose of enhancing both rope jumping and the schottische step.

1st Verse Part: Two-foot basic jump—slow time.

Chorus: Two-foot basic jump—fast time.

2nd Verse Part: Alternate basic foot step—slow time.

Chorus: Alternate basic foot step—fast time.

3rd Verse Part: Swing Step Forward—slow time.

Chorus: Swing Step Forward—fast time.

4th Verse Part: Swing Step Sideward—slow time.

Chorus: Swing Step Sideward—slow time.

DPE p. 410

Use music that possesses a rhythm that is steady, unchanging, and easy to hear.

Music that has a two-part format (a verse and chorus) is excellent as it gives students a natural break at which to change their routine.

Turn up the amplifier so the music is loud and easy to hear.

It may be necessary to take a short break and work with something like beanbags or play an inactive game, as children will tire easily in this activity.

Double Dutch activities can be used for developing a long-jump rope rhythmic routine.

Be patient. Some students will have more difficulty jumping to the rhythm than others.

PM—The student will be able to jump-rope to the rhythm of the music.

PM.—The student will be able to perform the routine to the schottische with the jump rope.

Cog.—The students will recognize the basic underlying beat and clap their hands to the rhythm after listening to a variety of records.

Aff.—The student will learn the value of overlearning a skill. Here is a chance to discuss the overlearning principle and explain that it is hard to listen for the rhythm if you haven't overlearned the skill of rope jumping. If you *have* overlearned rope jumping, you can easily listen to the music *without* thinking about rope jumping.

Cog.—The development of aerobic capacity involves basic elements: intensity, duration, and frequency of exercise. Students will understand each of the elements and how each can be manipulated to enhance fitness level.

B. *Ball Skills to Music*
1. Perform the following skills to the rhythm of the music:
   a. Bounce and catch.
   b. Bounce, clap, catch; bounce, turn, catch—also use toss.
   c. Dribble continuously in place and while moving.
   d. Work with a partner or in groups, passing one or more balls from one another in rhythm.
   e. Develop a routine utilizing the skills above.

DPE, pp. 368 – 372

Bounce a certain number of times and catch. Combine the bounces with various locomotor movements.

Form circles, triangles, and other patterns. Dribble forward, backward, sideward, stop and go.

Vary with bounce passes.

Hula hoops may also be used if more variety is desired.

PM.—The student will be able to bounce, pass, and catch the ball in rhythm to the music.

PM—The students will be able to develop creative routines utilizing themselves and partners.

Cog.—Rhythm and timing are important elements in motor skill performance. Discuss the need for learning rhythmic activities through correct practice and repetition.

MOVEMENT EXPERIENCE— CONTENT	ORGANIZATION AND TEACHING HINTS	EXPECTED STUDENT OBJECTIVES AND OUTCOMES

C. *Lummi Sticks*

1. Without sticks, learn the chant.
2. Issue sticks. Show: vertical taps, tap together. Work out a three-count routine: (1) vertical tap, (2) tap together, (3) rest beat. Sing the chant to this rhythm.
3. Organize by partners. Children sit cross-legged, facing, at a distance of 18–20". Work out the following routines:
   a. Vertical tap, tap together, partner tap right; vertical tap, tap together, partner tap left.
   b. Vertical tap, tap together, pass right stick; vertical tap, tap together, pass left stick.
   c. Vertical tap, tap together, toss right stick; vertical tap, tap together, toss left stick.
   d. Repeat a, b, c, except substitute an end tap and flip for the vertical tap and tap together (i.e., end tap, flip, partner tap right, end tap, flip, partner tap left).
   e. Vertical tap, tap together, pass right and left quickly; repeat.
   f. End tap, flip, toss right and left quickly, repeat.
   g. Right flip side, left flip in front, vertical tap in place, partner tap right; left flip side, right flip front, vertical tap in place, tap left.
   h. End tap in front, flip, vertical tap, tap together, toss right, toss left.
   i. Vertical tap, tap together, right stick to partner's left hand and left stick to own right hand. Repeat.
   j. Repeat previous routines, but reverse the circle.
   k. Devise own routines.

DPE, pp. 344 – 345

Most commercially available lummi stick music is written in measures of four beats (4/4). However, the traditional way is a three-beat measure (3/4) as described here. If a 4/4 rhythm is used, a pause or additional movement will have to be added to the routines listed.

The traditional chant is listed in the text. If using the chant, establish it early as it must carry the activity.

Copy the music and words onto a poster. A piano helps get the tune. Moderately slow beat.

Hold stick with thumb and fingers (not the first) at the bottom third of the stick.

Stress relaxed and light tapping.

Partners provide their own chanting. Two or three sets of partners can work in unison.

PM.—The student will get accustomed to the proper grip so it becomes automatic.

PM.—The student will be able to do the following: vertical tap, tap together, partner tap right (left), pass right (left), toss right (left), end tap, flip, toss right and left quickly; and he will put these together in rhythm to the chant.

Cog.—Water accounts for 70% of the body's weight. At least a quart of water must be ingested per day. Discuss how a great deal more must be ingested when one is involved in strenuous exercise. What problems arise when one doesn't drink enough water?

Cog.—Practicing skills incorrectly can make it difficult to learn them correctly later. Discuss the need for patience with one's self when learning new rhythmic activities. This prevents learning them incorrectly due to fear of failure and resultant peer pressure.

Cog.—All activities in sports involve rhythm. Most movements can be classified into even or uneven rhythm. Identify various sport skills and the underlying rhythm involved when they are performed correctly.

Cog.—The student will recognize and be able to do circling.

Aff.—People feel part of a group when they can perform mutual skills. Discuss how learning various physical skills allows people to interact with friends and people with similar interests.

GAME (5 – 7 MINUTES)

1. Alaska Baseball, p. 532
2. Addition Tag, p. 532

DYNAMIC PHYSICAL EDUCATION LESSON PLAN
Track and Field–Related Activities (Lesson 1)
Level II

Supplies and Equipment Needed:
Two stopwatches with neck lanyards (box for these for safety in the field)
Measuring boards for the four jumps
Starter (p. 716)
Pits for the jumps with takeoff boards
8–12 hurdles
Rope crossbar for high jump (p. 710)
High jump standards
Technique hints for each station (on poster boards)
Eight batons
Four sets of boxes and blocks for potato relay

MOVEMENT EXPERIENCE—CONTENT	ORGANIZATION AND TEACHING HINTS	EXPECTED STUDENT OBJECTIVES AND OUTCOMES

INTRODUCTORY ACTIVITY AND FITNESS DEVELOPMENT ACTIVITIES (9 – 11 MINUTES)

Stretching and Jogging

Combine the introductory and fitness activities during the track and field unit. This will help students understand how to stretch and warm up for demanding activity such as track and field.
Jog for 1–2 minutes
Standing Hip Bend   30 seconds
Sitting Stretch   30 seconds
Partner Rowing   60 seconds
Bear Hug (20 seconds
   each leg)   40 seconds
Side Flex (20 seconds
   each leg)   40 seconds
Trunk Twister   30 seconds
Jog for 2–3 minutes

DPE pp. 248 – 249

To prepare for strenuous activity, students should learn to warm up their body by walking or jogging, stretching, and finishing with jogging.

Avoid bouncing during the stretching activities. All stretching should be smooth and controlled movements.

Cog.—The student will be able to explain why stretching exercises and warm-ups are essential to track and field work.

PM.—The student will demonstrate the ability to put proper stress on muscles in stretching.

LESSON FOCUS (15 – 20 MINUTES)

Track and Field (1st meeting)

A. *Orientation*
  1. Goal is self-improvement and developing proper techniques.
  2. Each must accept responsibility for self-directed work. Try all activities.
  3. Learn from the general sessions and from the technique hints that are given at each station.
  4. You should rotate through two stations each day. The following period, you will participate in two other station activities. Please stay at your stations until the time is signaled for rotation.
  5. To measure the long jumps and the hop-step-and-jump, use the measuring tapes.

DPE pp. 659 – 670

Come to a central point. They should be ready to rest and listen.

Aff.—To succeed in track and field, one must work diligently and independently. Discuss the need for self-discipline in training.

Aff.—It is important to concentrate on good techniques, rather than performance, at this point. Discuss the importance of learning proper technique before worrying about maximum effort.

PM.—The student will demonstrate the ability to use the measuring tapes accurately.

191

MOVEMENT EXPERIENCE—CONTENT	ORGANIZATION AND TEACHING HINTS	EXPECTED STUDENT OBJECTIVES AND OUTCOMES

6. Use care with the stopwatches. They are expensive to purchase and also to repair. Put the lanyard around your neck when using stopwatches.
7. Announce the four groups. (Form groups according to formula on p. 665.)
 	
B. *Group Drills*
  1. Explain starting:
    a. Standing start
    b. Norwegian start
    c. Sprint start
  2. Starting practice by groups.
  3. Explain striding.
  4. Stride practice.
 	
C. *Station Orientation*
Place technique posters on cones at each station. Send a group to each station.
	Emphasize care for the watches. Show how they work and emphasize no winding.
	
	Explain that height is a factor and that this is one reason the groups are formed. They are important particularly in the high jump.
	
	Use an entire group at one time.
	
	Stride about 70 yd and return to start. Repeat several times.
		Cog.—The student will be able to explain how a stopwatch operates.
		
		Aff.—Acceptance of responsibility for care of equipment.
		
		Aff.—Acceptance by students of the group division is necessary if this approach is to work. Take time to discuss grouping, if deemed necessary.
		
		PM.—The student will demonstrate improvement in form, technique, and performance of:
		  Starting
		  Sprinting
		  Striding
		  Hop-step-and-jump
		  High jump
		  Relay and baton passing
		  Standing Long Jump (optional)
		  Potato Shuttle Race
		  Running Long Jump
		  Hurdling

Station 1
Starting and Sprinting
  1. Front foot 4–12" behind line.
  2. Thumb and first finger behind line, other fingers support.
  3. Knee of other leg placed just opposite front foot.
  4. On "get set," seat is raised, the down knee comes up a little, and the shoulders move forward over the hands.
  5. On "go," push off sharply and take short, driving steps.
Hop-Step-and-Jump
  1. Important to get the sequence and rhythm first, then later try for distance.
  2. Sprinting.
	Sprint 25 to 30 yd or so. Have one child use the starter and count out the rhythm of the start.
	
	Should be a gradual rise of the shoulders.
	
	Foul rule applies.
	
	The runner can sprint forward and then take a jump as a return activity.
		Cog.—The student will demonstrate knowledge about the points of technique of the above.
		
		Cog.—When sprinting, initial contact is made with the ball of the foot as compared with the heel or flat-footed contact made when running long distance. Discuss this and arm carry difference between sprinters and distance runners.

Station 2
Running High Jump
  1. Place bar low enough so all can practice.
  2. Approach at 45°.
  3. Good kick-up and arm action.
Baton Passing
  1. Decide on method of passing.
  2. Incoming runner passes with left hand to right hand of receiver.
  3. After receiving, change to the left hand.
  4. Estimate how fast to take off with respect to the incoming runner.
	Can begin with the scissors style.
	
	Use only two heights in beginning practice.
	
	No contest for height.
	
	Space runners.
	
	Change baton promptly.
	
	Avoid "blind" exchange.
		Cog.—Gravity and air resistance limit performances in the jumping events. Identify these factors and why altitude (Mexico City Olympics) has a positive impact on long jump performances.
		
		Cog.—The ratio of fast twitch versus slow twitch fibers is genetically determined. Fast twitch fibers contract rapidly and are useful in activities demanding speed and explosive power. Slow twitch fibers contract less quickly and are excellent for aerobic endurance activities. People are born with varying ratios and thus have a predisposition to succeed in activities in line with their given muscle fiber ratio.

MOVEMENT EXPERIENCE—CONTENT	ORGANIZATION AND TEACHING HINTS	EXPECTED STUDENT OBJECTIVES AND OUTCOMES
Station 3		
Running Long Jump	Stress the foul rule.	
1. Decide on jumping foot.	Hit with the jumping foot.	
2. Establish check point.	Use either activity.	
3. Control last four steps.		
4. Seek height.		
Standing Long Jump or the Potato Shuttle Race		
Station 4		Cog.—Knowledge of what interval training is and can do for performance.
Hurdling	Work for form.	
1. At beginning, use one or two hurdles.	Keep in the infield, keeping track clear.	
2. Leading foot is directly forward.	Begin in straightaway and stride around curve.	
Striding for Distance—Concluding Activity Interval Training	Best around the track.	
1. Repeat three to four times.		
2. Run 110 yd, walk 110 yd.		
Succeeding Meetings for the First Week		
1. Same introductory and fitness activity. Omit the orientation.		
2. Repeat the group drills—starting and striding. Make them shorter.		
3. Each group visits only two stations each meeting and the other two the next meeting.		
4. Finish with interval training.		

GAME ACTIVITY (5 – 7 MINUTES)

Potato Shuttle Relay, p. 666

DYNAMIC PHYSICAL EDUCATION LESSON PLAN
Track and Field–Related Activities (Lesson 2)
Level II

Supplies and Equipment Needed:
Four stopwatches with neck lanyards (box for these for safety in the field)
Measuring boards for the four jumps
Starter (p. 716)
Pits for the jumps with takeoff boards
8–12 hurdles
Stretch rope crossbar for high jump (p. 710)
High jump standards
Technique hints for each station (on poster boards)
Eight batons
Four sets—boxes and blocks for potato relay
Clipboards and pencils
Recording sheets for each group

MOVEMENT EXPERIENCE—CONTENT	ORGANIZATION AND TEACHING HINTS	EXPECTED STUDENT OBJECTIVES AND OUTCOMES

INTRODUCTORY ACTIVITY AND FITNESS DEVELOPMENT ACTIVITIES (9 – 11 MINUTES)

Stretching and Jogging

Combine the introductory and fitness activities during the track and field unit. This will help students understand how to stretch and warm up for demanding activity such as track and field.

Jog for 1–2 minutes
Standing Hip Bend   30 seconds
Sitting Stretch   30 seconds
Partner Rowing   60 seconds
Bear Hug (20 seconds
  each leg)   40 seconds
Side Flex (20 seconds
  each leg)   40 seconds
Trunk Twister   30 seconds
Jog for 2–3 minutes

DPE pp. 248 – 249

To prepare for strenuous activity, students should learn to warm up their body by walking or jogging, stretching, and finishing with jogging.

Avoid bouncing during the stretching activities. All stretching should be smooth and controlled movements.

Cog.—The student will be able to explain why stretching exercises and warm-ups are essential to track and field work.

PM.—The student will demonstrate the ability to put proper stress on muscles in stretching.

LESSON FOCUS (15 – 20 MINUTES)

Track and Field

Continue the same rotation plan as in week 1. Each group participates in two stations each meeting. Next meeting, visit the other two stations.

At each station, students will record the performances. Record all performances and circle the best one.

Station 1
Sprinting
1. 50-yd distance
2. 70-yd distance
3. Two trials
Hop-Step-and-Jump
1. Three trials
2. Record all three, circle best

DPE pp. 659 – 670

Stress legibility.

One watch.

Run individually.

Take best time.

Use starter.

PM.—The student will be able to perform creditably in the various events.

Cog.—Red blood cells pick up oxygen as they pass through the lungs. When exercising, a person breathes faster to bring more oxygen into the lungs. The heart beats faster to move more blood and transport oxygen to the muscles.

MOVEMENT EXPERIENCE—CONTENT	ORGANIZATION AND TEACHING HINTS	EXPECTED STUDENT OBJECTIVES AND OUTCOMES
Station 2 *High Jump* 1. Begin at 3 ft, raise 6" at a time 2. Two trials 3. Record best height made *Baton Passing*—Practice while waiting for high jump turn or when "out."	This increment keeps things moving. Use elastic shock cord for a crossbar. This eliminates the fear of the crossbar.	Cog.—Smoking causes the heart rate to jump 10–20 beats per minute. The blood vessels constrict and the heart must pump harder to get blood through them. Discuss how this can be a detriment to good health.
Station 3 *Running Long Jump* 1. Three trials 2. Record all three, circle best *Standing Long Jump* 1. Three trials 2. Record all three, circle best *Potato Relay*—One trial, run two races at a time.	Use foul rule. Watch for falling backward. Two watches.	
Station 4 *Hurdling* 1. Set up 60-yd hurdle course 2. Give two trials 3. Take best time *Striding*—Striding practice can be done while waiting for turns.	This can be omitted.	

GAME (5 – 7 MINUTES)

Relays Run as many as possible on a team. Repeat if enough time or change the type or distance.		PM.—The student will demonstrate the ability to cooperate in running the relay.

Note: It is possible to use the last meeting of track for a type of track and field meet. Use sprints, hurdles, and field events. Allow each to enter one track and one field event. Parents can be asked to help.

DYNAMIC PHYSICAL EDUCATION LESSON PLAN
Fundamental Skills Using Parachute Activity
Level II

Supplies and Equipment Needed:
  Parachute
  Cones
  Beanbags
  Jump ropes
  Basketballs or cageballs

MOVEMENT EXPERIENCE—CONTENT	ORGANIZATION AND TEACHING HINTS	EXPECTED STUDENT OBJECTIVES AND OUTCOMES

INTRODUCTORY ACTIVITY (2 – 3 MINUTES)

Creative Routine

Each student should develop his own warm-up routine. Emphasis should be on a balanced approach that touches all major muscle groups.

DPE pp. 223 – 224

It might be necessary to point out some activities to stimulate some of the youngsters.

Charts on the walls could be used to describe various warm-up activities.

PM.—The students will be able to physically warm themselves up in preparation for fitness activities.

FITNESS DEVELOPMENT ACTIVITY (7 – 8 MINUTES)

Hexagon Hustle

Outline a large hexagon with six cones. Place signs with directions on both sides of the cones. The signs identify the hustle activity students are to perform as they approach a cone.

Hustle	20 seconds
Push-Up from Knees	30 seconds
Hustle	20 seconds
Bend and Stretch	
(8 counts)	30 seconds
Hustle	20 seconds
Jumping Jacks (4 counts)	30 seconds
Hustle	20 seconds
Sit-Ups (2 counts)	40 seconds
Hustle	20 seconds
Double Leg Crab Kick	
(2 counts)	30 seconds
Hustle	20 seconds
Sit and Stretch (8 counts)	40 seconds
Hustle	20 seconds
Power Jumper	30 seconds
Hustle	20 seconds
Squat Thrust (4 counts)	30 seconds

Conclude the Hexagon Hustle with a slow jog or walk.

DPE p. 262

Examples of hustle activities that can be listed on signs are:
1. Jogging
2. Skipping and galloping
3. Hopping or jumping
4. Sliding
5. Running and leaping
6. Animal movements
7. Sport movements such as defensive sliding, running backwards, and carioca step.

During the hustle, faster moving students can pass to the outside of the hexagon.

Change directions regularly to keep students spaced evenly along the hexagon.

During the hustle, quality movement rather than speed is the goal.

Cog.—The student will be able to identify five exercises that stretch different body parts.

PM.—The student will be able to perform exercises to stretch the body.

Aff.—The student will be able to explain that stretching should be done slowly and with gradual force, rather than strong bouncing movements.

LESSON FOCUS (15 – 20 MINUTES)

Parachute Activities

1. Circular movements—Move utilizing the basic locomotor movements and holding the chute at various levels.

DPE pp. 433 – 436

Teach the proper terminology so students can identify the various activities.

Cog.— The student will be able to identify the various parachute activities by name.

MOVEMENT EXPERIENCE— CONTENT	ORGANIZATION AND TEACHING HINTS	EXPECTED STUDENT OBJECTIVES AND OUTCOMES

2. Shaking the Rug and Making Waves—Shaking the Rug should involve small, rapid movements, whereas Making Waves is large movements.
3. Making a Dome—Parachute should be on the floor and held with both hands. Make a dome by standing up and rapidly lifting the chute overhead.
   a. Punching Bag—Make a dome, stand on edge, and punch the air out.
   b. Make a Dome—Stand on the edge, and in a circular fashion, push the air around the parachute.
4. Mushroom—Similar to the Dome except three or four steps toward the center are taken by each student.
   a. Mushroom Release—All students release the chute at its peak of inflation.
   b. Mushroom Run—Make a mushroom, move in to center, release grip, and run around the inside of the chute back to place.
5. Activities with balls and beanbags
   a. Ball Circle—Use a basketball or cageball and make it circle around the outside of the chute. Add a second ball.
   b. Popcorn—Place six to ten beanbags on the chute and shake them into the air.
   c. Poison Snake—Place six to ten jump ropes on the chute. Divide the players in half. Try to shake the ropes so they touch a player on the opposing team.
   d. Cannon ball—Use a 24" cageball on the chute. On the command "load," lower the chute to the ground. On "fire," lift the chute and fire the ball into the air.
	Perform the activities with different grips.
	
	Various patterns can be made by having the class work in small groups around the chute.
	
	Try making a dome while moving in a circle.
	
	Teach the proper technique of standing and lifting the parachute to avoid back strain.
	
	Work for precision so that all students are together in their movement.
	
	Proper care of the chute should be taught so that it is not ripped.
	
	Many routines to music can be developed and incorporated with the various chute activities. Many folk dances can be done utilizing parachute activities which increases motivation for students.
		Aff.—The parachute requires group cooperation for successful implementation of the activities. Discuss the importance of working together to improve everybody's welfare.
		
		PM.—The student will be able to cooperatively perform the following activities:
		  1. Making Waves.
		  2. Making a Dome.
		  3. Popcorn.
		  4. Ball Circles.
		
		PM.—The student will be able to perform a simple folk dance incorporating the parachute.
		
		Cog.—When exercising in hot weather, the amount of clothes worn should be minimized. This is due to the fact that clothes prevent sweat from evaporating and cooling the body. On the other hand, when it is cold outside, the body should be clothed so body heat will be maintained.

GAME (5 – 7 MINUTES)

The following games are suggested:
1. Nonda's Car Lot, p. 528
2. Box Ball, p. 532

DYNAMIC PHYSICAL EDUCATION LESSON PLAN
Manipulative Skills Using Frisbees (Flying Discs)
Level II

Supplies and Equipment Needed:
- Cones
- One Frisbee per child
- Hoops
- Signs
- Indian clubs

MOVEMENT EXPERIENCE—CONTENT	ORGANIZATION AND TEACHING HINTS	EXPECTED STUDENT OBJECTIVES AND OUTCOMES

INTRODUCTORY ACTIVITY (2 – 3 MINUTES)

Four-Corners Movement

Lay out a square with a cone at each corner. As the child passes each corner, he changes to a different locomotor movement.

Challenge the students by declaring various qualities of movement (i.e., soft, heavy, slow, fast).

DPE pp. 245 – 246

Students do not have to stay in line but can pass if they are doing a faster moving movement.

Encourage variety of movements and performing some movements that require placing body weight on the hands.

PM.—The student will be able to perform light locomotor movements using three different qualities.

FITNESS DEVELOPMENT ACTIVITY (7 – 8 MINUTES)

Hexagon Hustle

Outline a large hexagon with six cones. Place signs with directions on both sides of the cones. The signs identify the hustle activity students are to perform as they approach a cone.

Hustle	25 seconds
Push-Up from Knees	30 seconds
Hustle	25 seconds
Bend and Stretch (8 counts)	30 seconds
Hustle	25 seconds
Jumping Jacks (4 counts)	30 seconds
Hustle	25 seconds
Sit-Ups (2 counts)	40 seconds
Hustle	25 seconds
Double Leg Crab Kick (2 counts)	30 seconds
Hustle	25 seconds
Sit and Stretch (8 counts)	40 seconds
Hustle	25 seconds
Power Jumper	30 seconds
Hustle	25 seconds
Squat Thrust (4 counts)	30 seconds

Conclude the Hexagon Hustle with a slow jog or walk.

DPE p. 262

Examples of hustle activities that can be listed on signs are:
1. Jogging
2. Skipping and galloping
3. Hopping or jumping
4. Sliding
5. Running and leaping
6. Animal movements
7. Sport movements such as defensive sliding, running backwards, and carioca step.

During the hustle, faster moving students can pass to the outside of the hexagon.

Change directions regularly to keep students spaced evenly along the hexagon.

During the hustle, quality movement rather than speed is the goal.

Cog.—The student will be able to identify five exercises that stretch different body parts.

PM.—The student will be able to perform exercises to stretch her body.

Aff.—The student will be able to explain that stretching should be done slowly and with gradual force, rather than strong bouncing movements.

MOVEMENT EXPERIENCE—CONTENT	ORGANIZATION AND TEACHING HINTS	EXPECTED STUDENT OBJECTIVES AND OUTCOMES

LESSON FOCUS (15 – 20 MINUTES)

Frisbees (Flying Discs)

1. Skills:
   a. Backhand Throw
   b. Underhand Throw
   c. Thumbs-Down Catch
   d. Thumbs-Up Catch

Practice the throwing and catching skills so youngsters will feel comfortable with the following activities.

2. Activities
   a. Throw the Frisbee at different levels to partner.
   b. Throw a curve—to the left, right, and upward. Vary the speed of the curve.
   c. Throw a bounce pass—try a low and a high pass.
   d. Throw the disc like a boomerang. Must throw at a steep angle into the wind.
   e. Throw the Frisbee into the air, run and catch. Increase the distance of the throw.
   f. Throw the Frisbee through a hoop held by a partner.
   g. Catch the Frisbee under your leg. Catch it behind your back.
   h. Throw the Frisbees into hoops that are placed on the ground as targets. Different-colored hoops can be given different values. Throw through your partner's legs.
   i. Frisbee bowling—One partner has an Indian club which the other partner attempts to knock down by throwing the Frisbee.
   j. Play catch while moving. Lead your partner so he doesn't have to break stride.
   k. See how many successful throws and catches you can make in 30 seconds.
   l. Frisbee Baseball Pitching—Attempt to throw the Frisbee into your partner's "Strike Zone."

DPE pp. 380 – 382

Partner formation.

Throw and catch with a partner—begin with short distances and gradually move apart as skill improves.

Give students plenty of room—their lack of skill will result in many inaccurate throws.

Offer a helping station for those students who have difficulty learning the basic throws.

Emphasize accuracy rather than distance in the early stages of throwing the Frisbee.

Use both dominant and nondominant hands.

For a straight throw, the disc should be parallel to the ground on release.

Remind students to focus their eyes on the disc as long as possible.

Encourage students to try different activities of their own creation.

PM.—The student will be able to perform the following skills:
   a. Backhand Throw.
   b. Underhand Throw.
   c. Thumbs-Down Catch.
   d. Thumbs-Up Catch.

Cog.—The student will be able to explain the effect that the angle of the disc upon release will have on its flight.

Cog.—Age plays a role on pulse rate. At birth, the heart rate is 130–140 beats per minute at rest. At maturity, the heart rate will have gradually slowed to a rate of 68–84 beats per minute.

PM.—The student will be able to catch the Frisbee five out of eight times.

Aff.—Frisbees are a recreational activity. Discuss the importance of learning leisure-time skills for the future.

GAME (5 – 7 MINUTES)

Try some Frisbee games (p. 546).
1. Frisbee Keep-Away.
2. Frisbee Through-the-Legs Target Throw.
3. Frisbee Golf—Use hula hoops for the cups. Establish pars for various distance holes.

DYNAMIC PHYSICAL EDUCATION LESSON PLAN
Softball-Related Activities (Lesson 1)
Level II

Supplies and Equipment Needed:
Station 1: 2 batting tees, 4 balls, 2 bats (whiffle balls and bats preferred)
Station 2: 1 ball for each 2 children (can use fleece balls or whiffle balls)
Station 3: 4 bases (home plates), 4 balls
Station 4: 2 balls, 2 bats
28-ft. parachute and 10–12 long jump ropes

MOVEMENT EXPERIENCE— CONTENT	ORGANIZATION AND TEACHING HINTS	EXPECTED STUDENT OBJECTIVES AND OUTCOMES

INTRODUCTORY ACTIVITY (2 – 3 MINUTES)

Long-Rope Routine

Form a loose column and hold a long jump rope in the right hand.
First signal: Run in a column with one child leading the way.
Second signal: Shift the rope overhead from right hand to left hand without stopping.
Third signal: Two inside children let go of rope, outside children begin turning the rope for the two who have released the rope. They continue jumping the rope until the next signal.
Fourth signal: The outside youngsters move to the inside positions and vice versa. The sequence is then repeated.

DPE, p. 222

Group youngsters by fours.

The sequence should be smooth with very little hesitation.

Youngsters can think of other activities to perform with the rope on the second signal.

May want to have students carry two long ropes and work on Double Dutch on the third and fourth signals.

PM.—The student will be able to jump the long rope ten times consecutively without a miss.

Cog.—The student will be able to develop one new idea to be used by his or her group on the second signal.

FITNESS DEVELOPMENT ACTIVITY (7 – 8 MINUTES)

Parachute Fitness

1. Jog in circle with chute held in left hand. Reverse directions and hold with right hand.
2. Standing, raise the chute overhead, lower to waist, lower to toes, raise to waist, etc.
3. Slide to the right; return slide to the left.
4. Sit and perform sit-ups - 30 seconds.
5. Skip for 20 seconds.
6. Freeze; face the center, and stretch the chute tightly with bent arms. Hold for 8–12 seconds. Repeat five to six times.
7. Run in place, hold the chute at waist level, and hit the chute with lifted knees.
8. Sit with legs under the chute. Do a seat walk toward the center. Return to the perimeter. Repeat four to six times.

DPE, pp. 244 – 245

Evenly space youngsters around the chute.

Use different grips to add variation to the activities.

Develop group morale by encouraging students to move together.

Use music to motivate youngsters.

To cool down, allow youngsters a minute to perform parachute stunts like the Dome or Mushroom.

PM.—The students will be able to perform the exercises together.

Aff.—There are many approaches and activities used to develop fitness. Discuss the need for variety in developing fitness programs. This is a good time to discuss the reasons we teach a broad range of activities with the class.

MOVEMENT EXPERIENCE— CONTENT	ORGANIZATION AND TEACHING HINTS	EXPECTED STUDENT OBJECTIVES AND OUTCOMES

9. Place the chute on the ground. Jog away from the chute and return on signal. Repeat for 30 seconds.
10. On sides with legs under the chute, perform Side Flex and lift chute with legs.
11. Lie on back with legs under the chute. Shake the chute with the feet.
12. Hop to the center of the chute and return. Repeat for 20 seconds.
13. Assume the push-up position with the legs aligned away from the center of the chute. Shake the chute with one arm while the other arm supports the body.
14. Sit with feet under the chute. Stretch by touching the toes with the chute. Relax with other stretches while sitting.

LESSON FOCUS (15 – 20 MINUTES)

Softball (Multiple Activity Station Teaching)

Divide class equally between stations.

DPE pp. 639 – 657

Squad formation.

Have signs at each of the stations giving both direction and skill hints.

Captain gathers equipment in designated spot before changing to next station.

Aff.—Willingness to cooperate at each station is crucial to the success of the lesson. Discuss and emphasize the importance of cooperation among peers.

Station 1
Batting
1. Weight on both feet.
2. Bat pointed over right shoulder.
3. Trademark up on swing.
4. Elbows up and away from body.
5. Begin with hip roll and short step.
6. Swing level.
7. Follow through.
8. Eyes on ball.

Batting from Tee
1. Stand back (3 ft) from tee, so when stepping forward, ball is hit in front.
2. Show three types of grips.

Divide squad—with one batter, a catcher (next batter), and one or more fielders.

Points to avoid:
1. Lifting the front foot high off the ground
2. Stepping back with the rear foot
3. Dropping the rear shoulder
4. Chopping down on the ball (golfing)
5. Dropping the elbows

For safety, whiffle balls and plastic bats are suggested when working in stations.

PM.—The student will be able to meet the ball squarely on the tee.

Cog.—The student will know the different points in good batting.

Cog.—Strenuous exercise causes blood pressure to go up. This occurs because the heart beats faster and more blood is trying to push its way through the vessels. Why do some people have high blood pressure even at rest?

Station 2
Throwing and Catching
1. Show grips.
2. How to catch—Stress "give," eyes on the ball.

Practice Throwing
1. Overhand.
2. Side arm.
3. Underhand toss.

One ball for each two players. Partners stand about 10 yd apart.

Suggest spacing to conform to skill.

Use "soft" softballs.

PM.—The students will be able to increase their catching potential and increase their accuracy in throwing (three styles).

Cog.—The student will be able to define and recognize good points of throwing and catching.

MOVEMENT EXPERIENCE— CONTENT	ORGANIZATION AND TEACHING HINTS	EXPECTED STUDENT OBJECTIVES AND OUTCOMES
Station 3 *Pitching Rules* 1. Face the batter, both feet on the rubber and the ball held in front with both hands. One step is allowed, and the ball must be delivered on that step. 2. Ball must be pitched underhanded. 3. No motion or fake toward the plate can be made without delivering the ball. 4. No quick return is permitted, nor can the ball be rolled or bounced toward the batter. 5. Practice both regular pitch and windmill.	Divide squad into two groups. Each has a catcher, pitcher, and "batter," who just stands in position. A home plate and pitching rubber are helpful. Stress legal preliminary position before taking one hand off the ball to pitch.	PM.—The student will be able to pitch in observance with the rules. Cog.—The student will know the rules governing pitching. PM.—The student will be able to pitch 50% of the balls into the strike zone. Cog.—Softball is not a very effective sport for exercising the cardiovascular system. Most of the time is spent sitting or standing. Therefore, there is little, if any, aerobic activity.
Station 4 *Throwing or Batting Fly Balls* 1. Begin with high throwing from the "batter." 2. Have the fielders return the ball with a one-bounce throw to the "batter." 3. Show form for high and low catch. Show sure stop for outfielders.	Divide squad into two groups.	PM.—The student will begin to handle (catch) easy fly balls with confidence. PM.—The fielders will improve in estimating flight of the ball and getting under it in time.

LEAD-UP GAMES (5 – 7 MINUTES)

1. Throw It and Run, p. 650 2. Two-Pitch Softball, pp. 650 – 651 3. Hit and Run, p. 651	Play in two groups, with squads against each other.	

DYNAMIC PHYSICAL EDUCATION LESSON PLAN
Softball-Related Activities (Lesson 2)
Level II

Supplies and Equipment Needed:
  Station 1: 2 bats, 2 softballs (whiffle balls and bats are preferred)
  Station 2: 2 plates, 2 softballs
  Station 3: 4 bases (regular diamond), ball, bat (optional)
  Station 4: 2 bats, 2 balls, home plates (optional)
  Parachute
  Tape player
  Music

MOVEMENT EXPERIENCE—CONTENT	ORGANIZATION AND TEACHING HINTS	EXPECTED STUDENT OBJECTIVES AND OUTCOMES

INTRODUCTORY ACTIVITY (2 – 3 MINUTES)

Squad Leader Movement

Squads move around the area, following a leader. When the last change is signaled, the last person goes to the head of the line and becomes the leader.

DPE p. 223

Encourage leaders to keep the squads moving and to offer challenging movements.

PM.—Each leader will be able to take her squad through at least two different movements.

FITNESS DEVELOPMENT ACTIVITY (7 – 8 MINUTES)

Parachute Fitness

1. Jog in circle with chute held in left hand. Reverse directions and hold with right hand.
2. Standing, raise the chute overhead, lower to waist, lower to toes, raise to waist, etc.
3. Slide to the right; return slide to the left.
4. Sit and perform sit-ups - 30 seconds.
5. Skip for 25 seconds.
6. Freeze; face the center, and stretch the chute tightly with bent arms. Hold for 8–12 seconds. Repeat five to six times.
7. Run in place, hold the chute at waist level, and hit the chute with lifted knees.
8. Sit with legs under the chute. Do a seat walk toward the center. Return to the perimeter. Repeat four to six times.
9. Place the chute on the ground. Jog away from the chute and return on signal. Repeat for 35 seconds.
10. On sides with legs under the chute, perform Side Flex and lift chute with legs.
11. Lie on back with legs under the chute. Shake the chute with the feet.
12. Hop to the center of the chute and return. Repeat for 25 seconds.

DPE, pp. 244 – 245

Evenly space youngsters around the chute.

Use different grips to add variation to the activities.

Develop group morale by encouraging students to move together.

Use music to motivate youngsters.

To cool down, allow youngsters a minute to perform parachute stunts like the Dome or Mushroom.

PM.—The student will be able to perform all the parachute exercises.

Cog.—The student will be able to state which parachute exercises are isometric and which are isotonic.

Aff.—Society rewards individuals who are fit. Bring some advertisements from magazines and show how companies try to sell their product using a physically fit model.

MOVEMENT EXPERIENCE— CONTENT	ORGANIZATION AND TEACHING HINTS	EXPECTED STUDENT OBJECTIVES AND OUTCOMES
13. Assume the push-up position with the legs aligned away from the center of the chute. Shake the chute with one arm while the other arm supports the body. 14. Sit with feet under the chute. Stretch by touching the toes with the chute. Relax with other stretches while sitting.		

LESSON FOCUS (15 – 20 MINUTES)

Softball Skills (Multiple Activity Station Teaching) Divide class evenly among the stations.	*DPE* pp. 639 – 657 For safety, whiffle balls and plastic bats should be used when teaching softball with the station format.	Aff.—Each player will work at the designated skill and attempt to improve her skill. Discuss the importance of practicing both strengths and weaknesses.
Station 1 *Game of Pepper* *Station 2* *Pitching and Umpiring* 1. Teach umpiring (by catcher) 　a. Right hand—strike 　b. Left hand—ball	Divide squad into two groups. Change batters every six swings. Stress easy underhand pitching. Need catcher and pitcher. Pitch to three batters and then rotate.	PM.—The players will be able to play this game successfully in order to develop throwing, catching, and striking skills. PM.—The student will be able to "strike out" two out of three batters. PM.—Umpires will gain in increased skill. PM.—The student will be able to demonstrate proper umpiring techniques in calling balls and strikes.
Station 3 *Infield Practice* 1. Throw around the bases clockwise and counterclockwise. 2. Roll ball to infielders and make the play at first. After each play, throw around the infield. 3. If enough skill, bat the ball to the infielders in turn.	Set up regular infield, staffed by squad. Rotate where needed.	PM.—The infielders will gain in skill in infield play. PM.—The infielders will learn to "play" the grounder at the most advantageous spot.
Station 4 *Batting Practice* Each batter takes six swings and then rotates to the field. Catcher becomes batter and pitcher moves up to catcher. Review stress points for batting.	Use the squad. Have hitter, catcher, pitcher, and fielders. Use two softballs to keep things moving. Pitcher must be able to serve up good pitches. Use a shorter distance for pitching.	Cog.—There are five major reasons that arteries become filled with cholesterol and become plugged: 1. Inactivity or lack of exercise 2. Obesity 3. Smoking cigarettes 4. Eating foods high in cholesterol 5. Living with a high level of stress or depression

LEAD-UP GAME

1. In a Pickle, p. 652
2. Beat Ball, p. 652
3. Kick Softball, pp. 651 – 652

DYNAMIC PHYSICAL EDUCATION LESSON PLAN— ALTERNATE
Football-Related Activities (Lesson 1)
Level II

Supplies and Equipment Needed:
8 footballs or foam rubber footballs
4 soccer balls or foam rubber balls
12 cones (for boundaries)
16 flags
16 pinnies

MOVEMENT EXPERIENCE— CONTENT	ORGANIZATION AND TEACHING HINTS	EXPECTED STUDENT OBJECTIVES AND OUTCOMES

INTRODUCTORY AND FITNESS DEVELOPMENT ACTIVITIES

This lesson may be substituted for any of the previous lessons. Use the introductory and fitness development activities given in the sequenced lesson plans.

LESSON FOCUS (15 – 20 MINUTES)

Football

DPE pp. 593 – 606

A. *Orientation* (first day)
   1. Concentrate on techniques.
   2. Basic organization is station teaching, except for group stance drills. Use proper stance in all drills.

B. *Stance Drills*
   1. Offensive stance (3 point)
      a. Feet shoulder width apart.
      b. Toes point ahead.
      c. Heel–toe relationship.
      d. One hand down.
      e. Look ahead.
   2. Defensive stance
      a. Four-point stance.
      b. Toes pointed ahead.
      c. Look ahead.
      d. Move rapidly forward.
         Orientation at each station.

Emphasize that stance is important.

Use stance drill with entire squad at one time; squads go in succession.

Go through four or five repetitions.

Cog.—The student will be able to describe why a good football player employs the proper stance. How does a stance affect stability and balance?

Station 1

Punting
1. Use soccer balls or foam rubber footballs.
2. Technique:
   a. Kicking foot forward.
   b. Short step with that foot.
   c. Long step with other foot.
   d. Good knee flexion.
   e. Keep an eye on the ball.

One ball for each two students.

Squad divides into partner activity.

Concentrate on form with a moderate distance.

PM.—The student will demonstrate the ability to use the two-step punting form.

Station 2

Centering
1. Use three footballs.
2. Technique:
   a. Feet well spread.
   b. Toes pointed ahead.
   c. Proper hand and finger position.
   d. Send to receiver about waist high.

It is easier to concentrate on form when using a soccer ball.

Cog.—The student will be able to tell when a punt is used in a football game and why it is used.

Cog.—Every play starts with a center pass. The student will be able to express the importance of accuracy to prevent fumbles and loose balls.

MOVEMENT EXPERIENCE—CONTENT	ORGANIZATION AND TEACHING HINTS	EXPECTED STUDENT OBJECTIVES AND OUTCOMES

Station 3
1. Use three footballs.
2. Technique (passing):
  a. Comfortable grip.
  b. Point foot in direction of pass.
  c. Turn partially sideways.
  d. Overhand motion.
3. Technique (catching):
  a. Relax fingers and hands.
  b. Bring ball into body.
  c. Little fingers together.
		PM.—The student will demonstrate the ability to center the ball so that centering does not interfere with the play.

Station 4 *Ball Carrying* 1. Use two footballs. 2. Each player has two flags. Show proper method of carrying ball. There probably will be no time for a game on the first day.	Divide squad into defensive and offensive players. Wait until player is completely through area before next player runs. Split the remainder of the time.	

C. *Second Day*
  1. Repeat introductory and fitness activities.
  2. Repeat Stance Drills.
  3. Station Practice:
    a. Squads 1 and 2 at stations 3 and 4.
    b. Squads 3 and 4 at stations 1 and 2.		

D. *Third Day* 1. Repeat introductory and fitness activities. 2. Combination Drill (10 minutes).	By squads. All squads use the drill. Allot enough space. All pass catchers run in the same direction—right to left or vice versa.	PM.—The student will exhibit the ability to coordinate football skills into a game situation.

LEAD-UP GAME (7 – 10 MINUTES)

1. Football End Ball, p. 600
2. Five Passes, p. 601

DYNAMIC PHYSICAL EDUCATION LESSON PLAN— ALTERNATE
Football-Related Activities (Lesson 2)
Level II

Supplies and Equipment Needed:
  8 footballs
  16 pinnies
  24 cones for marking boundaries (or substitutes)
  4 folding mats for the box ball
  Flags

MOVEMENT EXPERIENCE— CONTENT	ORGANIZATION AND TEACHING HINTS	EXPECTED STUDENT OBJECTIVES AND OUTCOMES

INTRODUCTORY AND FITNESS DEVELOPMENT ACTIVITIES

This lesson may be substituted for any of the previous lessons. Use the introductory and fitness development activities given in the sequence plans.

LESSON FOCUS (15 – 20 MINUTES)

MOVEMENT EXPERIENCE— CONTENT	ORGANIZATION AND TEACHING HINTS	EXPECTED STUDENT OBJECTIVES AND OUTCOMES
Football	*DPE* pp. 593 – 606	Cog.—The students will be able to verbalize the rules of football.
First Day	Each has two footballs.	
Orientation (5 minutes)	Select a good kicker for punting.	Aff.—The student will be able to accept the abilities of all in conducting the drills.
1. Review passing, catching, and centering skills.		
2. Divide by sex—squads 1 and 2, boys; squads 3 and 4, girls.		
Station Explanation		
1. Show combination drill.		
2. Show punt return drill.		
Station Activity		
1. Squads 1 and 2 to combination drill.		
2. Squads 3 and 4 to punt return drill.	Exchange positions.	
3. Rotate after 7 or 8 minutes.		
Game (10 minutes)		
1. Football Box Ball, p. 601		
a. Explain basic rules.		
b. Show scoring.		
Second Day		
Repeat introductory and fitness activities. Bring the group together for a brief orientation. Make this brief but to the point, answering questions about points brought out.		
Techniques and the Game of Box Ball	Two balls for each squad.	
Station Teaching		
1. Squads 1 and 2 to punt return.		
2. Squads 3 and 4 to combination drill.		
3. Exchange positions after 6 or 7 minutes.		
Game (15 minutes)		
Third Day		
Repeat the introductory and fitness activities.		
Bring together and explain *Speed Football* rules.	*DPE* p. 601	

207

MOVEMENT EXPERIENCE— CONTENT	ORGANIZATION AND TEACHING HINTS	EXPECTED STUDENT OBJECTIVES AND OUTCOMES
Each squad practices plays (5 minutes). *Speed Football* (15 minutes) 1. Squad 1 vs. 2. 2. Squad 3 vs. 4.	All squads. Two footballs for each squad. Two fields. Issue flags and pinnies.	PM.—The student will be able to reach the level of skill so that football-type games can be played with success. PM.—The student will have the ability to catch and pass to the extent that this game can be played successfully and pleasurably. Cog.—The student will show improvement in strategic maneuvering. Aff.—The students will be able to accept whatever role the captain assigns them in team play.

DYNAMIC PHYSICAL EDUCATION LESSON PLAN—ALTERNATE
Softball-Related Activities (Lesson 3)
Level II

Supplies and Equipment Needed:
Station 1: 2 bats, 2 balls, 2 tees
Station 2: 2 bases, 1 bat, 1 ball
Station 3: 2 pitching targets, 2 balls
Station 4: 1 bat, 2 balls

MOVEMENT EXPERIENCE— CONTENT	ORGANIZATION AND TEACHING HINTS	EXPECTED STUDENT OBJECTIVES AND OUTCOMES

INTRODUCTORY AND FITNESS DEVELOPMENT ACTIVITIES (2 – 3 MINUTES)

This lesson may be substituted for any of the previous lessons. Use the introductory and fitness development activities given in the sequence plans.

LESSON FOCUS (15 – 20 MINUTES)

Softball Skills (Multiple Activity Station Teaching)

Divide class equally among stations.

Station 1
1. Fungo or tee hitting for knocking out flies.
2. Review catching techniques.

Station 2
Bunting and Fielding
1. Bunting techniques
   a. Square around.
   b. Run the upper hand up the bat halfway.
   c. Hold the bat level.
   d. Just meet the ball.
   e. Direct the ball down either foul line.

Station 3
Pitching to Targets
1. Set up normal (35') pitching distance.
2. Each pitcher gets to pitch to three batters.
3. Score either walk or strikeout.
4. Review pitching rules.

Station 4
Hitting Practice
1. Need pitcher, batter, catcher, and fielders. Each batter gets six swings.
2. Review stress points for hitting.

DPE pp. 639 – 657

Squads form the basis for rotative activity.

Need a batter and fielders. If more than six on a squad, divide into two groups.

Use full squad—pitcher, catcher, first baseman, and the rest infielders. One batter is up. He gets three bunts. On the third bunt, he runs to first base. He then becomes a fielder. Establish a system of rotation.

Divide into two groups. Need batter, retriever, and scorer.

Full squad activity.

Controlled pitching is important. See that the batter has a good chance to hit.

Use two softballs.

Aff.—The student will be able to cooperate in practicing designated skills at the respective stations.

PM.—The student will develop enough skill to play Hit the Bat successfully.

Cog.—The student will be able to verbalize proper strategy in playing the ball with respect to the game.

PM.—The student will develop reasonable skill in bunting.

PM.—The student, as a pitcher, will be able to strike out two of three batters.

PM.—Out of six swings, the student will be able to hit solidly four times.

Cog.—The student will be able to recount the important stress points in hitting techniques.

LEAD-UP GAMES (5 – 7 MINUTES)

1. Beat Ball, pp. 652
2. Kick Softball, pp. 651 – 652
3. Two-Pitch Softball, pp. 650 – 651

PM.—The student will have developed enough skill to play these games successfully.

209

DYNAMIC PHYSICAL EDUCATION LESSON PLAN— ALTERNATE
Fundamental Skills Using Balance Beams and Manipulative Equipment Level II

Supplies and Equipment Needed:
  Balance-beam benches, mats for landing
  12 beanbags, hoops, wands, and playground balls
  Jump ropes

MOVEMENT EXPERIENCE— CONTENT	ORGANIZATION AND TEACHING HINTS	EXPECTED STUDENT OBJECTIVES AND OUTCOMES

INTRODUCTORY AND FITNESS DEVELOPMENT ACTIVITIES (2 – 3 MINUTES)

This lesson may be substituted for any of the previous lessons. Use the introductory and fitness development activities given in the sequenced lesson plans.

LESSON FOCUS ACTIVITY (15 – 20 MINUTES)

Balance-Beam Activities with Manipulative Equipment

A. *Activities to Self*
  1. Use one or two beanbags and toss to self in various fashions— around the body, under the legs, etc.
  2. Use a playground ball and toss to self.
  3. Bounce the ball on the floor and on the beam. Dribble the ball.
  4. Play catch with a partner.
  5. Balance a beanbag on various body parts. Use more than one bag.
  6. Jump-rope down the beam.
  7. Student's choice.

B. *Activities with Wands and Hoops*
  1. Carry a wand or hoop. Step over the wand or through the hoop in various fashions—forward, sideways, backward.
  2. Step over or go under wands or hoops held by a partner.
  3. Hula-hoop on various body parts while moving across the beam.
  4. Balance a wand on various body parts while moving across the beam.
  5. Balance a wand in one hand and twirl a hoop in the other hand and proceed across the beam.
  6. Student's choice.

C. *Challenge Activities*
  1. Hop the length of the beam.
  2. Walk the beam with the eyes closed. Spot the performer.

DPE pp. 422 – 424

Move deliberately, catching their balance after each step. Speed is not a goal.

Mats should be placed at the end of each beam to cushion the dismount and allow selected rolls and stunts.

Encourage quality dismounts. Students should pause at the end of the beam before dismounting.

Both sides of the body should receive equal treatment. If students walk with the left side leading, they should also walk with the right leading.

If the student steps off the beam, he should step back on at that point and continue to the end of the beam.

Students should look ahead at eye level, rather than at their feet.

Challenge the students to develop some of their own ideas and give them time to implement them.

Use return activities so students accomplish something on their way back to the beam.

PM.—The student will be able to walk the beam forward and backward while manipulating a piece of equipment.

Cog.—The student will be able to name five activities where balance is the major factor.

Aff.—Balance is affected a great deal by the auditory and visual senses. Experiment by trying various balance activities and eliminating some of the senses.

PM.—The student will be able to perform a full turn on the beam while balancing a wand on some body part.

MOVEMENT EXPERIENCE—CONTENT	ORGANIZATION AND TEACHING HINTS	EXPECTED STUDENT OBJECTIVES AND OUTCOMES
3. Perform some animal walks across the beam (i.e., Cat Walk, Lame Dog Walk, and Crab Walk).		
4. Walk to center of beam and do a complete body turn on one foot.	Allow students time to develop and practice activities of their choosing.	
5. Partners start on opposite ends of the beam and attempt to pass each other without losing their balance.		

GAME (5 – 7 MINUTES)

1. Hand Hockey, p. 533
2. Nine Lives, p. 534

DYNAMIC PHYSICAL EDUCATION LESSON PLAN— ALTERNATE
Fundamental Skills Using Climbing Ropes
Level II

Supplies and Equipment Needed:
  16 climbing ropes
  Tumbling mats

MOVEMENT EXPERIENCE—CONTENT	ORGANIZATION AND TEACHING HINTS	EXPECTED STUDENT OBJECTIVES AND OUTCOMES

INTRODUCTORY AND FITNESS DEVELOPMENT ACTIVITIES (2 – 3 MINUTES)

This lesson may be substituted for any of the previous lessons. Use the introductory and fitness development activities given in the sequenced lesson plans.

LESSON FOCUS (15 – 20 MINUTES)

Climbing Ropes

A. *Supported Pull-Ups*
  1. Kneel and pull to feet. Return.
  2. Sit, pull to feet, and back to seat.
  3. Stand, keep body straight while lowering body to the floor.

B. *Hangs*
  1. Sit, pull body off floor except for feet, and hold.
  2. Jump up, grasp the rope, and hang.
  3. Jump up, grasp the rope, and hang, and perform the following leg movements:
    a. One or both knees up
    b. Bicycling movement
    c. Half-lever
    d. Choice movement

C. *Climbing the Rope*
  1. Scissors grip:
    Place the rope inside the knees and outside the foot. Climb halfway up and practice descending using the reverse scissors grip before climbing to the top of the rope.
  2. Leg around rest:
    Wrap the left leg around the rope and over the instep of the left foot from the outside. Stand on the rope and instep with right foot.

DPE pp. 414 – 418

Place tumbling mats under all the climbing apparatus.

Caution students not to slide quickly down the rope to prevent rope burns.

Swinging on the ropes is motivating and should be done with bent arms.

The pull-up and hang activities are excellent lead-ups for students who are not strong enough to climb the rope.

Students should be encouraged to learn the various techniques of climbing and descending.

If there are only a few climbing ropes, it would be a good teaching technique to have the nonclimbing students work on another unit. Some good units are beanbags, hoops, wands, and/or playground balls.

Rope climbing is a very intense and demanding activity. A good idea is to break up the lesson focus with a game or relay. This will also offer leg development activity.

PM.—The student will be able to demonstrate proper techniques in the following activities:
  1. Climbing with the scissors grip
  2. Leg round rest
  3. Reverse scissors grip
  4. Instep squeeze

Cog.—The student will be able to describe the safety rules necessary when climbing ropes.

Aff.—Rope climbing demands a great deal of upper body strength. Discuss how muscular strength develops through overloading and increasing the demands placed on the body.

Cog.—Rope climbing is excellent for developing upper body strength. Discuss the major muscle groups that are used and developed when climbing ropes.

MOVEMENT EXPERIENCE—CONTENT	ORGANIZATION AND TEACHING HINTS	EXPECTED STUDENT OBJECTIVES AND OUTCOMES

D. *Descending the Rope*
   1. Reverse scissors grip
   2. Leg around rest
   3. Instep squeeze: The rope is squeezed between the insteps by keeping the heels together.

E. *Stunts Using Two Ropes*
   1. Straight arm hang: Jump up, grasp rope, and hang.
   2. Arms with different leg positions.
      a. Single and double knee lifts
      b. Half lever
      c. Full lever
      d. Bicycle—pedal feet like bicycle
   3. Pull-ups
      Same as pull-up on a single rope.
   4. Inverted hangs
      a. With feet wrapped around the ropes.
      b. With feet against the inside of the ropes.
      c. With the toes pointed and the feet not touching the ropes.

If other climbing equipment is available such as a horizontal ladder and/or exercise bar, many activities are offered in *DPE* pp. 420 – 422.

Two ropes, hanging close together, are needed.

Spotting should be done when students are performing inverted hangs on two ropes.

Cog.—The larger the diameter of the muscle, the greater the amount of force that can be generated. Identify various muscles of the body and their relative size.

PM.—The student will be able to perform the following two-rope activities:
   1. Straight-arm hang
   2. Hangs with different leg positions
   3. Pull-ups
   4. Inverted hangs
Aff.—Rope climbing favors those students who are small and carry little body fat. Discuss individual differences and how different sports favor certain types of body build.

GAME (5 – 7 MINUTES)

1. Nonda's Car Lot, p. 528
2. Indianapolis 500, p. 525

DYNAMIC PHYSICAL EDUCATION LESSON PLAN— ALTERNATE
Fundamental Skills Using Magic Ropes
Level II

Supplies and Equipment Needed:
6–10 magic ropes per class
Balls
Beanbags

MOVEMENT EXPERIENCE— CONTENT	ORGANIZATION AND TEACHING HINTS	EXPECTED STUDENT OBJECTIVES AND OUTCOMES

INTRODUCTORY AND FITNESS DEVELOPMENT ACTIVITIES (2 – 3 MINUTES)

This lesson may be substituted for any of the previous lessons. Use the introductory and fitness development activities given in the sequenced lesson plans.

LESSON FOCUS (15 – 20 MINUTES)

Magic Ropes

1. *Single-Rope Activities*
   a. Jump back and forth, feet uncrossed.
   b. Jump back and forth, feet crossed and uncrossed alternately.
   c. Jump back and forth, feet crossed.
   d. Hop back and forth over rope using both right and left foot in turn.
   e. Jump the rope and perform various body turns while jumping.
   f. Change body shapes and sizes while jumping.
   g. Crawl or slide under the rope.
   h. Alternate going over and under the rope.
   i. Crouch jump over the rope.
   j. Run and high jump (scissors kick) over rope.
   k. Choice—exploratory activity.
2. *Double Ropes*
   Ropes parallel to each other:
   a. Jump in one side, out other.
   b. Hop in one side, out other.
   c. Crouch jump in and out.
   d. Perform various animal walks in and out.
   e. Exploratory activity.
3. Ropes crossed at right angles to each other:
   a. Perform various movements from one to the other.
   b. Jump into one area, crawl out other.
4. One rope above other, create "barbed wire fence" effect:
   a. Step through ropes without touching.
   b. Crouch jump through.

DPE pp. 429 – 431

Divide the class into small groups of five or six members.

Start activities with the rope at a 6" height and progressively raise it to increase the challenge.

Emphasize the point that students are *not* supposed to touch the rope. The objective is body management and learning to control the body in space.

Rotate the rope holders.

Students should approach the rope from one end and perform their activities to the other end of the rope.

The child next in turn should begin movement when performing child is near the end of the rope.

Try holding one end near the floor and the other end 2–3 ft. high. Children then progress from the low end to the high and more difficult end.

PM.—The student will be able to hop back and forth from one end of the rope to the other without touching the rope at a height of 10".

Cog.—The student will understand and be able to recite why magic ropes are used in the program—to develop body management skills.

Aff.—Carbon monoxide in tobacco smoke reduces the physical endurance of the smoker. Discuss the detrimental effects of this habit.

MOVEMENT EXPERIENCE—CONTENT	ORGANIZATION AND TEACHING HINTS	EXPECTED STUDENT OBJECTIVES AND OUTCOMES

    c. Vary height and distance apart in which ropes are placed. Adds much excitement. Children are challenged not to touch the ropes.

5. Miscellaneous—Perform the activities with beanbag balanced on head or bouncing a ball.

6. Choice—exploratory activity.

GAME (5 – 7 MINUTES)

Since the magic ropes are a strenuous activity, it might be well to teach the games as an integral part of the lesson focus. In other words, teach 5–7 minutes of magic ropes and then take a break and teach a game. Then teach a few more magic rope activities and finish with a game.

The following are suggested:
1. Busy Bee, p. 526
2. Box Ball, p. 532

LESSON PLANS FOR THE SCHOOL YEAR
Developmental Level III

WEEK	INTRODUCTORY ACTIVITY	FITNESS DEVELOPMENT ACTIVITY	LESSON FOCUS ACTIVITY	GAME ACTIVITY	PAGE
1	Orientation and Class Management Games				220
2	Fastest Tag in the West	Teacher Leader Exercises	Soccer Skills (1)	Soccer Related	222
3	Move and Freeze	Teacher Leader Exercises	Soccer Skills (2)	Soccer Related	224
4	Popcorn	Hexagon Hustle	Soccer Skills (3)	Soccer Related	227
5	Run, Stop, and Pivot	Hexagon Hustle	Rhythmic Movement (1)	Triplet Stoop Pacman	229
6	European Running	Hexagon Hustle	Rhythmic Movement (2)	Tag Games	232
7	Hospital Tag	Circuit Training	Racket Sport Skills	Volley Tennis One-Wall Handball and Racketball	235
8	Medic Tag	Circuit Training	Football Skills (2)	Football Related	238
9	Pyramid Power	Circuit Training	Football Skills (2)	Football Related	241
10	Stretching	Jogging	Jogging Skills	Recreational Activities	243
11	Stretching	Jogging	Cross-Country Running	Recreational Activities	245
12	Partner Over and Under	Exercises to Music	Individual Rope-Jumping Skills (1)	Right Face One Base Tagball	247
13	Move and Manipulate	Exercises to Music	Tug-of-War Rope and Frisbee Skills	Frisbee Games and Tug-of-War Activities	249
14	New Leader	Exercises to Music	Hockey Skills (1)	Hockey Related	252
15	Group Over and Under	Exercises to Music	Hockey Skills (2)	Hockey Related	255
16	Four-Corners Sport Movement	Astronaut Drills	Basketball Skills (1)	Basketball Related	257
17	Beanbag Touch and Go	Astronaut Drills	Basketball Skills (2)	Basketball Related	260
18	Leapfrog	Astronaut Drills	Basketball Skills (3)	Basketball Related	262
19	Living Obstacles	Partner Aerobic Fitness and Resistance Exercises	Recreational Activities	Recreational Activities	264
20	Barker's Hoopla	Partner Aerobic Fitness and Resistance Exercises	Gymnastics and Climbing Rope Skills	Star Wars Flag Chase	266

WEEK	INTRODUCTORY ACTIVITY	FITNESS DEVELOPMENT ACTIVITY	LESSON FOCUS ACTIVITY	GAME ACTIVITY	PAGE
21	Following Activity	Parachute Fitness	Gymnastics and Juggling Skills	Team Handball Octopus Bomb the Pins	270
					275
22	Ball Activities	Parachute Fitness	Gymnastics and Bench Skills	Pin Knockout Over the Wall	
23	Rubber Band	Aerobic Fitness	Gymnastics and Balance-Beam Skills	Loose Caboose Octopus Fast Pass	279
24	Moving to Music	Aerobic Fitness	Manipulative Skills Using Wands and Hula Hoops	Jolly Ball Galactic Empire and Rebels Circle Hook-On	282
25	Vanishing Beanbags	Challenge Course Fitness	Volleyball Skills (1)	Volleyball Related	286
26	Marking	Challenge Course Fitness	Volleyball Skills (2)	Volleyball Related	289
27	European Running with Variations	Challenge Course Fitness	Rhythmic Movement (3)	Whistle Ball More Jump the Shot Variations	292
28	Popcorn	Continuity Drills	Rhythmic Movement (4)	Scooter Kickball Touchdown Chain Tag	296
29	Move, Exercise on Signal	Continuity Drills	Juggling Skills and Pyramids	Pyramid Building or Juggling	300
30	Long-Rope Routine	Continuity Drills	Relay Activities	Relaxation Activity	304
31	Stretching	Jogging	Track and Field Skills (1)	Shuttle Relays	306
32	Stretching	Jogging	Track and Field Skills (2)	Circular Relays	309
33	Stretching	Jogging	Track and Field Skills (3)	Shuttle/Circular Relays	311
34	Personal Choice	Squad Leader Exercises with Task Cards	Long-Rope Jumping Skills	Cageball Target Throw Sunday	312
35	Personal Choice	Squad Leader Exercises with Task Cards	Softball Skills (1)	Batter Ball Tee Ball Scrub (Work-Up)	315
36	Personal Choice	Squad Leader Exercises with Task Cards	Softball Skills (2)	Scrub (Work-Up) Slow Pitch Softball Babe Ruth Ball Three-Team Softball	318

WEEK	INTRODUCTORY ACTIVITY	FITNESS DEVELOPMENT ACTIVITY	LESSON FOCUS ACTIVITY	GAME ACTIVITY	PAGE
Alternate Lesson Plans					
A	Substitute	Substitute	Rhythmic Movement (5)	Scooter Kickball Sunday	320
B	Substitute	Substitute	Rhythmic Gymnastics	Touchdown Circle Hook-On Cageball Target Throw	322
C	Substitute	Substitute	Climbing Rope Skills	Whistle Mixer Touchdown Chain Tag	326

DYNAMIC PHYSICAL EDUCATION LESSON PLAN
Orientation and Class Management Games
Level III

Note: See Chapter 7 in *Dynamic Physical Education for Elementary School Children,* Tenth Edition

ORIENTATION LESSON PLAN

This week should be used to get students involved in the system you are going to use throughout the year. The following are reminders you might find useful in establishing your organizational schemes.

1. Tell the class what is expected with regard to entry and exit behavior. If you are using the squad method, it might be helpful to place four cones (one per squad) in the same area each day and ask the squads to get into line behind the cones.
2. If you organize the class into squads, get a class list and divide the class ahead of time. Try to equalize the number of boys and girls in each squad. If the squads are somewhat unequal in ability, changes can be made later. Name a captain for each squad and tell the class how often you are going to change captains (2–3 weeks is recommended). Give the captains various responsibilities so they have a chance to be a leader. An alternate can be designated to act as squad leader if the regular leader is absent.
3. Explain briefly the lesson plan format to the class. Each lesson will contain an introductory activity, fitness, lesson focus, and game activity. They will know what to expect and won't have to ask if "we're going to play a game today," etc.
4. When classes come to the activity area, explain briefly what you are going to do in the day's lesson. It should be short and concise, but they should know what you have planned for them.
5. Establish rules and expectations. Usually, basic rules state that students must listen when you are speaking and vice versa, and they must act in a socially sound manner, respecting the rights of other students.
6. If you are going to test, let the students know the reason for the test and exactly what it will involve on their behalf.
7. Emphasize the value of fitness and take them through a fitness routine. Set expectations high—it is easier to lower them later. Practice various formations such as open-squad and closed-squad, so they know what to do when you ask them to assume these positions. Try formations such as squares, triangles, and rectangles.
8. Discuss issue, distribution, and care of equipment and where and how it is to be stored. Students should play an integral part in handling equipment and should understand what is expected of them.
9. Decide how excuses for nonparticipation should be handled. Children should know where they go to be excused and where they go after they are excused.
10. Establish a signal to stop the class and gain attention. Usually a whistle and a hand signal are effective. Practice gaining the attention of the class with the signal during this orientation period. Activity should be started with a verbal command.
11. Select activities for this week in which you know all students will be successful. This is one of the best ways to develop enthusiasm for a program in its early stages. The corollary of this rule is to teach a few games and activities you enjoy.
12. The orientation week usually requires more explanation than is normal. After the first week, keep talking to a minimum and activity to a maximum. Remember that when you are talking or children are standing in line, there is no way they can learn and practice new physical skills.
13. Circulate among students as you develop movement experiences and skills. This allows for better individualized instruction and attention to the lesser skilled. Avoid spending the majority of teacher time "at the podium," in front of the class.
14. In each of the lessons read the reference areas in *Dynamic Physical Education* to provide an in-depth discussion of the activity.
15. Frequent reference should be made as needed to Chapter 7, "Effective Class Management," in *Dynamic Physical Education for Elementary School Children.* This chapter applies to all activities taught and offers strategies and techniques to enhance the teaching process.

16. Safety is an important issue to be covered in the first week. Children should receive safety rules to be followed when using large apparatus as well as similar rules for playground and gymnasium conduct. Rules should be posted in the gymnasium and throughout the school. See Chapter 9 in *Dynamic Physical Education* for an in-depth discussion on safety and liability.

17. It is crucial to the success of the teacher that good student management skills be developed early in the school year. During the first week, students should practice getting into various formations quickly and without talking, getting into groups of different sizes, and stopping on signal quickly (within 5 seconds). Games, such as those below, are excellent for teaching class management skills.

18. Express interest in your students and that you are anxious to learn their names. Inform them that you are going to ask them their names many times to expedite learning them. It also might be helpful to ask classroom teachers to put name tags on students before they come to physical education class. Having students write their names on a piece of masking tape is a quick and easy way to make name tags.

ACTIVITY

Play a few favorite games after a fitness routine has been introduced. The following games are excellent class management activities and offer the students a chance to get to know each other.

1. Whistle Mixer, p. 536
2. Loose Caboose, p. 534
3. Circle Hook-On, p. 537
4. Whistle Ball, p. 540
5. Touchdown, p. 539

DYNAMIC PHYSICAL EDUCATION LESSON PLAN
Soccer Skills (Lesson 1)
Level III

Supplies and Equipment Needed:
One ball per student (8" foam rubber balls or junior soccer balls)
Cones for marking areas for lead-up activities
Pinnies for soccer lead-up games
Jump ropes

MOVEMENT EXPERIENCE—CONTENT	ORGANIZATION AND TEACHING HINTS	EXPECTED STUDENT OBJECTIVES AND OUTCOMES

INTRODUCTORY ACTIVITY (2 – 3 MINUTES)

Fastest Tag in the West

Every player is a tagger. The object is to tag other players without being tagged yourself. Players who are tagged must sit or kneel and await the next game. If two or more players tag each other simultaneously, they are both/all "out."

DPE p. 222

An area at least 30 ft. by 50 ft. is recommended.

Restart the game frequently.

Vary the type of locomotor movement the class can use to chase and flee, or the part of the body that is tagged.

PM.—The student will be able to dodge/elude quickly without falling or colliding with another student.

Aff.—Fair play is of paramount importance in game activities. Discuss the importance of students' being their own referees in many games.

FITNESS DEVELOPMENT ACTIVITIES (7 – 8 MINUTES)

Teacher-Leader Exercises

Arm Circles	30 seconds
Push-Ups	30 seconds
Bend and Stretch	30 seconds
Treadmill	30 seconds
Sit-Ups	40 seconds
Single-Leg Crab Kick	30 seconds
Knee to Chest Curl	40 seconds
Run in Place	35 seconds
Standing Hip Bend	30 seconds

Conclude the routine with 2–4 minutes of jogging, rope jumping, or other continuous activity.

Increase the duration of exercises by 10–20% over the previous week.

DPE p. 258

Scatter formation.

Allow students to adjust the work load to their ability and fitness level. This implies that some students will perform more repetitions in the same amount of time.

Emphasize proper form and technique.

Rotate to different parts of the teaching area and help motivate students.

Cog.—Know why it is necessary to increase the number of repetitions (overload principle).

PM.—The student will be able to perform all activities at teacher established level.

Aff.—A positive attitude toward exercise and its value to people.

LESSON FOCUS (15 – 20 MINUTES)

Soccer

A. *Skills*
  1. Instep kick: Approach at 45° angle, top of instep meets ball. Place nonkicking foot alongside ball.
  2. Side of foot kick: Short distance kick; keep toe down. Use both the inside and outside of the foot.
  3. Sole of the foot trap: Use sole of foot to stop ball; make sure weight is placed on the non-receiving foot.

DPE pp. 617 – 637

Description of kicks and traps.

Partner or triangle formation, one ball for two or three children.

Keep head down, eyes on ball, follow through.

If short of gray foam balls, substitute 8 1/2" playground balls or soccer balls. Partially deflate the balls so they move more slowly and allow for increased success.

PM.—The student will be able to pass, kick, and trap the ball successfully at the end of the week.

Cog.—The student will be able to state two reasons why, in soccer activities, accuracy is much preferred over raw power and lack of control.

MOVEMENT EXPERIENCE— CONTENT	ORGANIZATION AND TEACHING HINTS	EXPECTED STUDENT OBJECTIVES AND OUTCOMES
4. Foot trap: Use side of foot, learn to "give" with leg so ball doesn't ricochet off foot.	8" foam rubber training balls are excellent substitutes as they remove the fear of being hurt by a kicked soccer ball. Make sure students handle the ball with their feet, not the hands. They should retrieve and move the balls with feet only.	

B. *Drills* (optional)
  1. Ball juggling
    a. Alternate feet.
    b. Twice with one foot, then other foot.
  2. Dribbling, marking, and ball recovery
  3. Body control (trapping)
    a. Inside of thigh.
    b. Chest.
  4. Dribbling and passing
	DPE pp. 623 – 628
	
	Individual work; let ball bounce once when changing feet.
	
	Pairs scattered; one has a soccer ball.
	
	Groups of two or three; one acts as a feeder (rotate feeders); girls should fold arms across chest for protection.
	
	Three-player shuttle drill.
		Aff.—Even in basic lead-up games, teamwork is necessary for success and enjoyment by all.
		
		Cog.—The student will be able to state the basic rules necessary for soccer lead-up games.

C. *Lead-Up Activities*
Discuss basic rules necessary for soccer lead-up games.
  1. Dribblerama (p. 630)
  2. Sideline Soccer (pp. 631 – 632)
  3. Line Soccer (pp. 633 – 634)
  4. Mini-Soccer (p. 634)
	DPE pp. 629 – 635
	
	One ball per player. All players dribble within a designated area without their ball touching anyone else's (Level 1); attempt to kick other players' ball out of area while retaining control of their own (Level 2).
	
	Encourage students to use their teammates on the sidelines.
	
	Rotate the active players often so all can participate. Time the length of participation rather than rotating after a score.
	
	Play Mini-Soccer if the class has played soccer in the past and is skilled in team play. If the game degenerates into "hogball," it may be too advanced for the class.
		Aff.—The student will learn to appreciate individual differences and show concern for the welfare of others.
		
		Aff.—Cooperation needs to be learned before students can compete with others. Discuss how it is impossible to have a competitive game if others choose not to cooperate and follow rules.

GAME (5 – 7 MINUTES)

Generally, the aforementioned lead-up games should be used as the game activity.

DYNAMIC PHYSICAL EDUCATION LESSON PLAN
Soccer Skills (Lesson 2)
Level III

Supplies and Equipment Needed:
One soccer ball per student (8" foam rubber balls or junior soccer balls)
Cones for marking areas for lead-up activities
Pinnies for soccer lead-up games
Tom-toms
Jump ropes

MOVEMENT EXPERIENCE—CONTENT	ORGANIZATION AND TEACHING HINTS	EXPECTED STUDENT OBJECTIVES AND OUTCOMES

INTRODUCTORY ACTIVITY (2 – 3 MINUTES)

Move and Freeze

1. Review the run, walk, hop, jump, leap, slide, gallop, and skip with proper stopping.
2. Practice moving and stopping correctly—emphasize basics of proper movement.
3. Add variety to the movements by asking students to respond to the following factors:
   a. Level—low, high, in-between.
   b. Direction—straight, zigzag, circular, curved, forward, backward, upward, downward.
   c. Size—large, tiny, medium movements.
   d. Patterns—forming squares, diamonds, triangles, circles, figure eights.

DPE p. 219

Scatter formation.

A tom-tom can be used. Otherwise, use a whistle to signal the stop.

Emphasize and reinforce creativity.

Change the various factors often and take time to explain the concepts the words describe if children cannot interpret them.

PM.—The student will be able to stop quickly under control.

Cog.—Know the elements involved in stopping quickly.

PM.—The student will be able to execute the various locomotor movements.

Cog.—The student will be able to interpret the concepts the words describe by moving the body in a corresponding manner.

PM.—The student will be able to move the body with ease throughout the range of movement varieties.

FITNESS DEVELOPMENT ACTIVITIES (7 – 8 MINUTES)

Teacher-Leader Exercises

Sitting Stretch	35 seconds
Push-Ups	35 seconds
Power Jumper	35 seconds
Jumping Jacks	35 seconds
Sit-Ups	45 seconds
Single-Leg Crab Kick	35 seconds
Knee to Chest Curl	45 seconds
Windmill	40 seconds
Trunk Twister	35 seconds

Conclude the routine with 2–4 minutes of jogging, rope jumping, or other continuous activity.

Increase the duration of exercises by 10–20% over the previous week.

DPE p. 258

Scatter formation.

Allow students to adjust the work load to their ability and fitness level. This implies that some students will perform more repetitions in the same amount of time.

Emphasize proper form and technique.

Rotate to different parts of the teaching area and help motivate students.

Cog.—The student will be able to explain verbally why correct form is important when performing fitness activities.

PM.—The student will be able to perform all activities at the teacher-established level.

MOVEMENT EXPERIENCE—CONTENT	ORGANIZATION AND TEACHING HINTS	EXPECTED STUDENT OBJECTIVES AND OUTCOMES

LESSON FOCUS (15 – 20 MINUTES)

Soccer

The soccer lesson works well in a circuit of instructional stations. Divide the skills into four to six stations and place the necessary equipment and instructions at each.

A. *Skills*
1. Outside foot kick: Use the outside of the foot. More of a push than a kick.
2. Dribbling: Move the ball with a series of taps. Start slowly and don't kick the ball too far away from the player.
3. Passing: Start passing the ball from a stationary position and then progress to moving while passing.
4. Goalkeeping/shooting: One player dribbles the ball 15–20 yd and shoots for a goal against a goalie from 15–20 yd away. The goalie, after stopping or retrieving the shot, becomes the dribbler/shooter, with the other player becoming the goalie on his end of the practice area.

B. *Drills*
1. Ball juggling
   a. Review Week 1
   b. Thigh—start with catch; add successive thigh volleys.
   c. Juggle with foot, thigh, head, thigh, and foot and catch.
2. Dribbling, moving, and passing drill
3. Heading, volleying, and controlling drill
4. Passing, guarding, and tackling drill

DPE pp. 617 – 637

One ball per two children—or triangle formation, one ball for each group of three children.

8" foam rubber training balls are useful for learning proper form in soccer activities.

Start expecting quality and accuracy in the kicks, passes, and traps.

Outside foot kick is used for short distances only.

Review the skills taught last lesson and integrate them into this lesson. Proper motor patterns can be learned only when they are reviewed and practiced many times.

Two beanbags spread 15–20 ft. apart on each side of the area for each pair of players; if the groups have three students, the third person can back up the goalie and rotate in after each shot on goal.

DPE pp. 623 – 628

Individual work. Be patient with these skills, as varying ability levels will appear.

Let students progress at their own rate.

Partner work: both partners repeat same maneuvers.

Groups of two to three: One player "feeds" the other two with soft underhand tosses; rotate feeders often.

Groups of four: Players need to learn to pass with both right and left feet. Defender should watch the ball, not the passer's feet.

PM.—The student will be able to kick, dribble, trap, and pass the soccer ball by the end of the week.

Cog.—The student will be able to describe the situations in which the outside foot kick should be used.

Aff.—When soccer is taught in a coed situation, students must appreciate individual differences.

Cog.—Flexibility is the range of motion at a joint. Flexibility is important in kicking activities as more force can be generated over a greater range of motion. Discuss the importance of stretching in order to lengthen connective tissue.

Aff.—Good passes can be easily handled by a teammate. Praise passes and teamwork.

Aff.—Teammates appreciate "soft tosses" when learning to execute chest and thigh traps, volleys, and heading.

PM.—The student will be able to pass without "telegraphing" his pass to a teammate.

MOVEMENT EXPERIENCE—CONTENT	ORGANIZATION AND TEACHING HINTS	EXPECTED STUDENT OBJECTIVES AND OUTCOMES
C. *Lead-Up Activities* Review basic rules necessary for soccer lead-up games. 1. Bull's-Eye (p. 630)	One ball per player. All players except one dribble balls throughout area. Player designated as "bull's-eye" attempts to chest pass (basketball skill) her ball at another ball; player whose ball is hit becomes new "bull's-eye."	Cog.—The student will be able to recite the basic rules of soccer. PM.—The student will practice and use the soccer skills learned previously. Cog.—Muscle soreness may occur from the breakdown of connective tissue. Excessive exercise (in relation to the amount of activity each person normally performs) may cause an imbalance in the breakdown–buildup process, and soreness will result. Students should understand the need for progressively increasing work load to minimize soreness.
2. Line Soccer (pp. 633 – 634)	This game has proved to aid in transition to positional play required in Mini-Soccer.	
3. Mini-Soccer (p. 634)	If game generates into "hogball," it may be too advanced for the class.	
4. Regulation Soccer (p. 635)	The regulation game should only be played if the class shows proficiency in Mini-Soccer.	

GAME (5 – 7 MINUTES)

Generally, the aforementioned games should be used as the game activity.

DYNAMIC PHYSICAL EDUCATION LESSON PLAN
Soccer Skills (Lesson 3)
Level III

Supplies and Equipment Needed:
  One soccer ball per student (8" foam rubber balls or junior soccer balls)
  Cones for marking areas for lead-up activities
  Pinnies for soccer lead-up games

MOVEMENT EXPERIENCE— CONTENT	ORGANIZATION AND TEACHING HINTS	EXPECTED STUDENT OBJECTIVES AND OUTCOMES

INTRODUCTORY ACTIVITY (2 – 3 MINUTES)

Popcorn

Students pair up with one person on the floor in push-up position and the other standing ready to move. On signal, the standing students move over and under the persons on the floor. The person on the floor changes from a raised to a lowered push-up position each time the partner goes over or under them. On signal, reverse positions.

DPE p. 223

Partner formation.

Encourage students to move as quickly as possible.

Challenge them to see how many times they can go over and under each other.

PM.—The student will be able to move quickly over, under, and around her partner.

Aff.—Warm-up activities only work when an individual motivates himself to move quickly and with intensity.

FITNESS DEVELOPMENT ACTIVITIES (7 – 8 MINUTES)

Hexagon Hustle

Outline a large hexagon with six cones. Place signs with directions on both sides on the cones. The signs identify the hustle activity students are to perform as they approach a cone.

Hustle	25 seconds
Push-Up from Knees	30 seconds
Hustle	25 seconds
Bend and Stretch (8 counts)	30 seconds
Hustle	25 seconds
Jumping Jacks (4 counts)	30 seconds
Hustle	25 seconds
Sit-Ups (2 counts)	40 seconds
Hustle	25 seconds
Double-Leg Crab Kick (2 counts)	30 seconds
Hustle	25 seconds
Sit and Stretch (8 counts)	40 seconds
Hustle	25 seconds
Power Jumper	30 seconds
Hustle	25 seconds
Squat Thrust (4 counts)	30 seconds

Conclude the Hexagon Hustle with a slow jog or walk.

DPE p. 262

Examples of hustle activities that can be listed on signs are:
  1. Jogging
  2. Skipping or galloping
  3. Hopping or jumping
  4. Sliding
  5. Running and leaping
  6. Animal movements
  7. Sport movements such as defensive sliding, running backwards, and carioca step

During the hustle, faster moving students can pass to the outside of the hexagon.

Change directions regularly to keep students spaced evenly along the hexagon.

During the hustle, quality movement rather than speed is the goal.

Cog.—It is necessary to increase the number of repetitions of activity to provide additional stress on the body and increase fitness levels.

PM.—The student will be able to perform one to two more repetitions of each exercise than he was capable of two weeks ago.

Aff.—Physically fit people are rewarded by society. Teachers, parents, and peers respond much more favorably to those fit and attractive.

MOVEMENT EXPERIENCE— CONTENT	ORGANIZATION AND TEACHING HINTS	EXPECTED STUDENT OBJECTIVES AND OUTCOMES

LESSON FOCUS (15 – 20 MINUTES)

Soccer

Since this is the third lesson of soccer, much emphasis should be placed on playing regulation soccer. Teach and/or review the following skills and devote the rest of the time to the game of soccer

1. *Skills*
   a. Punting—Hold ball in both hands in front of the body and kick the ball on the instep of the foot.
   b. Volleying—Practice using different parts of the body.
   c. Heading—Keep the eyes on the ball as long as possible before impact. Contact the ball with the forehead.
   d. Review any past rules and drills you find necessary for the success of the game activity.

2. *Lead-Up Activities*
   Mini-Soccer and/or Regulation Soccer—These should serve as the game activities, and thus other games are not offered.

DPE pp. 617 – 637

Students can work in pairs and practice kicking for accuracy to their partner.

Work in pairs and have a partner throw the ball toward different body parts to volley.

Use foam rubber balls for volleying and heading, as they are lighter and more comfortable for the students.

DPE pp. 629 – 635

Emphasize position play and teamwork. Change teams after an established period of time.

Cog.—In kicking activities, the swinging arc must be flattened. This can be accomplished by transferring the weight, moving ahead over a bent front knee, and reaching out during follow-through. Discuss how the arc should be flattened when kicking is performed.

PM.—The student will be able to punt the ball successfully five times.

PM.—The student will be able to volley and head the ball to a partner who is tossing the ball.

Cog.—The student will be able to state when volleying and heading are used in game situations.

Aff.—Soccer demands that players maintain their positions, rather than all chase the ball. Discuss the need for teamwork and the importance of all positions in the game.

Cog.—The angle of the rebound surface affects the rebound direction of the ball. Illustrate the necessity of adjusting the angle of the rebound surface to develop accuracy in kicking.

GAME (5 – 7 MINUTES)

Generally, the aforementioned games should be used as the game activity.

DYNAMIC PHYSICAL EDUCATION LESSON PLAN
Rhythmic Movement (Lesson 1)
Level III

Supplies and Equipment Needed:
 Tom-tom
 Cones
 Circuit training signs
 Tape player
 Music for rhythms

Dances Taught:
 E-Z Mixer
 Comin' Round the Mountain
 Jessie Polka
 Cotton-Eyed Joe
 Virginia Reel
 D'Hammerschmiedsgselln

MOVEMENT EXPERIENCE— CONTENT	ORGANIZATION AND TEACHING HINTS	EXPECTED STUDENT OBJECTIVES AND OUTCOMES

INTRODUCTORY ACTIVITY (2 – 3 MINUTES)

Run, Stop, and Pivot

The class runs, stops on signal, and pivots. Vary the activity by having the class pivot on the left foot or the right foot, by increasing the circumference, and by performing pivots in quick succession.

Students should continue running after the pivot. Movement should be continuous.

DPE p. 219

Emphasize correct form in stopping and absorbing force.

Make sure that students do not cross legs or lose balance while pivoting.

Allow a few moments for free practice.

Cog.—The student will be able to name sports such as basketball and baseball in which the pivot is used.

PM.—The student will be able to perform the pivot smoothly and correctly.

FITNESS DEVELOPMENT ACTIVITY (7 – 8 MINUTES)

Hexagon Hustle

Outline a large hexagon with six cones. Place signs with directions on both sides on the cones. The signs identify the hustle activity students are to perform as they approach a cone.

Hustle	30 seconds
Push-Up from Knees	30 seconds
Hustle	30 seconds
Bend and Stretch (8 counts)	30 seconds
Hustle	30 seconds
Jumping Jacks (4 counts)	30 seconds
Hustle	30 seconds
Sit-Ups (2 counts)	40 seconds
Hustle	30 seconds
Double-Leg Crab Kick (2 counts)	30 seconds
Hustle	30 seconds
Sit and Stretch (8 counts)	40 seconds
Hustle	30 seconds
Power Jumper	30 seconds
Hustle	30 seconds
Squat Thrust (4 counts)	30 seconds

Conclude the Hexagon Hustle with a slow jog or walk.

DPE p. 262

Examples of hustle activities that can be listed on signs are:
 1. Jogging
 2. Skipping and galloping
 3. Hopping or jumping
 4. Sliding
 5. Running and leaping
 6. Animal movements
 7. Sport movements such as defensive sliding, running backwards, and carioca step

During the hustle, faster moving students can pass to the outside of the hexagon.

Change directions regularly to keep students spaced evenly along the hexagon.

During the hustle, quality movement rather than speed is the goal.

Cog.—Circuit training should work all parts of the body, but no two similar parts in succession.

Cog.—In order that circuit training be effective, *quality* exercise must be performed at each station.

Cog.—The student will be able to accurately describe how overload is achieved (by increasing the length of activity at each station and decreasing the rest between stations).

MOVEMENT EXPERIENCE— CONTENT	ORGANIZATION AND TEACHING HINTS	EXPECTED STUDENT OBJECTIVES AND OUTCOMES

LESSON FOCUS (15 – 20 MINUTES)

Rhythms

Usually begin each lesson with a dance the students know and enjoy.

1. Listen to the music, clapping the rhythms and pointing out where changes occur.
2. Teach the basic skills used in the dance.
3. Practice the dance steps in sequence.
4. Practice with the music.

Make the rhythms unit an enjoyable one for students. Be enthusiastic when teaching rhythms.

1. E-Z Mixer (p. 341)

An American dance

Basic dance skills:
1. Walking
2. Elbow swing
3. Pivot (and walk to new partner)

Circle of partners facing CCW.

PM.—The student will develop the proper rhythm to perform this dance successfully.

Aff.—The student will accept new partners graciously.

2. Comin' Round the Mountain (p. 352)

An American dance

Basic dance skills:
1. Touch step
2. Step hop
3. Back-side-together

Circle of lines of three facing CCW.

As a change-of-pace activity, a simple game may be taught between dances.

PM.—The student will be able to put the parts of the dance together and perform it successfully.

3. Jessie Polka (pp. 352 – 353)

An American dance

Basic dance skills:
1. Two-step or polka step
2. Heel step
3. Touch step

Begin teaching the dance with students working individually.

As students grasp the dance sequence, suggest that they form groups of two or more in a conga line (one behind the other).

The person at the end of the line rushes to the front of the line on the last two two-steps (or polka steps).

Do not demand perfection when teaching dances. Children can be expected to make mistakes similar to learning any other physical skill.

PM.—The student will master the two-step (or polka step) and be able to apply it to other dances.

Aff.—Some appreciation of older American dances and culture will be acquired by the student.

Aff.—The students will accept a new group leader with good grace.

4. Cotton-Eyed Joe (p. 356)

An American dance

Basic dance skills:
1. Heel and toe step
2. Two-step
3. Two-step turning

PM.—The students will improve their technique in the two-step.

Aff.—Students will take pride in doing dances properly.

MOVEMENT EXPERIENCE—CONTENT	ORGANIZATION AND TEACHING HINTS	EXPECTED STUDENT OBJECTIVES AND OUTCOMES
	May want to teach the steps with the students scattered individually in the gym. After performing the dance steps to the music individually, progress to performing the dance in couples arranged in one large circle with the boys' (nonpinnie's) back to the center. Two-steps turning may be done solo.	
5. Virginia Reel (pp. 349 – 350)	An American dance. The reel is a carryover from the colonial days. It has many different forms. Basic dance steps: 1. The "reel" 2. Sashay The longways set should have not more than six couples. Each maneuver must be completed in eight counts. The eighth count in each series is actually a stop so the student can be in time for the next figure. Begin with slow tempo and gradually increase to normal tempo as students master the dance.	Aff.—Some appreciation of older American dances and culture will be acquired by the student. Cog.—The student will understand the need for correct timing. PM.—The student will be able to do the various figures and keep to reasonable time. PM.—The student will react to the call with the proper movement. PM.—The student will be able to perform the reel correctly.
6. D'Hammerschmiedsgselln ("The Journey Blacksmith") (p. 354)	A Bavarian dance Basic dance skills: 1. Clapping pattern 2. Step hops 3. Stars Play the music, pointing out where changes occur. Right and left hand stars are done while performing step hops. Begin by teaching the dance in partners. Practice the dance with the music. When students have grasped the dance sequence, groups of four may be formed. Vary the dance by performing it as a mixer.	PM.—The student will be able to add each part in turn and perform the dance successfully. Aff.—The student will enjoy dances he knows. Cog.—The student will be able to recognize and react to the changes as indicated in the music.

GAME (5 – 7 MINUTES)

1. Triplet Stoop, p. 537
2. Pacman, p. 540

DYNAMIC PHYSICAL EDUCATION LESSON PLAN
Rhythmic Movement (Lesson 2)
Level III

Supplies and Equipment Needed:
  Tom-tom
  Cones
  Circuit training signs
  Tape player
  Music for rhythms
  Pinnies

Dances Taught:
  Inside-Out Mixer
  Alley Cat
  Hora
  Hot Time in the Old Town Tonight
  Teton Mountain Stomp
  Kalvelis
  Limbo Rock

MOVEMENT EXPERIENCE—CONTENT	ORGANIZATION AND TEACHING HINTS	EXPECTED STUDENT OBJECTIVES AND OUTCOMES

INTRODUCTORY ACTIVITY (2 – 3 MINUTES)

European Running

Develop the ability to follow the leader, maintain proper spacing, and move to the rhythm of the tom-tom. Stop on a double beat of the tom-tom.

Variation: Have leader move in different shapes and designs. Have class freeze and see if they can identify the shape or formation.

DPE pp. 217 – 218

Single file formation with a leader.

Move in time to the beat of the tom-tom. Add clapping hands. Other movements may be added. The beat must be fast enough so students move at a fast trot with knees up.

PM.—The student will be able to move rhythmically with the beat of the tom-tom.

Cog.—The student will describe six sport and recreational activities in which the body moves rhythmically.

FITNESS DEVELOPMENT ACTIVITIES (7 – 8 MINUTES)

Hexagon Hustle

Outline a large hexagon with six cones. Place signs with directions on both sides on the cones. The signs identify the hustle activity students are to perform as they approach a cone.

Hustle	35 seconds
Push-Up from Knees	30 seconds
Hustle	35 seconds
Bend and Stretch (8 counts)	30 seconds
Hustle	35 seconds
Jumping Jacks (4 counts)	30 seconds
Hustle	35 seconds
Sit-Ups (2 counts)	40 seconds
Hustle	35 seconds
Double-Leg Crab Kick (2 counts)	30 seconds
Hustle	35 seconds
Sit and Stretch (8 counts)	40 seconds
Hustle	35 seconds
Power Jumper	30 seconds
Hustle	35 seconds
Squat Thrust (4 counts)	30 seconds

Conclude the Hexagon Hustle with a slow jog or walk.

DPE p. 262

Examples of hustle activities that can be listed on signs are:
1. Jogging
2. Skipping or galloping
3. Hopping or jumping
4. Sliding
5. Running and leaping
6. Animal movements
7. Sport movements such as defensive sliding, running backwards, and carioca step

During the hustle, faster moving students can pass to the outside of the hexagon.

Change directions regularly to keep students spaced evenly along the hexagon.

During the hustle, quality movement rather than speed is the goal.

Cog.—The student will be able to state which muscle groups are exercised at each circuit.

PM.—The student will be able to perform all exercises.

Aff.—Most fitness gains are made when the body is exercised past the point of initial fatigue. Briefly discuss the value of pushing one's self past the first signs of tiring.

MOVEMENT EXPERIENCE—CONTENT	ORGANIZATION AND TEACHING HINTS	EXPECTED STUDENT OBJECTIVES AND OUTCOMES
	LESSON FOCUS (15 – 20 MINUTES)	
Rhythms Usually begin each lesson with a dance the students know and enjoy.	1. Listen to the music, clapping the rhythms and pointing out where changes occur. 2. Teach the basic skills used in the dance. 3. Practice the dance steps in sequence. 4. Practice with the music.	
1. Inside-Out Mixer (pp. 353 – 354)	May use any record with a pronounced beat that has a moderate speed for walking. Basic skills: 1. Walking 2. Inside-out circle Circle of groups of three facing CCW. Begin with a slow tempo and gradually increase to normal speed. Center student may wear a pinnie for ease of identification. Mixers provide quick and easy accomplishment, thus reinforcing success through dance.	Cog.—The student will be able to recognize that dancing provides an enjoyable means of socialization.
2. Alley Cat (p. 351)	An American dance Basic dance steps: 1. Grapevine 2. Knee lifts All students should be scattered and face the same direction during instruction. When the routine has been repeated three times, the dancer should be facing the original direction.	PM.—The students will improve their techniques in the grapevine step to the point of utility in this dance. PM.—The dancer will be able to transfer the grapevine step learned in previous dances to this dance.
3. Hora (pp. 348 – 349)	Regarded as the national dance of Israel. It is a simple dance designed to express joy. There are two versions done in Israel, the Old Hora and the New Hora. The New Hora is more energetic. Basic dance steps: 1. Grapevine 2. Swing step Circle formation, hands joined (may be taught in a scattered formation first). Present both versions of the Hora. Master one before presenting the other. As a change of activity, a simple game may be taught between dances.	Aff.—The student will appreciate the culture of Israel as exemplified by this dance. PM.—The student will be able to do the Hora alone, in a circle, or in a line. PM.—The basic step will be mastered by the student so that it can be done automatically.

MOVEMENT EXPERIENCE—CONTENT	ORGANIZATION AND TEACHING HINTS	EXPECTED STUDENT OBJECTIVES AND OUTCOMES
4. Hot Time in the Old Town Tonight (p. 353)	An American dance Basic dance skills: 1. Two-step 2. Directional walking Single circle facing center. Begin with music at slow speed and gradually increase to normal speed.	Aff.—The student will take pride in doing dances correctly.
5. Teton Mountain Stomp (pp. 356 – 357)	An American dance Basic dance skills: 1. Step, close, step, stomp 2. Two-step 3. Banjo position 4. Sidecar position The banjo position resembles a swing position, with both hands joined and right hips adjacent. The sidecar position is the reverse of the banjo position, with left hips adjacent.	PM.—The student will be able to make smooth transitions from walking with a partner, to the banjo position, and then into the sidecar position. Aff.—The student will accept a new partner with the proper courtesy.
6. Kalvelis ("Little Blacksmith") (p. 355)	A Lithuanian dance Basic dance steps: 1. Polka step 2. Swing 3. Clapping pattern 4. Grand right and left The formation is a single circle, with partners facing the center. Use the polka step when performing the grand right and left in this dance. A new partner will be met at the completion of each grand right and left pattern.	PM.—The student will be able to transfer the polka step from previous dances to the present dance. PM.—The student will be able to put the parts of the dance together and make the partner change properly. Aff.—The student will accept new partners graciously.
7. Limbo Rock (p. 352)	An American dance Basic dance skills: 1. Touch step 2. Swivel step 3. Jump clap step Begin by teaching the steps with students scattered individually. Progress to a single circle of partners, or scattered with partners.	PM.—The student will develop the proper rhythm to perform this dance successfully.

GAME (5 – 7 MINUTES)

Use an active tag game for the close of this lesson.	(*DPE* p. 518)	

DYNAMIC PHYSICAL EDUCATION LESSON PLAN
Racket Sport Skills
Level III

Supplies and Equipment Needed:
  Rackets
  Yarn balls or whiffle balls
  Foam balls that bounce
  Used tennis balls
  Nets
  Targets
  Signs for circuit training
  Jump rope

MOVEMENT EXPERIENCE—CONTENT	ORGANIZATION AND TEACHING HINTS	EXPECTED STUDENT OBJECTIVES AND OUTCOMES

INTRODUCTORY ACTIVITY (2 – 3 MINUTES)

Hospital Tag

Students run around the area. When tagged, they must cover the area of their body with one hand. Students may be tagged twice, but they must be able to hold both tagged spots and keep moving. When a student is tagged three times, he must freeze. Restart the game after all students have been frozen.

DPE p. 222

Scattered formation.

Three or four taggers.

May vary locomotor movements.

Students keep moving even after they have been tagged.

PM.—Students will be able to dodge taggers effectively without falling.

Aff.—Students will freeze graciously and display good sportsmanship when tagged.

FITNESS DEVELOPMENT ACTIVITIES (7 – 8 MINUTES)

Circuit Training

Rope Jumping
Triceps Push-Ups
Agility Run
Body Circles
Hula Hoops
Partial Sit-Ups
Crab Walk
Tortoise and Hare
Bend and Stretch

Conclude circuit training with 2–4 minutes of walking, jogging, rope jumping, or other aerobic activity.

DPE pp. 259 – 262

Start with 30 seconds of exercise followed by 10 seconds of time to move and prepare for the next station.

Use signals such as "start," "stop," and "move up" to ensure rapid movement to the next station.

Move randomly from station to station to offer help for students who are not using correct technique.

Cog.—The student will be able to explain the need to exercise the arm and shoulder girdle area to increase strength in that region of the body.

Cog.—Water accounts for 70% of the body's weight. At least a quart of water must be ingested per day. Discuss how a great deal more must be ingested when one is involved in strenuous exercise. What problems arise when one doesn't drink enough water?

PM.—The student will be able to perform exercises and movements at this level.

LESSON FOCUS (15 – 20 MINUTES)

Racket Sports

The focus of this unit should be to give youngsters an introduction to tennis, badminton, and racketball. Proceed through the sequence of activities until they meet the developmental needs of students.

DPE pp. 378 – 380

Scatter formation.

Rackets and old tennis balls with holes punched in them work well. Also, the children can use their hands as paddles, and a fleece ball can be used.

Cog.—The student will be able to name five sports in which paddle skills are used.

PM.—The student will be able to control the paddle and ball in a variety of situations.

MOVEMENT EXPERIENCE—CONTENT	ORGANIZATION AND TEACHING HINTS	EXPECTED STUDENT OBJECTIVES AND OUTCOMES

1. Discuss the proper method of holding the racket using the forehand and backhand grips.
 	
2. Air dribble the ball and try the following challenges:
  a. How many bounces without touching the floor?
  b. Bounce it as high as possible. Perform a heel click (or other stunt) while the ball is in the air.
  c. Kneel, sit, and lay down while air dribbling.
3. Dribble the ball on the floor with the racket:
  a. Move in different directions—forward, backward, sideways.
  b. Move, using different steps such as skip, grapevine, gallop.
  c. Move to a kneeling, sitting, and supine position while continuing the dribble. Return to a standing position.
4. Bounce the ball off the racket and "catch" it with the racket.
5. Place the ball on the floor:
  a. Scoop it up with the racket.
  b. Roll the ball and scoop it up with the racket.
  c. Start dribbling the ball without touching it with the hands.
6. Self-toss and hit to a fence, net, or tumbling mat. This drill should be used to practice the forehand and backhand. The ball should be dropped so it bounces to waist level.
7. Partner activities:
  a. One partner feeds the ball to the other, who returns the ball with a forehand or backhand stroke.
  b. Stroke the ball back and forth to each other with one or more bounces between contact.
  c. Self-toss and hit. Drop the ball and stroke it to a partner 20–30 ft away. Partner does the same thing to return the ball.
  d. Partner throw and hit. One partner throws the ball to the other, who returns the ball by stroking it with the racket.
	This is a limited-movement activity; thus, break the activity into two parts separated by some running, rope jumping, or similarly physically demanding activity.
	
	Concentrate on control of the ball and quality of movement. Take your time going through activities.
	
	Use left hand as well as right in developing the racket skills.
	
	Foam rubber balls that bounce are excellent for these skills.
	
	Ask junior or senior high schools for their old tennis balls. They are "dead," which will be helpful in teaching some of these skills.
	
	Focus on correct technique of strokes rather than accuracy. Students have to swing with velocity if they are to learn proper form.
	
	If students have a difficult time controlling the ball, it might be helpful to use fleece balls.
	
	Allow time for student choice.
	
	"Give" with the paddle.
	
	Change the paddle from hand to hand while the ball is in the air.
	
	The foam balls are excellent, since they bounce but do not carry.
		Aff.—One way to improve skills is to experiment with different ways of performing them. Discuss the value of trying new activities rather than always practicing areas in which we are already skilled.
		
		Cog.—The angle of the paddle when the ball is struck will determine the direction that the ball will travel.
		
		Cog.—A paddle will give the student a longer lever with which to strike the ball, and thus more force can be applied to the ball which in turn will increase its speed.
		
		PM.—The student will be able to perform three partner activities.
		
		Aff.—People feel part of a group when they can perform mutual skills. Discuss how learning various physical skills allows people to interact with friends and people with similar interests.

MOVEMENT EXPERIENCE— CONTENT	ORGANIZATION AND TEACHING HINTS	EXPECTED STUDENT OBJECTIVES AND OUTCOMES

    e. Wall volley: If a wall is available, partners can volley against it.

8. Serving:

    a. Teach tennis serve without a racket. Use a yarn ball and practice hitting it with the open hand. The serve is similar to the overhand throwing motion. The toss is a skill that will need to be mastered prior to learning the striking motion.

    b. Teach the racketball serve in similar fashion. The hard, driving serve is done using a side-underhand throwing motion. The striking hand should be raised on the backswing. A small foam (Nerf) ball that bounces should be dropped to the floor and struck on the rebound.

    c. For a racketball lob serve, the ball is bounced and hit with an underhand motion. The ball is hit high on the wall and bounces to the back wall.

    d. The foam ball can be used for the badminton serve also. For this serve, the ball is dropped and hit with an underhand motion before it hits the floor.

    e. Depending on facilities, rackets can be used after the basic motion has been learned.

GAME (5 – 7 MINUTES)

There are many games that could be related to this unit. Suggestions are:

1. Volley tennis
2. One-wall handball
3. One-wall racketball
4. Serving as targets—use for all three sports

DYNAMIC PHYSICAL EDUCATION LESSON PLAN
Football Skills (Lesson 1)
Level III

Supplies and Equipment Needed:
  Signs for circuit training
  4–6 individual jump ropes (circuit training)
  8–12 junior footballs or foam rubber footballs
  4 soccer balls or foam rubber balls
  Audio player for circuit training
  12 cones (for boundaries)
  1 flag belt with flags per student
  1 pinnie per student (optional)
  Flag belts and flags

MOVEMENT EXPERIENCE—CONTENT	ORGANIZATION AND TEACHING HINTS	EXPECTED STUDENT OBJECTIVES AND OUTCOMES

INTRODUCTORY ACTIVITY (2 – 3 MINUTES)

Medic Tag

Three or four students are designated as "taggers." They try to tag the others; when tagged, a student kneels down as if injured. Another student (not one of the taggers) can "rehabilitate" the injured player, enabling her to reenter play.

DPE p. 222

Pinnies can be used to identify "taggers."

An area at least 30 ft by 50 ft is recommended.

Teacher designates means of "rehabilitation" (i.e., touching right shoulder and left knee; touching head—whereupon the injured must Crab Walk three steps).

Vary the types of locomotor movement the class can use to chase or flee.

Aff.—Self-responsibility is an integral part of many game activities. Discuss the importance of playing by the rules for the welfare of the entire class.

PM.—The student will be able to dodge/elude quickly without falling or colliding with another student.

FITNESS DEVELOPMENT ACTIVITIES (7 – 8 MINUTES)

Circuit Training

Rope Jumping
Triceps Push-Ups
Agility Run
Body Circles
Hula Hoops
Partial Sit-Ups
Crab Walk
Tortoise and Hare
Bend and Stretch

Conclude circuit training with 2–4 minutes of walking, jogging, rope jumping, or other aerobic activity.

DPE pp. 259 – 262

Increase to 35 seconds of exercise followed by 10 seconds of time to move and prepare for the next station.

Emphasize quality of movement rather than quantity and lack of technique.

Taped intervals of music and no music can be used to signal duration of exercise at each station and time to move to next station.

Cog.—Muscles atrophy without exercise and grow stronger with use. The student will be able to describe in his own words the need for exercises.

PM.—All students will be able to move and exercise through the circuit within 7 minutes.

MOVEMENT EXPERIENCE— CONTENT	ORGANIZATION AND TEACHING HINTS	EXPECTED STUDENT OBJECTIVES AND OUTCOMES

LESSON FOCUS (15 – 20 MINUTES)

Football

A. *Skills*
Introduce and practice the basic skills of football.
  1. Passing
  2. Catching
  3. Carrying the ball
  4. Centering
  5. Punting
  6. Stance

B. *Drills*
Practice football skills using the station format. Set up stations with a drill to be incorporated by students. Rotate students to at least two stations each day.

DPE pp. 593 – 606

Focus on the basic fundamentals. Offer brief explanation for the skills and allow time for practice.

Place critical points of technique on task cards at each station. Encourage students to analyze each other's technique.

Use foam rubber footballs during the first part of the drill so students learn proper technique without worrying about being hurt by the football.

  Station 1

Stance and Blocking

Offensive players use a 3 point stance with toes pointed forward and head up.

Defensive players use a 4 point stance with more weight on hands.

Blockers should avoid falling, and should stay on toes and in front of defensive player.

Use the Stance Drill with one student calling signals.

Once the stance is learned, practice blocking with emphasis on maintaining contact with the defensive player.

Cog.—The student will be able to describe why a good football player employs the proper stance. How does a stance affect stability and balance?

PM.—The student will be able to demonstrate correct blocking technique.

  Station 2

Centering and Carrying the Ball

Teach proper technique for long centering and T-formation centering.

Practice centering to a quarterback in the shotgun formation. The quarterback then practices carrying the ball.

Long centering is used for the shotgun formation and punting. When the football is centered to the quarterback in the T-formation, only one hand is used.

Use the Combination Drill to practice short and long centering.

Cog.—Every play starts with a center snap. The student will be able to express the importance of accuracy to prevent fumbles and loose balls.

PM.—The student will be able to center the ball to the quarterback (or punter) five consecutive times without a fumble.

  Station 3

Passing and Receiving

Begin practice with short passes to a stationary receiver.

Practice throwing to moving receivers, placing emphasis on leading the receiver with the pass.

Use the Combination Drill with emphasis placed on leading the receiver.

Practice throwing from under the center with a three-step drop.

Practice passing from the shotgun formation.

Rotate the center, quarterback, receiver, and ball chaser every five passes.

Aff.—Students will be able to understand the individual differences of others when participating in sport activities.

PM.—The student will be able to explain the importance of leading the receiver.

MOVEMENT EXPERIENCE—CONTENT	ORGANIZATION AND TEACHING HINTS	EXPECTED STUDENT OBJECTIVES AND OUTCOMES
Station 4 *Punting* Concentrate on technique rather than distance when teaching punting. Emphasize keeping the head down with the eyes on the ball. Drop the football rather than tossing it upward prior to the kick. C. *Lead-Up Games* Football End Ball, p. 600 Five Passes, p. 601 Speed Football, p. 601 Kick-Over, p. 601	For beginning punters, using a round foam rubber ball will be easier than kicking a football. The foam rubber footballs can be used after the basic components of kicking are learned.	Cog.—Students will be able to explain when and why punting is used in football. PM.—The student will demonstrate the ability to use the two-step punting technique.

GAME (5 – 7 MINUTES)

The football lead-up games listed above should be used for game activity.

DYNAMIC PHYSICAL EDUCATION LESSON PLAN
Football Skills (Lesson 2)
Level III

Supplies and Equipment Needed:
  Signs for circuit training
  4–6 individual jump ropes
  8 junior footballs or foam rubber footballs
  4 soccer balls or foam rubber balls
  12 cones
  1 flag belt with flags per student
  1 pinnie per student (optional)
  Audio player (circuit training)

MOVEMENT EXPERIENCE— CONTENT	ORGANIZATION AND TEACHING HINTS	EXPECTED STUDENT OBJECTIVES AND OUTCOMES

INTRODUCTORY ACTIVITY (2 – 3 MINUTES)

Pyramid Power

Students move throughout the area. On signal, they find a partner and build a simple partner support stunt or pyramid (i.e., double bear, table, hip–shoulder stand, statue). On the next signal, pyramids are quickly and safely dismantled and students move again.

DPE p. 223

Students should select a partner of similar size.

Remind students to stand on the proper points of support.

Prerecorded music with blank intervals works well here.

Aff.—Cooperation and consideration are integral components of all partner activities. Discuss the need to cooperate with and have compassion for others.

PM.—The student will be able to form two different pyramids.

Cog.—The student will know the proper points of support when forming pyramids.

FITNESS DEVELOPMENT ACTIVITIES (7 – 8 MINUTES)

Circuit Training

Rope Jumping
Push-Ups
Agility Run
Lower Leg Stretch
Juggling Scarves
Sit-Ups with Twist
Alternate Leg Extension
Tortoise and Hare
Bear Hug

Conclude circuit training with 2–4 minutes of walking, jogging, rope jumping, or other aerobic activity.

DPE pp. 259 – 262

Increase to 40 seconds of exercise followed by 10 seconds of time to move and prepare for the next station.

Hula hoops and juggling scarves placed at a station allow youngsters a chance to rest and are motivating activities.

This is the last week of circuit training. Encourage improvement of performance and technique.

Aff.—Most fitness gains are made when the body is exercised past the point of initial fatigue. Thus, briefly discuss the value of pushing one's self past the initial signs of fatigue.

PM.—The student will be able to complete each station with minimal resting.

LESSON FOCUS (15 – 20 MINUTES)

Football

A. *Drills*
Continue station work with skills delineated to stations as listed below. Rotate students to at least two stations each day.

DPE pp. 593 – 606

Place critical points of technique on task cards at each station. Encourage students to analyze each other's technique.

Aff.—Students will be able to evaluate the skill technique of peers after reviewing task cards.

MOVEMENT EXPERIENCE— CONTENT	ORGANIZATION AND TEACHING HINTS	EXPECTED STUDENT OBJECTIVES AND OUTCOMES
Station 1 **Stance and Blocking** Offensive players use a 3 point stance with toes pointed forward and head up. Defensive players use a 4 point stance with more weight on hands. Blockers should avoid falling, and should stay on toes and in front of defensive player.	Use the Stance Drill with one student calling signals. Once the stance is learned, practice blocking with emphasis on maintaining contact with the defensive player.	Cog.—The student will be able to describe why a good football player employs the proper stance. How does a stance affect stability and balance? PM.—The student will be able to demonstrate correct blocking technique.
Station 2 **Centering and Carrying the Ball** Teach proper technique for long centering and T-formation centering. Practice centering to a quarterback in the shotgun formation. The quarterback then practices carrying the ball.	Long centering is used for the shotgun formation and punting. When the football is centered to the quarterback in the T-formation, only one hand is used. Use the Combination Drill to practice short and long centering.	Cog.—Every play starts with a center snap. The student will be able to express the importance of accuracy to prevent fumbles and loose balls. PM.—The student will be able to center the ball to the quarterback (or punter) five consecutive times without a fumble.
Station 3 **Passing and Receiving** Begin practice with short passes to a stationary receiver. Practice throwing to moving receivers, placing emphasis on leading the receiver with the pass. Use the Combination Drill with emphasis placed on leading the receiver.	Practice passing after moving from under the center with a three-step drop. Practice passing from the shotgun formation. Rotate the center, quarterback, receiver, and ball chaser every five passes.	Aff.—Students will be able to understand the individual differences of others when participating in sport activities. PM.—The student will be able to explain the importance of leading the receiver.
Station 4 **Punting** Concentrate on technique rather than distance when teaching punting. Emphasize keeping the head down with the eyes on the ball. Drop the football rather than tossing it upward prior to the kick.	For beginning punters, using a round foam rubber ball will be easier than kicking a football. The foam rubber footballs can be used after the basic components of kicking are learned.	Cog.—Students will be able to explain simple elements of football strategy. PM.—The student will demonstrate the ability to use the two-step punting technique. Cog.—Students will be able to verbalize the basic rules of flag football. PM.—Students will be able to play football lead-up games without instructor supervision.
B. *Lead-Up Games* Speed Football, p. 601 Fourth Down, p. 601 Flag Football, p. 601		

GAME ACTIVITY (5– 7 MINUTES)

The football lead-up games listed above should be used for game activity.

DYNAMIC PHYSICAL EDUCATION LESSON PLAN
Jogging Skills
Level III

Supplies and Equipment Needed:
  One individual jump rope per child
  Manipulative equipment for jogging (as needed)
  Recreational and individual equipment as desired

MOVEMENT EXPERIENCE— CONTENT	ORGANIZATION AND TEACHING HINTS	EXPECTED STUDENT OBJECTIVES AND OUTCOMES

INTRODUCTORY AND FITNESS ACTIVITIES (9 – 11 MINUTES)

Stretching and Jogging

Combine the introductory and fitness activities during the track and field unit. This will help students understand how to stretch and warm up for demanding activity such as track and field.

Jog for 1–2 minutes
Standing Hip Bend	30 seconds
Sitting Stretch	30 seconds
Partner Rowing	60 seconds
Bear Hug (20 seconds each leg)	40 seconds
Side Flex (20 seconds each leg)	40 seconds
Trunk Twister	30 seconds

Jog for 2–3 minutes

DPE pp. 248 – 249

To prepare for strenuous activity, students should learn to warm up their body by walking or jogging, stretching, and finishing with jogging.

Avoid bouncing during the stretching activities. All stretching should be smooth and controlled movements.

Allow students to direct their warm-up activity. It is important that students be able to warm up without teacher direction.

Cog.—Static stretching involves stretching without bouncing. Stretches should be held for 15–30 seconds for maximum benefit.

Cog.—The student will be able to explain why stretching exercises and warm-ups are essential to track and field work.

PM.—The student will demonstrate the ability to put proper stress on muscles in stretching.

Cog.—The term *isometric* refers to maximum muscular effort exerted by pushing or pulling an immovable object.

LESSON FOCUS (15 – 20 MINUTES)

Jogging

A. Three types of jogging programs that can be used:
  1. *Jog-Walk-Jog*—In this method, the student jogs until he feels the need to rest, walks until somewhat rested, and then jogs again.
  2. *Jog a Set Distance*—The pace is varied depending on the body's reaction to the demands.
  3. *Increase the Distance*—The pace is maintained, but the distance is increased.

B. Take the students through jogging practice. Have them:
  1. Jog 110 yd, walk 55 yd, jog 110 yd, walk 55 yd, etc.
  2. Run 440 yd without stopping; increase distance.

DPE pp. 268 – 269

Teach children the proper style of running.

Start students at a short distance so they will not become discouraged.

Concentrate on teaching the values of jogging and encouraging students to start their own jogging program.

Works well on a 220-yd track.

Better endurance is needed for this procedure than for jog-walk-jog.

PM.—The student will be able to demonstrate proper jogging style.

PM.—The student will be able to jog 220 yd nonstop.

Aff.—Jogging is one of the best activities for developing cardiovascular endurance. Discuss the value of jogging for personal health.

Cog.—The student will be able to list three chronic effects jogging has on the body.

MOVEMENT EXPERIENCE— CONTENT	ORGANIZATION AND TEACHING HINTS	EXPECTED STUDENT OBJECTIVES AND OUTCOMES
3. Run for a specified distance in a random direction. A student may jog in any direction, but he should try to keep jogging. The advantage to this approach is that students won't race as they tend to do on a track. 4. Place a cone marker in the center of a circle that is 36 ft in radius. The object is to be as close to the cone as possible when a signal indicating elapsed time is given. This activity helps children learn time approximation regarding "pace." The children must jog outside the circle before reentering after pass by the center cone.	Cones may be used to mark circle. A good motivating technique is to jog across the state or the United States. The distance each student runs could be added together for a class total. "Train, don't strain."	Cog.—For exercise to have the most impact on the cardiovascular system, heart rate should reach the training state. This amounts to 70 to 85% of one's maximum heart rate. Maximum heart rate is 220 minus your age. Thus, if one is 10 years old, the training state will require a heart rate of 147–179. Compute the training rate for yourself. The student will learn to measure pulse rate and move the heart rate into the training state.
C. Encourage students to jog at a realistic pace. A good idea is to have them jog with a friend and talk while running. They should be able to run and talk comfortably. If not, they are running too fast. D. It is sometimes motivating for youngsters if they run with a piece of equipment (i.e., beanbag or jump rope). They can play catch with a ball or roll a hoop while jogging.	"Pace, not race." Don't praise the first few people leading the run if you are working on pace. The praise will cause the class to concentrate on winning rather than running for pace. Bring in high school track or cross-country runners to talk about their training.	

GAME: INDIVIDUAL OR RECREATIONAL ACTIVITY

Individual or recreational equipment can be put out for youngsters who wish a low-key closing activity. Some students may desire to continue jogging.

DYNAMIC PHYSICAL EDUCATION LESSON PLAN
Cross-Country Running
Level III

Supplies and Equipment Needed:
1 individual jump rope per child
Recreational and individual equipment as needed
8–12 cones for cross-country "funnel" (meet)
1 pinnie per student for meet (optional)

MOVEMENT EXPERIENCE—CONTENT	ORGANIZATION AND TEACHING HINTS	EXPECTED STUDENT OBJECTIVES AND OUTCOMES

INTRODUCTORY AND FITNESS DEVELOPMENT ACTIVITIES (9 – 11 MINUTES)

Stretching and Jogging

Combine the introductory and fitness activities during the track and field unit. This will help students understand how to stretch and warm up for demanding activity such as track and field.

Jog for 1–2 minutes

Standing Hip Bend	30 seconds
Sitting Stretch	30 seconds
Partner Rowing	60 seconds
Bear Hug (20 seconds each leg)	40 seconds
Side Flex (20 seconds each leg)	40 seconds
Trunk Twister	30 seconds

Jog for 2–3 minutes

DPE pp. 248 – 249

To prepare for strenuous activity, students should learn to warm up their body by walking or jogging, stretching, and finishing with jogging.

Avoid bouncing during the stretching activities. All stretching should be smooth and controlled movements.

Allow students to direct their warm-up activity. It is important that students be able to warm up without teacher direction.

Cog.—The student will be able to explain why stretching exercises are essential to track and field work.

PM.—The student will demonstrate the ability to put the proper stress on muscles in stretching.

Cog.—Flexors decrease the angle of a joint and extensors cause the return from flexion. Identify different flexor and extensor muscle groups and the joint they affect.

LESSON FOCUS (15 – 20 MINUTES)

Cross-Country Running

A. Discuss the sport of cross-country running and how it is scored.
   1. Seven members to a team.
   2. Lowest score wins.
   3. Total points for each team based on places finished in race.

B. Divide the class into equal teams based on estimated running times.

C. Depending on the age of youngsters, as well as their ability, teams can run different length courses. The following lengths are suggested:
   1. Beginning—3/4 mi
   2. Intermediate—1 1/2 mi
   3. Advanced—2 mi

D. Practice pace running by having students run 100 yd in different amounts of time (see chart on p. 669).

DPE pp. 668 – 669

Reinforce proper running style.

Intersperse the cognitive material with running and team practice. Don't sit for long (more than 2 minutes) without activity.

The number of students on each team should be equal, but seven are not necessary.

Time trials (informal) could be held so teams could be developed equally. A reasonable estimate of their distance running ability could be predicted by timing them over a short distance (50 yd). This distance should be covered in an all-out sprint.

DPE pp. 668 – 669

Cog.—The students will understand how to score a cross-country meet.

PM.—The student will be able to complete a run-walk over the cross-country course.

Aff.—Cross-country running places a burden on each member of the team to do her best, regardless of ability. Discuss the importance of self-competition as compared with competing against others of greater or lesser ability.

Cog.—The student will understand the importance of and need for "warming down" after strenuous activity.

Cog.—Students will understand how to score a cross-country meet.

MOVEMENT EXPERIENCE—CONTENT	ORGANIZATION AND TEACHING HINTS	EXPECTED STUDENT OBJECTIVES AND OUTCOMES
E. Explain and have the youngsters "warm down" after each course run.	This is a team sport, rather than individual activity; thus, the slowest runner on the team is as important as the fastest.	Aff.—Students who excel in cross-country running may be different from those who excel in team sports. Discuss individual differences regardless of the activity being analyzed.
F. Have a "mini" cross-country meet.	If walking is necessary, it should be done briskly.	

GAME (INDIVIDUAL OR RECREATIONAL ACTIVITY)

Since youngsters will finish at different times, individual equipment can be placed out so those youngsters who have completed the course and are warming down can be actively involved. Another good choice would be a recreational activity, such as Four-Square, Beanbag Horseshoes, and Sidewalk Tennis.

DYNAMIC PHYSICAL EDUCATION LESSON PLAN
Individual Rope Jumping Skills (Lesson 1)
Level III

Supplies and Equipment Needed:
  Individual jump ropes
  Exercise-to-music tape
  Cassette tape player
  Balls

MOVEMENT EXPERIENCE—CONTENT	ORGANIZATION AND TEACHING HINTS	EXPECTED STUDENT OBJECTIVES AND OUTCOMES

INTRODUCTORY ACTIVITY (2 – 3 MINUTES)

Partner Over and Under

Students pair up with one person on the floor and the other standing ready to move. On signal, the standing students move over, under, and/or around the person on the floor. On signal, reverse positions. Students on the floor can also alternate between positions such as curl, stretch, and bridge.

DPE p. 222

Partner formation.

Encourage students to move as quickly as possible.

Challenge them to see how many times they can go over and under each other.

As an additional challenge, bridges may move as long as they remain in a bridge position.

PM.—The student will be able to move quickly over, under, and around her partner.

Aff.—Warm-up activities only work when an individual motivates himself to move quickly and with intensity.

FITNESS DEVELOPMENT ACTIVITIES (7 – 8 MINUTES)

Exercises to Music

Forward Lunges	40 seconds
Alternate Crab Kicks	25 seconds
Windmills	35 seconds
Walk and do Arm Circles	20 seconds
Sit-Ups	30 seconds
Side Flex	25 seconds
Triceps Push-Ups	45 seconds
Two-Step or Gallop	15 seconds
Jumping Jack variations	25 seconds
Aerobic Bouncing and Clapping	35 seconds
Leg Extensions	40 seconds
Push-Ups	30 seconds
Walking to cool down	45 seconds

DPE p. 259

Students should know the exercises before trying to do them rhythmically.

Rhythmic sit-ups are four counts - knees, toes, knees, and down.

The exercise music should be taped prior to the routine. This frees the teacher to move and help students.

Voice instructions can be dubbed onto the tape to tell students when to change to a new exercise.

Cog.—The body starts to perspire in an attempt to maintain a constant temperature. The student will verbalize this in her own words.

PM.—The student will be able to perform all repetitions of the fitness activities.

Aff.—Regulation of body temperature is essential for comfort and safety. Discuss the many ways we attempt to regulate this temperature—more or fewer clothes, perspiring, swimming, fires.

LESSON FOCUS (15 – 20 MINUTES)

Individual Rope Jumping

1. Introduce the two basic jumps:
   a. Slow time
   b. Fast time
2. Introduce some of the basic step variations:
   a. Alternate foot basic step
   b. Swing step forward
   c. Swing step sideways
   d. Rocker step
   e. Spread legs, forward and backward

DPE pp. 404 – 410

Slow time—use a double rebound between each turn of the rope.

Fast time—one bounce for each turn of the rope.

Allow students to progress at their own rate. It is good to show the better jumpers some of the more difficult variations and allow them to practice by themselves.

PM.—Youngsters will be able to jump-rope to slow and fast time rhythm for 30–60 seconds.

Cog.—High-density lipoproteins (HDL) can slow the deposit of fat on arteries. The ratio of HDL to low-density lipoproteins (LDL) can be enhanced through exercise. Aerobic activity performed 30–45 minutes four times a week increases HDL levels in 7–10 weeks.

MOVEMENT EXPERIENCE— CONTENT	ORGANIZATION AND TEACHING HINTS	EXPECTED STUDENT OBJECTIVES AND OUTCOMES

f. Toe touch, forward and backward
g. Shuffle step
h. Cross arms, forward, backward
i. Double jump
3. Work out combinations—add cross-hands.
4. Teach how to go from rope turning forward to rope turning backward without stopping the rope.
5. Using an individual rope with one partner holding each end: Each partner turns, partners take turns jumping in while turning.
6. One partner holds and turns rope. Second partner jumps with partner.
7. With a partner, do "the wheel" using both individual ropes. Both partners jump.
8. Attempt combinations of jump rope variations.
9. Put combinations to music.

All of the variations can be done with the turning in a forward or backward direction.

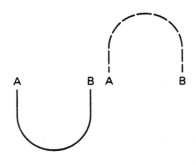

Partner A holds one of his rope handles in his left hand and one of Partner B's handles in his right hand. Partner B holds one of her rope handles in her right hand and one of Partner A's in her left hand.

GAME (5 – 7 MINUTES)

Aff.—Stress can be detrimental to a person's health. Discuss various situations that create stress among students. Discuss ways of coping with the stress.

Cog.—Some doctors estimate that young people eat 150–200 lb of sugar per year. Sugar offers "empty calories"—calories but no nutritional value. Eating too much sugar releases insulin to handle the extra sugar and soon depresses the blood sugar level to make you feel sluggish. Discuss the importance of reducing raw sugar intake.

Cog.—Students will understand that 10 minutes of rope jumping is equal to 30 minutes of jogging.

Aff.—Rope jumping is neither a male nor a female activity. It is performed by boxers, football players, and dancers for fitness development.

Play a less active game. The following are suggested:
1. Right Face, Left Face, p. 538
2. One Base Tagball, p. 542

DYNAMIC PHYSICAL EDUCATION LESSON PLAN
Tug-of-War Rope and Frisbee Skills
Level III

Supplies and Equipment Needed:
  Team tug-of-war rope
  Individual tug-of-war ropes
  Frisbees
  Music (for the exercise routine)
  Record player or cassette tape player
  Manipulative equipment
  Hoops
  Indian clubs

MOVEMENT EXPERIENCE—CONTENT	ORGANIZATION AND TEACHING HINTS	EXPECTED STUDENT OBJECTIVES AND OUTCOMES

INTRODUCTORY ACTIVITY (2 – 3 MINUTES)

Move and Manipulate

Each student is given a piece of equipment and moves around the area using locomotor movements. Students toss and catch the equipment while moving. On signal, the equipment is dropped, and students move over and around equipment.

DPE p. 221

Scatter formation.

Beanbags, fleece balls (yarn balls), hula hoops, or balls may be used.

Add many challenges while moving to both the locomotor movements and manipulative activities.

PM.—The student will be able to toss and catch an object while moving.

Cog.—The student will recite the fact that it is easier to toss and catch an object while standing stationary than while moving.

FITNESS DEVELOPMENT ACTIVITIES (7 – 8 MINUTES)

Exercises to Music

Forward Lunges	40 seconds
Alternate Crab Kicks	25 seconds
Windmills	35 seconds
Walk and do Arm Circles	20 seconds
Sit-Ups	30 seconds
Side Flex	25 seconds
Triceps Push-Ups	45 seconds
Two-Step or Gallop	15 seconds
Jumping Jack variations	25 seconds
Aerobic Bouncing and Clapping	35 seconds
Leg Extensions	40 seconds
Push-Ups	30 seconds
Walking to cool down	45 seconds

DPE p. 259

Students should know the exercises before trying to do them rhythmically.

Rhythmic sit-ups are four counts - knees, toes, knees, and down.

The exercise music should be taped prior to the routine. This frees the teacher to move and help students.

Voice instructions can be dubbed onto the tape to tell students when to change to a new exercise.

Cog.—The student will know each exercise by name.

PM.—The student will be able to pick up the beat of the music and stay with the rhythm while performing the exercises.

Aff.—Compare performances with those of the preceding week. Discuss the attitude that self-improvement is self-rewarding and motivates the learner to continue the effort.

Cog.—Oxygen debt occurs when the muscles need more oxygen than is being supplied. Anaerobic exercise usually creates an oxygen debt. Students should be able to distinguish anaerobic from aerobic activities.

LESSON FOCUS (15 – 20 MINUTES)

Tug-of-War Rope Activities

A. *Isometric Exercises*
  Make sure joints are bent and students aren't leaning.
  1. Standing—use the ends of ropes only and try to stretch the handle apart.

DPE pp. 388 – 391

Two parallel lines—this will allow you to start and stop them easily.

Make sure they hold their *maximum* effort for 8–10 seconds.

Force is applied to rope only, not partner.

249

MOVEMENT EXPERIENCE— CONTENT	ORGANIZATION AND TEACHING HINTS	EXPECTED STUDENT OBJECTIVES AND OUTCOMES

a. Use different hand positions and arm positions.
2. Partner Resistance Activities— start and stop on signal.
    a. Standing—sides facing each other and use both arms as well as right and left individually.
    b. Standing facing—use arms at various levels: above, below head, etc.
    c. Seated—sides facing, back to back, facing, legs elevated, etc. Also, hook on feet, knees—tug.
    d. Prone position—feet touching, heads toward each other, pull on ankle, push-up position pull, etc.
    e. On back—pull with feet, knees, arms.
    f. Develop other areas. Pupil choice.
	Start and stop on signal.
	
	Pull through the full range of motion.
	
	Rotate partners often.
		Cog.—Arteries, arterioles, and capillaries carry oxygenated blood to the muscles. Capillaries are so small and thin that oxygen passes right through the walls. At the same time, carbon dioxide is transferred from the body cells to the blood cells and carried back to the lungs to be expelled. The blood is transported back to the lungs in the veins. This system is called the circulatory system.
		
		PM.—The student will develop sufficient strength to hold her own with partner of equal size.
		
		Cog.—The student will be able to recite what tug-of-war ropes do for body development.

B. *Tug-of-War Activities*
1. Right, left, and both hands.
2. Leg pulls, elbows, pull between legs.
3. Tug with three body parts; on all fours.
4. Crab position, seal walk pull.
5. Line touch tug—(pull until you can touch the line behind you).
6. Partners facing, on signal, pick up partner's end of rope and pull.
    a. Begin in a push-up position.
    b. Start sitting crossed-leg fashion with hands on head.
    c. Touch a specified line before grabbing partner's end of rope.
7. Exploratory opportunity.
 	
C. *Tug-of-War Games*
1. Four way pull
2. Two against two pull
3. Japanese Tug-of-War
4. Hawaiian Tug-of-War
	The tug-of-war rope and Frisbee lesson has a dual lesson focus that may be approached in a variety of ways.
	  1. Alternate tug-of-war activities with Frisbee activities.
	  2. For each period, teach half of the lesson on tug-of-war ropes and half on Frisbees.
	  3. Teach 1 day of the week on tug-of-war ropes and the next day on Frisbees.
	When signal is given, place tug-of-war ropes on floor, ready for the next activity.
	
	Encourage gradual pulling to maximum effort rather than jerking.
	
	If grip is slipping—stop, renew grip, and proceed.
	
	Stress working safely with partner. Don't let go of the end of the tug-of-war rope abruptly.
	
	Establish lines to cross in order to win the tug-of-war.
	
	It might be a good idea to try a change-of-pace activity in the middle of the Tug-of-War lesson to pick up the tempo of the lesson. Try alternating tug-of-war ropes with Frisbee activities.
		Aff.—Even though tug-of-war ropes are competitive, cooperation is necessary to ensure an equal start and contest. Discuss the necessity of cooperation in all major sports.
		
		Cog.—The student will explain that maximum effort is required for best results in strength development.
		
		Aff.—A sense of fairness should be encouraged during this highly competitive activity. Take time to discuss the importance of fair play.

D. *Frisbees* (Flying Discs)
1. Skills
    a. Backhand throw
    b. Underhand throw
    c. Thumbs-down catch
	DPE pp. 380 – 382
	
	Partner formation.
		PM.—The student will be able to perform the following skills:
		1. Backhand throw
		2. Underhand throw
		3. Thumbs-down catch
		4. Thumbs-up catch

MOVEMENT EXPERIENCE— CONTENT	ORGANIZATION AND TEACHING HINTS	EXPECTED STUDENT OBJECTIVES AND OUTCOMES
d. Thumbs-up catch Practice the throwing and catching skills so youngsters will feel comfortable with the following activities.	Throw and catch with a partner. Begin with short distances and gradually move apart as skill improves.	
2. Activities a. Throw the Frisbee at different levels to partner. b. Throw a curve—to the left, right, and upward. Vary the speed of the curve. c. Throw a bounce pass—try a low and high pass. d. Throw the Frisbee like a boomerang. Must throw at a steep angle into the wind. e. Throw the Frisbee into the air, run and catch. Increase the distance of the throw. f. Throw the Frisbee through a hoop held by a partner. g. Catch the Frisbee under your leg. Catch it behind your back. h. Throw the Frisbees into hoops that are placed on the ground as targets. Different colored hoops can be given different values. Throw through your partner's legs. i. Frisbee bowling—One partner has an Indian club that the other partner attempts to knock down by throwing the Frisbee. j. Play catch while moving. Lead your partner so he doesn't have to break stride. k. See how many successful throws and catches you can make in 30 seconds. l. Frisbee Baseball Pitching— Attempt to throw the Frisbee into your partner's "Strike Zone."	Give students plenty of room—their lack of skill will result in many inaccurate throws. Emphasize accuracy rather than distance in the early stages of throwing the Frisbee. Use both dominant and nondominant hand. For a straight throw, the disc should be parallel to the ground on release. Remind students to focus their eyes on the disc as long as possible. Encourage students to try different activities of their own creation. Offer a helping station for those students who have difficulty learning the basic throws.	Cog.—The student will be able to explain the effect that the angle of the disc on release will have on its flight. Aff.—Frisbees are a recreational activity. Discuss the importance of learning leisure-time skills for the future. PM.—The student will be able to catch the Frisbee six out of eight times.

GAME (5 – 7 MINUTES)

Try some Frisbee games:
1. Frisbee Keep-Away
2. Frisbee Through-the-Legs Target Throw
3. Frisbee Golf—Use hula hoops for the cups. Establish pars for various distance holes.

Incorporate some tug-of-war activities:
1. Group tug-of-war using a long tug-of-war rope
2. Any of the tug-of-war games listed in the lesson (C)

DYNAMIC PHYSICAL EDUCATION LESSON PLAN
Hockey Skills (Lesson 1)
Level III

Supplies and Equipment Needed:
Hockey sticks and pucks (indoors) or whiffle balls (outdoors)
Beanbags, fleece balls (optional)
Exercise-to-music tape
Audiotape player
Tumbling mats for goals

MOVEMENT EXPERIENCE—CONTENT	ORGANIZATION AND TEACHING HINTS	EXPECTED STUDENT OBJECTIVES AND OUTCOMES

INTRODUCTORY ACTIVITY (2 – 3 MINUTES)

New Leader

Squads move around the area, following the squad leader. On signal, the last person can move to the head of the squad and become the leader. Various types of locomotor movements and/or exercises should be used.

Variation:
Assign each squad a specific area if desired. Each area could include a piece of equipment to aid in the activity (beanbag, fleece ball, etc.).

DPE p. 223

Squad formation. Encourage students to keep moving unless an exercise or similar activity is being performed.

Cog.—The student will be able to give two reasons why warm-up is necessary prior to strenuous exercises.

Aff.—The student will be capable of leading as well as following. Discuss the necessity of both in our society.

FITNESS DEVELOPMENT ACTIVITIES (7 – 8 MINUTES)

Exercises to Music

Side Flex (switch sides)	40 seconds
Trunk Twister	25 seconds
Rhythmic Sit-Ups	35 seconds
Slide/Skip	20 seconds
Jumping Jack variations	30 seconds
Triceps Push-Ups	25 seconds
Partial Curl-Ups	45 seconds
Gallop	15 seconds
Push-Ups	25 seconds
Aerobic Bouncing and Clapping	35 seconds
Leg Extensions	40 seconds
Walking to cool down	45 seconds

DPE p. 259

Students should know the exercises before trying to do them rhythmically.

Rhythmic sit-ups are four counts - knees, toes, knees, and down.

Students can lead the exercise-to-music routine while the instructor monitors student progress.

Voice instructions can be dubbed onto the tape to tell students when to change to a new exercise.

Cog.—The student will recognize the names of the activities and be able to demonstrate each one.

PM.—The student will be able to perform the exercises to the beat of the music on the tape.

LESSON FOCUS (15 – 20 MINUTES)

Hockey

A. *Skills*
 1. Review Gripping/Carrying of stick.
 2. Quick Hit and Side Fielding on the move—The hit is a short pass, usually following the dribble. Fielding is "catching" the puck or ball with stick.

DPE pp. 607 – 616

Keep stick below waist level to ensure accuracy and safety.

Do not lift the stick too high, and hit through the ball. Strive for accuracy.

Good fielding requires learning to "give" with the stick.

Begin with movement; if skills are lacking, return to stationary practice (front field).

Cog.—The student will be able to describe the meaning of the following terms: grip, carry, dribble, field, dodge, tackle, and drive.

PM.—The student will be able to perform each of the skills listed.

MOVEMENT EXPERIENCE—CONTENT	ORGANIZATION AND TEACHING HINTS	EXPECTED STUDENT OBJECTIVES AND OUTCOMES
3. Controlled Dribble—A series of short taps used to move the ball or puck in desired direction; use both sides of the blade. 4. Tackling—An attempt to intercept the ball from an opponent. 5. Dodging—Maintaining control of the ball while evading a tackler. Hold the ball as long as possible until one can determine which direction the tackler is going to move—then pass the puck or ball. 6. Driving—Hitting the ball or puck for distance or trying to score a goal. 7. Goalkeeping—The goalie should practice moving in front of the ball and bringing the feet together; turn the stick sideways.	Individual or partner work. Use a plastic puck indoors and a whiffle ball outdoors. Keep hands spread 10–14". The proper time to tackle is when the ball is *off* the opponent's stick. Assure students that it is impossible to make a successful tackle every time. Pass the ball to one side of the tackler and move self around the opposite side. The stick is raised higher (waist level) and the hands are brought together to give the player a longer lever. The goalie may kick the puck, stop it with any body part, or allow it to rebound off any body part. An 8-ft folding tumbling mat set on end makes an excellent goal.	Aff.—Safety and concern for others is important. Others can be hurt by wild swinging of the stick. Discuss the need for rules in all sports in order to protect the participants. PM.—The student will be able to control the ball while moving. Cog.—The distance over which a muscle contracts determines, in part, the amount of force to be generated. Various backswings and wind-ups are performed to increase the range of motion prior to contraction. Students will understand why preliminary movements are carried out in sports activities. PM.—The student will be able to demonstrate the proper manner of blocking a shot on goal.

B. *Drills*
  1. Dribbling
    a. Students in pairs—20 ft apart. One partner dribbles toward the other, goes around her and back to starting point. The first student then drives the ball to the second, who completes the same sequence.
    b. Students in threes—one student dribbles and dodges three cones spaced 10 ft apart; after clearing the last cone, "quick hit" to the next player, who fields and repeats in opposite direction.
  2. Passing and Fielding—Downfield Drill—Two or three files of players start at one end of area. One player from each file proceeds downfield, passing to and fielding from others until reaching end. Shoot on goal at this point. A goalie may be used.
  3. Dodging and tackling—Pairs—One partner dribbles toward the other, who tries to tackle; reverse roles if tackle is successful.
	DPE p. 612
	Students should also practice driving and fielding in this drill.
	Shuttle-type formation with two players starting on one side and one player on the other side.
	
	If two lines are used, have two or three drills going to decrease student "waiting" time.
	When finished, return around the outside to avoid interfering with next group, and rotate to a new line.
	Rotate goalies.
	Practice this drill at a moderate speed in early stages.
		PM.—The student will be able to drive the ball or puck without bringing the blade of the stick above the waist on the backswing or follow-through.
		Cog.—Hockey is a team game and passing is a needed skill. The student will be able to describe what factors make up a good pass.
		Aff.—In fine motor control skills, much practice is needed to approach a desirable level. Discuss the need for drills and repeated practice.

MOVEMENT EXPERIENCE—CONTENT	ORGANIZATION AND TEACHING HINTS	EXPECTED STUDENT OBJECTIVES AND OUTCOMES
C. *Lead-up Games*—These will suffice as the game activities. 1. Lane Hockey, p. 613 2. Goalkeeper Hockey, p. 614 3. Sideline Hockey, p. 614 This game is an excellent lead-up to regulation hockey.	May be played with two lines like "Line Soccer."	

DYNAMIC PHYSICAL EDUCATION LESSON PLAN
Hockey Skills (Lesson 2)
Level III

Supplies and Equipment Needed:
  Hockey sticks and pucks or whiffle balls
  Tumbling mats for goals
  Cones
  Exercise-to-music tape
  Audiotape player

MOVEMENT EXPERIENCE—CONTENT	ORGANIZATION AND TEACHING HINTS	EXPECTED STUDENT OBJECTIVES AND OUTCOMES

INTRODUCTORY ACTIVITY (2 – 3 MINUTES)

Group Over and Under

One half of the class is scattered. Each is in a curled position. The other half of the class leaps or jumps over the down children. On signal reverse the group quickly. In place of a curl, the down children can bridge and the others go under. The down children can also alternate between curl and bridge as well as move around the area while in bridged position.

DPE p. 222

Scatter formation.

Encourage the students to go over or under a specified number of classmates.

Vary the down challenges (i.e., bridge using two body parts, curl face down or on your side).

PM.—The student will be able to perform the activities of bridge, curl, leap, jump, and hop at a teacher-acceptable level.

Cog.—Warm-up loosens the muscles, tendons, and ligaments, decreasing the risk of injury. It also increases the flow of blood to the heart muscle.

FITNESS DEVELOPMENT ACTIVITIES (7 – 8 MINUTES)

Exercises to Music

Side Flex (switch sides)	40 seconds
Trunk Twister	25 seconds
Rhythmic Sit-Ups	35 seconds
Slide/Skip	20 seconds
Jumping Jack variations	30 seconds
Triceps Push-Ups	25 seconds
Partial Curl-Ups	45 seconds
Gallop	15 seconds
Push-Ups	25 seconds
Aerobic Bouncing and Clapping	35 seconds
Leg Extensions	40 seconds
Walking to cool down	45 seconds

DPE p. 259

Students should know the exercises before trying to do them rhythmically.

Rhythmic sit-ups are four counts - knees, toes, knees, and down.

The exercise music should be taped prior to the routine. This frees the teacher to move and help students.

Voice instructions can be dubbed onto the tape to tell students when to change to a new exercise.

Cog.—The overload principle dictates that to increase strength, one must perform progressively larger work loads. Duration, frequency, and intensity can be modified to progressively overload the system. Students should be able to develop work loads that are meaningful to their fitness levels.

LESSON FOCUS (15 – 20 MINUTES)

Hockey

A. *Review skills taught in previous lesson:*
  1. Quick hit/fielding
  2. Controlled dribble
  3. Tackling
  4. Dodging
  5. Driving
  6. Goalkeeping

DPE pp. 607 – 616

See previous hockey lesson plan for description and teaching hints.

PM.—The student will be able to perform the basic skills in hockey.

MOVEMENT EXPERIENCE— CONTENT	ORGANIZATION AND TEACHING HINTS	EXPECTED STUDENT OBJECTIVES AND OUTCOMES

B. *Introduce*
    1. Face-Off—The two players taking the face-off each face a sideline, with the right side facing the goal that they are defending. The players hit the ground and then each other's stick three times. Following the third stick hit, the ball/puck can be played.
    2. Jab Shot—This maneuver is a one-sided poke that attempts to knock the ball/puck away from an opponent. The jab shot is used only when a tackle is not possible.
	For safety purposes, keep the stick on the ground or floor when executing this skill.	Cog.—Wellness demands learning to cope with stressful situations. A study demonstrated that a 15-minute walk reduces tension more effectively than a tranquilizer. Students will understand the importance of exercise for stress reduction.
		
		 Cog.—The student will be able to explain the importance of practicing and developing basic hockey skills before playing a regulation game.

C. *Review the following drills:*
    1. Student dribbling in pairs.
    2. Dribbling and dodging through three cones with "quick hit" to next player.
    3. Downfield Drill—passing, fielding, and driving on the move.
    4. Partner dodging and tackling drill. Practice jab shot as well as tackling.
	See previous hockey lesson plan for a description of the drills reviewed.
	
	 Groups of three; shuttle-type formation.
	
	 Two or three drills going on simultaneously; two or three lines per drill (have players rotate lines).
	
	 Emphasize the importance of proper timing to facilitate a "clean" tackle. Tripping with the stick is illegal and should be avoided.	

D. *Introduce the following drills:*
    1. Three-on-Three Drill—Many goals can be set up and six students can work in small groups of three offensive and three defensive players.
    2. Shooting Drill—Mats are set up as goals (three or four on each end of the floor). Half of class on each half of the floor. Each team attempts to hit pucks into opponents' goals without crossing center line of gym. Use a large number of pucks.
    3. Face-Off Drill—groups of two.
      a. One stick per player, one puck or ball per group.
	In the three-on-three drill, the offensive team should concentrate on passing, dribbling, and dodging and the defense-tackling and good body position.
	
	 Use these drills as needed.
	
	 One of the players may cue as follows:
	 Floor—Stick
	 Floor—Stick
	 Floor—Stick
		PM.—The student will be able to successfully participate in the three-on-three drill.
		
		 Aff.—Violence in sport is evident, particularly in hockey. Discuss the need for ethics in sport including self-discipline, accepting one's own and others' feelings, and the immorality of physical violence.
		
		 PM.—The student will be able to play all positions in Regulation Elementary Hockey.
		
		 Cog.—The student will be able to recite the basic rules of Regulation Elementary Hockey.

E. *Lead-up games:*
 These are adequate for game activities if so desired.
    1. Sideline Hockey, p. 614
      This is an excellent lead-up game for regulation hockey.
    2 Regulation Elementary hockey, pp. 614 – 615
	Emphasize position play rather than everyone chasing the puck.
	
	 Teach the basic rules first and then play the regulation game. As the game progresses, the more subtle rules can be introduced. In other words, don't sit the class down and discuss rules for 5–10 minutes. Play the game and introduce them as necessary.
		Aff.—Teamwork and cooperation are important for a successful game of hockey. Discuss the importance of these two elements in all team sport activities.

DYNAMIC PHYSICAL EDUCATION LESSON PLAN
Basketball Skills (Lesson 1)
Level III

Supplies and Equipment Needed:
  One basketball or playground ball for each student
  Flags for Flag Dribble
  Pinnies for lead-up games
  Cones
  Hoops or individual mats
  Tape player
  Music

MOVEMENT EXPERIENCE—CONTENT	ORGANIZATION AND TEACHING HINTS	EXPECTED STUDENT OBJECTIVES AND OUTCOMES

INTRODUCTORY ACTIVITY (2 – 3 MINUTES)

Four-Corners Sport Movement

Lay out a square with a cone at each corner. Each cone should have a sign on each side delineating one of the following movements from the list below. As the students pass each corner, they change to the movement on the sign. On signal, change directions and do the movements on the other side of the cone.

Challenge the students with some of the following agility movements:
  1. Backward Running
  2. Long Leaps
  3. Carioca
  4. Front Crossover
  5. Back Crossover
  6. High Knee/Fast Legs
  7. Two slides, do a half turn, continue in the same direction leading with the other leg, etc.
  8. Sprinting
Challenge the students by declaring various qualities of movement, i.e., soft, heavy, slow, and fast.

DPE pp. 245 – 246

Students do not have to stay in line but can pass if they are doing a faster moving movement.

Encourage variety of movements and performing some movements that require placing body weight on the hands.

It may be necessary to return to the basic locomotor movements with some classes (i.e., running, sliding, skipping).

Aff.—The student will display proper courtesy when passing other students.

PM.—The student will be able to perform five agility movements with quality.

PM.—The student will be able to perform light locomotor movements using three different qualities.

FITNESS DEVELOPMENT ACTIVITIES (7 – 8 MINUTES)

Astronaut Drills

Perform the following activities, stopping only to do the exercises.

Walk while doing Arm Circles	25 seconds
Crab Full-Leg Extension	20 seconds
Skip sideways	25 seconds
Body Twist	30 seconds
Slide; change lead leg often	25 seconds
Jumping Jack variations	30 seconds
Crab Walk to center and back	25 seconds
Sit-Ups with Twist	25 seconds
Hop to center and back	25 seconds

DPE pp. 262 – 263

Use circle or scatter formation with ample space between youngsters. If a circle formation is used, establish a "passing lane" to the outside for faster students.

Change directions occasionally to keep students spread out.

Taped intervals of music and no music can be used to signal movement and stopping to do exercises.

Cog.—The student will be able to explain the need to exercise on all fours to increase arm and shoulder girdle strength.

PM.—The student will be able to perform the fitness activities at the beginning level.

Aff.—This routine is used by astronauts. They need to be fit, as fitness is extremely useful when unexpected demands are made on the body. Discuss some of these unexpected demands.

MOVEMENT EXPERIENCE— CONTENT	ORGANIZATION AND TEACHING HINTS	EXPECTED STUDENT OBJECTIVES AND OUTCOMES

Four Count Push-Ups 20 seconds Gallop Backwards 25 seconds Bear Hugs 30 seconds Grapevine Step (Carioca) 25 seconds Trunk Twisters 20 seconds Power Jumper 20 seconds	Emphasize quality movement over quantity. Allow students to adjust the work load pace. They should be able to move at a pace that is consistent with their fitness level.	
Cool down with stretching and walking or jogging for 2–3 minutes.		

LESSON FOCUS (15 – 20 MINUTES)

Basketball	*DPE* pp. 569 – 591	PM.—The student will be able to perform the following skills adequately:
A. *Review these passes:*	Organize by partners.	1. Push, baseball, underhand, and one-hand passes
1. Chest pass		2. Dribbling—right and left hands while moving
2. Bounce pass		3. Shooting—one-handed shot
3. Baseball pass		4. Catching—high and low passes
4. Underhand pass		
5. One-hand push pass		Cog.—A spinning object will rebound from the floor in the direction of its spin. Discuss how spin can be applied to a basketball (by applying force off-center) and be used to advantage.
B. *Introduce the two-handed overhead pass:*	Remain in partner formation.	Cog.—The student will be able to recite the basic rules of basketball in the following areas:
1. Fingers on the side of the ball, thumbs behind ball. The momentum comes from a forceful wrist and finger snap; ball takes slight downward path.		1. Dribbling 2. Traveling 3. Out of bounds 4. Jump ball
C. *Two-on-One Passing* (game)	Groups of three.	PM.—The student will be able to play Two-on-One Passing successfully as both a passer and a ball chaser.
1. Two players, spread out 15–20 ft apart.	Teach pivoting by player with ball to escape defensive pressure.	
	Rotate "ball chasers" frequently.	
2. A third player attempts to touch the ball while other two pass it back and forth.	Chest pass gets little or no practice in this drill.	Cog.—Ligaments are inelastic and do not contract. Joint injuries usually damage ligaments. When ligaments are stretched, they do not grow back to their regular length. Discuss the need for surgery to repair ligament damage.
D. *Dribbling* (each has a ball)		
1. Review rules—traveling, double dribble.		Cog.—Many backaches occur from weak abdominal muscles. This occurs due to the strength of psoas tilting the pelvis forward and creating excessive back arch. Discuss how back muscles are developed by walking and running, whereas the abdominal muscles must be strengthened using curl-ups, rowing, and partial curl-ups.
2. Review technique—wrist action, finger control, eyes ahead, knees bent.		
3. Figure-Eight Dribbling Drill	Shuttle-type formation; three or four players per group.	
a. Three cones spaced 5 ft apart.		
b. Weave in and out of cones, changing hands so that the hand opposite the obstacle is always used.		
4. Dribble-and-Pivot Drill		
a. Work in pairs.		
b. Three signals: Signal 1: dribble in any direction.		

MOVEMENT EXPERIENCE— CONTENT	ORGANIZATION AND TEACHING HINTS	EXPECTED STUDENT OBJECTIVES AND OUTCOMES

Signal 2: stop and pivot back and forth.
Signal 3: pass back to partner.
5. Practice fancy dribbling
  a. Behind back.
  b. Between legs.
	For a parallel stop, player can pivot on either foot; for a stride stop, pivot must be made on back foot.
	
	Use different types of passes.	

E. *One-Handed Shot*
1. Raise ball up to eye level, sight, and shoot (demonstrate).
2. Shoot from close position around the basket with partners alternating.
3. Add a short dribble and a shot.
4. Dribble and Shoot Drill (pp. 581 – 582)
  a. Use this drill to introduce the lay-up shot.
  b. Have students practice with right and left hands.
	If too many balls, alternate with dribbling or reduce the number of balls.
	
	Each can take two shots.
	
	This is preliminary to lay-up practice later.
	
	Stress points:
	1. Take off on the left foot when shooting with the right hand, and vice versa.
	2. Carry the ball in both hands until just before shooting.
	3. Aim at a spot on the backboard above the basket.
	4. Shoot with right hand when approaching the basket from the right side, and vice versa.	

F. *Flag Dribble* (p. 588) 1. Use half of basketball court area. 2. Students eliminated start another game on other half of court.	May be played by squads or team. (Be sure to designate with pinnies.) Maximizes practice for all students.	
G. *Group Defensive Drill* (p. 582) 1. Students slide as commanded. 2. Ball dribbling by leader may be substituted for verbal commands.	Sc er formation. D ot cross feet or bring them together. Keep sliding smooth (no bouncing). This serves as a good lead-up for the three-player weave drill.	Aff.—Basketball is a team sport demanding contribution from all members of the team. Discuss the importance of using all players without prejudice when developing plays and strategy.
H. *Passing on the Move*—Downfield Drill as described in hockey chapter (p. 612)	Have two or three drills going on simultaneously to maximize practice opportunities.	
I. *Captain Basketball* (p. 586)		Cog.—The students will be able to explain the rules of Captain Basketball and Sideline Basketball. PM.—The student will be able to play all positions in Captain Basketball.
J. *Sideline Basketball* (p. 587)		Cog.—Skill can be improved with practice. However, readiness will determine when the fastest improvement will occur. This indicates that students will develop their skills at different times, regardless of chronological age. Discuss the need to understand individual growth patterns.

GAME (5 – 7 MINUTES)

These are included in the lesson focus above.

DYNAMIC PHYSICAL EDUCATION LESSON PLAN
Basketball Skills (Lesson 2)
Level III

Supplies and Equipment Needed:
  Beanbags (one per student)
  Audiotape player for Astronaut Drills (optional)
  Pinnies for lead-up games
  1 basketball or playground ball per student

MOVEMENT EXPERIENCE— CONTENT	ORGANIZATION AND TEACHING HINTS	EXPECTED STUDENT OBJECTIVES AND OUTCOMES

INTRODUCTORY ACTIVITY (2 – 3 MINUTES)

Beanbag Touch and Go

Beanbags are spread throughout the area. On signal, students move and touch as many beanbags as possible. Different body parts can be specified for touching (i.e., "Touch five yellow beanbags with right knee").

DPE p. 221

Description of Beanbag Touch and Go.

Spread beanbags before class arrives, if possible.

Students may trace out a triangle, square, circle, etc., as they move around different bags.

PM.—The student will be able to perform challenges as designated by the teacher.

Cog.—Introductory activity should begin at a moderate level of intensity rather than an immediate all-out burst.

FITNESS DEVELOPMENT ACTIVITIES (7 – 8 MINUTES)

Astronaut Drills

Perform the following activities, stopping only to do the exercises.
Walk while doing

Arm Circles	30 seconds
Crab Full-Leg Extension	20 seconds
Skip sideways	30 seconds
Body Twist	30 seconds
Slide; change lead leg often	30 seconds
Jumping Jack variations	30 seconds
Crab Walk to center and back	30 seconds
Sit-Ups with Twist	25 seconds
Hop to center and back	30 seconds
Four Count Push-Ups	20 seconds
Gallop Backwards	30 seconds
Bear Hugs	30 seconds
Grapevine Step (Carioca)	30 seconds
Trunk Twisters	20 seconds
Power Jumper	20 seconds

Cool down with stretching and walking or jogging for 2–3 minutes.

DPE pp. 262 – 263

Use circle or scatter formation with ample space between youngsters. If a circle formation is used, establish a "passing lane" to the outside for faster students.

Change directions occasionally to keep students spread out.

Taped intervals of music and no music can be used to signal movement and stopping to do exercises.

Emphasize quality movement over quantity. Allow students to adjust the work load pace. They should be able to move at a pace that is consistent with their fitness level.

Cog.—The training effect occurs when the heart rate is elevated above 150–160 beats per minute. To achieve this level, we keep moving without much rest.

Aff.—Very little resting time occurs in Astronaut Drills. When one exercises for a long period of time, without rest, muscular and cardiovascular endurance is developed.

LESSON FOCUS (15 – 20 MINUTES)

Basketball

A. Review and use different drills to practice prior skills:
  a. Chest and bounce passes
  b. Two-hand overhead pass
  c. Dribbling and pivoting
  d. One-hand set shot
  e. Lay-up

DPE pp. 569 – 591

Try to organize the lesson focus period so that half of the time is spent practicing skills and half playing lead-up or skill-related games.

Cog.—Blood pressure measurements are recorded using two numbers. When your heart contracts, the pressure in the arteries is called systolic pressure. When the heart is relaxed and filling with blood, the diastolic pressure is recorded. Discuss how blood pressure is measured and what constitutes high blood pressure.

MOVEMENT EXPERIENCE—CONTENT	ORGANIZATION AND TEACHING HINTS	EXPECTED STUDENT OBJECTIVES AND OUTCOMES
f. Guarding Use some different drills such as the triangle passing drill, lay-up drill, file dribbling and pivoting drill, and the set-shot drill.	Practice lay-ups with both right and left hands from both sides of the basket. Don't turn every drill into a relay. Competition will often force children to think more about winning than polishing their skills. It takes a long time to learn basic skills. Don't be in a hurry to teach all activities, and allow plenty of review time.	Cog.—The reason backspin is put on a basketball when it is shot is that spin opposite to the direction of flight will cause the ball to remain closer to the backboard and increase the possibility of its dropping in. Discuss the effects of spin in the direction of flight and when it is used to advantage.

B. Introduce the Three Lane Rush Drill (p. 581)
  1. Use chest and/or bounce passes.
  2. "Lead" the receiver with the pass.
  3. Follow your pass, going behind the receiver; then cut for basket, awaiting receipt of a pass.
	Three-player weave may develop slowly in initial stage.
	
	Cutting for the basket ensures short, accurate passes.	

C. Review guarding and introduce the "Give and Go."
  1. Offensive–defensive drill with a post (p. 583)
    a. An offensive player, being guarded by a defensive player, passes the ball to a stationary post player.
    b. The offensive player tries to maneuver around or past the defensive player for a return pass and shot.
	Two groups can work at each basket (one per side). Rotate players after each shot.
	
	Try this drill without a defensive player first.
	
	Game selection depends on skill level of class.
		Cog.—Muscle fatigue occurs when muscles will no longer contract. Training will delay the onset and severity of fatigue. Discuss the effects of fatigue on athletic play and the importance of maintaining a high level of fitness.

D. Integrate some of the following lead-up games into each day's lesson focus and/or game activity.
  1. Captain Basketball (p. 586)
  2. Sideline Basketball (p. 587)
  3. Twenty-One (p. 587)
  4. One-Goal Basketball (p. 588)
  5. Basketball Snatch Ball (p. 589)
  6. Lane Basketball (p. 587)
	When playing lead-up games, encourage one-on-one guarding so that youngsters learn to stay with their opponent, rather than chasing the ball.	

GAME (5 – 7 MINUTES)

Included in lesson focus.

DYNAMIC PHYSICAL EDUCATION LESSON PLAN
Basketball Skills (Lesson 3)
Level III

Supplies and Equipment Needed:
Audiotape player for Astronaut Drills (optional)
1 basketball or playground ball per student
Pinnies for lead-up games
Flags

MOVEMENT EXPERIENCE— CONTENT	ORGANIZATION AND TEACHING HINTS	EXPECTED STUDENT OBJECTIVES AND OUTCOMES

INTRODUCTORY ACTIVITY (2 – 3 MINUTES)

Leapfrog

Two, three, or four children are used for this group activity. They form a curved line, with all except the last child in line taking the leapfrog position. The last child leaps over the other children in turn and, after going over the last child, gets down in position so that the others can leap him.

Variations:
1. Change the height of the leapfrog position—low, medium, high.
2. Increase the distance between the youngsters in the leapfrog position.
3. Add some locomotor movements or stunts that the youngster on the move must perform between leaps over each child.

DPE p. 223

Lines should curve to avoid running into other jumpers.

Stress good form on the jump as well as holding the down position with the hands on the knees.

Encourage, but don't force, youngsters to try the jump. If they are reticent, allow them to be in the down position and run around each student when it is their turn to jump.

PM.—The student will be able to crouch jump over the students in the down position.

Cog.—The student will be able to identify the elements necessary to land softly after jumping over a student.

Cog.—Reciprocal innervation is a dual set of messages to the muscles which tell one set to contract and the opposing set to relax. Discuss the importance of this process for efficient movement.

FITNESS DEVELOPMENT ACTIVITY (7 – 8 MINUTES)

Astronaut Drills

Perform the following activities, stopping only to do the exercises.
Walk while doing

Arm Circles	35 seconds
Crab Full-Leg Extension	20 seconds
Skip sideways	35 seconds
Body Twist	30 seconds
Slide; change lead leg often	35 seconds
Jumping Jack variations	30 seconds
Crab Walk to center and back	35 seconds
Sit-Ups with Twist	25 seconds
Hop to center and back	35 seconds
Four Count Push-Ups	20 seconds
Gallop Backwards	35 seconds
Bear Hugs	30 seconds
Grapevine Step (Carioca)	35 seconds
Trunk Twisters	20 seconds
Power Jumper	20 seconds

Cool down with stretching and walking or jogging for 2–3 minutes.

DPE pp. 262 – 263

Use circle or scatter formation with ample space between youngsters. If a circle formation is used, establish a "passing lane" to the outside for faster students.

Change directions occasionally to keep students spread out.

Taped intervals of music and no music can be used to signal movement and stopping to do exercises.

Emphasize quality movement over quantity. Allow students to adjust the work load pace. They should be able to move at a pace that is consistent with their fitness level.

PM.—The student will be able to perform all activities at the increased load level.

Cog.—The student will be able to verbalize in her own words the fact that regular exercise strengthens muscles and helps prevent joint and muscle injury.

MOVEMENT EXPERIENCE— CONTENT	ORGANIZATION AND TEACHING HINTS	EXPECTED STUDENT OBJECTIVES AND OUTCOMES

LESSON FOCUS (15 – 20 MINUTES)

Basketball

This lesson should focus on skills and drills listed in the first two lessons that the teacher has not yet introduced, along with review.

A. Introduce skills and/or drills listed in lessons one and two that have not yet been taught.

B. Review and use previously introduced drills to practice these skills:
   1. Three Lane Rush
   2. Guarding and "Give and Go."
   3. Lay-up shot
   4. One-handed set shot
      a. Introduce jump shot to those students who appear ready.
      b. Use the following games to teach shooting under pressure:
         1. Freeze Out (p. 588)
         2. Basketrama (p. 590)

C. Integrate some of the following lead-up games into each day's lesson focus and/or game activity:
   1. Sideline Basketball (p. 587)
   2. Flag Dribble (p. 588)
   3. One-Goal Basketball (p. 588)
   4. Basketball Snatch Ball (p. 589)
   5. Three-on-Three (p. 589)

DPE pp. 569 – 591

Try to organize the lesson so that half of the time is spent practicing skills and half playing lead-up to skill-related games.

Offensive-defensive drill with a post (p. 583) works well here.

GAME (5 – 7 MINUTES)

Included in lesson focus.

DYNAMIC PHYSICAL EDUCATION LESSON PLAN
Recreational Activities
Level III

Supplies and Equipment Needed:
  Individual jump ropes
  Equipment for recreational activities

MOVEMENT EXPERIENCE—CONTENT	ORGANIZATION AND TEACHING HINTS	EXPECTED STUDENT OBJECTIVES AND OUTCOMES

INTRODUCTORY ACTIVITY (2 – 3 MINUTES)

Living Obstacles

Half of the class is scattered. Each is in a bridged position. The remaining half of the class moves under, over, or around the obstacles. The bridges may move around the area while maintaining their bridged positions. On signal, reverse the group quickly.

DPE p. 222

Scatter formation.

Encourage students to go over, under, or around a specified number of "living obstacles."

Vary the down challenges (i.e., bridge using two body parts, do a side bridge).

PM.—The student will be able to move in a bridged formation.

Cog.—Warm-up loosens the muscles, tendons, and ligaments, decreasing the risk of injury. It also increases the flow of blood to the heart muscle.

FITNESS DEVELOPMENT ACTIVITY (7 – 8 MINUTES)

Partner Aerobic Fitness and Resistance Exercises

Students find a partner and lead each other in aerobic activities. Partners switch leader and follower roles after each partner resistance exercise. This routine assumes that students have previous aerobic fitness experience. If not, the aerobic activities will have to be led by the teacher.

Aerobic Fitness Activity	25 seconds
Arm Curl-Up	45 seconds
Aerobic Fitness Activity	25 seconds
Camelback	45 seconds
Aerobic Fitness Activity	25 seconds
Fist Pull Apart	45 seconds
Aerobic Fitness Activity	25 seconds
Scissors	45 seconds
Aerobic Fitness Activity	25 seconds
Butterfly	45 seconds
Aerobic Fitness Activity	25 seconds
Resistance Push-Up	45 seconds
Aerobic Fitness Activity	25 seconds
Knee Bender	45 seconds

Walk, stretch, and relax for a minute or two.

DPE pp. 263 – 266 lists aerobic fitness activities.

DPE pp. 256 – 258 describes partner resistance exercises.

During the time allowed for partner resistance exercises, both students should have the opportunity to complete each exercise.

If youngsters can't think of an aerobic activity, ask them to copy another student.

Youngsters should take 6–10 seconds to move through the full range of motion while their partner applies resistance.

PM.—The student will be able to apply the correct amount of resistance for his partner to perform with maximum effort through the full range of motion.

PM.—The student will be able to do the aerobic conditioning activities continuously for 45 seconds.

Cog.—Cardiovascular endurance is developed though the use of aerobic conditioning activities.

Cog.—The student will understand that partner resistance exercises develop strength.

Cog.—Physical activity appears to change the state of mind in a positive direction. People on regular exercise programs are more productive and better able to cope with stress. Discuss the importance of regular exercise and acceptable types of exercise to cause the above effect.

Cog.—Exercise increases the diameter and density of bones. Why would this be important? Why do bones become stronger in response to exercise?

MOVEMENT EXPERIENCE—CONTENT	ORGANIZATION AND TEACHING HINTS	EXPECTED STUDENT OBJECTIVES AND OUTCOMES

LESSON FOCUS (15 – 20 MINUTES)

Recreational Activities

The purpose of the recreation is to teach children activities that they can play during the time when school is not in session. Suggested activities are:
1. Shuffleboard
2. Four Square
3. Double Dutch rope jumping
4. Team Handball
5. Around the Key Basketball
6. Beach ball Volleyball (2 on 2)
7. Jacks
8. Marbles
9. Sidewalk Tennis
10. Horseshoes
11. Rope quoits
12. Tetherball
13. Tennis Volleyball

Emphasis should be placed on teaching the rules of the activities so children can enjoy them on their own time.

It might be useful to set up the activities at four different stations and rotate students from one station to the next.

If you know a traditional game played by children in your area for many years, now is a good time to teach it.

PM.—The student will be able to play at least four of the given activities.

Cog.—The student will be able to recite the rules for playing four or more of the activities.

Aff.—Recreational activities can be an excellent release for reducing stress. Relaxation demands playing for enjoyment and personal pleasure. Adults spend millions of dollars searching for activities that are relaxing and rewarding.

GAME (5 – 7 MINUTES)

Since the activities above are recreational in nature, the game period should be included in the lesson focus.

DYNAMIC PHYSICAL EDUCATION LESSON PLAN
Gymnastics and Climbing Rope Skills
Level III

Supplies and Equipment Needed:
20–24 beanbags
Hoops
Tumbling mats
Climbing ropes (as available)
Other climbing apparatus (optional)
Manipulative equipment (optional)
4 Indian clubs
One jump rope per child
Flags

MOVEMENT EXPERIENCE—CONTENT	ORGANIZATION AND TEACHING HINTS	EXPECTED STUDENT OBJECTIVES AND OUTCOMES

INTRODUCTORY ACTIVITY (2 – 3 MINUTES)

Barker's Hoopla

Place one hoop in each of the four corners and the middle of a square playing area. A distance between hoops of 25–30 ft is challenging. Five or six beanbags are placed in each hoop. There are five teams, one beside each hoop (home base). The object is to steal beanbags from other hoops and return them to the hoop that is home base. Variation: Beanbags must be taken *out* of home base hoop and placed in other hoops.

DPE p. 540

Watch for collisions.

The type of locomotion used may be changed to add variety.

Only one bag at a time may be taken. Bag may be released only when hand is vertically over home base hoop.

Aff.—The student will develop an appreciation for playing by the rules without extrinsic motivation factors.

PM.—The student will be able to dodge or evade quickly without falling or colliding.

FITNESS DEVELOPMENT (7 – 8 MINUTES)

Partner Aerobic Fitness and Resistance Exercises

Students find a partner and lead each other in aerobic activities. Partners switch leader and follower roles after each partner resistance exercise. This routine assumes that students have previous aerobic fitness experience. If not, the aerobic activities will have to be led by the teacher.

Aerobic Fitness Activity	30 seconds
Arm Curl-Up	45 seconds
Aerobic Fitness Activity	30 seconds
Camelback	45 seconds
Aerobic Fitness Activity	30 seconds
Fist Pull Apart	45 seconds
Aerobic Fitness Activity	30 seconds
Scissors	45 seconds
Aerobic Fitness Activity	30 seconds
Butterfly	45 seconds
Aerobic Fitness Activity	30 seconds
Resistance Push-Up	45 seconds
Aerobic Fitness Activity	30 seconds
Knee Bender	45 seconds

Walk, stretch, and relax for a minute or two.

DPE pp. 263 – 266 lists aerobic fitness activities.

DPE pp. 256 – 258 describes partner resistance exercises.

During the time allowed for partner resistance exercises, both students should have the opportunity to complete each exercise.

If youngsters can't think of an aerobic activity, ask them to copy another student.

Youngsters should take 6–10 seconds to move through the full range of motion while their partner applies resistance.

PM.—The student will be able to perform all the exercises.

Cog.—The student will be able to recite the fact that resistance should be offered throughout the full range of motion for maximum benefit.

Cog.—Partner resistance exercises are used to develop strength. Aerobic conditioning activities are needed for endurance development.

PM.—The student will be able to perform the aerobic conditioning activities continuously for 60 seconds.

MOVEMENT EXPERIENCE—CONTENT	ORGANIZATION AND TEACHING HINTS	EXPECTED STUDENT OBJECTIVES AND OUTCOMES

LESSON FOCUS (15 – 20 MINUTES)

Gymnastics and Climbing Ropes

A. *Gymnastics*

Six groups of activities are found in this lesson to insure that youngsters receive a variety of experiences. Pick a few activities from each group and teach them alternately. For example, teach one or two tumbling and inverted balances, then one or two balance stunts, followed by individual stunts, etc. Do not place excessive time on one group of activities at the expense of another.

1. Tumbling and Inverted Balances
   a. Forward and Backward Roll Combinations
   b. Back Extension
   c. Headstand Variations
   d. Handstand Against a Wall
2. Balance Stunts
   a. V-Up
   b. Push-Up Variations
   c. Flip-Flop
3. Individual Stunts
   a. Wall Walk-up
   b. Skier's Sit
   c. Rocking Horse
   d. Heel Click (Side)
4. Partner and Group Stunts
   a. Double Scooter
   b. Eskimo Roll (Double Roll)
   c. Tandem Bicycle
   d. Circle High Jump
5. Partner Support Stunts
   a. Back Layout
   b. Front Sit
   c. Flying Dutchman
6. Combatives
   a. Hand Wrestle
   b. Finger Fencing
   c. Touch Knees
   d. Grab the Flag
   e. Rooster Fight

DPE pp. 481 – 497

Scatter as many tumbling mats as possible throughout the area in order to avoid waiting lines.

Do not perform many repetitions of tumbling and inverted balances. For most children, limiting the number of forward or backward roll repetitions to four or five will prevent fatigue and injury.

There is usually a wide range of ability among youngsters in this lesson. If necessary, start at a lower level than listed here to assure students find success.

Teach youngsters to stand on the hips and shoulders when doing partner support stunts.

DPE pp. 499 – 504

Rotate partners to prevent one student from dominating another. For safety, use starting and stopping signals to ensure fair starts and fast stops.

PM.—The student will be able to perform a forward and a backward roll.

PM.—The student will be able to perform the basic headstand.

PM.—The student will be able to balance his body in the balance stunts and manage it easily in the individual stunts.

Cog.—The student will be able to recite the stress points necessary to know in performing the forward and backward roll.

Cog.—The student will be able to state the key points necessary to spot the headstand.

Aff.—Tumbling is an excellent activity as it teaches children to control their bodies in various situations. Discuss the courage and perseverance gymnasts must have to meet success.

Cog.—Wellness refers to taking care of one's self for better health. It places the responsibility for good health on the individual rather than a doctor. Discuss various facets of wellness and making responsible decisions for better health.

Cog.—Stability and balance can be increased by (1) keeping the body weight over the base of support, (2) increasing the size of the base of support, and (3) lowering the center of gravity. Identify this process being performed in the stunts and tumbling activities.

Aff.—Combatives are a good example of "one on one" competition. Discuss the need for self-control and good sportsmanship.

B. *Climbing Ropes*
   1. Supported Pull-Ups
      a. Kneel and pull to feet. Return.
      b. Sit, pull to feet, and back to seat.
      c. Stand, keep body straight while lowering body to the floor.

DPE pp. 414 – 418

Place tumbling mats under all the climbing apparatus.

Caution students not to slide quickly down the rope to prevent rope burns.

The pull-up and hang activities are excellent lead-ups for students who are not strong enough to climb the rope.

PM.—The student will be able to demonstrate proper techniques in the following activities:
   1. Climbing with the scissors grip
   2. Leg around rest
   3. Reverse scissors grip
   4. Instep squeeze
Cog.—The student will be able to describe the safety rules necessary when climbing ropes.

MOVEMENT EXPERIENCE— CONTENT	ORGANIZATION AND TEACHING HINTS	EXPECTED STUDENT OBJECTIVES AND OUTCOMES

2. Hangs
   a. Sit, pull body off floor except for feet, and hold.
   b. Jump up, grasp the rope, and hang.
   c. Jump up, grasp the rope and hang, and perform the following leg movements:
      1. One or both knees up
      2. Bicycling movement
      3. Half lever
      4. Choice movement
3. Climbing the Rope
   a. Scissors grip
      Place the rope inside of the knee and outside the boot. Climb halfway up and practice descending using the reverse scissors grip before climbing to the top of the rope.
   b. Leg around rest—Wrap the left leg around the rope and over the instep of the left foot from the outside. Stand on the rope and instep with right foot.
4. Descending the Rope
   a. Reverse scissors grip
   b. Leg-around rest
   c. Instep squeeze—The rope is squeezed between the insteps by keeping the heels together.
5. Stunts Using Two Ropes
   a. Straight arm hang—Jump up, grasp rope, and hang.
   b. Arms with different leg positions.
      1. Single and double knee lifts
      2. Half lever
      3. Full lever
      4. Bicycle—pedal feet like bicycle
   c. Pull-ups—same as pull-up on a single rope
   d. Inverted hangs
      1. With feet wrapped around the ropes
      2. With feet against the inside of the ropes
      3. With the toes pointed and the feet not touching the ropes
6. Swinging and Jumping
   The student should reach high and jump to a bent-arm position while swinging.
   a. Swing and jump. Add one half and full turns.
   b. Swing and return.
   c. Swing and jump for distance or land on a target.

ORGANIZATION AND TEACHING HINTS

Students should be encouraged to learn the various techniques of climbing and descending.

If there are only a few climbing ropes, it would be a good teaching technique to have the nonclimbing students work on another unit.

If such large apparatus is unavailable, other units that work well include hoops, wands, playground balls, and rope jumping.

Two ropes, hanging close together, are needed.

Spotting should be done when students are performing inverted hangs on two ropes.

Swinging on the ropes should be done with bent arms and with knees tucked.

Caution the person waiting in line to wait out of the way until the person before her is completely finished.

EXPECTED STUDENT OBJECTIVES AND OUTCOMES

Aff.—Rope climbing demands a great deal of upper body strength. Discuss how muscular strength develops through overloading and increasing the demands placed on the body.

Cog.—Rope climbing is excellent for developing upper body strength. Discuss the major muscle groups that are used and developed when climbing ropes.

Cog.—The larger the diameter of the muscle, the greater the amount of force that can be generated. Identify various muscles of the body and their relative size.

PM.—The student will be able to perform the following two-rope activities:
1. Straight arm hang
2. Hangs with different leg positions
3. Pull-ups
4. Inverted hangs

Aff.—Rope climbing favors those students who are small and carry little body fat. Discuss individual differences and how different sports favor certain types of body build.

MOVEMENT EXPERIENCE— CONTENT	ORGANIZATION AND TEACHING HINTS	EXPECTED STUDENT OBJECTIVES AND OUTCOMES

GAME (5 – 7 MINUTES)

1. Star Wars, (p. 539)
2. Flag Chase, (p. 536)

DYNAMIC PHYSICAL EDUCATION LESSON PLAN
Gymnastics and Juggling Skills
Level III

Supplies and Equipment Needed:
Parachute
Scarves
Balls for juggling
Tumbling mats
8 foam balls (8 1/2")
Bowling pins or Indian clubs
Playground balls

MOVEMENT EXPERIENCE—CONTENT	ORGANIZATION AND TEACHING HINTS	EXPECTED STUDENT OBJECTIVES AND OUTCOMES

INTRODUCTORY ACTIVITY (2 – 3 MINUTES)

Following Activity

One partner leads and performs various kinds of movements. The other partner follows and performs the same movements. This can also be used with squad organization, with the squad following a leader.

DPE p. 222

The leaders should be changed often. Use a whistle to signal the changes of roles.

Partner or squad formation.

Encourage good reproduction of the leader's movements.

PM.—Be able to follow and accurately reproduce the movements of the leader.

Aff.—People must be able to lead as well as follow at times. Briefly discuss the need for cooperation between people.

FITNESS DEVELOPMENT (7 – 8 MINUTES)

Parachute Fitness

1. Jog in circle with chute held in left hand. Reverse directions and hold with right hand.
2. Standing, raise the chute overhead, lower to waist, lower to toes, raise to waist, etc.
3. Slide to the right; return slide to the left.
4. Sit and perform sit-ups - 40 seconds.
5. Skip for 25 seconds.
6. Freeze, face the center, and stretch the chute tightly with bent arms. Hold for 8–12 seconds. Repeat five to six times.
7. Run in place, hold the chute at waist level, and hit the chute with lifted knees.
8. Sit with legs under the chute. Do a seat walk toward the center. Return to the perimeter. Repeat four to six times.
9. Place the chute on the ground. Jog away from the chute and return on signal. Repeat for 35 seconds.
10. On sides with legs under the chute. Perform Side Flex and lift chute with legs.

DPE, pp. 244 – 245

Evenly space youngsters around the chute.

Use different grips to add variation to the activities.

Develop group morale by encouraging students to move together.

Use music to motivate youngsters.

To cool down, allow youngsters a minute to perform parachute stunts like the Dome or Mushroom.

Cog.—The student will be able to explain that maximum effort must be exerted if the exercise is going to be of any value.

PM.—The student will be able to demonstrate one new partner resistance exercise to the class.

PM.—The student will be able to perform each aerobic conditioning activity continuously for 75–90 seconds.

Cog.—Sweating occurs when the body is overheated due to stress in an attempt to maintain a constant body temperature. The student will be able to explain why the body sweats.

MOVEMENT EXPERIENCE— CONTENT	ORGANIZATION AND TEACHING HINTS	EXPECTED STUDENT OBJECTIVES AND OUTCOMES

11. Lie on back with legs under the chute. Shake the chute with the feet.
12. Hop to the center of the chute and return. Repeat for 25 seconds.
13. Assume the push-up position with the legs aligned away from the center of the chute. Shake the chute with one arm while the other arm supports the body.
14. Sit with feet under the chute. Stretch by touching the toes with the chute. Relax with other stretches while sitting.

LESSON FOCUS (15–20 MINUTES)

Gymnastics and Juggling

A. *Gymnastics*

Six groups of activities are found in this lesson to insure that youngsters receive a variety of experiences. Pick a few activities from each group and teach them alternately. For example, teach one or two tumbling and inverted balances, then one or two balance stunts, followed by individual stunts, etc. Do not place excessive time on one group of activities at the expense of another.

1. Tumbling and Inverted Balances
   a. Freestanding Handstand
   b. Cartwheel and Round-Off
   c. Judo Roll
   d. Advanced Forward and Backward Roll Combinations
   e. Gymnastic Routines
2. Balance Stunts
   a. Long Reach
   b. Toe Jump
   c. Handstand Stunts
3. Individual Stunts
   a. Walk-Through
   b. Jump-Through
   c. Circular Rope Jump
   d. Bouncer
4. Partner and Group Stunts
   a. Stick Carries
   b. Two-Way Wheelbarrow
   c. Partner Rising Sun
   d. Triple Roll
5. Partner Support Stunts
   a. Knee-and-Shoulder Balance
   b. Press
   c. All-Fours Support
6. Combatives
   a. Palm Push
   b. Bulldozer
   c. Breakdown
   d. Elbow Wrestle
   e. Leg Wrestle

DPE pp. 481 – 497

Scatter as many tumbling mats as possible throughout the area in order to avoid waiting lines.

For most children, limiting the number of forward or backward roll repetitions to four or five will prevent fatigue and injury.

There is usually a wide range of ability among youngsters in this lesson. If necessary, start at a lower level than listed here to assure students find success.

After students learn the basic activities, emphasize three phases of correct performance:
1. Starting Position
2. Execution
3. Finishing Position

DPE pp. 499 – 504

Rotate partners to prevent one student from dominating another. For safety, use starting and stopping signals to ensure fair starts and fast stops.

Cog.—Momentum needs to be developed and applied when performing rolls. The student will be able to name three ways of developing momentum (i.e., tucking, starting from a higher point, preliminary raising of the arms).

PM.—The student will be able to perform at least two of the activities in each of the groups.

Aff.—Tumbling and stunts are activities in which there is a wide range of student ability which is evident to others. Discuss the sensitivity of the situation and the need to understand the shortcomings of others.

Cog.—The center of weight must be positioned over the center of support in balance stunts. The student will be able to describe and demonstrate this in his or her own fashion.

Cog.—Certain sports and activities offer a greater degree of aerobic conditioning. Contrast activities such as basketball, jogging, bicycling, rope jumping, and swimming with bowling, golf, softball, and football.

Aff.—Many people take drugs to help them handle stress. Unfortunately, they avoid dealing with the cause of stress. Drugs are short-term solutions and ultimately cause more problems than they solve. Discuss how drugs can cause physiological and psychological changes and addiction.

MOVEMENT EXPERIENCE—CONTENT	ORGANIZATION AND TEACHING HINTS	EXPECTED STUDENT OBJECTIVES AND OUTCOMES

B. *Juggling with Scarves* Scarves are held by the fingertips near the center. To throw the scarf, it should be lifted and pulled into the air above eye level. Scarves are caught by clawing, a downward motion of the hand, and grabbing the scarf from above as it is falling.
 1. *Cascading*—Cascading is the easiest pattern for juggling three objects. The following sequence can be used to learn this basic technique.
   a. One scarf. Hold the scarf in the center. Quickly move the arm across the chest and toss the scarf with the palm out. Reach out with the other hand and catch the scarf in a straight down motion (clawing). Toss the scarf with this hand using the motion and claw it with the opposite hand. Continue the tossing and clawing sequence over and over.
   b. Two scarves. Hold a scarf with the fingertips in each hand. Toss the first one across the body as described above.
   c. Three-scarf cascading. A scarf is held in each hand by the fingertips as described above. The third scarf is held with the ring and little finger against the palm of the hand. The first scarf to be thrown will be from the hand that is holding two scarves.
 2. *Reverse Cascading*—Reverse cascading involves tossing the scarves from the waist level to the outside of the body and allowing the scarves to drop down the midline of the body.
   a. One scarf.
   b. Two scarves.
   c. Three scarves.
 3. *Column Juggling*—Column juggling is so named because the scarves move straight up and down as though they were inside a large pipe or column and do not cross the body.
	DPE pp. 372 – 375
	
	 Scarf juggling should teach proper habits (e.g., tossing the scarves straight up in line with the body rather than forward or backward).
	
	 Many instructors remind children to imagine that they are in a phone booth or large refrigerator box—to emphasize tossing and catching without moving.
	
	 The fingers, not the palms, should be used in throwing and catching the objects.
	
	 Throwing the objects too high and away from the body is a problem students need to overcome.
	
	 Verbal cues such as "toss, claw, toss, claw" are helpful.
	
	 To perform three-scarf column juggling, begin with two scarves in one hand and one in the other hand.
		Cog.—The student will be able to state the sequence of throwing the scarves in cascading with three objects.
		
		 PM.—The student will be able to consistently toss the objects up and directly in front of the body.
		
		 Aff.—Students must accept the fact that the more difficult the skill, the more practice it takes to learn.
		
		 Discuss the complexity of juggling and the need for applied and repetitive practice.
		
		 Aff.—Discuss the fact that accomplishing the skill once is not a goal. Performing the skill many times correctly is a goal of people who excel at skills.

MOVEMENT EXPERIENCE—CONTENT	ORGANIZATION AND TEACHING HINTS	EXPECTED STUDENT OBJECTIVES AND OUTCOMES

4. *Showering*—Start with two scarves in the right hand and one in the other. Begin by throwing the first two scarves from the right hand. Toss the scarves in a large circle away from the midline of the body and overhead as high as possible. As soon as the second scarf is released, toss the scarf across to the left hand and throw it in the same path with the right hand. All scarves are caught with the left hand and passed to the right hand.

5. *Juggling Challenges*
   a. While cascading, toss a scarf under one leg.
   b. While cascading, toss a scarf from behind the back.
   c. Instead of catching one of the scarves, blow it upward with a strong breath of air.
   d. Begin cascading by tossing the first scarf into the air with a foot. Lay the scarf across the foot and kick it into the air.
   e. Try juggling three scarves with one hand. Do not worry about establishing a pattern, just catch the lowest scarf each time. Try both regular and reverse cascading as well as column juggling.
   f. While doing column juggling, toss up one scarf, hold the other two, and make a full turn. Resume juggling.
   g. Try juggling more than three scarves (up to six) while facing a partner.
   h. Juggle three scarves while standing beside a partner with inside arms around each other. This is easy to do since it is regular three-scarf cascading.

6. *Juggling with Balls*—Two balls can be juggled with one hand, and three balls can be juggled with two hands. Juggling can be done in a crisscross fashion, which is called cascading, or it can be done in a circular fashion, called showering. Cascading is considered the easier of the two styles and should be the first one attempted.

Showering is more difficult than cascading because of the rapid movement of the hands. There is less time allowed for catching and tossing. The scarves move in a circle following each other. It should be practiced in both directions for maximum challenge.

Students easily become frustrated with this skill. It is a good idea to allow short bouts of practice. For example, 4–5 minutes of practice followed by a game would avoid long periods of failure. Further practice could be continued after the game for another 4–5 minutes.

After the basic skill of juggling is mastered, different types of objects can be used (i.e., pins, rings, and beanbags).

MOVEMENT EXPERIENCE—CONTENT	ORGANIZATION AND TEACHING HINTS	EXPECTED STUDENT OBJECTIVES AND OUTCOMES

GAME (5 – 7 MINUTES)

Try some of these games:
1. Team Handball, p. 545
2. Octopus, p. 543
3. Bomb the Pins, p. 536

DYNAMIC PHYSICAL EDUCATION LESSON PLAN
Gymnastics and Bench Skills
Level III

Supplies and Equipment Needed:
1 8 1/2" playground ball per student
Tape player (aerobic dance)
Tumbling mats
6 benches
Parachute
Indian clubs

MOVEMENT EXPERIENCE— CONTENT	ORGANIZATION AND TEACHING HINTS	EXPECTED STUDENT OBJECTIVES AND OUTCOMES

INTRODUCTORY ACTIVITY (2 – 3 MINUTES)

Ball Activities

Each student has an 8 1/2" playground ball. The balls can be dribbled as in basketball or as in soccer. On signal, students stop, balance on one leg, pass the ball under the leg and around back and overhead, maintaining control and balance.

Variations:
1. Toss ball up in place of dribble.
2. Play catch with a friend while moving.
3. Have a leader challenge the class to try different stunts and manipulative actions.

DPE p. 221

Emphasis should be on movement rather than ball skill activities.

Spread the playground balls throughout the area so the time needed to secure and put away equipment is minimized.

Cog.—The student will explain the concept of making a toss that leads the catcher so he can move into the path of the ball.

PM.—The students will be able to toss the balls in front of themselves so movements are not interrupted.

FITNESS DEVELOPMENT ACTIVITY (7 – 8 MINUTES)

Parachute Fitness

1. Jog in circle with chute held in left hand. Reverse directions and hold with right hand.
2. Standing, raise the chute overhead, lower to waist, lower to toes, raise to waist, etc.
3. Slide to the right; return slide to the left.
4. Sit and perform sit-ups - 45 seconds.
5. Skip for 30 seconds.
6. Freeze, face the center, and stretch the chute tightly with bent arms. Hold for 8–12 seconds. Repeat five to six times.
7. Run in place, hold the chute at waist level, and hit the chute with lifted knees.
8. Sit with legs under the chute. Do a seat walk toward the center. Return to the perimeter. Repeat four to six times.
9. Place the chute on the ground. Jog away from the chute and return on signal. Repeat for 45 seconds.

DPE, pp. 244 – 245

Evenly space youngsters around the chute.

Use different grips to add variation to the activities.

Develop group morale by encouraging students to move together.

Use music to motivate youngsters.

To cool down, allow youngsters a minute to perform parachute stunts like the Dome or Mushroom.

Cog.—It is interesting to measure the breathing rate at rest and during and after exercise. Why does breathing rate vary?

Aff.—Many experts feel people are overweight due to lack of activity rather than eating too much. Discuss why this might be true.

Aff.—Goals should be set based on a person's capability. Discuss some types of goals students might set to maintain physical fitness. Some examples might be:
1. Jog 1–1 1/2 miles daily.
2. Do 10 push-ups daily.
3. Jump-rope for 10 minutes daily.
4. Play basketball every day for 30 minutes.
5. Run 30 miles in a month.

MOVEMENT EXPERIENCE—CONTENT	ORGANIZATION AND TEACHING HINTS	EXPECTED STUDENT OBJECTIVES AND OUTCOMES

10. On sides with legs under the chute. Perform Side Flex and lift chute with legs.
11. Lie on back with legs under the chute. Shake the chute with the feet.
12. Hop to the center of the chute and return. Repeat for 30 seconds.
13. Assume the push-up position with the legs aligned away from the center of the chute. Shake the chute with one arm while the other arm supports the body.
14. Sit with feet under the chute. Stretch by touching the toes with the chute. Relax with other stretches while sitting.

LESSON FOCUS (15 – 20 MINUTES)

Gymnastics and Benches

A. *Gymnastics*
Six groups of activities are found in this lesson to insure that youngsters receive a variety of experiences. Pick a few activities from each group and teach them alternately. For example, teach one or two tumbling and inverted balances, then one or two balance stunts, followed by individual stunts, etc. Do not place excessive time on one group of activities at the expense of another.

1. Tumbling and Inverted Balances
   a. Straddle Press to Handstand
   b. Handstand Variations
   c. Headspring
   d. Walking on the Hands
   e. Walk-Over
2. Balance Stunts
   a. Handstand Stunts
   b. Front Seat Support
   c. Elbow Balance
3. Individual Stunts
   a. Pretzel
   b. Jackknife
   c. Heel and Toe Spring
   d. Single-Leg Circle
4. Partner and Group Stunts
   a. Quintuplet Roll
   b. Dead Person Lift
   c. Injured Person Carry
   d. Merry-Go-Round
5. Partner Support Stunts
   a. Angel
   b. Side Stand
   c. Partner Pyramids
6. Combatives
   a. Catch-and-Pull Tug-of-War
   b. Stick Twist
   c. Toe Touch
   d. Crab Contest
   e. Shoulder Shove
   f. Power Pull

DPE pp. 481 – 497

Scatter as many tumbling mats as possible throughout the area in order to avoid waiting lines.

For most children, limiting the number of forward or backward roll repetitions to four or five will prevent fatigue and injury.

Many of these activities are difficult. Do not hesitate to start at a level lower than listed here to assure students find success.

Avoid asking all students to perform in front of others. Allow students to work individually.

Teach youngsters to stand on the hips and shoulders when doing partner support stunts.

DPE pp. 499 – 504

Rotate partners to prevent one student from dominating another. For safety, use starting and stopping signals to ensure fair starts and fast stops.

PM.—The student will be able to perform a forward and backward roll with at least two variations.

The student will be able to perform at least two activities from each of the categories.

Cog.—The student will be able to describe proper positioning of the hands and knees in partner support and pyramid activities.

Cog.—The student will be able to name at least three safety principles that are important tumbling and inverted balance activities.

Aff.—Tumbling is an excellent activity for overcoming personal fear of harm from the activities. Discuss how many athletes must conquer various fears and take risks in order to succeed.

Cog.—When a forward roll is started, the center of gravity is moved outside the base of support. This causes momentum to be developed in the direction of the roll. What skills demand that the performer move into an unstable position?

PM.—The student and his partner will be able to originate and demonstrate two partner support activities.

MOVEMENT EXPERIENCE—CONTENT	ORGANIZATION AND TEACHING HINTS	EXPECTED STUDENT OBJECTIVES AND OUTCOMES

B. *Benches*
1. Basic Tumbling Skills
   a. Forward Roll
   b. Backward Roll
   c. Forward Roll to a Walkout
   d. Cartwheel
2. Locomotor Movements
   a. Gallop.
   b. Jump on and off the bench.
   c. Hop on and off the bench.
   d. Jump or hop over the bench.
3. Movements alongside the benches—Proceed alongside the bench in the following positions.
   a. Prone position—hands on bench.
   b. Supine position—hands on bench.
   c. Turn over—proceed along bench, changing from prone to supine position with hands on bench.
   d. All of the above positions performed with the feet on the bench.
4. Scooter movements—sit on bench and proceed along bench without using hands.
   a. Regular scooter—feet leading.
   b. Reverse scooter—legs trailing.
   c. Seat walk—walk on the buttocks.
5. Crouch jumps.
   a. Straddle jump.
   b. Regular jump.
   c. One hand—two feet.
   d. One hand—one foot.
6. Jump dismounts.
   a. Single jump—forward or backward.
   b. Jump with turns—1/2, 3/4, or full.
   c. Jackknife.
   d. Jackknife split.
   e. Heel or knee slap.
7. Jump followed by a stunt.
   a. Jump—forward roll.
   b. Back jump—back roll.
   c. Side jump—side roll.
   d. Shoulder roll.
   e. Cartwheel.
8. Allow students time to develop their own routines on the benches including dismounts and return activities.

DPE pp. 425 – 427

Benches should be placed near the mats they will be used with so the transition is smooth and time efficient.

Extend lead foot high into air after each gallop as a "chasse" lead-up.

Six benches, one group behind each bench.

Place a mat at end of bench for dismounts.

Use a dismount at the end of each activity. See numbers 6 and 7 for suggestions.

Have the next person in line begin when the person in front of him is halfway across the bench.

Have the youngsters perform a return activity on the way back to their line.

Speed is not the goal. Move deliberately across the bench.

Keep the limbs on the floor as far away as possible from the bench to achieve maximum developmental effect.

Use the dismounts to add variety to each of the previous activities. Proper dismounting should be encouraged and can be associated with gymnastic routines.

PM.—The student will be able to perform the forward roll on the bench.

PM.—The student will be able to perform the locomotor movements across the bench.

Cog.—The student will be able to identify which bench activities develop arm and shoulder girdle strength.

Cog.—The student will be able to describe why quality of movement is necessary on the benches to ensure beneficial results.

Cog.—Increased fat causes the heart to have to work harder. The resting pulse rate of an obese person is often 10 beats per minute faster than a normal weight individual. This amounts to approximately 14,000 extra beats per day due to excessive fat.

Cog.—Flexing at the ankles, knees, and hips is important when landing after a dismount. This increases the time over which the force is absorbed. Students should understand the importance of absorbing force for a stable landing and minimizing the risk of injury.

MOVEMENT EXPERIENCE—CONTENT	ORGANIZATION AND TEACHING HINTS	EXPECTED STUDENT OBJECTIVES AND OUTCOMES

GAME (5 – 7 MINUTES)

1. Pin Knockout, p. 543
2. Over the Wall, p. 542

DYNAMIC PHYSICAL EDUCATION LESSON PLAN
Gymnastics and Balance-Beam Skills
Level III

Supplies and Equipment Needed:
  Tape player for aerobic dance
  Tumbling mats
  Six balance beams
  Manipulative equipment to be used on balance beams
  Cones
  Balls

MOVEMENT EXPERIENCE— CONTENT	ORGANIZATION AND TEACHING HINTS	EXPECTED STUDENT OBJECTIVES AND OUTCOMES

INTRODUCTORY ACTIVITY (2 – 3 MINUTES)

Rubber Band

Students begin from a central point with the teacher. On signal, students move away from the teacher with a designated movement such as run, hop sideways, skip backward, double-lame dog, or carioca. On signal, they sprint back to the central point.

DPE p. 223

Be sure plenty of room exists away from starting point.

Repeat this cycle several times.

Students can perform one or two stretching activities after returning to central point.

PM.—The student will be able to perform all of teacher-designated movements at an adequate level.

Cog.—The student will know the meaning of all movements called out by the teacher.

FITNESS DEVELOPMENT ACTIVITY (7 – 8 MINUTES)

Aerobic Fitness (suggested routine)

1. Rhythmic run with kick—24 counts
2. Bounce forward and backward with clap—24 counts
3. Rhythmic 4-count sit-ups—24 counts
4. Crab Kick Combinations—24 counts
Repeat steps 1–4 four times.
5. Jumping Jack variations—24 counts
6. Knee lifts turning—24 counts
7. Side bends—24 counts
8. Leg extensions (seated)—24 counts
Repeat steps 5–8 four times.
9. Directional run (changing formations)—24 counts
10. Bounce with body twist—24 counts
11. Side leg raises (alternate legs)—24 counts
12. Rhythmic push-ups—24 counts
Repeat steps 9–12 four times.

Run randomly, jump turn, and say "YEA!" to finish.

DPE pp. 263 – 266

Perform the routine for 7 1/2 minutes.

May be done in scattered formation or in a circle.

A follow-the-leader approach is excellent.

Use music that stimulates students to exercise.

Alternate bouncing and running movements with flexibility and strength development movements.

While performing rhythmic running movements, students can move into different formations.

Place cue cards on the wall that list steps, number of repetitions, and "cue words."

Smile and have a good time—students will believe you enjoy fitness activity.

Variations may be made in the suggested routines.

PM.—The student will be able to perform all of the exercises in time to the music by the end of the week.

Cog.—The student will be able to recognize all of the exercises by name by the end of the week.

Cog.—The blood is transported back to the lungs in the veins. This system is called the circulatory system.

Cog.—The body adapts rapidly to hot, humid conditions. Within two weeks of practice and training in heat, the body will adapt and become more efficient. Primarily, the body sweats more rapidly and to a greater extent. The evaporation of sweat effectively cools the body. Discuss adaptation and the important role of sweating to maintain a constant body temperature.

MOVEMENT EXPERIENCE— CONTENT	ORGANIZATION AND TEACHING HINTS	EXPECTED STUDENT OBJECTIVES AND OUTCOMES

LESSON FOCUS (15 – 20 MINUTES)

Gymnastics and Balance Beam Activities

A. *Gymnastics*
Review activities taught in previous gymnastics lesson plans. Present a wide variety of activities from each of the following activities:
   a. Tumbling and Inverted Balances
   b. Balance Stunts
   c. Individual Stunts
   d. Partner and Group Stunts
   e. Partner Support Stunts
   f. Combatives

B. *Balance Beams*
   1. Move across the beam in various directions, using the following movements:
      a. Slide
      b. Heel and toe
      c. Tiptoes
      d. High Kicks
      e. Grapevine
      f. Dip Step
      g. Student choice
   2. Balance objects such as beanbags, erasers, or wands while walking across beam. (Exploratory approach.)
   3. Use various equipment:
      a. Play catch with beanbags. Try different throws and movements.
      b. Bounce a playground ball and catch it, dribble it, play catch with a partner.
      c. Step over a wand, go under a wand, change directions.
      d. Go through a hoop.
      e. Jump-rope with an individual jump rope.
   4. Half-and-Half Movements— Utilizing previously learned movements, the student goes halfway across the beam using a selected movement and then changes to another movement to travel to second half.
   5. Movement Sequences
      a. Repeat the half-and-half movements, adding a particular challenge or stunt in the center. Examples include:

DPE pp. 481 – 497

Scatter as many tumbling mats as possible throughout the area in order to avoid waiting lines.

There is usually a wide range of ability among youngsters in this lesson. If necessary, start at a lower level than listed here to assure students find success.

DPE pp. 499 – 504

DPE pp. 422 – 424

Balance beams should be placed near the mats they will be used with so the transition is smooth and time efficient.

Use at least six benches with equal numbers of students behind each bench.

Stress student choice and exploration.

Place a target on the wall in front of the beams. Ask students to visually focus on the targets while walking the beams.

Use a mat at the finishing end of the beam for students to perform their dismounts.

Assign a return activity for students so they are busy off as well as on the beam.

DPE pp. 413 – 414 (return activities)

Stress quality of the movement across the bench as well as during the dismount.

If a child falls, have her step back on the beam and continue. This will ensure her of the same amount of practice as the gifted child.

Make sure each student performs a dismount. The dismount will discourage the student from running across the beam and will closely simulate the competitive balance-beam event.

A jumping box or other type of box placed near the front of each beam allows for efficient pick-up and put-away of manipulative equipment.

Aff.—Learning gymnastics skills helps a student's total body control. Discuss specific physical activities that require different amounts of body control.

PM.—The student will know proper spotting techniques when needed.

Cog.—The student will know that high-difficulty gymnastic stunts should only be attempted with teacher spotting when learning.

M.—The student will be able to balance themselves and an object while walking across the beam; a desirable goal would be for neither the object nor the child to fall off.

Cog.—For increased balance control, widen the base of support and lower the center of gravity. Discuss the impact of the narrow base of support found on balance beams.

Cog.—Balance is a learned activity. The student will be able to explain that practice and concentration are necessary for improvement.

Cog.—The student will be able to explain how changing arm and leg positions or direction of movement creates a new balance task for the body.

Aff.—Awareness of the status and prestige given to a skilled performer. Discuss the payoff when one is skilled, such as friends, money, prizes, etc.

Cog.—Balance activities are best performed when performers are relaxed. Increased leg strength also plays an important part in balance. Encourage practice at home where there is little fear of falling and embarrassment.

MOVEMENT EXPERIENCE—CONTENT	ORGANIZATION AND TEACHING HINTS	EXPECTED STUDENT OBJECTIVES AND OUTCOMES

1. Balances—Front Balance (p. 457), Backward Balance (p. 457), Seat Balance (p. 472).
2. Stunts—Walk Through (p. 485), Finger Touch (p. 472).
3. Challenges—Make a full turn, jump kicking up heels; do a push-up.

6. Allow student exploration.

GAME (5 – 7 MINUTES)

Play a game that is active. Try to introduce new games rather than falling back on a few that both you and the class know well. The following are suggested:
1. Loose Caboose, p. 534
2. Octopus, p. 543
3. Fast Pass, p. 536

DYNAMIC PHYSICAL EDUCATION LESSON PLAN
Manipulative Skills Using Wands and Hula Hoops
Level III

Supplies and Equipment Needed:
  Taped music (for the introductory activity)
  Taped music (for the aerobic dance routine)
  Wands
  Hula hoops
  Cassette recorder
  Cageball
  Tom-tom
  Deck tennis rings

MOVEMENT EXPERIENCE—CONTENT	ORGANIZATION AND TEACHING HINTS	EXPECTED STUDENT OBJECTIVES AND OUTCOMES

INTRODUCTORY ACTIVITY (2 – 3 MINUTES)

Moving to Music

Use different types of music to stimulate various locomotor and non-locomotor movements. Dance steps such as the polka, two-step, schottische, and grapevine could be practiced.

DPE p. 221

If students have difficulty sensing the rhythm, a tom-tom may be used to aid them.

Emphasis should be placed on synchronizing the movement with the music.

Cog.—The student will be able to recognize the difference between 3/4 and 4/4 rhythm.

PM.—The student will be able to move, in time with the music, to six different rhythms.

Cog.—People need to warm up psychologically so they "feel" like moving. Discuss the importance of movement in setting the right frame of mind for fitness development activity.

FITNESS DEVELOPMENT ACTIVITY (7 – 8 MINUTES)

Aerobic Fitness (suggested routine)

1. Bounce and do arm circles—24 counts
2. Grapevine step with clap—24 counts
3. Curl-Up variations—24 counts
4. Treadmill combinations—24 counts
Repeat steps 1–4 four times.
5. Forward and side stride hops—24 counts
6. Knee lift and kick combinations—24 counts
7. Rhythmic windmills—24 counts
8. Leg extensions (seated)—24 counts
Repeat steps 5–8 four times.
9. Rhythmic run with knee lift on every fourth beat—24 counts
10. Rock side to side with double bounce on each side—24 counts
11. Rhythmic push-ups (try them in the reverse position!)—24 counts
12. Bear hugs—24 counts
Repeat steps 9–12 four times.

Bounce turn and clap, jump up, and say "HEY!" to finish.

DPE pp. 263 – 266

Perform the routine for 8 minutes.

This is the final week of aerobic dance.

Students should be given the opportunity to lead.

Groups of four to six may be formed to create aerobic dance routines.

Use music that stimulates students to exercise.

Smile and have a good time; students will get a positive feeling about fitness activities.

Aff.—Leadership demands an increase in responsibility. Leaders must be concerned for the welfare of others as well as themselves. Discuss how the squad captain determines the work load for the rest of the group.

PM.—The student will be able to perform the exercises at an increased work load (longer duration) than the previous week.

Cog.—One measure often used to measure fitness is to count the pulse rate after exercise within 2 or 3 minutes. It might be interesting to measure pulse rate at various intervals after exercise. The more fit one is, the faster pulse rate returns to normal.

Aff.—A well-balanced diet provides fuel for physical activity. Discuss the basics of a good diet and the need for such.

MOVEMENT EXPERIENCE—CONTENT	ORGANIZATION AND TEACHING HINTS	EXPECTED STUDENT OBJECTIVES AND OUTCOMES
		PM.—The student will be able to work in small groups and create aerobic dance routines by the end of the week. Cog.—Aerobic training increases maximal oxygen intake. A large part of the increase is due to increased stroke volume of the heart. More blood is pumped per heart beat due to increased capacity of the heart and stronger contractions. How is the heart strengthened?

LESSON FOCUS (15 – 20 MINUTES)

Wands Select some activities from each of the three groups: exercises, stunts, and partner activities.	*DPE* pp. 382 – 386	

A. *Exercises Using Wands*
 1. Standing isometrics:
  a. Push hands together; chest high, overhead, behind seat.
  b. Pull hands apart; chest high, overhead, behind seat.
 2. Wand overhead, with straight arms:
  a. Bend right, left, forward.
 3. Wand twist:
  a. Twist right, left.
  b. Bend right, left.
 4. Long sitting, wand overhead:
  a. Touch toes with wand.
	Watch posture. Stress good effort. Hold for 8 seconds.
	
	Stress full bends. Reach beyond toes.
		Aff.—Wand stunts demand a great deal of flexibility. Often, girls are more successful at flexibility than boys. This is an opportune time to discuss individual differences as well as ability differences between sexes.
		
		Cog.—The students will be able to explain in their own words that frequent stretching makes possible a wider range of motion and conserves energy.

B. *Wand Stunts*
 1. Wand catch:
  a. Practice different combinations.
  b. Do four-way routine.
 2. Thread needle—V-Seat:
  a. Legs crossed.
  b. Legs together.
  c. Combination.
 3. Thread needle—standing:
  a. Front–back, reverse side-to-side.
  b. Add Shoulder Stretcher.
 4. Grapevine:
  a. First stage.
  b. Second stage—step out.
  c. Reverse.
 5. Back Scratcher:
  a. First stage—down back.
  b. Second stage—down over seat.
 6. Wand Whirl:
  a. Practice standing wand.
  b. Grab with hand, grab with one finger.
  c. Do right and left turns.
	Do one each way. Keep balance.
	
	Stress not touching the wand.
	
	Hold wand in fingertips.
	
	Allow kneeling, may be better for some. Use demonstration.
	
	Crossed-hands position, palms up. Use demonstration.
	
	Secure some skill in standing wand.
	
	Stick will slip. Must control.
	
	Do *not* reverse jump. Get height. Practice without stick.
	
	Keep distances short.
		Cog.—It appears to be impossible to improve reaction time. Reaction time is the time it takes to initiate a response to a signal. However, movement time can be improved through increasing strength, shortening the length of a lever, and decreasing the distance to be moved. Movement time is the time it takes to move a certain distance. Discuss a skill and what could be modified to improve movement time.
		
		Cog.—Knowledge of results is important when learning motor skills. Performers can evaluate their movements and make modifications for improvement. Discuss various aspects of a skill students should analyze to improve their performance.
		
		PM.—The student will be able to perform 6 of the 11 wand stunts.

MOVEMENT EXPERIENCE—CONTENT	ORGANIZATION AND TEACHING HINTS	EXPECTED STUDENT OBJECTIVES AND OUTCOMES

7. Twist under:
    a. Right hand, left hand.
    b. Twist right, left; reverse.
 8. Jump stick
 9. Wand balances
    a. Student choice—back of hand, shift back to front, change hands, sit, lie. Get up. Try balances on foot.
 10. Crab leap
    a. Alternating feet.
 11. Long reach—Perform with the wand in both the left and right hand in turn.		

C. *Partner Activities*
    1. Partner catch—one wand, two wands
    2. Partner change
      a. Simple exchange
      b. Spin
    3. Partner rowing
      a. Seated, legs spread, feet against feet
      b. Overhand grip, row back and forth.
    4. Stick twist—face, arms overhead, overhand grip
    5. Wand Wrestle—one hand outside
    6. Chinese Pull-Up
      a. Sit, facing, knees straight, soles against soles
      b. Bend forward, grasp wand
    7. Wring the Dishrag
    8. Ring toss with deck tennis rings—alternate back and forth
	Distances short, use one step. Gradually increase distance. Add turns.
	
	 Hold wand instead of hands.
	
	 Try to get opponent to shift grip.
	
	 Try to wrestle stick away.
	
	 Stress equal start.
	
	 Both hands either inside or out.
	
	 Keep distances short at first.
		Cog.—Teaching a skill in parts is effective when the skill is complex and contains many individual skills, and the learner has limited memory span. Explain and demonstrate to youngsters how skills can be taught in parts and then put together as a complete task.
		
		 Cog.—Practice sessions should be short when tasks are difficult and performers young. Also, when excessive repetition is demanded, sessions should be kept short. Students will understand the need for short practice sessions, distributed evenly over a long period of time.

Hoops
    1. Move through a hoop held by a partner. Challenge by varying the height and angle of the hoop. Do Rabbit and Frog Jumps through the hoop.
    2. Hula-hoop using various body parts such as waist, neck, knees, arms, and fingers.
      a. While hula-hooping on the arms, try to change the hoop from one arm to the other.
      b. Change hoop from one partner to another while hula-hooping.
      c. Try leg-skippers—hula-hoop with one leg and jump the hoop with the other leg.
    3. Jump rope with the hoop—forward, sideways, backward. Begin with a back-and-forth swing.
	DPE pp. 386 – 388
	
	 Scatter formation.
	
	 Hula-hooping demands that body parts are moved back and forth, *not* in a circle.
	
	 Have the class place their hoops on the floor when you desire their attention.
	
	 When jumping through hoops, encourage children to hold them loosely to prevent falls.
	
	 Use the hoop as a home area for children. This will keep them in a designated area.
	
	 The reverse spin must be taught and practiced. Many students find it to be a difficult skill.
	
	 When throwing and catching two hoops, each partner should throw one and then progress to both hoops being thrown at the same time by one partner.
		PM.—The students will be able to hula-hoop on at least one part of their bodies.
		
		 PM.—The students will be able to place a reverse spin on the hoop, causing it to return to them.
		
		 Aff.—Many students will not immediately be able to hula-hoop or apply the reverse spin. Discuss the value of continued practice versus the alternative of quitting and never learning the skill.
		
		 Aff.—Discuss the value of learning a skill simply for one's own enjoyment and satisfaction.

MOVEMENT EXPERIENCE—CONTENT	ORGANIZATION AND TEACHING HINTS	EXPECTED STUDENT OBJECTIVES AND OUTCOMES

4. Roll hoop and run alongside it. Run in front of it.
5. Roll hoop with a reverse spin to make it return to the thrower.
6. Roll with a reverse spin and see how many times partner can go through it.
7. Roll with a reverse spin, jump the hoop, and catch it as it returns.
8. Roll with a reverse spin, kick it into the air, and catch.
9. Balance the hoop on your head, try to walk through it ("thread the needle") forward, backward, and sideward.
10. Use the hoop as a cowboy lasso, standing, sitting, or lying down.
11. Try partner activities:
   a. Play catch with hoop.
   b. Hula-hoop on one arm, toss to partner, who catches it on one arm.
   c. Use two hoops for catching.
   d. Hoop with one hoop and play catch with other.

GAME (5 – 7 MINUTES)

Play an active game, as wands and hula hoops do not require much aerobic activity.

The following are suggested:
1. Jolly Ball, p. 537
2. Galactic Empire and Rebels, p. 543
3. Circle Hook-On, p. 537

DYNAMIC PHYSICAL EDUCATION LESSON PLAN
Volleyball Skills (Lesson 1)
Level III

Supplies and Equipment Needed:
  One beanbag per student
  Apparatus for the Challenge Course
  Volleyball trainers or foam training balls, one for each student
  Cones
  Nets
  Hoops

MOVEMENT EXPERIENCE— CONTENT	ORGANIZATION AND TEACHING HINTS	EXPECTED STUDENT OBJECTIVES AND OUTCOMES

INTRODUCTORY ACTIVITY (2 – 3 MINUTES)

Vanishing Beanbags

Beanbags (one per student) are spread throughout the area. Students move throughout the area. On signal, they find a beanbag and sit on it. On the next signal or command, the students move again, with a few beanbags being removed during the interval. On signal, they once again sit on a beanbag. The object is to try not to be left without a beanbag more than five times.

DPE p. 222

Spread bags before class arrives, if possible.

Vary the locomotor movements and body parts to be placed on the bags.

Hoops may be substituted for beanbags.

PM.—The student will be able to move throughout the area without falling or bumping.

Aff.—Sportsmanship is necessary when students are put in self-officiating situations. Discuss the need for fair play in this and other activities.

FITNESS DEVELOPMENT (7 – 8 MINUTES)

Challenge Course Fitness

Design a course around the perimeter of the area using the following ideas:
Step on jumping box, dismount to tumbling mat, and do a forward roll.
Run and weave through four wands held upright by cones.
Handwalk across a horizontal ladder or do a flexed-arm hang from a climbing rope for 5 seconds.
Step on and off three jumping boxes (small-large-small).
Agility run through hoops.
Perform jump turns.
Leap over a magic rope held taut with two chairs or jumping boxes.
Hop on one foot.
Do a Log Roll across a tumbling mat.
Alternate going over and under six obstacles (cones and wands or hoops).
Crouch jump or scooter movements the length of a balance-beam bench.
Slide through a parallel tumbling mat maze (mats stood on their sides).

DPE p. 263

Design a Challenge Course that exercises all body parts.

Emphasize moving through the Challenge Courses with quality movements. The goal is fitness, not how fast youngsters can move through the course.

Distribute youngsters throughout the course rather than lining them up to start at one point. Faster moving youngsters can pass a station one time only.

Stop the class at regular intervals to perform flexibility and strength development activities for the shoulder girdle and abdominal region.

Change directions periodically. This will help prevent a build-up of students at slower moving stations.

Cog.—The student will be able to design a Challenge Course that exercises all parts of the body.

PM.—The student will be able to accomplish all the challenges successfully.

Aff.—Many different methods for developing and maintaining physical fitness are used in this curriculum. Discuss the importance of people's analyzing their likes and dislikes as they find an approach to fitness that best suits them.

PM.—The student will be able to negotiate all obstacles successfully while traveling around the Challenge Course at least three times within the allotted time.

MOVEMENT EXPERIENCE— CONTENT	ORGANIZATION AND TEACHING HINTS	EXPECTED STUDENT OBJECTIVES AND OUTCOMES

LESSON FOCUS (15 – 20 MINUTES)

Volleyball

A. *Skills*
  1. *Underhand Serve*
  Face the net with the foot opposite the serving hand positioned slightly forward and the weight on the rear foot. Hold the ball waist high in the opposite hand. When serving, step forward with the opposite foot, swinging the serving hand forward with an underhand motion.
  2. *Overhand Pass*
  Position the feet in an easy, comfortable manner with the knees bent. Cup the forefingers and thumbs close together forehead high with elbows out. Ball contact is made at eye level by the force of spread fingers and arm and leg extension.
  3. *Forearm Pass* (Bump)
  Move rapidly to the spot where the ball is descending to ensure an accurate volley. Clasp the hands together so the forearms are parallel to the floor and the elbows are reasonably locked. While awaiting the ball, hold the forearms and hands between the knees. When contacting the ball, swing the forearms slightly upward with rapid leg extension. Contact is made with the forearms or fists.
  4. *Setup*
  Raise the ball with a soft, easy pass to position 1 or 2 ft above the net and about 1 ft away from it. Usually the overhand pass is used for the setup. The player who taps to the "setter" must make an accurate, easily handled pass.

B. *Drills*
  1. Partner work—Positioned about 20 ft apart, two players practice the underhand serve back and forth, catching the ball after each serve.

DPE pp. 671 – 682

Practice with a partner serving back and forth or against a wall.

Contact can be made with an open hand or with the fist. (Encourage student exploration.)

Foam balls (8 1/2") or beach balls increase success in early stages of learning.

It should appear as if the player is "looking through the window."

Do not contact the ball with the palm of the hands.

Again, foam balls (8 1/2") or beach balls are suggested in the beginning stages.

Do not swing the arms above waist high or the ball will travel backward.

Forearm contact is generally more accurate than fist contact.

Practice in groups of four to six.

The pass to the setter is usually a bump.

The setup is generally the second hit in a series of three.

DPE pp. 676 – 677

After the correct skill pattern is established, the receiver sets a target for the server by moving forward, backward, or to one side or the other.

Work in groups of two or three, depending on the number of balls and available wall space. If no wall space is available, one partner tosses the ball to the receiver. Following the volley by the receiver, the tosser catches the ball and the partners trade roles.

PM.—The student will be able to perform the following skills adequately:
  1. Underhand serve
  2. Overhand pass
  3. Bump
  4. Setup

Cog.—The student will be able to recite the basic rules of volleyball in the following areas:
  1. Scoring
  2. Rotation
  3. Violations

Cog.—The student will know why forearm contact is preferred over fist contact when executing the bump.

Aff.—Teamwork is essential for group success. Discuss the need for cooperation among teammates before success in a competitive situation can be achieved.

Aff.—Cooperation is necessary when partner and group work are used to learn skills.

MOVEMENT EXPERIENCE— CONTENT	ORGANIZATION AND TEACHING HINTS	EXPECTED STUDENT OBJECTIVES AND OUTCOMES
2. Individual work—Stand 6 ft from a wall; throw the ball to the wall and volley it to the wall with an overhand pass. The player then catches the ball and gives it to his partner. Use the same drill to teach the forearm pass (bump). Allow two passes against the wall before a catch is made.		
3. Individual work—Standing 6 ft from the wall, toss the ball against the wall and alternate an overhand pass with a bump.		
4. Group work—Two groups of students scatter on opposite sides of the net. The children serve volleyballs from back of the baseline and recover balls coming from the other team.	Eight to ten balls are needed. The action is informal and continuous. The game Shower Service Ball (p. 679) may be played here.	
C. *Lead-Up Games* 1. Keep It Up (p. 679)—An 8 1/2" foam ball or beach ball may accelerate skill acquisition in the early stages.	The same player may not volley the ball twice in succession. Groups count the volleys aloud so their progress is known.	PM.—The student will be able to participate successfully in the lead-up games.
2. Mini-Volleyball (pp. 679 – 680)— This game is played with three players per side. Extra players should be rotated in. When the ball is served, the two front line players drop back to receive the serve, and the back line player moves forward to become the setter. The ball is set for one of the front line players to spike. Variation: Rotation Mini-Volleyball.	Other players may assist the ball over the net on the serve. Beach balls may be substituted. Foam balls (8 1/2") work well in the learning stages of this game. The back line player is *not* allowed to spike in this game. Students must be taught to call the ball and talk constantly to maintain position balance and keep the ball in play.	
3. Regulation Volleyball (p. 680)— This game follows regulation rules. In the beginning stages, it is suggested that the server receive a second serve if the first one fails. Emphasis on teamwork should include encouraging back court players to pass to front court players.	The serving distance may be shortened if needed. Do not allow the game to become Ping-Pong Volleyball, in which the ball is merely batted back and forth with no attempt at a setup.	Cog.—The student will know the three referee calls and their meanings: 1. Side out 2. Point 3. Double foul

GAME (5 – 7 MINUTES)

These are included in the lesson focus above.

DYNAMIC PHYSICAL EDUCATION LESSON PLAN
Volleyball Skills (Lesson 2)
Level III

Supplies and Equipment Needed:
Challenge Course equipment
Volleyball trainers and/or foam (8 1/2") training balls (one per student)
Three or four volleyball standards
Two or three volleyball nets

MOVEMENT EXPERIENCE— CONTENT	ORGANIZATION AND TEACHING HINTS	EXPECTED STUDENT OBJECTIVES AND OUTCOMES

INTRODUCTORY ACTIVITY (2 – 3 MINUTES)

Marking

"Mark" by touching partner; after touch, reverse and the other partner attempts to mark.

Variations:
1. Use the eight basic locomotor movements.
2. Use positions such as Crab Walk, Puppy Dog Walk, etc.
3. Allow a point to be scored only when they touch a specified body part (i.e., knee, elbow, left hand).
4. Use signal to freeze, then student attempts to "mark" (or tag) partner. Reverse roles.
5. Use a whistle signal to change partners' roles. (If chasing partner, reverse and attempt to move *away* from the other.)

DPE p. 222

Encourage students to "watch where they are going" so they won't run into each other.

Partners should be somewhat equal in ability.

Change partners once or twice.

PM.—The students will be able to move with enough agility and quickness to allow them to catch as well as evade their partners.

Cog.—The student will be able to verbalize a simple reason for warm-up prior to strenuous activity.

FITNESS DEVELOPMENT (7 – 8 MINUTES)

Challenge Course Fitness

Design a course around the perimeter of the area using the following ideas:
Step on jumping box, dismount to tumbling mat, and do a forward roll.
Run and weave through four wands held upright by cones.
Handwalk across a horizontal ladder or do a flexed-arm hang from a climbing rope for 5 seconds.
Step on and off three jumping boxes (small-large-small).
Agility run through hoops.
Perform jump turns.
Leap over a magic rope held taut with two chairs or jumping boxes.
Hop on one foot.
Do a Log Roll across a tumbling mat.
Move through a tunnel made with jumping boxes covered by a tumbling mat.
Crouch jump or scooter movements the length of a balance-beam bench.
Slide through a parallel tumbling mat maze (mats stood on their sides).

DPE p. 263

Design a Challenge Course that exercises all body parts. Allow students an opportunity to develop new challenge ideas.

Emphasize moving through the Challenge Courses with quality movements. The goal is fitness, not how fast youngsters can move through the course.

Distribute youngsters throughout the course rather than lining them up to start at one point. Faster moving youngsters can pass a station one time only.

Stop the class at regular intervals to perform flexibility and strength development activities for the shoulder girdle and abdominal region.

Change directions periodically. This will help prevent a build-up of students at slower moving stations.

Cog.—Challenge Courses were a common way of developing fitness in the armed services.

PM.—All students should be able to run the Challenge Course three times.

Aff.—There is no easy way to fitness. It demands self-discipline. Discuss the importance of possessing a positive attitude toward activity in later life.

P.M.—The student will be able to do all Challenge Course movements with adequate skill.

MOVEMENT EXPERIENCE—CONTENT	ORGANIZATION AND TEACHING HINTS	EXPECTED STUDENT OBJECTIVES AND OUTCOMES

LESSON FOCUS (15 – 20 MINUTES)

Volleyball

A. *Skills*

1. *Review and use different drills to practice prior skills.*
   a. Underhand serve
   b. Overhand pass
   c. Bumping (forearm pass)
   d. Setup

2. *Introduce the overhand serve.* Stand with the opposite foot in front and the opposite side of the body turned somewhat toward the net. Toss the ball straight up with the opposite hand so it comes down in front of the shoulder on the serving side. The striking hand comes forward, contacting the ball 1 ft or so above the shoulder. Weight transfer is an essential part of this skill. Contact is made with the fingertips (pads of fingers) or with the fist.

3. *Introduce blocking.* A member of the defensive team forms a screen by extending hands and arms straight up while jumping straight up. The ball is not struck, but rebounds from the blocker's stiffened hands and arms.

B. *Drills*

1. Individual work—Volley the ball directly overhead and catch. Try two consecutive volleys before the catch. Next, alternate a bump with an overhand pass before the catch. Finally, try to keep ball going five or six times in a row with one kind of volley; alternate kinds of volleys.

2. Individual work—Volley the ball 15 ft overhead, make a full turn, and pass the ball again. Vary with other stunts (i.e., touching the floor, a heel click, clapping the hands at two different spots).

DPE pp. 671 – 682

"Opposite" refers to the hand or side opposite the serving hand or side.

The floater—a serve made with the fingertips that has no spin—is difficult for opponents to handle.

The blocker should leave as little space as possible between himself and the net.

This is a basic volleying drill that should be given ample work before proceeding to others.

Allow student choice in selecting stunts.

Cog.—The "floater" is the most difficult variation of the overhand serve for the receiver to handle.

Cog.—The student will demonstrate understanding of when to use blocking.

PM.—The student will show increased proficiency in the following skills:
1. Underhand serve
2. Overhand pass
3. Jumping
4. Setup

Aff.—The student will show increasing appreciation for the importance of teamwork in the game of volleyball.

PM.—The student will demonstrate an improvement in the skill of spiking.

Aff.—Volleyball skills require diligence and patience. Discuss continued practice versus the alternative of quitting and never learning difficult skills.

MOVEMENT EXPERIENCE—CONTENT	ORGANIZATION AND TEACHING HINTS	EXPECTED STUDENT OBJECTIVES AND OUTCOMES

3. Partner work—Players are 10 ft apart. One player tosses the ball to the other, who volleys it back to the first player, who catches it. After several volleys by one player, exchange tossers. Players can try to keep the ball going back and forth with a designated number of volleys before one player catches the ball.

Many sequences of volleys are possible in this drill. Movement problems such as the following can be presented: "See if you and your partner can each execute a bump, then an overhand pass, then a bump before the catch."

4. Partner work—One partner serves to the other, who volleys the ball back. Exchange responsibilities after several serves and return volleys.

5. Group work—Setup should be reviewed from the previous lesson with a ball tosser, setter, and ball retriever. A blocker can be added if sufficient skill exists.

Practice in groups of four to six depending on available balls and net space.

Rotate positions following each attempt.

C. *Lead-Up Games*
1. Mini-Volleyball (pp. 679 – 680)
2. Regulation Volleyball (p. 680)
3. Three-and-Over Volleyball (p. 680). This game adds emphasis to the basic offensive strategy to be used in volleyball. The rules are the same as in Regulation Volleyball, except that the ball must be played twice before going over the net on the third volley. Violation of this rule results in a loss of serve or point.
4. Rotation Mini-Volleyball (pp. 680 – 681)

See previous volleyball lesson for game details.

PM.—The student will be able to participate successfully in the lead-up games.

GAME (5 – 7 MINUTES)

These are included in the lesson focus above.

DYNAMIC PHYSICAL EDUCATION LESSON PLAN
Rhythmic Movement (Lesson 3)
Level III

Supplies and Equipment Needed:
  Tom-tom
  Apparatus for the Challenge Course
  Tape player and music
  Tinikling poles
  Pinnies
  Chalk or jump rope

Dances Taught:
  Jugglehead Mixer
  Ten Pretty Girls
  Klumpakojis
  Tinikling

MOVEMENT EXPERIENCE—CONTENT	ORGANIZATION AND TEACHING HINTS	EXPECTED STUDENT OBJECTIVES AND OUTCOMES

INTRODUCTORY ACTIVITY (2 – 3 MINUTES)

European Running with Variations

1. Run lightly counterclockwise.
2. Clap hands on every fourth beat.
3. Stamp foot on every second beat.
4. On signal, make a complete turn, using four running steps.
5. On signal, stop, pivot, and move in the opposite direction.
6. Appoint a student to lead the class through various formations.

DPE pp. 217 – 218

Variations should be tried after the class has mastered the quality requirements of rhythm, spacing, and staying in line.

At times, stop the drumbeat and have the class continue running. The patter of their feet is a good measure of their success in the activity.

Cog.—Skilled runners do not need the beat of the tom-tom, but can keep time with the leader.

PM.—The student will be able to perform the variation and maintain the proper rhythm at the same time.

FITNESS DEVELOPMENT ACTIVITY (7 – 8 MINUTES)

Challenge Course Fitness

Design a course around the perimeter of the area using the following ideas:
Step on jumping box, dismount to tumbling mat, and do a forward roll.
Run and weave through four wands held upright by cones.
Handwalk across a horizontal ladder or do a flexed-arm hang from a climbing rope for 5 seconds.
Step on and off three jumping boxes (small-large-small).
Agility run through hoops.
Perform jump turns.
Leap over a magic rope held taut with two chairs or jumping boxes.
Hop on one foot.
Do a Log Roll across a tumbling mat.
Alternate going over and under six obstacles (cones and wands or hoops).
Crouch jump or scooter movements the length of a balance-beam bench.
Slide through a parallel tumbling mat maze (mats stood on their sides).

DPE p. 263

Change some of the challenges and add new ones designed by students.

Emphasize moving through the Challenge Courses with quality movements. The goal is fitness, not how fast youngsters can move through the course.

Distribute youngsters throughout the course rather than lining them up to start at one point. Faster moving youngsters can pass a station one time only.

Stop the class at regular intervals to perform flexibility and strength development activities for the shoulder girdle and abdominal region.

Change directions periodically. This will help prevent a build-up of students at slower moving stations.

Cog.—Challenge Courses were a common way of developing fitness in the military services.

Cog.—Smoking increases the amount of carbon monoxide inhaled. Carbon monoxide limits the amount of oxygen that can be carried by the blood to the cells. Discuss how smoking could reduce physical performance.

Cog.—The student will be able to explain that in order to support stronger muscles, larger bones are developed. Muscles grow when exercised regularly, and bones become stronger in response to the increased stress.

Cog.—Young people who have completed college and want to teach, find it extremely difficult to secure a position if they are 25% overweight. Discuss how obesity affects the perceptions of people.

PM.—The student will be able to go through the Challenge Course at least four times.

292

MOVEMENT EXPERIENCE—CONTENT	ORGANIZATION AND TEACHING HINTS	EXPECTED STUDENT OBJECTIVES AND OUTCOMES
	Repeat the Challenge Course for the duration of the 7–8 minute fitness development section.	
	Some of the challenges may be changed if desired to increase motivation.	
	This is the final week of this fitness routine.	

LESSON FOCUS (15 – 20 MINUTES)

MOVEMENT EXPERIENCE—CONTENT	ORGANIZATION AND TEACHING HINTS	EXPECTED STUDENT OBJECTIVES AND OUTCOMES
Rhythms Begin each lesson with a dance the students know and enjoy.	1. Listen to the music, clapping the rhythms and pointing out where changes occur. 2. Teach the basic skills used in the dance. 3. Practice the dance steps in sequence. 4. Practice with the music. Make the rhythms unit an enjoyable one for students. Be enthusiastic when teaching rhythms.	
1. Jugglehead Mixer (p. 356)	An American dance Beginning with a mixer will help break the ice, and help pave the way for more difficult dances. Basic dance steps: 1. Two-step 2. Elbow swing Circle of couples facing CCW, boys (nonpinnies) on the inside. A variety of dances are listed. Time allowances will determine the number that will be taught.	PM.—The students will improve their techniques in the two-step to the point of utility in this dance. Aff.—The students will enjoy this dance since it has a fun aspect. PM.—The student will become more skilled in performing turns.

MOVEMENT EXPERIENCE— CONTENT	ORGANIZATION AND TEACHING HINTS	EXPECTED STUDENT OBJECTIVES AND OUTCOMES

2. Ten Pretty Girls (pp. 351 – 352)	An American dance
	
	Basic dance steps:
	  1. Front, side, back step
	  2. Swing step
	Arms or hands may be linked.
	
	Begin with the music at slow tempo. As students become familiar with the dance, the tempo may be turned up to normal speed.
	
	For each repetition of the dance, begin on alternate feet.
	
	Groups of three in the circle; the center person moves forward on the three stamps.
		PM.—The student will improve in the front, side, back step.
		
		Aff.—The student will take pride in doing dances properly.
		
		Aff.—The student will accept a new partner with proper courtesy.

3. Klumpakojis (pp. 350 – 351)	A Lithuanian dance
	
	Basic dance steps:
	  1. Walking
	  2. Stars
	  3. Polka step
	Double circle, partners facing CCW.
	
	At intervals during Part IV of the dance, shout "Hey, hey" or "Yahoo" spontaneously.
		Cog.—The student will be able to recognize and react to the changes as indicated in the music.

4. Tinikling (pp. 345 – 348)
  a. Teach the Dance Rhythm
    1. Teach the basic step rhythm using two parallel chalked lines or jump ropes.
    2. Practice a two-count weight transfer rocking sideways on the left and right feet.
    3. When students can shift the weight from side to side, introduce the uneven rhythm. This is a similar rocking motion where one hop is done on the left foot and two on the right.
    4. Practice the uneven rhythm moving in and out of the ropes, lines on the floor, or stationary poles.
	A dance from the Philippines
	
	Small-group formations.
	
	Since 5th and 6th grade students have previously had a taste of the tinikling dance, progress through the beginning steps should be made quickly.
	
	The initial step is used only to get the dance under way.
	
	Make sure the sticks go together on the *down*-beat, as this is an auditory cue for the dancer.
	
	This dance takes some time to learn. Don't be impatient, and allow them enough time to practice.
	
	Make sure that the people handling sticks are rotated often.
	
	The sticks should be kept low or the dancer's legs may be caught.
	
	Eyes should be up, not looking at feet or poles.
	
	Partners face, holding hands with the side to the poles. Begin with the foot nearest the poles.
	
	Students should be given some time to practice these skills as they are rather difficult to master.
		Cog.—The student will know the origin of the dance.
		
		PM.—The student will be able to perform the basic tinikling step as well as move the sticks to the proper rhythm.
		
		Aff.—Dancing is an activity that has been done for many years, in many cultures. Discuss the possibilities as to why this occurs.

MOVEMENT EXPERIENCE— CONTENT	ORGANIZATION AND TEACHING HINTS	EXPECTED STUDENT OBJECTIVES AND OUTCOMES

MOVEMENT EXPERIENCE— CONTENT

b. Teach the Pole Rhythm
  1. Teach the pole rhythm by practicing a three-count clapping rhythm cued by the teacher with a tom-tom. The rhythm is clap (hands together); down (slap top of legs); down (same as previous).
  2. Clap the rhythm to the record. Slow the music down in the early learning stages.
  3. Allow everyone to practice the rhythm with the poles and no dancers.
  4. Add dancers doing the basic step.
c. Practice other steps and the circle movement.
  1. Crossover step: begin with the right foot.
  2. Rocker step: face the poles.
  3. Circle the poles.
  4. Cross step.
d. Formation dancing.
  1. Line of poles individually; with a partner.
  2. Square formation.
e. Variations
  1. Bouncing ball to self or to a partner.
  2. Individual rope jumping while performing the tinikling dance.

ORGANIZATION AND TEACHING HINTS

Various pole formations:

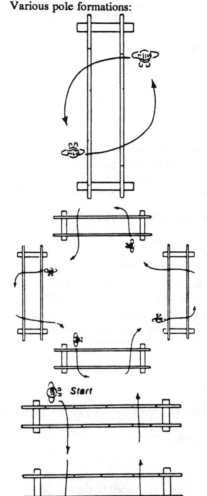

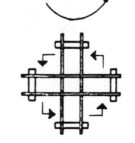

GAME (5 – 7 MINUTES)

EXPECTED STUDENT OBJECTIVES AND OUTCOMES

Aff.—One of the important facets to positive social adjustment is accepting individual differences. Discuss the importance of accepting others as they are and avoiding comparing, judging, and disapproving other's performances.

Aff.—All sports activities contain rhythmic elements. Discuss the need for smooth, continuous rhythm in some of these activities: basketball, football, ice skating, track and field, etc.

Cog.—The student will be able to master at least two of the other steps.

Cog.—Motor skills are classified as open and closed. When the environment is constantly changing, the skill is open. If spatial factors and the environment do not change, the skill is closed. Identify examples of closed and open skills.

PM.—The student will be able to bounce and pass the ball in a rhythmic manner.

PM.—The student will be able to jump rope in a rhythmic manner while performing the dance.

1. Whistle Ball, p. 540
2. More Jump the Shot Variations, p. 541

DYNAMIC PHYSICAL EDUCATION LESSON PLAN
Rhythmic Movement (Lesson 4)
Level III

Supplies and Equipment Needed:
  Individual jump ropes
  Tape player and music
  Beanbags
  Fleece balls or yarn balls
  Hula hoops
  Pinnies
  Scooters

Dances Taught:
  Jiffy Mixer
  Horse and Buggy Schottische
  Oh Johnny
  Doudlebska Polka
  Korobushka
  Alunelul

MOVEMENT EXPERIENCE— CONTENT	ORGANIZATION AND TEACHING HINTS	EXPECTED STUDENT OBJECTIVES AND OUTCOMES

INTRODUCTORY ACTIVITY (2 – 3 MINUTES)

Popcorn

Students pair up with one person on the floor in push-up position and the other standing ready to move. On signal, the standing students move over and under the persons on the floor. The person on the floor changes from a raised to a lowered push-up position each time the partner goes over or under them. On signal, reverse positions.

DPE p. 223

Scatter formation.

Beanbags, fleece balls (yarn balls), hula hoops, or balls may be used.

Add many challenges while moving to both the locomotor movements and manipulative activities.

PM.—The student will be able to toss and catch an object while moving.

Cog.—The student will recite the fact that it is easier to toss and catch an object while standing stationary than while moving.

FITNESS DEVELOPMENT ACTIVITY (7 – 8 MINUTES)

Continuity Drills

Students alternate jump rope activity with exercises done in two-count fashion. Exercises are done with the teacher saying "Ready" and the class answers "One-two" and performs a repetition of the exercise. Teachers or students can lead.

Rope jumping - forward	25 seconds
Double Crab Kick	30 seconds
Rope jumping—backward	25 seconds
Partial Bent-Knee Sit-Up	45 seconds
Jump and slowly turn body	25 seconds
Push-Ups	45 seconds
Rocker Step	25 seconds
Sit and Twist	30 seconds
Swing-Step forward	25 seconds
Side Flex	30 seconds
Free jumping	35 seconds
Sit and stretch	45 seconds

DPE p. 262

Use scatter formation.

Taped intervals of music and no music can be used to signal rope jumping (with music) and performing exercises (without music).

A number of enjoyable chants can be used (i.e., "Physical education" followed by a two-count response and repetition "is fun!").

Allow students to adjust the work load to their fitness level. This implies resting if the rope jumping is too strenuous.

PM.—The student will be able to perform the exercises with rhythm and in unison with the rest of the class.

Cog.—Exercise, if demanding enough, will cause the training effect to occur in a short period of time. Discuss the fact that 10 minutes of rope jumping is equal to 30 minutes of jogging.

Aff.—With the class moving together and "sounding like a team," it is a good time to discuss pride in group accomplishment.

MOVEMENT EXPERIENCE— CONTENT	ORGANIZATION AND TEACHING HINTS	EXPECTED STUDENT OBJECTIVES AND OUTCOMES

LESSON FOCUS (15 – 20 MINUTES)

Rhythms

Begin each lesson with a dance the students know and enjoy.

1. Listen to the music, clapping the rhythms and pointing out where changes occur.
2. Teach the basic skills used in the dance.
3. Practice the dance steps in sequence.
4. Practice with the music.

Make the rhythms unit an enjoyable one for students. Be enthusiastic when teaching rhythms.

A number of dances are listed. Time allowances will determine the number that will be taught.

Do not demand perfection when teaching dances. Children can be expected to make mistakes similar to learning any other physical skill.

1. Jiffy Mixer (p. 353)

An American dance

Basic dance steps:
1. Heel-and-toe step
2. Chug step
3. Walking

This dance may be introduced in a single circle facing inward. As the dance steps are grasped, progress to a double circle of partners facing with the boy's (nonpinnie's) back to the center. Add moving on to a new partner.

Create a less formal atmosphere when performing mixers.

Mixers provide quick and easy accomplishment, thus reinforcing success through dance.

Cog.—The student will be able to recognize and react to the changes as indicated in the music.

PM.—The student will be able to put the parts of the dance together and make the partner change properly.

2. Horse and Buggy Schottische (pp. 354 – 355)

An American dance

Basic dance skills:
1. Schottische step
2. Horse and buggy formation

Couples should practice in groups of four until they have mastered the dance. Then the groups of four can be put together into a circular formation.

This takes some practice.

PM.—The student will become more skilled in the schottische step.

PM.—The student will be able to apply the schottische to the horse and buggy formation.

MOVEMENT EXPERIENCE— CONTENT	ORGANIZATION AND TEACHING HINTS	EXPECTED STUDENT OBJECTIVES AND OUTCOMES
3. Oh Johnny (p. 358)	An American dance Basic dance skills: 1. Circle the ring 2. Partner and corner swing 3. Allemande left with the corner gal 4. Do-si-do 5. Promenade This is a singing call that eliminates the need for a caller. Partners may be boy–girl or pinnie–nonpinnie. Corners become new partners for the next verse of the dance. Begin practice at slow tempo. This is a mixer. Partners change after each verse of the dance.	Cog.—The student will recognize the proper figure on call. PM.—The students will be able to perform all of the basic square dance steps smoothly.
4. Doudlebska Polka (pp. 358 – 359)	A Czechoslovakian dance Basic dance skills: 1. Polka step 2. Clapping pattern 3. La, la, la step May be done in one large circle of partners, or in several smaller circles of partners scattered around the area. Any dancers without a partner go to the "lost and found" department in the center. They may reenter during the clapping portion of the dance.	PM.—The student will be able to apply the polka step in this dance. Aff.—Students will be able to accept new partners with the proper courtesies.
5. Korobushka (pp. 357 – 358)	A Russian dance Basic dance steps: 1. Schottische step 2. Balance step 3. Walking step Double circle, partners facing, boy's (nonpinnie's) back to the center. Review dances students have learned previously. This is an enjoyable endeavor for youngsters and allows them to see progress they have made.	Aff.—The student will develop some appreciation of the Russian culture. PM.—The student will be able to perform the schottische step well enough to employ it in this dance and in other dances.

MOVEMENT EXPERIENCE— CONTENT	ORGANIZATION AND TEACHING HINTS	EXPECTED STUDENT OBJECTIVES AND OUTCOMES
6. Alunelul ("ah-loo-NAY-loo") (p. 357)	A Romanian dance The dance is called "Little Hazelnut." Stomping represents breaking hazelnuts. Basic dance steps: 1. Stomp 2. Step behind step Stomps should be made close to supporting foot. Dancers should be scattered, moving individually. After the dance steps have been learned, lines (side by side) may be formed with students holding the shoulder of the dancer(s) beside them. Do not demand perfection when teaching dances. Children can be expected to make mistakes similar to learning any other physical skill. As a change-of-pace activity, a tag game (or other simple game) may be taught between dances.	Aff.—The student will begin to develop an appreciation for folk dancing. PM.—The student will be able to put the parts of the dance together and perform it successfully.

GAME (5 – 7 MINUTES)

1. Scooter Kickball, p. 538
2. Touchdown, p. 539
3. Chain Tag, p. 541

DYNAMIC PHYSICAL EDUCATION LESSON PLAN
Juggling Skills and Pyramids
Level III

Supplies and Equipment Needed:
  Juggling scarves
  Fleece balls
  Foam tennis balls
  Individual jump ropes
  Tumbling mats
  Tape player
  Music

MOVEMENT EXPERIENCE—CONTENT	ORGANIZATION AND TEACHING HINTS	EXPECTED STUDENT OBJECTIVES AND OUTCOMES

INTRODUCTORY ACTIVITY (2 – 3 MINUTES)

Move, Exercise on Signal

Students do a locomotor movement, stop on signal, and perform an exercise such as the following suggested activities:
  1. Push-Ups
  2. Curl-Ups
  3. Crab Kick
Variations
  4. V-Ups
  5. Treadmills

DPE p. 219

Many different exercises may be done. These should be selected to add challenge to this activity.

Vary the locomotor movements by adding quality (slow–fast, high–low) or direction.

PM.—The student will be able to perform the basic exercises on command.

PM.—The student will be able to perform the locomotor movement variations as well as the designated exercises.

Aff.—The body should be gradually warmed up, rather than moving into demanding activity immediately. Discuss this with the class with regard to need to self-pace and gradually work toward maximum output. Incorporate this principle into your teaching by demanding more as the introductory and fitness work progresses.

PM.—The student will be able to stop quickly with good balance.

FITNESS DEVELOPMENT ACTIVITY (7 – 8 MINUTES)

Continuity Drills

Students alternate jump rope activity with exercises done in two-count fashion. Exercises are done with the teacher saying "Ready" and the class answers "One-two" and performs a repetition of the exercise. Teachers or students can lead.

Rope jumping - forward	30 seconds
Double Crab Kick	30 seconds
Rope jumping—backward	30 seconds
Partial Bent-Knee Sit-Up	45 seconds
Jump and slowly turn body	30 seconds
Push-Ups	45 seconds
Rocker Step	30 seconds
Sit and Twist	30 seconds
Swing-Step forward	30 seconds
Side Flex	30 seconds
Free jumping	40 seconds
Sit and stretch	45 seconds

DPE p. 262

Use scatter formation.

Taped intervals of music and no music can be used to signal rope jumping (with music) and performing exercises (without music).

A number of enjoyable chants can be used (i.e., "Physical education" followed by a two-count response and repetition "is fun!").

Allow students to adjust the work load to their fitness level. This implies resting if the rope jumping is too strenuous.

Cog.—Two misconceptions prevail in regard to weight control. One is that exercise burns a small amount of calories and thus has no impact on weight, and the other is that exercise increases appetite. This ignores the fact that if a mile were run every day, the person would burn 12 lb of fat in a year. Activity does not appear to significantly increase appetite.

PM.—The student will be able to perform the exercises correctly and respond in unison with the rest of the class.

MOVEMENT EXPERIENCE—CONTENT	ORGANIZATION AND TEACHING HINTS	EXPECTED STUDENT OBJECTIVES AND OUTCOMES
		Cog.—When a person exercises regularly, additional capillaries form in the muscle tissue so that the muscle cells are better supplied with blood. The student will be able to describe this occurrence in her own words. Discuss the importance of regular exercise and acceptable types of exercise to cause the above effects.

LESSON FOCUS (15 – 20 MINUTES)

Juggling Activities
 	
A. *Juggling with Scarves*—Scarves are held by the fingertips near the center. To throw the scarf, it should be lifted and pulled into the air above eye level. Scarves are caught by clawing, a downward motion of the hand, and grabbing the scarf from above as it is falling.
  1. *Cascading*—Cascading is the easiest pattern for juggling three objects. The following sequence can be used to learn this basic technique.
    a. One scarf. Hold the scarf in the center. Quickly move the arm across the chest and toss the scarf with the palm out. Reach out with the other hand and catch the scarf in a straight-down motion (clawing). Toss the scarf with this hand using the motion and claw it with the opposite hand. Continue the tossing and clawing sequence over and over.
    b. Two scarves and one hand. Hold the scarves with the fingertips in one hand. Toss the first scarf upward. As the first scarf reaches its zenith, toss the second scarf and catch the first one. Continue.
    c. Two scarves and two hands. Hold a scarf with the fingertips of each hand. Toss the first one across the body as described above. Toss the second scarf across the body in the opposite direction.
	DPE pp. 372 – 376
	
	Scarf juggling should teach proper habits (e.g., tossing the scarves straight up in line with the body rather than forward or backward).
	
	Many instructors remind children to imagine that they are in a phone booth or large refrigerator box—to emphasize tossing and catching without moving.
	
	The fingers, not the palms, should be used in tossing and catching the objects.
		Cog.—The student will be able to state sequence of throwing the scarves in cascading with three objects.
		
		PM.—The student will be able to consistently toss the objects up and directly in front of the body.
		
		Aff.—Students must accept the fact that the more difficult the skill, the more practice it takes to learn.
		
		Discuss the complexity of juggling and the need for applied and repetitive practice.
		
		Aff.—Discuss the fact that accomplishing the skill once is not a goal. Performing the skill many times correctly is a goal of people who excel at skills.

MOVEMENT EXPERIENCE—CONTENT	ORGANIZATION AND TEACHING HINTS	EXPECTED STUDENT OBJECTIVES AND OUTCOMES

d. Three-scarf cascading. A scarf is held in each hand by the fingertips as described above. The third scarf is held with the ring and little fingers against the palm of the hand. The first scarf to be thrown will be from the hand that is holding two scarves.

2. *Reverse Cascading*—Reverse cascading involves tossing the scarves from the waist level to the outside of the body and allowing the scarves to drop down the midline of the body.
   a. One scarf.
   b. Two scarves.
   c. Three scarves.

3. *Column Juggling*—Column juggling is so named because the scarves move straight up and down as though they were inside a large pipe or column and do not cross the body.

4. *Showering*—Start with two scarves in the right hand and one in the other. Begin by throwing the first two scarves from the right hand. Toss the scarves in a large circle away from the midline of the body and overhead as high as possible. As soon as the second scarf is released, toss the scarf from the left to the right hand and throw it in the same path with the right hand. All scarves are caught with the left hand and passed to the right hand.

5. *Juggling Challenges*
   a. While cascading, toss a scarf under one leg.
   b. While cascading, toss a scarf from behind the back.
   c. Instead of catching one of the scarves, blow it upward with a strong breath of air.
   d. Begin cascading by tossing the first scarf into the air with a foot. Lay the scarf across the foot and kick it into the air.
   e. Try juggling three scarves with one hand. Do not worry about establishing a pattern, just catch the lowest scarf each time. Try both regular and reverse cascading as well as column juggling.

To perform three-scarf column juggling, begin with two scarves in one hand and one in the other hand.

Showering is more difficult than cascading because of the rapid movement of the hands. There is less time allowed for catching and tossing. The scarves move in a circle following each other. It should be practiced in both directions for maximum challenge.

MOVEMENT EXPERIENCE—CONTENT	ORGANIZATION AND TEACHING HINTS	EXPECTED STUDENT OBJECTIVES AND OUTCOMES

f. While doing column juggling, toss up one scarf, hold the other two, and make a full turn. Resume juggling.

g. Try juggling more than three scarves (up to six) while facing a partner.

h. Juggle three scarves while standing beside a partner with inside arms around each other. This is easy to do since it is regular three-scarf cascading.

B. *Juggling with Balls*—Two balls can be juggled with one hand, and three balls can be juggled with two hands. Juggling can be done in a crisscross fashion, which is called cascading, or it can be done in a circular fashion, called showering. Cascading is considered the easier of the two styles and should be the first one attempted.

Students easily become frustrated with this skill. It is a good idea to allow short bouts of practice. For example, 4–5 minutes of practice followed by a game would avoid long periods of failure. Further practice could be continued after the game for another 4–5 minutes.

After the basic skill of juggling is mastered, different types of objects can be used (i.e., pins, rings, and beanbags).

Pyramids

Emphasis in this lesson is on smaller pyramid groups. Stunts using only two performers should be practiced as a preliminary to pyramid building with three students. Groups larger than three are not recommended since that increases the potential for accidents.

DPE p. 496

The problem-solving approach can be used to encourage children to devise different pyramids.

Use about two thirds of the lesson focus time teaching juggling and one third forming pyramids.

Place a number of signs or pictures around the area to encourage different types of pyramids.

GAME (5 – 7 MINUTES)

Instead of a game activity, use the game time for additional work on pyramids or juggling.

DYNAMIC PHYSICAL EDUCATION LESSON PLAN
Relay Activities
Level III

Supplies and Equipment Needed:
   Long jump ropes (16 ft)
   Individual jump ropes
   Cones
   Tom-tom
   Equipment for relays
   Tape player
   Music

MOVEMENT EXPERIENCE—CONTENT	ORGANIZATION AND TEACHING HINTS	EXPECTED STUDENT OBJECTIVES AND OUTCOMES

INTRODUCTORY ACTIVITY (2 – 3 MINUTES)

Long-Rope Routine

Students begin in a loose column composed of four people holding the long jump rope in their right hand (held down to their right side).

First signal: Jog lightly in a column with one child leading.

Second signal: Shift the rope overhead from the right side to the left side, transferring the rope to the left hand while still jogging.

Third signal: The two inside students release the rope and the two outside students begin turning the rope. The two inside students jump the rope until the next signal.

Fourth signal: The outside students move to the inside positions to jump while the inside students move out to turn the rope. The sequence is repeated.

DPE, p. 220

Use a tom-tom to signal changes.

Students should be in groups of four.

May want to have students carry two long ropes and work on Double Dutch on the third and fourth signals.

Students should move through the sequence with little hesitation.

Students may create their own activity for the second signal.

Students should change end holders without stopping the rope.

Challenge students to work on stunts and Double Dutch.

PM.—The student will be able to jump the long rope 10 times consecutively without a miss.

Cog.—The student will be able to develop one new idea to be used by his group on the second signal.

FITNESS DEVELOPMENT ACTIVITY (7 – 8 MINUTES)

Continuity Drills

Students alternate jump rope activity with exercises done in two-count fashion. Exercises are done with the teacher saying "Ready" and the class answers "One-two" and performs a repetition of the exercise. Teachers or students can lead.

Rope jumping - forward	35 seconds
Double Crab Kick	30 seconds
Rope jumping—backward	35 seconds
Partial Bent-Knee Sit-Up	45 seconds
Jump and slowly turn body	35 seconds
Push-Ups	45 seconds
Rocker Step	35 seconds
Sit and Twist	30 seconds
Swing-Step forward	35 seconds

DPE p. 262

Use scatter formation.

Taped intervals of music and no music can be used to signal rope jumping (with music) and performing exercises (without music).

Other exercises can be substituted to add variation to the activity.

Allow students to adjust the work load to their fitness level. This implies resting if the rope jumping is too strenuous.

PM.—The student will be able to perform the exercises with rhythm and in unison with the rest of the class.

PM.—The student will be able to jump-rope for 25 seconds without stopping.

Aff.—Lack of exercise is one of the key factors in heart disease. Symptoms of heart disease are often found in young people, and thus fitness activities may help retard this health problem. Discuss heart disease and the role of exercise.

MOVEMENT EXPERIENCE— CONTENT	ORGANIZATION AND TEACHING HINTS	EXPECTED STUDENT OBJECTIVES AND OUTCOMES

Side Flex	30 seconds
Free jumping	45 seconds
Sit and stretch	45 seconds

LESSON FOCUS (15 – 20 MINUTES)

Relays

Introduce a variety of relays. The following are listed in sequence from easy to difficult:

Partner Relays, p. 551
Carry and Fetch Relay, p. 550
Attention Relay, p. 557
Corner Fly Relay, p. 555
Pass and Squat Relay, p. 555
Rescue Relay, p. 556
Circular Attention Relay, p. 557
Potato Relays, p. 552
Tadpole Relay, p. 555
Three Spot Relay, pp. 551 – 552
Jack Rabbit Relay, p. 554

Teach relays with learning to understand the concept of cooperation, competition, playing under stress, and abiding by certain rules in mind, rather than teaching various skills.

Team should contain four to eight members. Change leaders often.

Rotate students into different squads so the makeup of each squad changes.

Have the children sit down when they are finished.

Put the least talented students in the middle of the squad so they do not stand out.

Emphasis should be on student enjoyment rather than winning at all costs.

PM.—The student will be able to participate in the relays at an adequate level.

Aff.—Relays involve performing under stress. Explain what happens to athletic performance when stress is too great. Mention the fear of looking stupid and being embarrassed.

Cog.—The importance of winning sometimes supersedes the reasons for participating in competitive activities. Discuss participating for enjoyment, skill development, and fitness maintenance.

GAME (5 – 7 MINUTES)

Since relays are spirited and competitive, it might be a good idea to spend a few minutes doing something relaxing.

DYNAMIC PHYSICAL EDUCATION LESSON PLAN
Track and Field Skills (Lesson 1)
Level III

Supplies and Equipment Needed:
  Two stopwatches with neck lanyards (box for these for safety in the field)
  Measuring tapes for the four jumps
  Starter (p. 716)
  Pits for the jumps with takeoff boards
  8–12 hurdles
  Stretch rope crossbar for high jump (p. 710)
  High jump standards
  Technique hints for each station (on poster boards)
  Eight batons
  Four sets of boxes and blocks for potato relay

MOVEMENT EXPERIENCE—CONTENT	ORGANIZATION AND TEACHING HINTS	EXPECTED STUDENT OBJECTIVES AND OUTCOMES

INTRODUCTORY AND FITNESS DEVELOPMENT ACTIVITIES (9 – 11 MINUTES)

Stretching and Jogging

Combine the introductory and fitness activities during the track and field unit. This will help students understand how to stretch and warm up for demanding activity such as track and field.

Jog for 1–2 minutes.

Standing Hip Bend	30 seconds
Sitting Stretch	30 seconds
Partner Rowing	60 seconds
Bear Hug (20 seconds each leg)	40 seconds
Side Flex (20 seconds each leg)	40 seconds
Trunk Twister	30 seconds

Jog for 2–3 minutes.

DPE pp. 248 – 249

To prepare for strenuous activity, students should learn to warm up their body by walking or jogging, stretching, and finishing with jogging.

Avoid bouncing during the stretching activities. All stretching should be smooth and controlled movements.

Allow students to direct their warm-up activity. It is important that students be able to warm up without teacher direction.

Cog.—The student will be able to explain why stretching exercises and warm-ups are essential to track and field work.

PM.—The student will demonstrate the ability to put proper stress on muscles in stretching.

LESSON FOCUS (15 – 20 MINUTES)

Track and Field—1st Meeting

A. *Orientation*
  1. Goal is self-improvement and developing proper techniques.
  2. Each must accept responsibility for self-directed work. Try all activities.
  3. Learn from the general sessions and from the technique hints that are given at each station.
  4. You should rotate through two stations each day. The following period you will participate in two other station activities. Please stay at your stations until time is signaled for rotation.

DPE pp. 659 – 670

Come to a central point. They should be ready to rest and listen.

Instructional charts listing two or three technique hints and, if possible, a diagram or picture should be posted for each event.

Emphasize care for the watches and show how they work.

Explain that height is a factor and that this is one reason the groups are formed. They are important particularly in the high jump.

Aff.—To succeed in track and field, one must work diligently and independently. Discuss the need for self-discipline in training.

Aff.—It is important to concentrate on good techniques, rather than performance at this point. Discuss the importance of learning proper technique before worrying about maximum effort.

PM.—The student will demonstrate the ability to use the measuring tapes accurately.

Cog.—The student will be able to explain how a stopwatch operates.

Aff.—Acceptance of responsibility for care of equipment.

MOVEMENT EXPERIENCE— CONTENT	ORGANIZATION AND TEACHING HINTS	EXPECTED STUDENT OBJECTIVES AND OUTCOMES
5. To measure the long jumps and the hop-step-and-jump, use the measuring tapes. 6. Use care with the stopwatches. They are expensive to purchase and also to repair. Put the lanyard around your neck when using stopwatches. 7. Announce the four groups. (Form groups according to formula on p. 665.)		Aff.—Acceptance by students of the group division is necessary if this approach is to work. Take time to discuss grouping, if deemed necessary.

B. *Group Drills*
  1. Explain starting:
    a. Standing start
    b. Norwegian start
    c. Sprint start
  2. Starting practice by groups.
  3. Explain striding.
  4. Stride practice.
	Use an entire group at one time.	

C. *Station Orientation*
Take the entire group to each station and explain what is to be done.
	Stride about 70 yd and return to start. Repeat several times.	PM.—The student will demonstrate improvement in form, technique, and performance of:
		    Starting
		    Sprinting
		    Striding
		    Hop-step-and-jump
		    High jump
		    Relay and baton passing
		    Standing Long Jump (optional)
		    Potato Shuttle Race
		    Running Long Jump
		    Hurdling

Station 1
Starting and Sprinting
  1. Front foot 4–12" behind line.
  2. Thumb and first finger behind line, other fingers support.
  3. Knee of other leg placed just opposite front foot.
  4. On "get set," seat is raised, the down knee comes up a little, and the shoulders move forward over the hands.
  5. On "go," push off sharply and take short, driving steps.
Hop-Step-and-Jump (Triple Jump)
  1. Important to get the sequence and rhythm first, then later try for distance.
  2. Sprinting.
	Sprint 25–30 yd or so. Have one child use the starter and count out the rhythm of the start.
	
	Should be a gradual rise of the shoulders.
	
	Foul rule applies.
	
	The runner can sprint forward and then take a jump as a return activity.
		Cog.—The student will demonstrate knowledge about the points of technique of the above.
		
		Cog.—When sprinting, initial contact is made with the ball of the foot as compared with the heel or flat-footed contact made when running long distance. Discuss this and arm carry differences between sprinters and distance runners.

MOVEMENT EXPERIENCE—CONTENT	ORGANIZATION AND TEACHING HINTS	EXPECTED STUDENT OBJECTIVES AND OUTCOMES

Station 2

Running High Jump
1. Keep stretch rope low enough so all can practice.
2. Approach at 45°.
3. Good kick-up and arm action.

Can begin with the scissors style.

Use only two heights in beginning practice. Avoid competition.

Cog.—Gravity and air resistance limit performances in the jumping events. Identify these factors and why altitude (Mexico City Olympics) has a positive impact on long jump performances.

Baton Passing
1. Decide on method of passing.
2. Incoming runner passes with left hand to right hand of receiver.
3. After receiving, change to the left hand.
4. Estimate how fast to take off with respect to the incoming runner.

Space runners

Change baton promptly.

Avoid "blind" exchange.

Cog.—The ratio of fast twitch versus slow twitch fibers is genetically determined. Fast twitch fibers contract rapidly and are useful in activities demanding speed and explosive power. Slow twitch fibers contract less quickly and are excellent for aerobic endurance activities. People are born with varying ratios and thus have a predisposition to succeed in activities in line with their given muscle fiber ratio.

Station 3

Running Long Jump
1. Decide on jumping foot.
2. Establish check point.
3. Control last four steps.
4. Seek height.
Standing Long Jump or the Potato Shuttle Race (p. 666)

Stress the foul rule.

Hit with the jumping foot.

Use either activity.

Station 4

Hurdling
1. At beginning, use one or two hurdles.
2. Leading foot is directly forward.
Striding for Distance
Concluding Activity Interval Training
1. Repeat three or four times.
2. Run 110 yd, walk 110 yd.
Succeeding meetings for the first week:
1. Same introductory and fitness activity. Omit the orientation.
2. Repeat the group drills—starting and striding. Make them shorter.
3. Station activity—Each group visits only two stations each meeting and the other two the next meeting.
4. Finish with interval training.

Practice striding along the hurdles before going over them.

Keep in the infield, keeping track clear.

Begin in straightaway and stride around curve.

Best around the track.

Cog.—Knowledge of what interval training is and can do for performance.

GAME ACTIVITY (5 – 7 MINUTES)

Shuttle Relays, p. 662

DYNAMIC PHYSICAL EDUCATION LESSON PLAN
Track and Field Skills (Lesson 2)
Level III

Supplies and Equipment Needed:
Four stopwatches with neck lanyards (box for these for safety in the field)
Measuring tapes for the four jumps
Starter (p. 716)
Pits for the jumps with takeoff boards
8–12 hurdles
Stretch rope crossbar for high jump (pp. 710)
High jump standards
Technique hints for each station (on poster boards)
Eight batons
Four sets of boxes and blocks for potato relay
Clipboards and pencils
Recording sheets for each group

MOVEMENT EXPERIENCE— CONTENT	ORGANIZATION AND TEACHING HINTS	EXPECTED STUDENT OBJECTIVES AND OUTCOMES

INTRODUCTORY AND FITNESS DEVELOPMENT ACTIVITIES (9 – 11 MINUTES)

Stretching and Jogging

Combine the introductory and fitness activities during the track and field unit. This will help students understand how to stretch and warm up for demanding activity such as track and field.

Jog for 1–2 minutes.

Standing Hip Bend	30 seconds
Sitting Stretch	30 seconds
Partner Rowing	60 seconds
Bear Hug (20 seconds each leg)	40 seconds
Side Flex (20 seconds each leg)	40 seconds
Trunk Twister	30 seconds

Jog for 2–3 minutes.

DPE pp. 248 – 249

To prepare for strenuous activity, students should learn to warm up their body by walking or jogging, stretching, and finishing with jogging.

Avoid bouncing during the stretching activities. All stretching should be smooth and controlled movements.

Allow students to direct their warm-up activity. It is important that students be able to warm up without teacher direction.

Cog.—The student will be able to explain why stretching exercises and warm-ups are essential to track and field work.

PM.—The student will demonstrate the ability to put proper stress on muscles in stretching.

LESSON FOCUS (15 – 20 MINUTES)

Track and Field

Continue the same rotation plan as in week 1. Each group participates in two stations each meeting. Next meeting, visit the other two stations.

At each station, students can record their performances.

Station 1
Sprinting
1. 60 yd distance
2. 75 yd distance
3. Two trials

DPE pp. 659 – 670

Stress legibility.

One watch.

Run individually.

Take best time.

Use starter.

PM.—The student will be able to perform creditably in the various events.

MOVEMENT EXPERIENCE—CONTENT	ORGANIZATION AND TEACHING HINTS	EXPECTED STUDENT OBJECTIVES AND OUTCOMES

Hop-Step-and-Jump
  1. Three trials
  2. Record performances
		Cog.—Red blood cells pick up oxygen as they pass through the lungs. When exercising, a person breathes faster to bring more oxygen into the lungs. The heart beats faster to move more blood and transport oxygen to the muscles.

Station 2
High Jump
  1. Begin at 3 ft, raise 6" at a time
  2. Two trials
  3. Record performances
 	
Baton Passing—Practice while waiting for high jump turn or when "out."
	This increment keeps things moving.	Cog.—Smoking causes the heart rate to jump 10–20 beats per minute. The blood vessels constrict and the heart must pump harder to get blood through them. Discuss how this can be a detriment to good health.

Station 3
Running Long Jump
  1. Three trials
  2. Record all three, circle best
Standing Long Jump
  1. Three trials
  2. Record performances
 	
Potato Relay—One trial, run two races at a time.
	Use foul rule.
	
	Watch for falling backward.
	
	Two watches.	

Station 4
Hurdling
  1. Set up 60-yd hurdle course
  2. Give two trials
  3. Record best time
 	
Striding—Striding practice can be done while waiting for turns.
	Practice striding beside the hurdles before going over them.
	
	This can be omitted.	

GAME OR FUN ACTIVITY (5 – 7 MINUTES)

Circular Relays, p. 662	Four members per team. Run around a 200-m or 220-yd track.	PM.—The student will demonstrate the ability to cooperate in running the relay.

DYNAMIC PHYSICAL EDUCATION LESSON PLAN
Track and Field Skills (Lesson 3)
Level III

Supplies and Equipment Needed:
Four stopwatches with neck lanyards (box for these for safety in the field)
Measuring tapes for the four jumps
Starter (p. 716)
Pits for the jumps with takeoff boards
8–12 hurdles
Rope crossbar for high jump (p. 710)
High jump standards
Technique hints for each station (on poster boards)
Eight batons
Four sets of boxes and blocks for potato relay
Clipboards and pencils
Recording sheets for each group

MOVEMENT EXPERIENCE—CONTENT	ORGANIZATION AND TEACHING HINTS	EXPECTED STUDENT OBJECTIVES AND OUTCOMES

INTRODUCTORY AND FITNESS DEVELOPMENT ACTIVITIES (9 – 11 MINUTES)

Stretching and Jogging

Combine the introductory and fitness activities during the track and field unit. This will help students understand how to stretch and warm up for demanding activity such as track and field.

Jog for 1–2 minutes.

Standing Hip Bend	30 seconds
Sitting Stretch	30 seconds
Partner Rowing	60 seconds
Bear Hug (20 seconds each leg)	40 seconds
Side Flex (20 seconds each leg)	40 seconds
Trunk Twister	30 seconds

Jog for 2–3 minutes.

DPE pp. 248 – 249

To prepare for strenuous activity, students should learn to warm up their body by walking or jogging, stretching, and finishing with jogging.

Avoid bouncing during the stretching activities. All stretching should be smooth and controlled movements.

Allow students to direct their warm-up activity. It is important that students be able to warm up without teacher direction.

Cog.—The student will be able to explain why static stretching is more effective than ballistic stretching for track and field warm-up.

PM.—The student will demonstrate flexibility during stretching.

LESSON FOCUS (15 – 20 MINUTES)

Track and Field

1. Utilize the last week of this unit to conduct a track and field meet. The same rotation plan and groups of students started the previous two weeks can be continued for the meet.
2. Utilize the same stations, events, number of trials, and scoring procedures outlined in last week's track and field lesson.

DPE pp. 659 – 670

Parents can be asked to help.

PM.—The student will demonstrate proper form and improving performance in track and field events.

Aff.—Students develop their skills at different rates, regardless of chronologic age. Discuss the need for sensitivity to individual growth patterns.

PM.—The students will work independently and diligently to keep the meet running on schedule.

GAME OR FUN ACTIVITY (5 – 7 MINUTES)

Shuttle and/or Circular Relays, p. 662. These may be omitted depending on the time needed for the meet.

DYNAMIC PHYSICAL EDUCATION LESSON PLAN
Long-Rope Jumping Skills
Level III

Supplies and Equipment Needed:
  Squad leader exercise task cards
  Long jump ropes (16')
  Music for rope jumping
  Cageball
  Balls

MOVEMENT EXPERIENCE—CONTENT	ORGANIZATION AND TEACHING HINTS	EXPECTED STUDENT OBJECTIVES AND OUTCOMES

INTRODUCTORY ACTIVITY (2 – 3 MINUTES)

Personal Choice

Students select the type of introductory activity they wish to use in order to warm up. They may use one they have previously learned in class, or they may create one of their own. Emphasis should be on a balanced approach that works all major muscle groups.

Encourage students to keep moving.

It may be necessary to point out some activities to stimulate some of the youngsters.

PM.—The student will be able to create a warm-up routine that will physically warm her up for fitness activities.

Cog.—The student will be able to develop a balanced warm-up routine.

FITNESS DEVELOPMENT ACTIVITY (7 – 8 MINUTES)

Squad Leader Exercises with Task Cards

The class is divided into groups of five to seven students. Each group is given a task card that lists eight to ten exercises. One of the group members serves as the leader and leads them in one of the exercises. Each time an exercise is completed, the card is passed to another person in the squad. Start with 25 seconds of exercise followed by 10 seconds to pass the card to the next person.

Suggested exercises:
  Sitting Stretch
  Push-Ups
  Body Circles
  Jumping Jack variations
  Crab Kick combinations
  Partial Curl-Ups
  Treadmills
  Toe Touchers
  Leg Extensions

Whenever the group is not doing an exercise, they should walk or jog.

DPE p. 259

Aerobic activities such as jogging or rope jumping may be used between strength exercises in order to develop the cardiovascular system.

Taped intervals of music and no music can be used to signal exercise (music) and passing the card to the next person (no music).

A goal of squad leader exercises is to allow students the opportunity to lead other students. Teachers should give students freedom to modify the exercises.

Cog.—The student will be able to recognize the exercises by name.

Cog.—The student will be able to describe how overload is achieved (by increasing the number of repetitions of each exercise and by decreasing the amount of rest between each set of exercises).

PM.—The student will be able to do *quality* work on all exercises listed on the task cards.

MOVEMENT EXPERIENCE— CONTENT	ORGANIZATION AND TEACHING HINTS	EXPECTED STUDENT OBJECTIVES AND OUTCOMES

LESSON FOCUS (15 – 20 MINUTES)

Long-Rope Jumping

A. *Single Long-Rope Activities*
1. Review previously learned jumping skills.
2. Have more than one youngster jump at a time. Students can enter in pairs or triplets.
3. Jump while holding a beanbag or playground ball between the knees.
4. While turning rope, rotate under the rope and jump. Continue jumping and rotate back to the turning position.
5. Play catch with a playground ball while jumping.
6. Do the Egg Beater: Two or more long ropes are turned simultaneously. The ropes are aligned perpendicular to each other; the jumper jumps the rope where they cross.
7. Try combinations of three or four ropes turning. The ropes are aligned parallel to each other and students jump and move through to the next rope.

B. *Double Long-Rope Activities*
1. Basic jump on both feet. Land on the balls of the feet, keeping ankles and knees together with hands across the stomach.
2. Jogging Step. Run in place with a jogging step. Increase the challenge by circling while jogging.
3. Scissors Jump. Jump to a stride position with the left foot forward and the right foot back about 8 in. apart. Each jump requires reversing the position of the feet.
4. Straddle Jump. Jump to the straddle position and return to closed position. Try a Straddle Cross Jump by crossing the legs on return to the closed position. The straddle jumps should be performed facing away from the turners.
5. Turnaround. Circle left or right using the basic jump. Begin circling slowly at first and then increase speed. To increase the challenge, try the turnaround on one foot.

DPE pp. 399 – 404

Organize youngsters in two groups of four or five.

Design some type of rotation plan so all youngsters get a chance to jump and turn.

Make sure youngsters know the difference between entering front and back door.

Youngsters who have problems jumping should face one of the turners and key their jumps to both the visual and audio cues (hand movement and sound of the rope hitting the floor).

When turning Double Dutch, rotate the hands inward toward the midline of the body (right forearm counterclockwise and left forearm clockwise). Students should concentrate on the sound of the ropes hitting the floor so that they make an even and rhythmic beat.

Double Dutch turning takes considerable practice. Take time to teach it as a skill that is necessary for successful jumping experiences.

When entering, stand beside a turner and run into the ropes when the back rope (farther from the jumper) touches the floor. Turners should be taught to say "go" each time the back rope touches the floor.

Concentrate on jumping in the center of the ropes facing a turner. Use white shoe polish to mark a jumping target.

Aff.—The student will appreciate the great deal of time and practice needed to become skilled at jumping rope.

Cog.—Physical activity appears to change the state of mind in a positive direction. People on regular exercise programs are more productive and better able to cope with stress. Discuss the benefits of aerobic activities such as rope jumping.

PM.—The student will be able to jump-rope with proper form in time to the music.

PM.—The student will master at least two of the more difficult maneuvers.

MOVEMENT EXPERIENCE— CONTENT	ORGANIZATION AND TEACHING HINTS	EXPECTED STUDENT OBJECTIVES AND OUTCOMES

6. Hot Peppers. Use the Jogging Step and gradually increase the speed of the ropes.
7. Half Turn. Perform a half turn with each jump. Remember to lead the turn with the head and shoulders.
8. Ball Tossing. Toss and catch a playground ball while jumping.
9. Individual Rope Jumping. Enter Double Dutch with an individual rope and jump. Face the turner and decrease the length of the individual jump rope.

Exit the ropes by facing and jumping toward one turner and exiting immediately after jumping. The exit should be made as close to the turner's shoulder as possible.

When students are having trouble with Double Dutch, allow them opportunity to return to single rope jumping.

The jumper must jump twice as fast as each rope is turning.

GAME (5 – 7 MINUTES)

Select a less active game.
1. Cageball Target Throw, p. 541
2. Sunday, p. 539

DYNAMIC PHYSICAL EDUCATION LESSON PLAN
Softball Skills (Lesson 1)
Level III

Supplies and Equipment Needed:
  Station 1: 2 batting tees, 4 balls, 2 bats
  Station 2: 2 balls
  Station 3: 4 bases (home plates), 4 balls
  Station 4: 2 balls, 2 bats
  Exercise task cards
  Station signs
  Tape player
  Music

MOVEMENT EXPERIENCE—CONTENT	ORGANIZATION AND TEACHING HINTS	EXPECTED STUDENT OBJECTIVES AND OUTCOMES

INTRODUCTORY ACTIVITY (2 – 3 MINUTES)

Personal Choice

Students select the type of introductory activity that they wish to use in order to warm up. They may use one they have previously learned in class, or they may create one of their own. Emphasis should be on a balanced approach that works all major muscle groups.

Encourage students to keep moving.

It may be necessary to point out some activities to stimulate some of the youngsters.

PM.—The student will be able to create a warm-up routine that will physically warm him up for fitness activities.

FITNESS DEVELOPMENT (7 – 8 MINUTES)

Squad Leader Exercises with Task Cards

The class is divided into groups of five to seven students. Each group is given a task card that lists eight to ten exercises. One of the group members serves as the leader and leads them in one of the exercises. Each time an exercise is completed, the card is passed to another person in the squad. Use 30 seconds of exercise followed by 10 seconds to pass the card to the next person.

Suggested exercises:
  Sitting Stretch
  Push-Ups
  Body Circles
  Jumping Jack variations
  Crab Kick combinations
  Partial Curl-Ups
  Treadmills
  Toe Touchers
  Leg Extensions

Whenever the group is not doing an exercise, they should walk or jog.

DPE p. 259

Aerobic activities such as jogging or rope jumping may be used between strength exercises in order to develop the cardiovascular system.

Taped intervals of music and no music can be used to signal exercise (music) and passing the card to the next person (no music).

A goal of squad leader exercises is to allow students the opportunity to lead other students. Teachers should give students freedom to modify the exercises.

Cog.—Know why it is necessary to increase the number of repetitions (overload principle).

PM.—The student will be able to perform all exercises at teacher-established levels.

Aff.—The students will demonstrate the self-discipline needed for independent group work.

MOVEMENT EXPERIENCE— CONTENT	ORGANIZATION AND TEACHING HINTS	EXPECTED STUDENT OBJECTIVES AND OUTCOMES

LESSON FOCUS (15 – 20 MINUTES)

Softball (Multiple Activity Station Teaching)

Divide the class equally among the stations.

Use whiffle balls and plastic bats if safety or lack of space is a concern.

DPE pp. 639 – 657

Squad formation.

Have signs at each of the stations giving both direction and skill hints.

Captain gathers equipment in designated spot before changing to next station.

Aff.—Willingness to cooperate at each station is crucial to the success of the lesson. Discuss and emphasize the importance of cooperation among peers.

Station 1

Batting
1. Weight on both feet.
2. Bat pointed over right shoulder.
3. Trademark up on swing.
4. Elbows up and away from body.
5. Begin with hip roll and short step.
6. Swing level.
7. Follow through.
8. Eyes on ball.

Divide squad, with one batter, a catcher (next batter), and one or more fielders.

Points to avoid:
1. Lifting the front foot high off the ground.
2. Stepping back with the rear foot.
3. Dropping the rear shoulder.
4. Chopping down on the ball (golfing).
5. Dropping the elbows.

PM.—The student will be able to meet the ball squarely on the tee.

Cog.—The student will know the different points in good batting.

Cog.—Strenuous exercise causes blood pressure to go up. This occurs because the heart beats faster and more blood is trying to push its way through the vessels. Why do some people have high blood pressure even at rest?

Batting from Tee
1. Stand back (3 ft) from tee, so when stepping forward, ball is hit in front.
2. Show three types of grips.

Fungo Hitting
1. Students can be given this option instead of tee hitting.
2. Toss the ball up, regrasp the bat, and hit the ball.

This is a higher level batting skill than tee hitting.

Rotate batters, catchers, fielders.

Station 2

Throwing and Catching
1. Show grips.
2. How to catch—Stress "give," eyes on ball.

This will be review for most students.

Use "soft" softballs.

Rotate infield positions, including the "ball roller."

Set up regular infield staffed by a squad.

PM.—The students will be able to increase their catching potentials and increase their accuracy in throwing (three styles).

Cog.—The student will be able to define and recognize good points of throwing and catching.

Practice Activity
1. Throw around the bases clockwise and counterclockwise using the following throws:
   a. Overhand throw
   b. Sidearm throw
   c. Underhand toss
2. If enough skill, roll the ball to the infielders and make the throw to first. After each play, the ball may be thrown around the infield.

MOVEMENT EXPERIENCE— CONTENT	ORGANIZATION AND TEACHING HINTS	EXPECTED STUDENT OBJECTIVES AND OUTCOMES

Station 3

Pitching Rules

1. Face the batter, both feet on the rubber, and the ball held in front with both hands. One step is allowed and the ball must be delivered on that step.
2. Ball must be pitched underhanded.
3. No motion or fake toward the plate can be made without delivering the ball.
4. No quick return is permitted, nor can the ball be rolled or bounced toward the batter.
5. Practice both regular pitch and windmill.

Divide squad into two groups. Each has a catcher, pitcher, and "batter," who just stands in position.

A home plate and pitching rubber are helpful.

Stressed legal preliminary position before taking one hand off the ball to pitch.

Rotate positions regularly.

PM.—The student will be able to pitch in observance with the rules.

Cog.—The student will know the rules governing pitching.

PM.—The student will be able to pitch 50% of the balls into the strike zone.

Cog.—Softball is not a very effective sport for exercising the cardiovascular system. Most of the time is spent sitting or standing. Therefore, there is little, if any, aerobic activity.

Station 4

Throwing or Batting Fly Balls

1. Begin with high throwing from the "batter."
2. Have the fielders return the ball with a one-bounce throw to the "batter."
3. Show form for high and low catch. Show sure stop for outfielders.
4. After initial stages, allow fungo hitting of fly balls if the "batter" is capable.

Divide squad into two groups.

Leave a bat at the station.

PM.—The student will begin to handle (catch) easy fly balls with confidence.

PM.—The fielders will improve in estimating flight of the ball and getting under it in time.

LEAD-UP GAME (5 – 7 MINUTES)

1. Batter Ball, pp. 652 – 653
2. Tee Ball, p. 654
3. Scrub (Work-Up), pp. 654 – 655

DYNAMIC PHYSICAL EDUCATION LESSON PLAN
Softball Skills (Lesson 2)
Level III

Supplies and Equipment Needed:
  Station 1: 2 bats, 4 softballs
  Station 2: 3 plates, 3 softballs
  Station 3: 4 bases (regular diamond), ball, bat
  Station 4: 4 bats, 4 balls, home plates (optional)
  Exercise task cards
  Tape player
  Music

MOVEMENT EXPERIENCE—CONTENT	ORGANIZATION AND TEACHING HINTS	EXPECTED STUDENT OBJECTIVES AND OUTCOMES

INTRODUCTORY ACTIVITY (2 – 3 MINUTES)

Personal Choice

Students select the type of introductory activity they wish to use in order to warm up. They may use one they have previously learned in class, or they may create one of their own. Emphasis should be on a balanced approach that works all major muscle groups.

Encourage students to keep moving.

It may be necessary to point out some activities to stimulate some of the youngsters.

PM.—The student will be able to create a warm-up routine that will physically warm her up for fitness activities.

FITNESS DEVELOPMENT (7 – 8 MINUTES)

Squad Leader Exercises with Task Cards

The class is divided into groups of five to seven students. Each group is given a task card that lists eight to ten exercises. One of the group members serves as the leader and leads them in one of the exercises. Each time an exercise is completed, the card is passed to another person in the squad. Use 40 seconds of exercise followed by 10 seconds to pass the card to the next person.

Suggested exercises:
  Bend and Twist
  Push-Ups
  Triceps
  Knee Curl
  Tortoise and Hare
  Crab Full-Leg Extension
  Partial Curl-Ups
  Treadmills
  Toe Touchers
  Leg Extensions

Whenever the group is not doing an exercise, they should walk or jog.

DPE p. 259

Aerobic activities such as jogging or rope jumping may be used between strength exercises in order to develop the cardiovascular system.

Taped intervals of music and no music can be used to signal exercise (music) and passing the card to the next person (no music).

A goal of squad leader exercises is to allow students the opportunity to lead other students. Teachers should give students freedom to modify the exercises.

Cog.—The student will be able to verbalize why correct form is important when performing exercises.

PM—The student will perform all exercises at the teacher-established level.

MOVEMENT EXPERIENCE— CONTENT	ORGANIZATION AND TEACHING HINTS	EXPECTED STUDENT OBJECTIVES AND OUTCOMES

LESSON FOCUS (15 – 20 MINUTES)

Softball Skills (Multiple Activity Station Teaching) Divide the class equally among the stations. Use whiffle balls and plastic bats if safety or lack of space is a concern.	*DPE* pp. 639 – 657	Aff.—Each player will work at the designated skill and attempt to improve his skill. Discuss the importance of practicing both strengths and weaknesses.
Station 1 *Game of Pepper*—Practice bunting as well as half swings.	Divide squad into two groups. Change batters every six swings. Stress easy underhand pitching.	PM.—The players will be able to play this game successfully in order to develop throwing, catching, and striking skills.

Station 2
Pitching and Umpiring
  1. Teach umpiring.
    a. Right hand—strike
    b. Left hand—ball
	Need catcher, pitcher, batter, and umpire.
	
	Pitch to three batters and then rotate.
	
	The batter does not swing at the ball during umpiring practice.
		PM.—The student will be able to "strike out" two out of three batters.
		
		PM.—Umpires will gain increased skill.
		
		PM.—The student will be able to demonstrate proper umpiring techniques in calling balls and strikes.

Station 3
Infield Practice
  1. Roll ball to infielders and make the play at first. After each play, throw around the infield.
  2. If enough skill, bat the ball to the infielders in turn.
	Set up regular infield, staffed by squad. Rotate where needed.	PM.—The infielders will gain in skill in infield play.
		
		PM.—The infielders will learn to "play" the grounder at the most advantageous spot.

Station 4
Batting Practice
Each batter takes six swings and then rotates to the field. Catcher becomes batter and pitcher moves up to catcher.
 	
Review stress points for batting.
	Use the squad. Have hitter, catcher, pitcher, and fielders.
	
	Use two softballs to keep things moving.
	
	Pitcher must be able to serve up good pitches. Use a shorter distance for pitching.
		Cog.—There are five major reasons that arteries become filled with cholesterol and become plugged:
		  1. Inactivity or lack of exercise
		  2. Obesity
		  3. Smoking cigarettes
		  4. Eating foods high in cholesterol
		  5. Living with a high level of stress or depression

LEAD-UP GAMES (5 – 7 MINUTES)

  1. Scrub (Work-Up), pp. 654 – 655
  2. Slow Pitch Softball, p. 655
  3. Babe Ruth Ball, p. 655
  4. Three-Team Softball, p. 656

DYNAMIC PHYSICAL EDUCATION LESSON PLAN—
ALTERNATE
Rhythmic Movement (Lesson 5)
Level III

Supplies and Equipment Needed:
Lummi sticks
Tape player and music

Dances Taught:
Lummi Sticks
Klumpakojis
Korobushka

MOVEMENT EXPERIENCE—CONTENT	ORGANIZATION AND TEACHING HINTS	EXPECTED STUDENT OBJECTIVES AND OUTCOMES

INTRODUCTORY AND FITNESS DEVELOPMENT ACTIVITIES (9 – 11 MINUTES)

This lesson may be substituted for any previous lessons. Use the introductory and fitness development activities given in the sequenced lesson plans.

LESSON FOCUS (15 – 20 MINUTES)

Rhythms

A. *Lummi Sticks*
1. Without sticks, learn the chant.
2. Issue sticks. Show: vertical taps, tap together. Work on a three-count routine: (1) vertical tap, (2) tap together, (3) rest beat.
3. Organize by partners. Children sit Indian fashion, facing, at a distance of 18–20". Work out the following routines:
   a. Vertical tap, tap together, partner tap right; vertical tap, tap together, partner tap left.
   b. Vertical tap, tap together, pass right stick; vertical tap, tap together, pass left stick.
   c. Vertical tap, tap together, toss right stick; vertical tap, tap together, toss left stick.
   d. Repeat a, b, c, except substitute an end tap and flip for the vertical tap and tap together (i.e., end tap, flip, partner tap right, end tap, flip, partner tap left).
   e. Vertical tap, tap together, pass right and left quickly; repeat.
   f. End tap, flip, toss right and left quickly; repeat.
   g. Right flip side–left flip in front, vertical tap in place, partner tap right; left flip side–right flip in front, vertical tap in place, tap left.

DPE pp. 344 – 345

Various lummi stick rhythms records are available for teaching lummi stick activities.

Teach the various tap sequences to the students individually before organizing them in partners.

Hold stick with thumb and fingers (not the first) at the bottom third of the stick.

Stress relaxed and light tapping.

Partners provide their own chanting. Two or three sets of partners can work in unison.

This is called circling.

Allow time for devising own routines.

Cog.—The student will be able to sing the Lummi Stick Chant.

Cog.—Practicing skills incorrectly can make it difficult to learn them correctly later. Discuss the need for patience with one's self when learning new rhythmic activities. This prevents learning them incorrectly due to fear of failure and resultant peer pressure.

PM.—The student will get accustomed to the proper grip so it becomes automatic.

PM.—The student will be able to do the following—vertical tap, tap together, partner tap right (left), end tap, flip, toss right (left), end tap, flip, toss right and left quickly—and put these together in rhythm to the chant.

Cog.—The student will recognize and be able to do circling.

MOVEMENT EXPERIENCE— CONTENT	ORGANIZATION AND TEACHING HINTS	EXPECTED STUDENT OBJECTIVES AND OUTCOMES

h. End tap in front, flip, vertical tap, tap together, toss right, toss left.

i. Vertical tap, tap together, right stick to partner's left hand and left stick to own right hand. Repeat.

j. Repeat previous routines, but reverse the circle.

k. Devise own routines.

B. *Klumpakojis*   *DPE* pp. 350 – 351

C. *Korobushka*   *DPE* pp. 357 – 358

GAME (5 – 7 MINUTES)

Use an active game:
1. Scooter Kickball, p. 538
2. Sunday, p. 539

DYNAMIC PHYSICAL EDUCATION LESSON PLAN—
ALTERNATE
Rhythmic Gymnastics
Level III

Supplies and Equipment Needed:
Record player (or cassette tape player) and records (or tapes)
Jump ropes
Hula hoops
8 1/2" playground balls
Ribbons
Posters

MOVEMENT EXPERIENCE—CONTENT	ORGANIZATION AND TEACHING HINTS	EXPECTED STUDENT OBJECTIVES AND OUTCOMES

INTRODUCTORY AND FITNESS DEVELOPMENT ACTIVITIES (9 – 11 MINUTES)

This lesson may be substituted for any of the previous lessons. Use the introductory and fitness development activities given in the sequenced lesson.

LESSON FOCUS (15 – 20 MINUTES)

Rhythmic Gymnastic Activities

Rhythmic gymnastics involves the combination of manipulating hand-held apparatus and graceful body movements to music. The apparatus used are jump ropes, hoops, 8 1/2" playground balls, and ribbons. Individual routines utilize one piece of apparatus and are 1–1 1/2 minutes long. Group routines utilize one or two different types of apparatus and are 2 1/2–3 minutes long.

A. *Basic Rope Movements*
1. Single and double jumps forward and backward.
2. Circles on each side of the body holding both ends of the rope.
3. Figure-eight swings:
   a. Holding both ends of rope.
   b. Holding the center of the rope and swinging the ends.
4. Pendulum swing rope and jump.
5. Skip over rope turning forward or backward.
6. Run over turning rope.
7. Schottische over turning rope.
8. Cross rope over body and jump.
9. Holding the ends and center of the rope:
   a. Kneel and horizontally circle the rope close to the floor.
   b. Stand and circle the rope overhead.

DPE pp. 392 – 395

Present a variety of ideas to students that may be useful in creating a routine.

Discuss differing degrees of difficulty of movements presented.

Avoid working in lines.

Emphasize covering the entire 40 ft x 40 ft area when choreographing a routine.

Be sure to provide students with ample time to practice skills individually. DO NOT ask student to perform dance and manipulative skills in front of others until they have become comfortable with the activities.

To create a group routine, use a poster at each station and divide the children into each groups at each station:

Station 1
Combine five different jump rope movements together.

Station 2
Combine five movements together. One must go close to or on the floor.

Station 3
Combine four movements together and one tossing movement.

Station 4
Combine four movements together and one toss to a partner.

Aff.—The student will develop an appreciation for the amount of skill needed to perform a quality rhythmic gymnastic routine.

PM.—The student will be able to master a minimum of five jump rope skills that could be used in a rhythmic routine.

Cog.—The student will be able to correctly name at least five jump rope skills.

Aff.—The student will realize that more difficult skills require more time and practice to master. Discuss the need for repetitive practice.

PM.—The student will contribute to the creation of a 2 1/2–3 minute group rope routine.

PM.—The student will perform in the group routine created by the class.

MOVEMENT EXPERIENCE—CONTENT	ORGANIZATION AND TEACHING HINTS	EXPECTED STUDENT OBJECTIVES AND OUTCOMES

10. Perform a body wrap with the rope. (Hold one end on the hip, wrap the rope around the body with the other hand.)
11. Upon completing a backward turning rope jump, toss the rope with both ends into the air and catch it.
12. Run while holding both ends in one hand and circling the rope backward on the side of the body. Toss and catch the rope while performing this.
13. While performing a dance step, toss and catch the rope.
14. Hold both ends of the rope and swing the rope around the body like a cape.
15. Perform leaps while circling the rope on one side.
16. Hook rope around foot and make shapes with the body and foot–rope connection.
17. Have students explore and create more movements.

Have each group teach its combination to another group until the entire class learns the routine. Put the routine to music.

B. *Basic Hoop Movements*
   1. Swings
      a. Across the body.
      b. With body lean.
      c. Around body and change hands.
      d. Across body and change hands.
      e. Overhead, change hands, swing down.
      f. Form a figure eight.
      g. Create poses using hoop and body.
   2. Spins
      a. In front of the body.
      b. On the floor.
      c. Spin and kick one leg over and turn around.
   3. Circling
      a. Extend arm straight in front of body. Circle on hand between thumb and first finger.
      b. While swaying from side to side.
      c. Horizontal circle overhead.
      d. Hold both sides of hoop and circle in front of body.
      e. Circle around waist (hula-hoop).
   4. Tossing and catching
      a. One or two handed.
      b. Directional tosses.
      c. Toss overhead from hand to hand.
      d. Circle on side of body, toss into air, and catch.

The hoop movements should appear to be a graceful extension of the body.

To create a group routine, utilize student creativity in small groups to combine movements together. Then have each group teach its combination to another group, etc., until the students have created a group routine.

The movement of the hoop should be flowing.

Must always be in total control of the hoop.

All manipulative skills and movements should be coordinated with the music.

PM.—The students will create a group routine combining movements learned in class and those invented individually. The routine will be set to music.

PM.—The students will be able to perform at least five activities with a hoop.

PM.—The students will be able to place a backspin (reverse spin) on the hoop, causing it to return to them.

PM.—The students will be able to coordinate body movements and hoop movements with the musical accompaniment to create a rhythmic hoop routine.

MOVEMENT EXPERIENCE—CONTENT	ORGANIZATION AND TEACHING HINTS	EXPECTED STUDENT OBJECTIVES AND OUTCOMES

5. Rolling
  a. And run along side of the hoop.
  b. And run through.
  c. And jump over.
  d. Roll over one arm, across the chest to the other arm.
  e. Roll up the front of the body.
  f. Roll down the back of the body.
	The hoop must always roll without bouncing.	

6. Jumping
  a. As with jump rope.
  b. With a pendulum swing.
  c. Side to side.
  d. Leap through.
	Group and individual routines may be created in the same manner as the other apparatus described above.	PM.—The students will be able to create an individual or group routine by combining movements and setting them to music.

C. *Ball Skills*
1. Rolling
  a. Under bent legs.
  b. Around the body.
  c. Down the legs.
  d. Down the arms.
  e. Down legs, lift legs to toss the ball off toes and into air, and catch.		

2. Bouncing
  a. Adapt basketball dribbling drills with graceful body movements.
  b. Execute locomotor dance type movements while bouncing.
3. Toss and catch ball in a variety of body positions.
4. Add locomotor movements to tosses and catches.
5. Perform body waves with the ball.
6. Throw the ball in a variety of ways (also bounce).
7. Allow for student exploration.
	When throwing, the movement should flow from the feet through the body to the fingertips.
	
	The ball should rest in the hand and not be grasped by the fingers. Fingers should be slightly bent.
	
	Bounces should be caught noiselessly.
		PM.—The students will be able to perform ball activities with the ball resting in their hands rather than grasping the ball.

D. *Basic Ribbon Movements*
1. Swings
  a. Across and in front of body.
  b. Overhead from side to side.
  c. Swing it up and catch the end.
  d. While holding both ends, the ribbon can be swung up, around, and over the body.
2. Circling
  a. At different levels.
  b. Vertical or horizontal.
  c. In front of the body.
  d. Around the body.
  e. Run while circling overhead, leap as ribbon is circled down.
	The wand may be held in one or both hands.
	
	Hold the wand lightly with the index finger pointing down the wand.
	
	The ribbon should be a graceful extension of the body movements.
	
	Try stations to develop creative routines:
	
	Station 1
	Combine three or four movements. One must travel forward. One must be a figure eight.
	
	Station 2
	Combine three or four different movements. One must go to the floor. One must travel backward.
		Cog.—The students will understand the differences between the categories of ribbon movements.
		
		Aff.—Rhythmic gymnastics skills are activities in which there is a wide range of student ability. Discuss the sensitivity of the situation and the need to understand the shortcomings of others.

MOVEMENT EXPERIENCE— CONTENT	ORGANIZATION AND TEACHING HINTS	EXPECTED STUDENT OBJECTIVES AND OUTCOMES

    f. Add dance steps and turns.
    g. Figure eights.
    h. Figure eight and hop through the loop when wand passes side of body.
  3. Zigzag patterns
    a. Execute in air in front, around, and behind body.
    b. Run backward while zigzagging in front of body.
    c. Run forward while zigzagging behind body low or high.
  4. Spirals
    a. Execute around, in front, or beside the body while performing locomotor dance steps.
    b. Execute while performing forward rolls, backward rolls.
  5. Tosses
    a. The wand can be tossed and regrasped while performing dance, locomotor, or preacrobatic movements.
  6. Exchanges
    a. During group routines, ribbon is handed or tossed to partner.
E. Add dance steps to any of the skills listed.
  Dance steps may include:
  1. Chassé
  2. Runs, walks
  3. Schottische, polka, two-step, bleking, waltz
  4. Locomotor movements—skip, hop, gallop, slide, leap, jump, etc.
  5. Body waves
  6. Various turns—pirouette, tour-de-basque, tour jeté, fouetté

Station 3
Combine four movements. One must travel forward. One must include a toss. One must turn in a circle.

Station 4
Combine four movements. One must include a leap. One must travel forward with the ribbon moving behind you. One must be a ribbon exchange. End in a pose.

Create the feeling that the entire body is coordinated with the ribbon.

After students learn the basic manipulative and dance skills, begin to stress proper form.

Students may work in small groups and help each other. They can give constructive feedback to others.

Cog.—The students will be able to explain that when choreographing a rhythmic gymnastic routine, it must be at least 1 minute long and not more than 1 minute 30 seconds in length.

PM.—The students will be able to combine dance and manipulative skills successfully in order to create a rhythmic gymnastics routine.

GAME   (5 – 7 MINUTES)

1. Touchdown, p. 539
2. Circle Hook-On, p. 537
3. Cageball Target Throw, p. 541

DYNAMIC PHYSICAL EDUCATION LESSON PLAN—
ALTERNATE
Climbing Rope Skills
Level III

Supplies and Equipment Needed:
  Climbing ropes
  Tumbling mats (placed under the climbing ropes)
  Beanbags
  Hoops
  Wands
  Balls (optional)

MOVEMENT EXPERIENCE—CONTENT	ORGANIZATION AND TEACHING HINTS	EXPECTED STUDENT OBJECTIVES AND OUTCOMES

INTRODUCTORY AND FITNESS DEVELOPMENT ACTIVITIES (9 – 11 MINUTES)

This lesson may be substituted for any of the previous lessons. Use the introductory and fitness development activities given in the sequenced lesson.

LESSON FOCUS (15 – 20 MINUTES)

Climbing Ropes

A. *Supported Pull-Ups*
  1. Kneel and pull to feet. Return.
  2. Sit, pull to feet, and back to seat.
  3. Stand, keep body straight while lowering body to the floor.

B. *Hangs*
  1. Sit, pull body off floor except for feet, and hold.
  2. Jump up, grasp the rope, and hang.
  3. Jump up, grasp the rope and hang, and perform the following leg movements:
    a. one or both knees up
    b. bicycling movement
    c. half-lever
    d. choice movement

C. *Climbing the Rope*
  1. Scissors grip:
     Place the rope inside of the knee and outside the foot. Climb halfway up and practice descending using the reverse scissors grip before climbing to the top of the rope.
  2. Leg around rest:
     Wrap the left leg around the rope and over the instep of the left foot from the outside. Stand on the rope and instep with right foot.

DPE pp. 414 – 418

Place tumbling mats under all the climbing apparatus.

The pull-up and hang activities are excellent lead-ups for students who are not strong enough to climb the rope.

Students should be cautioned to descend the rope *slowly* to prevent rope burns.

Students should be encouraged to learn the various techniques of climbing and descending.

Rope climbing is a very intense and demanding activity. A good idea is to break up the lesson focus with a game or relay. This will also offer leg development activity.

Cog.—The student will be able to describe the safety rules necessary when climbing ropes.

PM.—The student will be able to demonstrate proper techniques in the following activities:
  1. Climbing with the scissors grip
  2. Leg around rest
  3. Reverse scissors grip
  4. Instep squeeze

Aff.—Rope climbing demands a great deal of upper body strength. Discuss how muscular strength develops through overloading and increasing the demands placed on the body.

Cog.—Exercise increases the diameter and density of bones. Why would this be important? Why do bones become stronger in response to exercise?

326

MOVEMENT EXPERIENCE—CONTENT	ORGANIZATION AND TEACHING HINTS	EXPECTED STUDENT OBJECTIVES AND OUTCOMES

D. *Descending the Rope*
  1. Reverse scissors grip
  2. Leg around rest
  3. Instep squeeze:
   The rope is squeezed between the insteps by keeping the heels together.
	If there are only a few climbing ropes, it would be a good teaching technique to have the nonclimbing students work on another unit. Some good units are beanbags, hoops, wands, and/or playground balls.	Cog.—Rope climbing is excellent for developing upper body strength. Discuss the major muscle groups that are used and developed when climbing ropes.
		
		Cog.—The larger the diameter of the muscle, the greater the amount of force that can be generated. Identify various muscles of the body and their relative size.

E. *Stunts Using Two Ropes*
  1. Straight arm hang: Jump up, grasp rope, and hang.
  2. Arms with different leg positions
   a. Single and double knee lifts
   b. Half lever
   c. Full lever
   d. Bicycle—pedal feet like bicycle
  3. Pull-Ups
   Same as pull-up on a single rope.
  4. Inverted hangs
   a. With feet wrapped around the ropes.
   b. With feet against the inside of the ropes.
   c. With the toes pointed and the feet not touching the ropes.
	Spotting should be done when students are performing inverted hangs on two ropes.	

F. *Swinging and Jumping*
  The student should reach high and jump to a bent-arm position while swinging.
  1. Swing and jump. Add one half and full turns.
  2. Swing and return.
  3. Swing and jump for distance or land on a target.
	Swinging on the ropes should be done with bent arms and with knees tucked.
	
	Caution the person waiting in line to wait out of the way until the person before her is completely finished.
		PM.—The student will be able to perform the following two-rope activities:
		  1. Straight arm hang
		  2. Hangs with different leg positions
		  3. Pull-Ups
		  4. Inverted hangs
		
		Aff.—Rope climbing favors those students who are small and carry little body fat. Discuss individual differences and how different sports favor certain types of body build.

GAME (5 – 7 MINUTES)

Suggest an active game:
 1. Whistle Mixer, p. 536
 2. Touchdown, p. 539
 3. Chain Tag, p. 541

Apparatus and Equipment Sources

One of the problems encountered when developing a program is purchasing the equipment and apparatus. The following list is offered as an aid to the teacher and lists the majority of items needed to equip a well-balanced program. All items are listed by priority in two categories—materials and/or supplies and capital outlay. Priority is based on cost, need, and versatility of the item as evaluated by the authors. In other words, the first piece of equipment listed (playground balls) can be used to facilitate the most units and is the most versatile and useful piece of equipment. Another important listing is the quantity needed for each item. In many cases, too few pieces of equipment are purchased. This list documents the fact that to develop a quality physical education program, a minimum amount of equipment is needed. Finally, many of the items can be constructed in an effort to keep costs down. See Chapter 33 of *Dynamic Physical Education for Elementary School Children* for specifications and construction hints.

The Robert Widen Company has demonstrated its reliability to furnish quality products. Equipment is shipped quickly and the quality is guaranteed. The address is:

The Robert Widen Company
P.O. Box 2075
142 North Cortez
Prescott, AZ 86301

A current price list is available upon request. Local inventory is maintained on most items. Call (602) 445-7390. United Parcel Service shipment on inventoried items will be made within 72 hours of order receipt.

RANK	MATERIAL/SUPPLY ITEM DESCRIPTION	QUANTITY NEEDED (Class Size of 36)
1	8 1/2" playground balls	36
2	6" x 6" beanbags	72
3	Jump ropes (plastic segments)	
	7 ft	30
	8 ft	30
	9 ft	9
	16 ft	12
4	Hula hoops	
	30" diameter	36
	36" diameter	36
	Segmented hoops available	
5	Wands	
	36" length	36
6	Traffic cones	
	12"— vinyl glo	20
7	Tambourine	1
8	Plastic rackets	36
9	Sponge balls—2 1/2"	36
10	Fleece balls—4"	36
11	8 1/2" foam rubber balls	36
12	Floor hockey sets	3
13	Hockey pucks	36
14	Plastic fun or whiffle balls—3"	36
15	Individual mats—carpet, rubber backed, 2 ft x 4 ft	36
16	Garden hose—plastic, 50 ft x 5/8" for partner tug-of-war ropes	2
17	Nylon rope—1/4", 200 ft	1
18	Magic stretch ropes	12
19	Beach balls—18" to 20"	36
20	Soccer balls	18
21	Basketballs—junior size	18
22	Measuring tapes—165 ft fiberglass	2
23	Hand pump	1
24	Footballs—junior size	18
25	Flags, football	36
26	Jumping boxes—8" high	36
27	Jumping boxes—16" high	6
28	Flying discs	36
29	Juggling scarves	36
30	Pinnies—snap on	36
31	Cageball—24"	1

RANK	MATERIAL/SUPPLY ITEM DESCRIPTION	QUANTITY NEEDED
32	Ball bags—nylon mesh	12
33	Volleyball nets	2
34	Tug-of-war rope—50 ft	1
35	Baseball bats—plastic	12
36	Softballs (soft)	18
37	Bats—wooden	3
38	Stopwatches	
	Sweep second hand	2
	Digital	2
39	Batons—plastic or aluminum	12
40	Scooterboards—18"	12
41	Indian clubs	9
42	Lummi sticks	72 pr.
43	Balloons—large	72

RANK	MATERIAL/SUPPLY ITEM DESCRIPTION	QUANTITY NEEDED
1	Tumbling mats—4 ft x 8 ft, 1-1/2" thick, 4 Velcro attachments	8
2	Balance-beam bench	6
3	Parachute and storage bag	1
4	Climbing ropes on tracks with beam fittings (8 ropes)	2 sets
5	Utility gym standards	2
6	Field marker	1
7	Push ball—48"	1
8	Climbing apparatus—trestle tree	1
9	Cassette tape player or record player	1